THE UPROOTED OF THE WESTERN SAHEL

Migrants' Quest for Cash in the Senegambia

Lucie Gallistel Colvin
Cheikh Ba
Boubacar Barry
Jacques Faye
Alice Hamer
Moussa Soumah
Fatou Sow

PRAEGER SPECIAL STUDIES • PRAEGER SCIENTIFIC

Library of Congress Cataloging in Publication Data
Main entry under title:

The Uprooted of the western Sahel.

  Bibliography: p.
  1. Migration, Internal--Senegambia. 2. Rural-urban
migration--Senegambia. 3. Urbanization--Senegambia.
4. Senegambia--Population. I. Colvin, Lucie Gallistel,
1943-   .
HB2125.5.A3U67   304.8'2'09663   81-5005
ISBN 0-03-057599-0   AACR2

Published in 1981 by Praeger Publishers
CBS Educational and Professional Publishing
A Division of CBS, Inc.
521 Fifth Avenue, New York, New York 10175 U.S.A.

123456789   145   987654321

Printed in the United States of America

ACKNOWLEDGMENTS

An offering of kola with deep gratitude is due the many who shared in the making of this study. The team members who struggled with the subject, the mix of disciplines, and the crosscultural academic and bureaucratic niceties with intellectual vitality and grace are the miracle that made patterns emerge from the great jumble of lives, policies, and events touched in the study. Their names as they appear on the individual chapters mark each scholar's unique contribution, but they perhaps do not reflect how fully this work is the result of a sharing of insights. As our periodic day-long seminars dragged into their second and third years, our original time commitments had long since been exceeded, but the work continued to draw us together. Many colleagues who do not appear as authors also contributed. Their thoughts and hospitality were very meaningful, particularly Junkung Keita, Moulie Gibril, M. S. Singal, George Lowe, C. Y. Lele, and Jack Dalton in Banjul; Victor Martin and Charles Becker in Kaolack; Abdoulaye Bara Diop, Mamadou Niang, Pathe Diagne, André Lericollais, Betty and Jack Schafer, David Shear, Sam Rea, Fred Galanto, and David Rawson in Dakar; Pap Cyr Diagne in Saint Louis; Oumar Ba, Abdoul Idy, Isselmou Ould Mohamed Sy and Ch. Sidi Abderrahmane in Nouakchott; Rokiatou Keita, Hamady Sow, Susan Caughman, and Gerry Goodrich in Bamako; and, on the other side of the ocean, Joel Gregory, Georges Sabagh, David T. Lewis, Bruce Fuller, Louis Cantori, W. B. Lamousé-Smith, Allan Howard, David Gisselquist, and Franklin Mendels.

The U.S. Agency for International Development (AID) funded this research. We thank the agency both for recognizing the importance of development of the issues in this study and for giving the team a liberal mandate to treat the subject with intellectual independence. Neither the data nor the views expressed in the study represent the official views of the Agency for International Development or the U.S. government.

The University of Maryland Baltimore County (UMBC) was the American institutional base for this project, and its administrators deserve heartfelt thanks for their support. The chairman and members of the African American Studies Department provided the example and inspiration for the project and continuing collegial interchange. The cartography laboratory, computer center, library, graduate school, and UMBC Press each contributed invaluable technical and financial aid.

The Institut Fondamental d'Afrique Noire offered office space and served as a base for the project in Senegal, for which we are deeply appreciative. The personnel of that establishment all contributed to the realization of the research, but we would particularly like to thank Director Amar Samb, our regretted colleague Camara Laye, research assistants Oumar Gueye and Martial Dieme, and secretary Arlette Traore. We thank also the rector of the university and the Direction Générale à la Recherche Scientifique et Technique for administrative support.

When this study was completed, a seminar to discuss it was held at the Institut Africain pour le Développement Economique et la Planification in Dakar, June 6-8, 1980. We are most grateful to our gracious hosts, as well as to the sponsors, the Secrétariat d'Etat à la Recherche Scientifique et Technique and AID, and the many colleagues in attendance whose critical comments added much to the subject.

The Gambian Division of Central Statistics and its parent Ministry of Economic Planning and Industrial Development have a lively interest in migration-related issues, which translated into collaboration with this project on a Gambian National Migration Survey. The personnel of the division most efficiently and genially collaborated in developing the questionnaire and conducted the field enumeration for that survey. Particular thanks are due Dr. Langley, the Permanent Secretary, and the directors, field supervisors, and enumerators of Central Statistics. Alexander Mogeilnicki of the University of Pennsylvania Population Studies Center conducted the computer programming of the data, and he expects to develop it further in his Ph.D. dissertation. The results of that survey are only incompletely incorporated in the Gambian chapter of this book due to limitations of space. That chapter reflects the views of the author, not of the statistics division or of the Gambian government. The official report of the survey will be published soon.

The present study is being issued in French and English versions, so that five of the chapters had to be translated from French to English and eight from English to French. The fine group of translators included Susan Ryan, Aminata Sow, Christiane Velasco-Sarr, and Susan Nam. The French version of the manuscript has been under the supervision of Boubacar Barry, and the English under Lucie Colvin. Typing has been a monumental task involving multiple drafts. Janet Gethman worked night and day to produce a professional final English version, while Susan Hahn, Eleanor Latini, Towanda Campbell, and many others made sense of our scribblings as the work was going on.

Ultimately our families all suffered some strains during this demanding project. For their forebearance and support we thank each member individually.

CONTENTS

Page

ACKNOWLEDGMENTS iii

LIST OF FIGURES, MAPS, AND TABLES ix

LIST OF ACRONYMS xiii

PART I: INTRODUCTION AND
HISTORICAL BACKGROUND

Chapter

1 INTRODUCTION AND REGIONAL HISTORICAL
BACKGROUND 3
by Lucie Gallistel Colvin

Research Program and Sources 7
Theoretical Approach 9
Methodology 21
Notes 24

2 ECONOMIC ANTHROPOLOGY OF PRECOLONIAL
SENEGAMBIA FROM THE FIFTEENTH THROUGH
NINETEENTH CENTURIES 27
by Boubacar Barry

Introduction 27
Senegambia from the Fifteenth to Seventeenth Century 28
Impact of the Slave Trade in the Eighteenth Century 39
Senegambia in the Nineteenth Century: Readjustments
after the Atlantic Trade and the Colonial Conquest 47
Conclusion 54
Notes 54

3 LABOR AND MIGRATION IN COLONIAL SENEGAMBIA 58
by Lucie Gallistel Colvin

Borders 59
Changing Forms of Labor and Occupational
Distribution 61

New Types of Mobility   63
The Changing Geographic Configuration of Migration   65
The Contemporary Economic Geography of the
    Senegambia   76
Notes   80

PART II: COUNTRY STUDIES

4   SENEGAL   83
     by Lucie Gallistel Colvin

     Urban Growth   89
     Drought and the Urban Growth Spurt   92
     Zonal Patterns of Migration within Senegal   96
     International Immigration   97
     Historical Overview: Migration and Public Policy
         in Senegal   100
     Notes   111

5   NORTHERN SENEGAL   113
     by Cheikh Ba

     Preface by Lucie Gallistel Colvin   113
     Introduction   118
     Regional Migration in Northern Senegal   121
     Historic Migration Patterns in Northern Senegal   123
     Current Migration Characteristics and Conditions   125
     Migration and Environmental Changes: Future
         Prospects   132
     Conclusion   133
     Resume   134
     Notes   134

6   ZONAL APPROACH TO MIGRATION IN THE
     SENEGALESE PEANUT BASIN   136
     by Jacques Faye

     Introduction   136
     Methodology   137
     The Peanut Basin   138
     Questionnaire   140
     The Questions   140
     Execution of the Survey   141

Analysis of Data   141
Distribution of Different Migrations in the Peanut
    Basin   142
Seasonal Inmigration at the End of the Rainy
    Season: Firdus   145
Dry Season Migration toward the Urban Centers:
    The Noran   150
The Major Migratory Zones of the Peanut Basin   151
The Central and North-Central Peanut Basin   154
The Old Peanut Basin   155
Western and Northern Border Zones of the Peanut
    Basin   155
Conclusion   156
Notes   158

7 REGIONAL MIGRATIONS IN SOUTHEASTERN
   SENEGAL, INTERNAL AND INTERNATIONAL   161
   by Moussa Soumah

The Geographical Framework   162
Land Use and Population Distribution   165
Migratory Movements   167
The Economic Perspective   173
The Social Perspective   174
Conclusion   178
Migration Questionnaire   179
Notes   180

8 DIOLA WOMEN AND MIGRATION: A CASE STUDY   183
   by Alice Hamer

Statement of the Problem   183
Review of Literature   184
Methodology   185
Findings   186
Recommendations   201
Notes   202

9 MIGRATION TO DAKAR   204
   by Fatou Sow

Introduction: Migration and the Drought   204
Migration Typology   207

Chapter		Page
	Migration to Dakar	210
	Conclusion	239
	Notes	241
10	MAURITANIA	244
	by Lucie Gallistel Colvin	
	Urbanization	250
	Policy Implications of Migration in Mauritania	258
	Notes	259
11	MALI	260
	by Lucie Gallistel Colvin	
	Emigration	263
	Urbanization	267
	Is Rural Development the Cure for the Rural Exodus?	271
	Migration and Public Policy in Mali	273
	Infrastructure: Transportation and Communications	274
	Rural Development	276
	Marketing, Price Policy, and Taxation	277
	Rural Development Planning	280
	Urban Policy	281
	Educational and Health Policy	282
	Notes	284
12	THE GAMBIA	287
	by Lucie Gallistel Colvin	
	Urbanization	296
	Rural-rural Migration	296
	Characteristics of Migrants	300
	Migration and Public Policy in the Gambia	310
	Notes	312

PART III: POLICY IMPLICATIONS

13	MIGRATION AND PUBLIC POLICY IN THE SENEGAMBIA	317
	by Lucie Gallistel Colvin	
	Geography	321
	The Economy	329

Chapter   Page

    Education   331
    Health Care   335
    Rural Development   335
    Urban Policy   337
    Migration Policy   339
    Receiving Areas: Policy Alternatives   340
    Coping with Ecological- and Disaster-related
      Migration   342
    Notes   343

BIBLIOGRAPHY   344

ABOUT THE AUTHORS   387

LIST OF FIGURES, MAPS, AND TABLES

Figure   Page

  1.1 Birth Rates, Death Rates, and Rates of Natural
       Increase for the World and Regions: 1976

  1.2 The Population Explosion: Where the People
       Are Likely to Be in the Year 2000   16

  4.1 Population Growth in Senegal   86

 12.1 Growth of Banjul-Kombo Saint Mary   290

 12.2 Population Growth in the Gambia   291

 12.3 Foreign-Born Population of the Gambia by
       Country of Birth   301

 12.4 Age-Sex Profile of Gambian Internal Migrants   307

 12.5 Age-Sex Profile of Foreign-Born Migrants in the
       Gambia   308

 12.6 Age-Sex Profile of Recent Migrants in the Gambia 309

Map		Page
1.1	World Population Density Pattern 1978	13
1.2	World Population Growth Pattern 1976	14
2.1	Fulbe Movements and Portuguese Penetration, Fifteenth and Sixteenth Centuries	31
2.2	Precolonial States of Northern Senegambia, circa 1850	41
3.1	Nineteenth Century West African Commercial Regions	66
3.2	Major Migratory Regions of West Africa in the 1920s	68
3.3	Major Migratory Regions of West Africa in the 1950s	70
3.4	Major Migratory Regions of West Africa in the 1970s	71
3.5	Migration in Senegambia, 1500–1850	72
3.6	Migration in Senegambia, 1900; Inmigration to Commercial Peanut Zones	73
3.7	Migration in Senegambia in the 1920s	74
3.8	Migration in Senegambia in the 1950s	75
4.1	Ethnic Groups of Senegal	88
5.1	Ecological Zones of Senegal	120
6.1	Nawetan Client Farmer Movements in the Senegalese Peanut Basin	143
6.2	Senegal's Peanut Basin Seasonal Migrations	146
6.3	Senegal's Peanut Basin	148
7.1	Rainfall in Senegal: Annual Averages and Average Number of Days, 1931–60	164

Map   Page

7.2   The Upper Gambia/Faleme Migratory Basin   170

7.3   International Migration from Guinea to Senegal   175

8.1   The Trip from Thionk Essil to the Gambia   191

9.1   Cape Verde Peninsula   213

10.1   Mauritania, Administrative Regions   246

12.1   The Gambia   288

13.1   Growth of Senegambian Capital Cities, 1900-76   323

Table

1.1   Estimated Crude Birth Rates by Major Less
       Developed Regions   17

1.2   Average Annual Rate of Growth in the World
       and Its Major Less Developed Regions   18

2.1   Consolidated Capacity Estimates tor the Slave
       Exports of Senegambia   42

2.2   Slave Exports from Senegambia, 1711-1810   43

3.1   Hierarchy of Urban Functions and Size in the
       Senegambia   78

4.1   Population Growth in Senegal by Region, 1960-76   87

4.2   Urban Growth in Senegal, 1955-76   91

4.3   Drought and Urban Growth in Senegal   94

4.4   Foreign-Born Africans in Senegal by Region of
       Residence, 1971 and 1976   98

4.5   African Immigrants to Senegal Claiming Senegalese
       Nationality versus Nationality of Origin   99

Table   Page

4.6   A Comparison of the Average Hourly Salaries
       of the Senegalese Peasant, Dakar Laborer,
       and French Laborer   102

4.7   Centralization of Skilled Humanpower in Senegal   105

5.1   Rainfall, 1944-73   124

10.1   Population Growth in Mauritania by Region,
       1965-77   247

10.2   Mauritanian Population by Region and Nomadic
       or Sedentary Lifestyle   248

10.3   Urban Growth in Mauritania, 1961-77   251

10.4   Employment in Mauritania, 1973   252

10.5   Phases of Growth of Nouakchott, 1961-77   253

11.1   Regional Population Growth in Mali   262

12.1   Components of 1963-73 Intercensal Growth in the
       Gambia: Three Hypotheses   292

12.2   Population of Gambian Towns, 1963 and 1973   297

12.3   Percent of Gambians and Immigrants Having
       Primary Education, 1973 and 1978   303

12.4   Geographic Centralization of Educated Gambians
       (1978 National Migration Sample Survey)   304

13.1   Population Growth in the Senegambia by Country,
       1960 to 1976   318

LIST OF ACRONYMS

AID	The (United States) Agency for International Development
AOF	Afrique Occidentale Francaise (Former French West Africa)
ANF	Archives Nationales de France (Paris)
ANS	Archives Nationales du Sénégal (Dakar)
ASECNA	Agency for the Security of Air Navigation
BCEAO	Banque Centrale des Etats de l'Afrique de l'Ouest
BCEOM	Bureau Central d'Etudes pour l'Equipement d'Outre-Mer
BEPC	Brevet d'Etudes du Premier Cycle
BREDA	Bureau Régional d'Education en Afrique (United Nations, Dakar)
CILSS	Comité Interétats pour la Lutte contre la Sécheresse Sahelienne
CNRS	Centre National de Recherche Scientifique (France)
ECOWAS	Economic Community of West African States
ENEA	Ecole Nationale d'Economie Appliquée
HLM	Habitations à Loyer Modéré
IBRD	International Bank for Reconstruction and Development
IFAN	Institut Fondamental d'Afrique Noire (University of Dakar)
ILO	International Labour Office (United Nations)
ISCO	International Standard Classification of Occupations
MIFERMA	Les Mines de Fer Mauritanienne
OCA	Office de Commercialisation de l'Arachide (Senegal)
OECD	Organization for Economic Cooperation and Development
OERS	Organisation des Etats Riverains du Sénégal
OMVG	Organisation pour la Mise en Valeur du Fleuve Gambie
OMVS	Organisation pour la Mise en Valeur du Fleuve Senegal
ONCAD	Office National de Coopération et d'Assistance pour le Développement

OPAM	Office des Produits Agricoles du Mali
SAED	Société d'Aménagement et d'Exploitation des terres du Delta
SICAP	Société Immobilière du Cap Vert
SODEVA	Société de Développement et de Vulgarisation Agricole
SOMIEX	Société Malienne d'Importation et d'Exportation
SOMIMA	Société Minière de la Mauritanie
SONADIS	Société Nationale de Distribution (Senegal)
SONEES	Société Nationale des Eaux et Electricité (Senegal)
SOTRAC	Société des Transports en Commun (Senegal)
UNDP	United Nations Development Program
UNESCO	United Nations Economic, Social, and Cultural Organization
UNFPA	United Nations Fund for Population and Agriculture

I

INTRODUCTION AND HISTORICAL BACKGROUND

1

INTRODUCTION AND REGIONAL HISTORICAL BACKGROUND

Lucie Gallistel Colvin

Migration is one of the outstanding consequences of the economic and demographic transformations that have overtaken the western Sahel in the twentieth century. It touches every village and every national economy, but often in very different ways. The most commented upon trend (and rightly so) is the drift from farms to cities. Senegambian cities are growing at a record rate, unequalled in their own historical experience and unparalleled on the other continents of the world. Only in other parts of Africa are similar rates of urbanization observed. The other three major migratory trends are the movement of farmers from hinterland areas to the frontiers of cash-crop zones, the augmentation of the agricultural labor force in cash-crop zones by migrant client farmers, and the sedentarization of nomadic herders.

Economically, these patterns reflect a maldistribution of wealth and economic opportunity on two levels, internationally between developed and developing countries, and internally between urban residents vis-à-vis rural, cash-croppers vis-à-vis subsistence farmers, and farmers vis-à-vis herders. The rural exodus has the effect of reducing the disparity in wealth and opportunity between rural and urban populations but, at the same time, reducing overall production of both food stuffs and commercial crops. Internal Senegambian migration, of course, does nothing to equalize international disparities. Only the tiny but rapidly growing proportion of migrants to Europe taps into the wage structure of the developed world and repatriates some of that wealth.

Demographically, the current pattern of migration reflects a bulge in population growth that began in the 1920s and accelerated rapidly in the period following World War II. Colonial and immediately postcolonial health interventions focused on epidemic diseases, sharply reducing mortality but without introducing general health care. Fertility, which had traditionally been high and necessarily so to offset unusually elevated mortality rates, continues to be high because of cultural sanctions and continuing health insecurity.

As a result, family and village economic structures that had evolved when an average of two dependent children per wife survived are severely strained by the present average of three to four surviving children per wife. The strains are greater in the urban areas where each child represents an additional mouth to feed and school supplies to purchase out of a single salary. But they are also felt in rural areas quite severely. Where child care can no longer be met by the traditional extended family, the demand for day care centers has arisen. Rural farm women have traditionally done an important part of the agricultural labor. When extended families were larger and children more widely spaced, the older children, grandmothers, and other wives were able to share child care. But fragmentation of the family is evident in rural as well as urban areas. Rural areas with long and intense involvement in cash cropping show a smaller average family size than those on the periphery of the cash economy.[1] Both men and women are seeking entry into the cash economy. In urban areas, they compensate by working at multiple occupations when a single salary does not suffice. In rural areas, they grow cash crops on personal plots and many migrate at least seasonally in search of cash wages or profit from petty trade. This, in turn, increases the burden of agricultural labor on the aged and on women and children. The quest for cash is the dominant theme among both rural-rural and urban migrants. In the early colonial period at the turn of the century, attempts to introduce European currency were thwarted by the resistance of a still vital traditional economy, a resistance broken only by forcible taxation, labor recruitment, and commercial monopolies. Eighty years later, the traditional economy is everywhere in decline, and the cash economy has become an element in every family's economic outlook. Money is a necessity for taxes, clothing, transportation and customary celebrations, as well as an opportunity to earn bride price, radios, sewing machines, bicycles, and other consumer goods.

Studying migration leads one into the lives of masses of individuals and households, where policies decided in Dakar, Paris, and other Senegambian and Western capitals affect families' ability to function. To see why people move, one must learn why they think they will be better off in one locality of a region than in another.

Urbanization is historically and logically irreversible. This book examines in detail the historical evidence and implications of that conclusion for the countries of the western Sahel. Sedentarization of formerly transhumant herders is likewise inevitable over the long term, as the abundant land and fragile ecology that sustained their economy is eroded by expanding human and animal population. In both cases, it is important to slow the process as much as possible immediately, but future planning will have to look to structural alternatives.

When this research was being proposed, it was hypothesized that rural-urban drift intensified during the recent Sahelian drought and that one should measure the reverse migration and/or reduction in migratory trends that might have accompanied the return of normal rainfall. The team's observations confirm that there was a drought-related influx and only a minimal return movement. Instead of dissipating, urban population bulges moved slowly from outlying cities toward the regional center of Cap Vert/Thiès in the last years of the drought. However, the drought-related spurt in urbanization is small compared with the continuing high rate of rural-urban drift related to deeper causes. Research on the uprooting process, in this book and elsewhere, shows that every serious economic dislocation in the countryside contributes to permanent urban migration. Even beneficent rural development projects, in the context of present rural-urban inequalities, increase the probability of participants ending up in the city, merely by introducing them to new lifestyles. Autocratic new rural development project structures and those that provide too low a participant income—both common trends—are particularly likely to augment rather than diminish the rural exodus.

One of the dilemmas that rural-urban migration poses for development in the western Sahel is that it reduces productivity of both food and cash crops without offsetting it by a countervailing increase in productivity in urban areas. The cities of the Sahel are colonial cities and, from their earliest development on, have had a focus on admistrative, commercial, and transportation functions rather than on productivity. Thus, by moving to the cities, rural residents increase their access to wealth and opportunity but decrease their productivity. New migrants' urban consumption, meager as it is, is above that of rural residents. And while they often work harder at tougher jobs than the urban-born, the jobs they work at do not involve production. This has been a source of frustration for governments and development agencies in the Sahel.

Yet the greatest danger in migration policy is in attacking urbanization itself, instead of its causes. Policies designed to diminish migration in economically troubled countries frequently have only caused further dislocations in production. This is because it is difficult to affect the nonproductive forms of migration without affecting the other forms necessary for the functioning of the agricultural system. Seasonal labor is essential to agriculture in large areas of Senegal, the Gambia, southern Mauritania, and western Mali. The clearing and settling by migrants of new agricultural frontiers of the peanut basin and cotton basin are also contributing substantially to agricultural productivity, in Senegal and Gambia particularly.

One important question explored in this study is whether and how the expanding frontier can provide relief to the overpopulated areas of the peanut basin and an alternative to rural-urban migration. The inner frontier of central Senegal is attracting Wolof migrants from the old northern peanut basin and from those areas increasingly desertified by the recent drought. Similarly, Mandinka farmers from the exhausted Badibus/Kerewan peanut zone are settling and clearing west and east of there. The farthest frontier in Senegal Oriental and the Gambian Upper River is attracting Fulbe migrants from the declining rural economies of Futa Jallon in Guinea and the middle Senegal basin and diverse other settlers from relatively sparsely populated outlying areas of Senegal, neighboring Mali, and Mauritania.

This expanding agricultural frontier is one of the last in the world, having counterparts only in other areas of Africa, Australia, the Asian tundra, and South America. But it is rapidly coming to a close as the available fertile land will be exhausted within the next decade. The frontier has nearly closed in the Gambia, and it is rapidly extending into eastern Senegal and the upper Casamance.

Just as Africa is the last continent to have expanding agricultural frontiers, it is also the last continent to have open borders. As the agricultural frontiers close, the borders may be expected to follow. Traditional Senegambian hospitality and generosity have been nourished on a sparse population in relation to relatively generous resources. As land resources are expropriated and an awareness of scarcity becomes acute, governments and citizens of the area can be expected in the near future to reconsider policies affecting land and opportunity allocation.

Another historically and economically important pattern of migration that is currently declining rapidly in the Senegambia is nomadic pastoralism. While the social and economic impact of the sedentarization of nomads requires separate study, this book is able to confirm that it is happening in Senegal, Gambia, and, most notably, Mauritania. In the latter country, because the majority of the population only a decade ago was dependent on pastoral transhumance, the collapse of the herding economy has consequences of national scope, unique to the area. Between the 1965 census and the 1976 census, the nomadic proportion of the population of Mauritania decreased from 65 percent to 33 percent. The combined

influences of drought, war, economic modernization, and the emancipation of slaves are permanently transforming the relationship of
people to the land. Many of the former nomads are settling in the
cities, where the rate of growth of urban population from 1965 to
1976 was 10 percent per year (compared with 23 percent for the
capital city of Nouakchott and 7 percent for francophone Africa as
a whole). Some former nomads have settled along roads and at deep
wells, while others have settled the agricultural areas of southern
Mauritania. Still others have joined the traditional emigration into
commercial occupations, which takes Mauritanians throughout the
western Sahel.

RESEARCH PROGRAM AND SOURCES

The team that conducted the study was interdisciplinary, comprised of three social and economic historians, two geographers,
and two sociologists. The theoretical and conceptual literature on
which we have drawn and our choice of methods are also interdisciplinary.

Our initial task was to describe and analyze population movements within the Senegambia in relation to the past and present
economy of the region as a whole and of each zone in it. During an
initial three months of weekly seminars in October through December of 1977, the team surveyed the monographic literature on each
area and the theoretical literature on migration from each discipline.
We divided the region geographically into zones, selected unanswered
questions and problems for further research, and established research teams under the direction of each researcher. Geographer
Cheikh Ba concentrated on the pastoralists of northern Senegal.
Rural sociologist Jacques Faye surveyed the departure and receiving zones of the peanut basin. Geographer Moussa Soumah focused
on the far frontier of middle and upper Casamance and eastern
Senegal, while historian Alice Hamer explored the rapidly expanding
migration of women from the lower Casamance. Sociologist Fatou
Sow, whose area was the central metropolis of Dakar, brought migration studies in that area up to date with a socioeconomic survey
of the most recently settled bidonvilles (shanty towns). Historian
Boubacar Barry provided a regional economic history to the end of
the nineteenth century, while Lucie Colvin, also an economic historian, traced the economic and demographic changes within the
region in the colonial and postcolonial periods. She also did the
research for all parts of the region falling outside of Senegal.

Although the region is multinational, problems of logistics and
cost prohibited coordinated field research in all six of the countries

concerned. We originally proposed to AID a systematic data collection effort involving a uniform questionnaire and multiple pas-
sages through overlapping sampling districts. When this appeared
too costly, we were asked instead to synthesize existing data and
focus on policy questions. Nevertheless, some new field research
was in Senegal and Gambia. Monographs and recent census reports
in two of the remaining countries made it possible to do reasonably
detailed country studies for Mauritania and Mali. Since neither of
the two complete Gambian censuses included questions related to
migration, more detailed data was desired for that country. The
Senegambian Migration Study happened to fall just five years after
the last decennial census, so the migration project and the Gambian
Central Statistics Division decided on a collaborative National
Sample Census and Migration Survey. The field enumeration was
conducted in May of 1978, and the data processing was completed in
1979 by Alexander Mogielnicki, of the University of Pennsylvania
Population Studies Center, under the auspices of the Senegambia
Migration Study. A preliminary report of the results is contained
in the Gambian chapter of this book, and more complete analysis is
expected in the Ph. D. dissertation of Mogielnicki.

Census data from the 1970 round of censuses had been expected to provide the data base for the postcolonial analyses in
Senegal, Mali, and Mauritania, all of which conducted censuses in
1976. Delays in processing resulted in only global data being
available in provisional reports until the very end of this study.
Mauritania's provisional report includes some analysis of the data,
while Senegal's and Mali's provisional results included only gross
tabulations for administrative districts and regions. In Mali, use
of the data for historical trends was further hindered by the non-
comparability of the geographic units used in the 1976 census and in
the 1960/61 sample census. Census data for six rural regions of
Senegal have recently been published in unedited form, permitting
some more detailed analysis. For certain questions, comparable
data was made available to the study for the Cap Vert region, permitting some urban-rural comparisons. Historical census data is
available in the archives for Senegal and Gambia, providing a good
picture of the historical evolution of urbanization and overall population growth. Changes in the boundaries of census reporting districts made it almost useless for rural zones. No census data and
only very rough economic statistical estimates are available for
Guinea and Guinea Bissau. This unfortunately led to their limited
mention in this study, even though Guinea has long been a major
source of migrants into its neighboring countries.

Statistical portraits of the countries of Senegambia are also
available in annual statistical summaries published by their respec-

tive departments of statistics and in official four- and five-year plans. In most cases, however, these summaries have not yet been corrected to reflect the much larger populations found in each country in the 1976 census. The reports of various international organizations listed in the bibliography also provided useful, although occasionally contradictory, data. Those that generate their own statistical estimates include the (UNFPA), the (IBRD), the (ILO), (UNESCO), and the (UNDP).

Overall statistics on migration in West Africa have recently been compiled in a monumental study by K. C. Zachariah of the IBRD and Julien Condé of the Organization for Economic Cooperation and Development.[2] This multivolume study is intentionally limited to a statistical description and does not attempt to analyze the migratory flows. It is also limited to the nine West African countries for which data were available, three of which (Senegal, Gambia, and Mali) are included in our study. Recent works of interpretation of migration also tend to apply to West Africa as a whole or to the Sahel as a whole, without considering the regional focuses that migration patterns reflect. Among the major recent studies are the work by Samir Amin and Daryll Forde, Modern Migrations in Western Africa; two small volumes published by the Comité d'information Sahel, Qui de se nourrit de la famine en Afrique? and Les migrations africaines; and John C. Caldwell's The Sahelian Famine and its Demographic Consequences.[3] Individual themes within the scope of our migratory study have also been the subject of particular studies. On urbanization, a most recent and provocative study published by the World Bank is entitled, "Urban Growth and Economic Development in the Sahel."[4] The most comprehensive works on sedentarization of nomads in this area are the ongoing studies of Charles Toupet, a geographer at the University of Dakar.[5]

The economic data on which the Senegambia migration study is based come from government statistical services, published in a variety of forms in periodic reports. We have also used the United Nations and International Monetary Fund trade statistics and a very interesting compilation of price data contained in the study, "Marketing, Price Policy, and Storage of Food Grains in the Sahel: A Survey," by the working group on marketing, price policy, and storage of the Comité Interétats pour la Lutte contre la Secheresse Sahelienne (CILSS) and the Club du Sahel.[6]

THEORETICAL APPROACH

This study was designed to explore the policy implications of migratory patterns in the Senegambia in the context of their unique social and economic history, not to develop a new theoretical approach to migration. The assembly of an interdisciplinary team of six senior researchers and a graduate student working together on a common problem over more than a year's time reflects the assumption that no one theoretical approach was adequate in exploring all of the policy areas involved in migration. Previous studies of migration in Africa have primarily been the domain of economists, geographers, demographers, and, on the microlevel, of anthropologists. Economists have focused on the radical inequalities between urban and rural incomes and opportunities in explaining the causes of migration. The economic consequences include urban labor surpluses and rural labor shortages. J. Harris and R. Sabot have constructed a model for analyzing this aspect, which, however, for lack of appropriate data in Africa, proves difficult in practical application.[7] Elliott Berg has analyzed the costs and benefits of labor migration for governments, employers, and migrants in the Senegambia.[8] A highly debated economic issue is the economic benefit of migrants' remittances to sending communities. The most recent consensus seems to be that remittances are often substantial and even essential to the economic survival of sending zones and countries but that those left behind are rarely able to transform remittances into productive activities to stimulate economic growth.

In the present book, we explore the applicability of these theories to specific local zones within the Senegambia—some of which are receiving immigrants, others primarily sending, and others both receiving and sending different types of migrants—in relation to the needs of migrants and the local economy. We believe that in linking our study of migratory patterns to the historical evolution of public policy and to current policy alternatives we contribute a new methodological approach to the study of migration. Establishing in the abstract that income inequalities or rapid population growth stimulate migration is of limited use if there is no conceivable combination of policy alternatives or development scenarios that could alter those circumstances. More important is what geographic, economic, educational, demographic, and health policies might mitigate the negative consequences.

Similarly, in the area of demography, this study tests existing demographic theory against Senegambian realities. Demographers point out that rapid surges in growth of rural populations are accompanied by high rates of outmigration as younger sons find out that slots in the rural economy cannot expand fast enough to absorb them.[9] Demographic methods also reveal the effect of migration on the age-sex structure of the populations in sending and receiving zones.[10] Since modern migration has historically involved young adults, with males predominating, receiving areas benefit from the increase in active males, showing a lower ratio of dependent (younger than 15 years and older than 65 years) to active (15-65 years) populations. Sending areas, by contrast, tend to have female-predominant sex ratios and a high proportion of dependents.

John Caldwell, in a major study in Ghana from 1962 through 1964, examined both the stated motivations and results of migration for individuals and the socioeconomic correlates of variations in volume of migration.[11] He found that the greater the distance from a rural area to the next large center, the greater the proportion of outmigrants. We discuss this same relationship in the Senegambia as an aspect of regional and national peripherality. The major exception to this pattern is that in every Senegambian country there are old cash-crop zones near the major centers that have reached a point of soil exhaustion and overpopulation, leading to intense outmigration. Caldwell also found a direct correlation between outmigration and the size of the source village, the economic condition of the household (wealthier ones having more outmigration), the presence of relatives in urban areas, the amount of education, literacy, knowledge of English, family size, and birth rank. He also found, as did we, a tendency for diversification in the traditional single young adult male predominance among migrants.

Among the geographers, pioneering work has been done by R. Mansell Prothero, who initially developed a typology of traditional and modern varieties of migration in Africa according to the purposes, distances, ecological changes, and timing involved.[12] Akin Mabogunje has drawn on this and developed it, focusing on the Nigerian experience and on urbanization in a regional context.[13] William Hance, in turn, recapitulates the theoretical literature and catalogs the current African patterns on a continentwide basis.[14]

Perhaps the most interesting overall perspective on migration and its historical variants comes from J. Beaujeu-Garnier's Geography of Population.[15] She explores the psychosocial as well as the better known socioeconomic causes and consequences of migration in a world historical context. Among the socioeconomic factors, she emphasizes the roles of absolute poverty and of populations living so close to the margin of survival that any localized problem or catastrophe can set off an exodus. Such areas, throughout the underdeveloped world, are juxtaposed to attractive zones of visible prosperity. Beaujeu-Garnier also notes the role of disruption of the economic equilibrium in rural areas as a result of historic changes and policies, taking her examples, however, from the agricultural revolution in Europe rather than from contemporary less developed countries.

The western Sahel shares with the rest of Africa a unique econodemographic situation. Overall population density is still rather low, and urbanization and industrialization are among the least advanced in the world. Fertility, mortality, overall population growth and migration rates are all higher than in other areas of the world (see Maps 1.1 and 1.2, Figures 1.1 and 1.2, and Tables 1.1 and 1.2). This book explores the determinants of these variables and their short term prospects in the western Sahel. It also considers, at some length, their policy implications. Even though theoretical models in all of the other social sciences are built on historic analysis, it has been customary in African development planning to apply these models as if knowledge of the local history were unnecessary or irrelevant. Economic and demographic theory explain, in a scientific sense, most variation in migratory rates. However, that knowledge alone provides very little insight into the policy implications of migration. It is necessary to know how related policies have evolved historically, how and to what degree they can be changed, and the magnitude of social changes that could be expected from such policy changes. In the following chapters, we provide historical background to the many aspects of life that are altered in the process of migration, to the interrelationship between macro- and microinstitutional changes, and to the interactions between local government budgets and policies and current migratory trends. We include history of the geographic evolution of the transportation and communications patterns in the area; of occupational specialization by sex, age, and ethnicity; of labor supply in relation to such specialization; of education, health, and migration control.

There is sometimes confusion over what constitutes the region called Senegambia and why it should be chosen as the region for study. Historians of the area do not share the same confusion. Historically, it emerges clearly as a distinct economic region over the last 1,000 years, comprising the basins of the two rivers: the Senegal and the Gambia. Today, political borders creating the separate nations of Senegal, Gambia, Mali, Mauritania, Guinea, and Guinea Bissau have left the area without any organizational coherence. The only organizations that reflect the historic unity of the region today are the Organisation pour la Mise en Valeur du Fleuve Sénégal (OMVS) and the Organisation pour la Mise en Valeur du Fleuve Gambie (OMVG), that is, the international organizations created to plan the development of the Senegal and Gambia river basins. Development planning, politics, administration, and the collection of statistics on populations all take place within national borders. However, when it comes to realizing a development project, the implementers are faced with an economy that still continues to function on a regional basis.

MAP 1.1

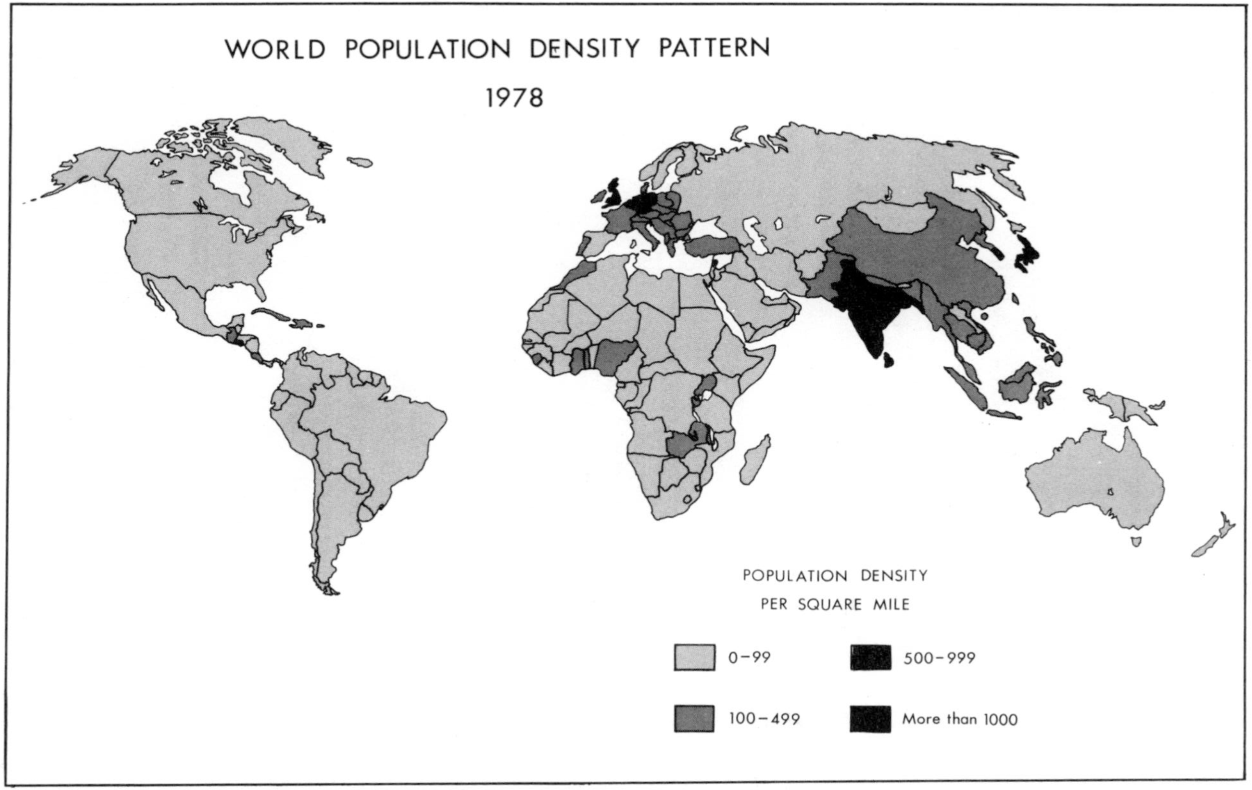

WORLD POPULATION DENSITY PATTERN

1978

POPULATION DENSITY
PER SQUARE MILE

▨ 0-99		■ 500-999	
▨ 100-499		■ More than 1000	

Source: U.S. Bureau of Census, World Population, 1977 (Washington, D.C.: Bureau of Census, 1977).

MAP 1.2

WORLD POPULATION GROWTH PATTERN
1976

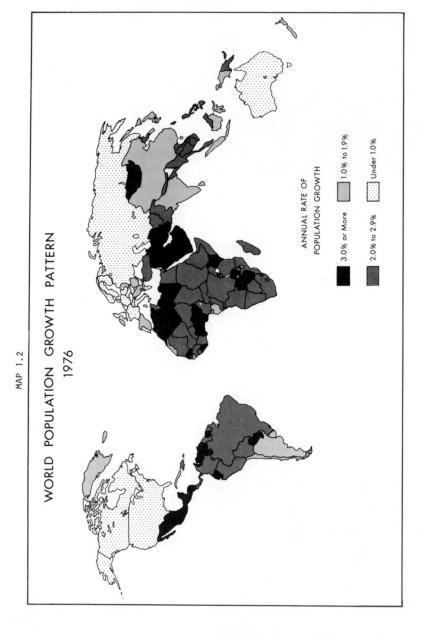

ANNUAL RATE OF
POPULATION GROWTH

3.0% or More
2.0% to 2.9%
1.0% to 1.9%
Under 1.0%

Source: U.S. Bureau of Census, World Population, 1977 (with revisions of the West African data).

14

FIGURE 1.1

Birth Rates, Death Rates, and Rates of Natural Increase
for the World and Regions: 1976

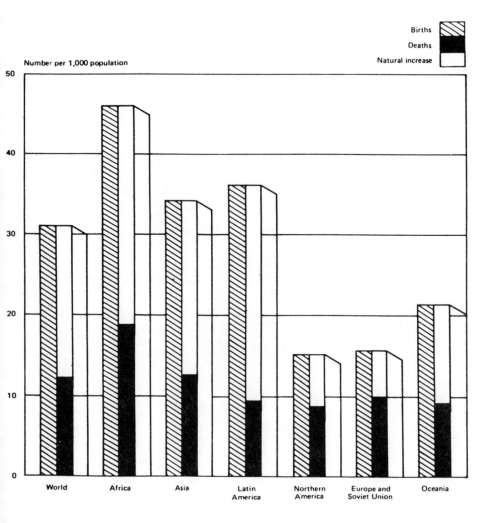

Source: U.S. Bureau of Census, World Population, 1977,
Figure 5.

FIGURE 1.2

The Population Explosion:

Where the People Are Likely to Be in the Year 2000

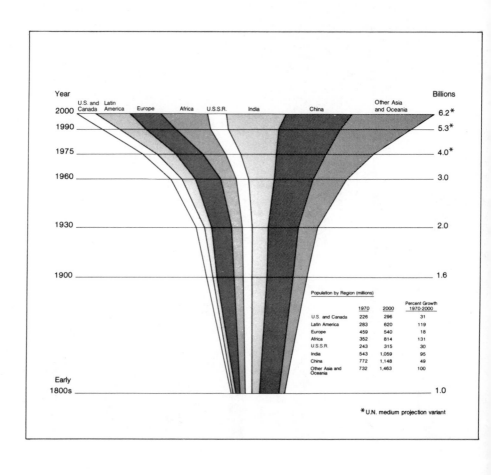

Source: U.S. Department of State, Bureau of Public Affairs,
"International Population Policy," Current policy no. 171,
April 29, 1980.

TABLE 1.1

Estimated Crude Birth Rates by Major Less Developed Regions
(in percentages)

	1950–55	1955–60	1960–65	1965–70	1970–75	Percent Decline 1950–75
World total	35.6	34.6	33.7	32.1	31.5	11.5
Less developed regions	42.1	40.9	39.9	38.4	39.5	10.9
Developed regions	22.9	21.9	20.5	18.1	17.2	24.9
Africa	48.1	48.0	47.7	47.2	46.3	3.7
Latin America	41.0	40.5	39.5	38.1	36.9	10.0
East Asia	35.6	30.9	28.5	27.0	26.2	26.4
South Asia	44.0	45.1	44.8	42.9	41.9	7.1
Southeast Asia	44.7	45.6	44.9	43.4	42.4	7.0
South Asia	43.9	45.1	44.9	42.7	41.7	7.5
Southwest Asia	46.2	45.9	44.1	43.5	42.8	7.4

Source: United Nations, Levels of Trends of Fertility Throughout the World, 1950–1970; Population Studies, 1959 (New York, 1977). Cited by Dudley Kirk, "World Population Numbers and Rates: The Range of Difference," Presentation to the Population Association of America annual meeting, Philadelphia, April 26, 1979.

TABLE 1.2

Average Annual Rate of Growth in the World and Its Major Less Developed Regions
(in percentages)

	1950–55	1955–60	1960–65	1965–70	1970–75	1975–77
World total	1.8	2.0	2.0	2.0	1.9	1.9
Excluding China	1.7	1.9	1.9	1.9	1.9	1.9
More developed	1.3	1.3	1.2	1.0	0.9	0.7
Less developed	2.1	2.3	2.3	2.4	2.4	2.3
Excluding China	2.1	2.3	2.4	2.8	2.4	2.4
Africa	2.1	2.3	2.5	2.6	2.7	2.8
Asia	2.0	2.2	2.1	2.3	2.2	2.1
Latin America	2.6	2.8	2.8	2.7	2.6	2.6

Source: U.S. Bureau of Census, World Population, 1977, Table 2.

Migration patterns are just one reflection of this. By charting the ensemble of individual movements from one point to another, one can see that the tendencies are actually regional with a central focus on Dakar. What nationally based studies show as the movements of Mauritanians toward Senegal or Malians toward Senegal or Senegalese toward the Gambia in fact are part of the same flows as internal migration. Similarly, an analysis of the movement of meat in the form of animals or of slaughtered meat, or of cereal products, or of imports reflects this regional movement rather than simply a national one. Again, the focus is on Dakar. Similarly, if one analyzes communications patterns, the number of telephone calls, the number of passenger miles, the number of freight miles in particular directions, the number of passengers moving into and out of the airports and ports or along the railroads, the amount of currencies flowing in different directions and the overall directions of trade, again this regional structure appears. Yet the tendency today and since the colonial period is toward the fragmentation of this region along national lines and toward restructuring the communications and transportation patterns that served the earlier regional economy.

Regional history enables us to trace the changes in concentration of economic activity and population density—from the river valleys of the interior in the ninth through sixteenth centuries toward the coastal areas as European commerce expanded on the seas from the fifteenth century on—illustrating the evolution of this region historically and its economic roots in the period prior to the colonial conquest of the area. The subsequent chapter on the colonial era shows how the river valleys that had originally been the focus of regional integration were first supplanted by the railroads and port and then by the road structure built during the colonial period. At the same time, the introduction of the cash economy and its peculiar migration patterns in colonial Senegambia is explored. Applying geographic theory to this historical evolution, we can see that a hierarchy of functions and size evolved among the cities of the region and show how the evolving export/import focus of the economy translated into spatial patterns. We see the evolution of a dendritic pattern of regional development early in the colonial period, with Dakar as the region's primate city. Goods, currency, transportation networks, and people all flowed toward Dakar. The economic and demographic hinterland from which they flowed followed the contours of the precolonial commercial network around 1900, then expanded to include additional French-ruled areas as far east as Upper Volta. We have traced the growth of this hinterland from the early colonial period to its peak in the mid-1950s and the gradual fragmentation and shrinking of this hinterland since that period.

The borders of the region for each period have been traced
by studying the intensity and direction of flow of goods, currency,
and people, following the method of transactional analysis proposed
by political scientist, Karl Deutsch.[16] The framework for the
political analysis of regions proposed by Louis Cantori and Steven
Spiegel is also useful.[17] Their analysis focuses on the contrasting
political positions of the economically and politically dynamic cores
of regions and the weaker periphery. Since the areas of economic
dynamism are also attracting inmigration and the peripheral areas
are losing population, this distinction is useful in studying population
policy and the related inequalities of economic development within
the region. Part II of the book is a portrait of the region today.
Chapter 4 sets out the global geographic tendencies within the region, the distribution of cities, the infrastructure, both existing
and planned, and the economic activities and their complementarity
in the flows of people, goods, and money over the last three decades.

On a microeconomic level, the geographers and agronomists
on our team also helped us to understand the changing patterns of
land use. In Chapter 5, Colvin and Ba show how, in the River Valley and Ferlo of northern Senegal, competing patterns of land use
are obliging nomads to sedentarize and are making some traditional
agricultural patterns untenable. Rural socioeconomic studies allowed us to show the institutional erosion that accompanies high
rates of outmigration from rural areas and becomes, in turn, a
cause of outmigration. Institutional deterioration due to the absence
of large portions of the men in the active working and decision-
making ages must be taken into account in the formulation of economic development plans for areas such as the Senegal river basin.
A similar pattern of institutional breakdown and economic stagnation
is observable in other border provinces with high outmigration, including the Casamance, the hinterland areas of eastern Mauritania,
the Kayes region of Mali, and Futa Jallon in Guinea.

In contrast, the peanut basin, which Jacques Faye explores
in Chapter 6, shows a much more complex migratory pattern. The
densely populated but deteriorating areas close to Dakar show high
rates of outmigration toward Dakar, counterbalanced in part by
inmigration of seasonal client (and occasionally wage) farm labor.
A much smaller stream of pioneers from the same area moves away
from the center to settle the expanding frontier. They dominate the
frontier, engaging client farmers from the more peripheral border
provinces to supplement their labor supply.

In Chapter 7, Moussa Soumah examines the border provinces,
Senegal Oriental and Upper Casamance, which supply the more dynamic cash-crop zones with migrant labor and themselves receive
migrant settlers from still farther hinterland areas across neighbor-

ing borders. Alice Hamer, in Chapter 8, focuses on a rather unique pattern of institutionalized, seasonal, urban migration of young women from the Lower Casamance, escaping a highly authoritarian, hard-working, traditional milieu in search of cash and a few years of freedom. Again, the trend is clearly connected with the peripherality of the homeland. If more cash opportunities were available locally, the outmigration would probably be reduced.

The central pole of attraction in the region, Dakar, is the subject of Fatou Sow's chapter. Because of the multitude of earlier studies on the city, including some she had conducted, her research focuses on conditions in the most recently settled migrants' sections. She shows how these have been pushed to the geographic as well as socioeconomic periphery of the city by slum clearance and urban planning.

The subsequent three chapters, 10 through 12, are studies of the outlying countries of the region: Mauritania, Mali, and Gambia. In each case, a discussion of the country's geographic relationship to the regional economy is followed by a demographic profile; a portrait of migratory patterns related to the zonal, national, and regional economy; and, finally, a history of related policies and alternatives.

Part III, Chapter 13, draws together for analysis the policy implications of migratory and related economic patterns in the region as a whole. Policies directly concerning human movements (residence, citizenship, border crossing) turn out to be the least important in current circumstances. A much more urgent need is coordinated economic and demographic growth policies, which will enable economic growth to accelerate, distribute its benefits more equitably between countryside and city, and make a harmonized deceleration of mortality/fertility and overall population growth feasible for both nations and families in the Senegambia. The policy areas that most directly affect migration patterns are considered in the following order: the geography of development, economics, education, health care, rural development, urban policy, and migration policy.

METHODOLOGY

The methods used in this study varied from researcher to researcher, and all were discussed thoroughly in the seminar. The seminar itself was our unifying methodology. We lacked the funding for a coordinated regional survey research, and we also hoped that it would not be necessary because the censuses conducted in Senegal, Mauritania, and Mali in 1976 would provide most of the statistical data we might have sought. We therefore selected individual questions and areas for more detailed research by each researcher and his team, which we knew not to be covered in the census questionnaires. The methods selected and their rationales are presented in each chapter.

The main data available from the censuses are place of birth as opposed to nationality or place of current residence. Those enumerated are also usually classified as "residents absent," "residents present," and "visitors." This allows some measurement of the volume of out- and inmigration. However, the time limits chosen to define statuses, absent or present or visitor, varied from country to country. And in no case, except the Gambia National Migration Survey, is the destination of absentees or the origin of visitors recorded.

There were some problems with the use of census and macroeconomic data. The most fundamental of the problems with the censuses was that most of the completed analyses have not yet been published. When this study was proposed early in 1977, it was predicted that the 1976 census results would be published within that year. As of this writing in October of 1979, only provisional results are available on the national level for the three major censuses. In addition to provisional national tallies, Senegal has published crude data tables for six of its eight regions, not including the central urban Cap Vert region. These provisional reports are very important and did allow us to update the global demographic picture of the region. What they did not allow was the kind of detailed analysis of fluctuations in the intensity of flows that we had hoped to be able to measure.

Our work with the census questionnaires and provisional reports also allowed us to comment on the potential usefulness of the as yet unpublished data. In general, the censuses in the Francophone countries used considerably more detailed questionnaires than those adopted in Anglophone Gambia, but they were correspondingly slower to be analyzed and published. In both areas, lack of adequate mapping and publication of maps was a serious problem to the users of the data. It was also difficult to compare data from one decennial census with the next because the boundaries of the census districts were allowed to change for administrative convenience. When this happens, the potentially valuable historical analysis of local changes is lost and historical changes can be observed only at national or provincial levels. Moreover, in some countries an individual had to move only from one small province or district to another in order to be classed as a migrant, while in others a much larger interregional movement was required. So long as the defining districts within which movement takes place vary so enormously in size, the statistics on volume of migration are not comparable from one country to another.

The most serious problem for creating a regional picture of migratory patterns is that the migratory region's boundaries do not correspond to those of any nation. In order to see accurately the boundaries of the region from census data, one would need the data to be published at a small district level, which is usually not done. Only Mauritania is attempting this. It would also be necessary for the directions of migration to be included in the census questionnaire. A question on place of previous residence and time of last move was included in the Mauritanian census and may provide very interesting results. It was not included in any of the other censuses. Therefore, in the Gambia National Migration Survey, which we conducted in the course of this study in collaboration with the Gambia government, a five-year seasonal history of moves was collected, showing seasonal patterns of movement, longer term movements, directions of movement, and motives.

Another difficulty is that many of the socioeconomic aspects of migration, which might in theory be drawn from analysis of the census questionnaires, will probably never be published. There is no statistical analysis of the educational and occupational breakdown of migrants as opposed to stable residents. No income data were collected in any of the countries. When the question of collecting income data is raised, statisticians frequently—and perhaps rightly—complain that the data would be of poor quality. We would argue that it would nevertheless, be far better than no data on this subject. Even if the data were inaccurate, by the time the same question had been asked in a second census, one would at least see changes over time.

The occupational question on the census questionnaires might eventually provide the most useful data for the socioeconomic analysis of migration. It is not, however, currently published for migrants as opposed to stable residents. At present, all countries are using the International Standard Classification of Occupations (ISCO) issued by the U.N. International Labour Office as part of a general movement toward uniform definitions in censuses and national accounts. Unfortunately, this international classification of occupations is uniquely unsuitable for an analysis of Senegambian economies. It lumps from 70 to 80 percent of the population together as farmers and herders and ignores the sharp seasonal variation in activity found in predominantly rural populations. Some countries using it have classified homemakers as unemployed even when they farm from six to twelve hours per day in the rainy season and account for a substantial proportion of the agricultural produce. And it excludes children younger than 15 who are responsible for a

substantial amount of work in these very young populations. Moreover, milking and the sale of milk are classed as "housework" even
though they are the core of the pastoral economy, apparently because they are done by women. In the Gambia National Migration
Survey, we attempted to correct this by instructing enumerators to
record a person's main source of income as his/her primary occupation. Nevertheless, the ISCO was interpreted differently in each
part of the region. Its inappropriate categories make the census
data useless as a basis for estimates of labor supply and demand
in the traditional economy.

Finally, historians and sociologists are interested in the evolution of social structures in relation to migration, specifically the
sociological components of the rural exodus. Empirical observation
suggests that all groups in traditional society participate in the
rural exodus, although the push factors of inadequate land and/or
opportunity in the village may be greater for persons of slave and
caste origin. The issue is so sensitive to rural residents and
policy makers alike that questions relating to social origin are excluded from censuses as they were in this study's field research.
It surfaced, however, spontaneously in interviews in Mauritania
and is discussed in existing sociological literature on Senegal,
Gambia, and Mali.

In summary, we have used existing census data in this study
and have drawn some rather startling conclusions about accelerated
rates of growth, urbanization, and sedentarization of nomads from
it. For the interpretation of those data, however, we relied primarily on pooling the extensive knowledge of monographic literature
and the individual research of the team members.

NOTES

1. Abdoulaye Bara Diop, "La famille rurale wolof: Mode
de résidence et organisation socio-économique," Bulletin de
l'I.F.A.N., ser. B, 36 (1974): 147-63.
2. "Demographic Aspects of Migration in West Africa,"
henceforth referred to as "Migration in West Africa," World Bank
Working Paper, Washington, D.C., June 1978.
3. Amin and Forde (London: Oxford University Press, 1974);
Comité d'information Sahel (Paris: Maspero, 1975 and 1976);
Caldwell (Washington: Overseas Liaison Committee, December
1975).
4. Prepared by Michael A. Cohen, assisted by S. A. Agunbidae, Danielle Antelin, and Anne De Mautort, World Bank Working
Paper 315, January 1979.

5. See bibliography.

6. Ann Arbor: Center for Research on Economic Development, University of Michigan, August 1977.

7. "Urban unemployment in LDCs: Toward a more general search model," paper presented to the research workshop on Rural-Urban Labor Market Interactions, Employment and Rural Development Division, Development Economics Department, IBRD, Washington, D. C., February 5-7, 1976. See also J. Harris and M. Todaro, "Migration, Unemployment, and Development: A Two-Sector Analysis," American Economic Review (March 1971) and R. Sabot, Economic Development, Structural Change and Urban Migration (Oxford: Clarendon Press, 1976).

8. "The Economics of the Migrant Labor System," in Urbanization and Migration in West Africa, ed. Hilda Kuper (Berkeley: University of California Press, 1965). Also "Backward Sloping Labor Supply Functions in Dual Economies—the Africa Case," Quarterly Journal of Economics 75 (1961): 468-92.

9. See Margaret Wolfson, Changing Approaches to Population Problems (Paris: Organization for Economic Cooperation and Development, 1977).

10. See John C. Caldwell, ed., Population Growth and Socioeconomic Change in West Africa (New York: Columbia University Press for the Population Council, 1975); Pierre Cantrelle et al., eds., Population and African Development (Dolhein, Belgium: Ordina Editions, 1974); John C. Caldwell and Chukuka Okonjo, eds., The Population of Tropical Africa (New York: Columbia University Press, 1968); and William Brass et al., The Demography of Tropical Africa (Princeton: Princeton University Press, 1968).

11. African Rural-Urban Migration: The Movement to Ghana's Towns (New York: Columbia University Press, 1969).

12. Geography of Africa (Boston: Routledge and Kegan Paul, 1973). See also K. M. Barbour and R. M. Prothero, Essays in African Population (New York: Praeger, 1962).

13. Regional Mobility and Resource Development in West Africa (Montreal: McGill University Press, 1972); Urbanization in Nigeria (London: University of London Press, 1968); "Migration and Urbanization," in Population Growth, ed. John C. Caldwell (New York: Columbia University Press, 1975), chap. 7.

14. Population, Migration, and Urbanization in Africa (New York: Columbia University Press, 1970).

15. (New York: St. Martin's Press, 1964).

16. Karl Deutsch, The Analysis of International Relations (Englewood Cliffs, N. J.: Prentice-Hall, 1968); Karl Deutsch and Haywood Alker, Mathematical Approaches to Politics (San Francisco, 1973); I. R. Savage and Karl W. Deutsch, "A Statistical

Model of the Gross Analysis of Transaction Flows," Econometrica 28 (July 1960): 551-72.

17. Louis Cantori and Steven Spiegel, The International Politics of Regions: A Comparative Approach (Englewood Cliffs, N.J.: Prentice-Hall, 1970).

2

ECONOMIC ANTHROPOLOGY OF PRECOLONIAL SENEGAMBIA FROM THE FIFTEENTH THROUGH THE NINETEENTH CENTURIES

Boubacar Barry

INTRODUCTION

Historically, Senegambia extended far beyond the present frontiers of Senegal and included the two complete basins of the Senegal and Gambia Rivers from their sources in the upper plateaus of the Futa Jalon to their openings onto the Atlantic Ocean. It was a vast area with the northern boundary north of the Senegal river basin, the southern one at the Rio Grande, and the eastern one at the Bafing.

All aspects of the region have reached their present form with the influences of history and economics, and only by considering this great geographic whole can one today understand the problems of economic integration in relation to the present frontiers of Senegal, Gambia, Mauritania, Mali, Guinea Bissau, and Guinea Conakry. This region lies at the junction of two great historical fronts of West Africa: the Sahara and the Sudan. But it has also been strongly subjected to the effects of a third front, that of the ocean, with the arrival of Europeans at the end of the fifteenth century. This last influence, which without a doubt dominated the period of the fifteenth through nineteenth centuries, led to the establishment of European bases on the coast and to trading in slaves, gum arabic, leather, gold, and ivory. For that reason, the integration process of Senegambia into a capitalist economy was instrumental in the socioeconomic and political evolution of this area.

The Atlantic slave trade that dominated the area in this period substantially influenced mainland population trends, leading to decrease rather than growth and showing westward and southward migratory movements. The trade also contributed to the physiognomy of the states, which were very fragmented, and to a regression in economic production. In general, opposition between theocratic states that were multinationally oriented and militaristic monarchies hostile to militant Islam and dependent on the Atlantic trade constitutes the fabric of Senegambian history in the era of mercantile colonialism.

The aim of this chapter is to analyze the historical background of the area in order to understand the modern phenomenon of migration with regard to economic development. It was, in fact, during the course of this long period of time that present populations became established. We will retrace the production methods along the large commercial axes and explore the socioeconomic dynamics of the formation of the local states under the influence of the Atlantic trade dominated by France, Portugal, England, and Holland. This will enable us to understand better the various changes that the Senegambian societies endured during the initial long precolonial period and then during colonization and, finally, the questions posed today by the potential economic integration of the fragmented postcolonial nation-states with their artificial frontiers.

A study of this area's evolution, particularly in its economic and demographic aspects, is greatly limited by the scarcity of quantitative data in the archives and written documents for early precolonial Senegambia. Nevertheless, we have used numerous monographies covering most of the historical regions of Senegambia. [1] There is still no historical synthesis for the whole area. The only regional study, that by Philip Curtin, [2] for all its merits, sins on a very important point. This is that the author neglected, for obvious ideological reasons, to study and interpret all the consequences of Atlantic slave trade that dominated Senegambian societies.

SENEGAMBIA FROM THE FIFTEENTH TO THE SEVENTEENTH CENTURY

For a long time, practically up to the fifteenth century, Senegambia was a dependency of the Sudan and of the Sahara—before being subjected to the influence of the ocean with the arrival of the Europeans.

Sudanese and Saharan Dependency

As Yves Person has said in relation to the Sudanese world, Senegambia is a dead end, a cul de sac where cultural waves from the east, the epicenter of Sudanese civilization, come to expire on the beaches of an ocean that leads nowhere. But very soon, at least from the eighth century onward, innovations came from the north, from the Saharan front of Islam.[3] Whereas the Saharan front, through transsaharan trade, assured an opening to the north for Senegambia (Tekrur and Silla) toward the Mediterranean world, the Sudanese, with its Islamic elements, was felt essentially along the River Gambia.

In fact, the influence of the Sahara was confined to the northern region of Senegambia, in particular the Senegal river basin where sedentary people bartered their foodstuffs and slaves for horses, salt, and products made in Maghrib, which were carried in small lots by camel caravans. In this northern zone of Senegambia, a notable tendency was the gradual displacement of black people from the north toward the south as a result of progressive aridness in the Sahel zones and of pressure from the Arabo-Berber nomads of the eastern Sahara. Against this background in the eleventh century, the Almoravid movement took place, and its Islamic militancy left lasting traces on the banks of the Senegal River before embarking on the conquest of Morocco and the Iberian peninsula.

However, the major part of Senegambia remained a direct dependency of western Sudan, which had a marked influence until and even after the fifteenth century. This influence, particularly from Mali, was the origin of the transformation of lineage societies into states and of the insertion of Senegambia into the long-distance trade circuits of the Sudan.

In fact, the Mandinka who already controlled the gold mines of Bure and Bambuk, tried very early on to control the salt mines of the ocean coast. And so, at the height of its power, Mali began veritable colonization along the Gambian River. To the south, the Mandinka founded Gabu (Guinea Bissau), Niumi, Niani, and Wuli along the river by pushing back or assimilating the autochthonous people of the Bajar group. The Mandinka were also the ancestors of the Gelewar dynasty who founded the Siin and Salum kingdoms in Serer territory. To escape Mali hegemony, which spread to most of Senegambia, the Jola concentrated in the Casamance swamps. However, in the middle of the fourteenth century, a succession crisis following the death of Mansa Suleyman in 1360 led to the establishment of the Jolof Empire, which grouped together a rather loose federation of the Wolof kingdoms of Jolof, Walo, Kajor, and Bawol. Jolof, founded by Ndaadyaan Ndyaay, thus dominated most of Senegambia and made Mali retreat toward the south of the River Gambia.

However, Jolof hegemony burnt out quickly and broke up permanently in the middle of the sixteenth century following a Fulbe invasion led by Koli Tengela. This invasion completely overturned the political balance of Senegambia.[4] Beginning about 1450, the Fulbe

of the Sahel had crossed the River Gambia to settle on the high
plateau of Futa Jalon. From there, around 1490, the Denyanke,
led by Tengela and his son, Koli Tengela, set off again. They
crossed over the Gambia again and overthrew the Malinkes of Wuli
and other dependencies of Mali; then they conquered Gajaga and the
Tukulor country, which became known as Futa Toro. This movement, well illustrated by Map 2.1, involved one of the largest population movements to our knowledge in the history of Senegambia
since the fifteenth century. Alvarez de Almada described this "Futa
invasion, which crossed the River Gambia from north to south, raz-
ing everything as far as the Rio Grande where the Fulas were defeated by the Beafadas. The invaders filled in the River Gambia
with stones at a place called 'the Fula crossing,' twelve leagues
above Lame, in order to cross it."[5] The impressive number of
Koli's companions, which increased with the addition of local inhabitants along the way, is confirmed by Lemos Colho and Joao de
Barros. In any case, because of its size, the invasion drastically
changed the demographic map of the whole of Senegambia. The movement, which departed from the Sudan, affected successively Bundu,
Futa Jalon, the Rio Grande, the Gambia, and the Senegal river basin,
leaving behind at each step numerous of Koli's traveling companions.
(See Map 2.1.)

This vast population movement took place at a time when
Senegambia was about to be involved in Portuguese trade, gradually
putting an end to its dependence on the Sudan. But before launching
into this new era dominated by the Atlantic trade, it would be best
to describe the political, economic, and social structures of Senegambia, which were to be greatly changed during the course of the
following centuries.

Political, Economic, and Social Organization
of Senegambian Societies

Despite the diversity of population—Wolof, Tukulor, Fulbe,
Peul, Mandinka, Serer, and so forth—this area had a certain unity
of social and political organization, due to having had the same influences over the centuries. The influence of the Mandinka and of
Islam is evident in the transition of these societies from a lineage-
based political organization into states. Thus the monarchical state
confirmed the hierarchization of the society, which had been based
either on a matrilinear (Wolof and Serer) or on a patrilinear system
(Fulbe, Tukulor, and Mandinka). In both cases, the social and
political organization rested on a subordinate relationship between
a free class and a nonfree class. The Sudanese influence introduced

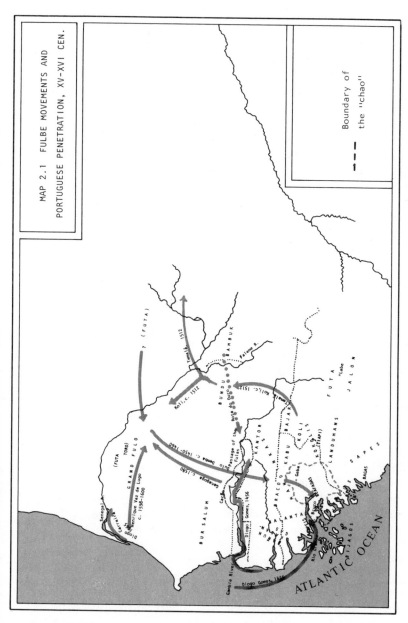

MAP 2.1 FULBE MOVEMENTS AND
PORTUGUESE PENETRATION, XV-XVI CEN.

Boundary of
the "chao"

Source: A. Texeira da Mota, "Fulas e Beafadas no Rio Grande no Seculo XV," _Academia das Ciencias de Lisbao_ (1970): 921.

31

a system of endogamous occupational castes, which ranked at the bottom of the freeborn. Oligarchical political structures were closely linked to the social system. Most of these were monarchies elected by a college of nobles (Seb Ak Baor in Walo, the Grand Jaraf in the Jolof and Sin). Power was greatly limited in practice by many rights to which the various social groups, even those in the servile class, were entitled.

Because of lack of documents, however, it is difficult to unravel the political, social, and economic dynamics of Senegambia before its contact with Europe. Senegambian societies were, in the large majority, essentially agricultural with a self-sufficient domestic economy, except for certain nomadic Fulbe groups that traveled down the banks of the River Senegal between the plateau of Futa Jalon to the Ferlo. The fundamental characteristic of this self-sufficient economy was, according to Claude Meillassoux,

> the knowledge of agricultural and artisanal techniques in order to use a fairly high level of productivity to meet the food demands necessary to maintain and reproduce its members as well as to repeat the agricultural cycle. Using the land as a means of production, which yields its product at term due to the prior investment of energy. Using human energy as the dominant source of energy in agricultural and artisanal labor. Using individual agricultural production methods that need no more than the investment of individual labor. [6]

Meillassoux continues,

> Production was thus founded on a certain collectivism based on the lineage or its substitute, the extended family. The land, being indissociable from the relationship of production and reproduction which enabled its use, could not be subjected to "appropriation" for itself by which it would be separated from the social context which gave it an economic use and worth. [7]

Land was a patrimony belonging jointly to members of the domestic community in which the self-sufficient economy, far from being at a subsistence level, was integrated into regional and foreign trade.

First there was the exchange of agricultural produce with produce from animals. This complementarity was a permanent factor that ruled relations between the sedentary people of the River Senegal and the nomadic Berbers of present-day Mauritania. It was due to the Berbers that the river valley was linked to transsaharan trade, trading slaves for horses and also gold for manufactured products from the Maghrib. Although, since the rise of Mali, the River Senegal was slightly off the main transsaharan trade routes, its whole length did constitute an important trade axis. The inhabitants of the delta of the River Senegal traded salt from the rich salt mines of Ganjol and salt fish for millet with the people of Futa Toro and the upper river basin, as far upstream as Kayes. Similarly, the northeastern part of Senegambia was linked to the long trade routes, which ended at the trading centers of the River Niger, by the Soninkes of Gajaaga who monopolized the gold trade of Bambuk. The Soninke were spread throughout the area, and Gajaaga was the terminal for various trade routes supplied by horse from the east, by donkey from the south, and by camel from the north. At the same time, it was a distribution point for trade along the River Senegal.[8]

The second Senegambian commercial axis was the River Gambia, dominated by the exchange of salt from Gabu and the coast for the textiles of Mali and kola from the forests. This trade was the monopoly of Mandinka Jula and Jaxanke Jula, who came from Ja on the Niger River. They settled towns from the gold mines of Bambuk up to the Lower Gambia and along toward the forests in the south, in Sierra Leone. It was they who, along with the Soninke (in reality, western Jula), assured the liaison of the east-west route between the upper Niger and the upper Gambia and then the north-south kola route across Futa Jalon.[9]

This long-distance trading was limited to luxury products— salt, gold, kola, horses, textiles—and slaves. It reflected the complementarity of the natural zones of West Africa, that is, forest, savannah, and desert, in relation to which Senegambia was until then a sort of cul de sac and an outlet. This long-distance trading was monopolized by communities of specialist merchants often confused with the ethnic groups of the same names, the Zwaya Berbers, the Jaxankes, and the Soninkes. The trade was also associated with Islam. This is because there was a certain demarcation between the military-political groups that ruled countries and the Muslim trading communities that were semi-autonomous enclaves linked together across national boundaries.[10] This was the heritage of the merchant Islam of the medieval empires of the Sudan, which in Senegambia did not have the opportunity to change fundamentally the sociopolitical structures of the different kingdoms that were already established. So the absence of an important dynamic merchant class did not alter the mode of production of the domestic economies insofar as the only resource, the land, was the common patrimony of the various communities that had about the same level of productivity throughout

Senegambia. We should say that, with the exception of the River Senegal where the population density was high very early on, the question of land has never been a big problem because shifting cultivation, the model that predominated in the area, entailed the gradual displacement of population. Moreover, the fact that there was plenty of free land explains to a great extent the ability to absorb and integrate foreigners in the various communities of Senegambia. Thus the question of land was largely not involved in conflicts between communities or states, with the exception of the constant conflict between nomadic and sedentary people.

However, it is evident that well before the fifteenth century the Lamanate system, the earliest method of land tenure, had already been replaced by a system of fiefs and charters developed by the rising monarchies of Walo, Kajor, Sin, Futa, and so on, with the tribute due superiors becoming higher and higher. However, as suggested by Abdoulaye Bara Diop, monarchy does not fundamentally change the inalienable right to the land. Rather, the kings, while respecting the right of the Lamans, the landowners, took more and more of the free land to distribute to relatives and allies among their entourages (warriors, nobles, marabouts) and even had to encroach on the land of the Lamanate. This gave rise to a system of fiefs and charters and led very quickly to the feudalization of tenure. But the pattern of land ownership did not alter under monarchies in one fundamental aspect, which seems to us to be the distinction between ownership and right of usufruct, so that eminent domain existed only when these two rights belonged to one and the same person.[11] So, with this self-sufficient economy, as Pathe Diagne says,

> The wealth is in the granaries, and in the herds, of course, but prestige is in the blood, in the birthright. For this peasant aristocracy which had not completely abandoned working the land, material equality was a fact. But hierarchical rank and status remained of foremost importance and explained, as Boubacar Ly suggested so correctly, that the feeling of honor was an essential stimulant to social dynamism.[12]

However, the simple needs of the more privileged classes and the relative poverty of the aristocracies in power did not preclude the emergence, from this period on, of tensions and contradictions within the Senegambian societies based on inequality and the hierarchization of the various social groups.

The internal dynamics outlined here profoundly accelerated and reinforced from the end of the fifteenth century in the wake of Senegambia's contact with European maritime powers. This external factor is important in explaining the political, social, and

economic transformation insofar as the precapitalist Senegambian
societies endured the assault of Europe while it was in full capitalist evolution and created locally a veritable economic and political
domination, which radically altered the course of their destiny.
From that time onward, the evolution of Senegambia could no longer
be understood without considering this external influence. It was
dominated by European trade, which conquered the international
market by monopolizing trade with Asia, Africa, and America from
the fifteenth century onward.

Atlantic Trade and Restructuring of the States

The arrival of Europeans on the coast, particularly the Portuguese at the end of the fifteenth century, radically changed the course
of this area's history. The maritime fringe became the principal
front of acculturation. The installation of the Portuguese at Arguin
around 1445 was the first victory of the boat over the caravan, which
meant that trade was diverted away from traditional trading routes
to the profit of Atlantic trade. The Portuguese, in their pursuit of
gold, attempted to penetrate the Sudan by the waterways of the River
Senegal and, particularly, of the River Gambia. Ultimately, the
failure of an attempt to construct a fort in 1488 on the banks of the
River Senegal, the difficulty of navigating the Felou Falls area of
the Senegal River, and Mandinka domination in Gambia meant that
the Portuguese had to trade on the coast and at the two deltas without acquiring a territorial base. This trade in gold, ivory, leather,
and slaves marked the beginning of a profound remodeling of the
political map of Senegambia.
In fact, during the fifteenth and sixteenth centuries, Portuguese
trade changed the destiny of this cul de sac; it became the main access of the whole hinterland of the Sudan toward the sea. From that
time on, Senegambia would also be subjected to external demands
and be somewhat transformed according to these demands, which
would determine not only the internal evolution of the area but also
the form European colonization would take.
Originally, the establishment of the Portuguese at Arguin and
at the mouth of the Senegal and Gambia Rivers was intended to divert
the gold from the Sudan toward the Atlantic. The River Gambia,
specifically Kuntaur, was the principal outlet for the declining Mali
empire. Nevertheless, it is difficult to evaluate the amount of gold
traded from the mines of Bambuk (between the Faleme and the Bafing)
and Bure (on the upper Niger) via Senegambia. Philip Curtin estimates, with every necessary reservation on his figures, that the export of gold did not exceed 35 kgs per year for the sixteenth and

seventeenth centuries, and that only in good years.[13] We must also include in the Senegambian market the Arguin trading center that, through the nomadic camel drivers, would certainly be supplied from Bambuk. Vitorino Magalhaes Godinho estimates the annual ceiling of receipts from Arguin during the last quarter of the fifteenth century and the first quarter of the sixteenth as between 20 and 25 kgs, that is, from 5,500 to 7,000 cruzados.[14] He adds that from 1542 the trading station was utterly spoiled by illicit trading, the amount of which is difficult to assess, and also by the fact that the Portuguese could from then onward trade directly at the mouth of the Senegal and Gambia Rivers.[15]

The arrival of the Portuguese by sea and river in Upper Gambia, not far from the foothills of Futa Jalon, represented a turning point in the history of Sudanese gold, which they poured into the Kuntaur market. This new commercial route gave access to the coast from the River Senegal from as far away as Sierra Leone and was a contributing factor in the severance of the Bambuk and Bure regions from the Niger river basin and the Sahara to become a permanent part of Senegambia. Our research suggests that the trade of Senegambia has been underestimated and was in fact highly coveted by different European powers from the sixteenth century on.[16]

Apart from gold, the leather trade was very important before the slave trade era. In the sixteenth century, Senegambia exported between 6,000 and 7,000 skins per year, reaching a peak of 150,000 skins in 1660 because of the high demand from Europe.[17] Coelho notes that around 1660 from 35,000 to 40,000 skins per year were loaded at the port of Rufisque.[18]

To this we must add the trade of beeswax and ivory. According to Coelho, the Afro-Portuguese dealing between Cacheu and Goree brought between 1,500 and 2,000 quintals of ivory and beeswax to the Dutch. In 1673, non-Portuguese trade represented about 3,000 quintals of beeswax and ivory per year. After 1685, the English companies became the principal exporters, with 20 or 30 tons of beeswax and from 20 to 30 tons of ivory per boat.[19]

Lastly, there is the slave trade, and one often forgets Senegambia's importance in this during the course of the fifteenth through seventeenth centuries. As far as Curtin is concerned, Senegambia was certainly the first source of slaves shipped directly to Europe by sea and continued to be the principal source during the sixteenth century. But he estimated the number of slaves as between 250 and 1,000 per year for the period 1526-50, and two centuries later the figure was about the same for the coastal region encompassing the Wolof, Fulbe, Serer, and the Mandinkas of Gambia. So, as the overall volume of the West African slave trade toward America increased, the Senegambian proportion dropped from 20 percent to

less than 1 percent of the total.[20] It is evident that Curtin underestimated beyond measure the substantial demographic depression
caused by the slave trade in Africa and, in particular, in the case
of Senegambia. Larenzo Coelho told of a ship leaving Arguin in
August 1513 that alone transported 145 slaves, and Godinho estimated the annual traffic at from 800 to 1,000 from this faraway
Saharan locality, which had been established in order to divert trade
from the caravan routes to the benefit of the Portuguese.[21] Unfortunately, we lack figures for this trade, which was important during
the early development of the Cape Verde Islands, of Madeira, and,
later, at the beginning of the sugar economy, of the Antilles because
of the geographic position of Senegambia. Pereira estimated Portuguese trade around 1500 at more than 3,500 slaves between the
Senegal River and Sierra Leone, and the Portuguese authorities estimated trade at Cacheu before 1640 at 3,000 slaves per year.[22] In
1660, pointing out the advantages of Portuguese trade in the Fleuve,
Lavanha mentioned that slaves represented the essential part of the
traffic.[23] Moreover, trading with the Cape Verde Islands was possible because slaves had been transported there from Senegambia.
In 1582, the population of Pogo and Santiago consisted of 1,608
whites, 400 free slaves, and 13,700 slaves who specialized in the
cotton industry for the Senegambian market.[24] These people would
give rise to the Afro-Portuguese community (Lancados or Tangomaos),
which played an important role in interregional trade in kola, textiles,
and salt between Senegambia and the coast of Upper Guinea and linked
the River Gambia by boat to the forest zone of Sierra Leone.

In exchange for gold, ivory, beeswax, and slaves, the Senegambians received European products from the Portuguese and,
later, in the seventeenth century, from the French, the Dutch, and
the English. These were mostly cheap jewelry, firearms, spirits,
iron bars, and textiles that were mainly destined for the ruling
classes, often to the detriment of local industry. Le Maire gives
us an idea of trade in Senegal in 1682 in the following terms.

> In exchange for these negros one gave cotton material,
> copper, tin, iron, spirits, and some glass bangles.
> Profit on this trade was 800%. Leather, ivory and
> gum arabic was taken to France and the slaves were
> sent to the French islands of America to work on sugar
> plantations. The best slaves went for 10 francs each
> and could be sold for more than a hundred ecus, so the
> expense was less for the purchase than for transporta-
> tion because of the high cost of ships.[25]

This is not the place to give the exact amount of imports from Senegambia, but we want to show the unequal exchange conditions that

were established from the beginning between the Europeans and the Senegambians and, particularly, the consequences of this trading on the historical political, social, and economic development of this area.

First, concerning the political aspect, from the second half of the sixteenth century, under the influence of the Atlantic trade, a structuring of the countries of Senegambia began. In fact, the Jolof empire was shaken up by the massive Fulbe invasion of Koli Tengela and disintegrated under the influence of the Portuguese trade that, by benefiting the coastal states, accelerated political fragmentation of Senegambia. Between 1530 and 1550, the coastal province of Kajor proclaimed its independence from the Jolof with Amari Ngone as first damel (king). [26] This example was soon followed by Walo and Bawol, leaving the original Jolof isolated in the interior because of lack of a direct link with the Atlantic trade that had become all-important. It was this same process that brought about the independence of the Sin and Salum kingdoms during the sixteenth century.

After the breakup of this large Jolof region, the damel of Kajor, Amari Ngone, tried to impose his hegemony by annexing Bawol (he took the title of the Damel-Teñ) and one part of Walo, the mouth of the River Senegal. But, very early on, the Bawol-Kajor crisis at the turn of the seventeenth century led to the rising to power of the Denanke kingdom of the "Grand Ful," which in its turn extended its domination over the major part of Senegambia. The Denanke dynasty reached its peak at the beginning of the eighteenth century under the reign of Samba Lamu. At that time, Futa Toro, by occupying the mouth of the river and a part of the Sahel, maintained its twofold orientation toward the Sudan and the Atlantic. [27] In the meantime, the magnificent Mali empire was in the process of collapsing, but it managed to maintain its authority over one part of the River Gambia after 1550 following the fragmentation of the Jolof. But, soon left to themselves, the Mandinkas of the west divided into small principalities on both banks of the Gambia: Niumi, Wuli, and Badibu. Only Gabu, in Guinea Bissau and the Casamance, were to have a large enough territory to attempt imposing their hegemony along the south bank of the Gambia. [28] Political fragmentation was the most important occurrence in Senegambia in the second half of the sixteenth century. The Atlantic trade contributed to it up to the colonial conquest by accelerating the breakdown of the socioeconomic and political structures.

As for the socioeconomic aspect, despite its relative unimportance, the Atlantic trade was the object of bitter competition between the English, Dutch, and French, which directly threatened Portuguese monopoly from the beginning of the seventeenth century. Their arrival in connection with the development of the slave trade, which had become the cornerstone of colonial mercantilism, led to the partition of Senegambia into zones of influence, in each of which a fortified post was constructed. From 1621, the Dutch had been established at Goree, followed by the French at Saint-Louis in 1659, the English in Gambia in 1668, and, finally, the Portuguese who remained confined to Cacheu. The setting up of trading stations over all the coast linked by ports of trade completed the reorientation of Senegambian trade toward the sea. Moreover, from the end of the eighteenth century on, the slave trade created an unstable atmosphere of wars and incessant organized uprisings, often by the aristocracies against their own subjects.

Directing the trading route toward the sea and intensifying the slave trade led to the beginning of a vast marabout movement from Mauritania, led by Nāsir ad-Dīn, between 1673 and 1677. The movement embodied simultaneously the defense of the transsaharan trading interests and the desire to put an end to the human drain generated by the Atlantic slave trade. This vast movement encompassed Mauritania, Futa Toro, and the kingdoms of Jolof, Kajor, and the Walo. It was eventually reversed by a coalition of the French from Saint-Louis and the overthrown aristocracies. This victory prevented any possibility of creating a vast political whole and marked the triumph of Atlantic trade and the birth of military aristocracies engaged in the slave trade, which became the principal activity during the eighteenth century.[29]

IMPACT OF THE SLAVE TRADE IN THE EIGHTEENTH CENTURY

From the second half of the seventeenth century on, sugar cane development in the New World led to an increase in the slave trade, which became the mainstay of African trade during the whole eighteenth century. Since the sixteenth century, Senegambia had been a considerable source of servile humanpower, and it would continue to steadily feed the market in the Antilles because of its geographic position. This trade was extremely important, although in the eighteenth century Senegambia became a smaller or even negligible source compared with the rest of the African coast, which saw "the biggest shipments of men that had ever taken place on the surface of the seas."[30]

The Slave Trade Era and the Demographic Drain

Because of lack of adequate documentation, it is unfortunately difficult to obtain an idea of the population of Senegambia in order to measure correctly the extent of the demographic drain from this region with the slave trade. Apart from attempts by Curtin and Mbaye Guèye and the adjustments made by Charles Becker and V. Martin, there is no methodical study on the slave trade as to the number of slaves exported from the whole of Senegambia. At any rate, Curtin has attempted to give us a detailed study of the number of slaves, although his results are often incorrect because he omits numerable sources and because he is predisposed to lower the available figures considerably by not taking into account the illegal trade. According to Table 2.1, Curtin estimates the export capacity from Senegambia between 1681 and 1810 at 304,330 slaves, which for the eighteenth century gives a potential total of 259,900 slaves (between 1711 and 1810).[31]

Thus, according to Curtin, during the eighteenth century the annual rate of possible slave exports from Senegambia varied between 1,000 for the period 1793-1800 and 4,090 for the period 1724-1735.[32]

Curtin gives the data in Table 2.2 for actual slave exports between 1711 and 1810 from calculation of shipping data and reaches the overall figure of 181,800 slaves, 77,600 for the French trade and 104,200 for the English trade.[33] The figures go from 259,000 to 181,800—or a difference of 78,100—slaves between the capacity estimates and the actual data for the period 1711-1810. Moreover, the annual average between 1721 and 1730 out of a total of 22,500, according to Table 2.2, would be 2,250 slaves. This reduces to almost half the forecasts of Table 2.1, which gave the figure of 4,090 slaves per year in 1730.

Jean Suret-Canale has already shown the merits of Curtin's work and also his guilty silence on the slave trade and its effects on Senegambian societies.[34] Better yet, Charles Becker has clearly shown the flimsiness of the figures put forward by Curtin from embarcations of certain years. Thus, by using other available data for several years, Becker estimates about 500,000 slaves instead of the 304,330 slaves suggested by Curtin.[35] Charles Becker thought it preferable to look for results from meticulous enquiries on the slave trade in the archives of port towns to obtain definite figures.

So far as I am concerned, it is obvious that the arbitrary choice of slave figures by Curtin, which reduced by almost half the estimates already calculated from the lowest figures, cannot contribute correctly to assessing the demographic drain that occurred with the trade.

The most important point is not, in fact, the number of slaves per se, but rather the consequences of this economy, founded on human hunting, that created a permanently unstable situation unfavorable to productive activities not to mention the effects of the demographic bleeding.

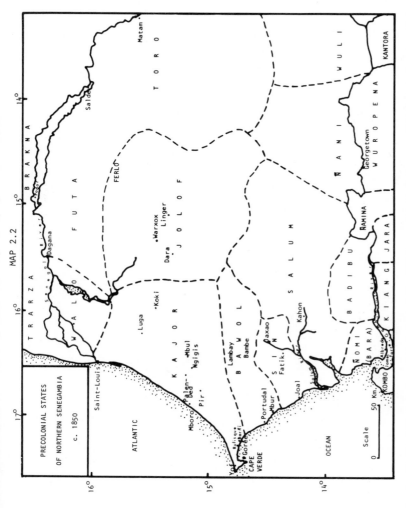

MAP 2.2

PRECOLONIAL STATES

OF NORTHERN SENEGAMBIA

c. 1850

Source: Lucie Gallistel Colvin, "Kajor and Its Diplomatic Relations with Saint-Louis of Senegal, 1963–1861" (Ph.D. dissertation, Columbia University, 1972), p. 17.

TABLE 2.1

Consolidated Capacity Estimates for the Slave Exports of Senegambia

Date of Estimate	Distribution of Slaves by Embarkation Point					Total Annually	Applied to Years	Total for Period
	Saint-Louis	Gajaaga	Goree	French Gambia	English Gambia			
1687	100	—	500	750	—	1,350	1681–89	12,150
1693	200	—	200	500	—	900	1690–1704	13,500
1716	—	2,380*	—	—	750	3,130	1705–16	32,160
1718	50	600	470	400	750	2,270	1717–23	15,890
1730	—	1,090*	—	—	3,000	4,090	1724–35	49,080
1741	—	900*	—	—	2,140	3,040	1736–46	33,440
1753	500	550	540	—	1,000	2,590	1747–60	36,260
1766	1,110*	—	425	—	1,511	3,050	1761–67	21,350
1769–78	1,500*	—	300	—	1,500	3,300	1768–78	36,300
1779–88	—	1,716	—	—	1,050	2,800	1779–92	39,200
1795	—	—	—	—	1,000	1,000	1793–1800	8,000
1802–10	—	700	—	—	—	700	1801–10	7,000
Total								304,330
Total 1711–1810								259,900

*Only combined totals are available for these years.

Source: Philip Curtin, Economic Change in Precolonial Africa: Senegambia in the Era of the Slave Trade (Madison: University of Wisconsin Press, 1975), p. 162.

TABLE 2.2

Slave Exports from Senegambia, 1711–1810

Dates	French Exports	British Exports	Total
1711–20	10,300	20,600	30,900
1721–30	13,400	9,100	22,500
1731–40	12,300	13,900	26,200
1741–50	7,700	17,300	25,000
1751–60	6,300	16,200	22,500
1761–70	2,300	11,800	14,100
1771–80	4,000	8,100	12,100
1781–90	17,400	2,900	20,300
1791–1800	3,400	2,800	6,200
1801–10	500	1,500	2,000
Total	77,600	104,200	181,800

Source: Philip Curtin, Economic Change in Precolonial Africa: Senegambia in the Era of the Slave Trade (Madison: University of Wisconsin Press, 1975), p. 163.

Consequences of the Slave Trade

From the strong resistance of the slave traders to abolition of the slave trade during the nineteenth century, it is clear that this was very important throughout the eighteenth century, which was truly the slave trade era. In fact, this "economic commodity" was the basis of the mercantile policy of the European powers and took priority in the African trade. On this point, Senegambia as a whole was no exception to the rule. Study of Senegambian trade confirms this hypothesis.

A look at French trade profits in Senegambia according to the report on Senegalese trade dated April 23, 1723 gives the following figures.[36]

Type of Merchandise	Purchase Price in Senegal (livres tournois)	Selling Price in France (livres franc)	Profit (livres franc)
8,000 quintals of gum arabic	6/qal 48,000 35/qal	—	232,000
2,000 Negroes	120/ea 240,000 800/ea	1,600,000	1,360,000
400 quintals of ivory	72/qal 28,800 150/qal	60,000	31,200
1,000 quintals of beeswax	64/qal 64,000 —	200,000	136,000
10,000 skins	10 pieces 5,000 3/10 pieces	35,000	300,000
50 gold marcs	512/marc 25,600 1000/marc	50,000	24,400
Total	411,400	1,945,000	2,083,600

The company could make a profit every year of 2,083,600 livres franc from its business with Senegal. Deduct expenses for food and salaries for employees in the colony (estimated at 200,000 lt/yr) and equipping seven vessels (60,000 per boat or 420,000). These two items include the sum of 620,000 to be deducted from 1,813,600 of profit, leaving for the Compagnie des Indes 1,193,600 of profit in an ordinary year.

These estimates for the French trade alone clearly show the preponderance of the slave trade. Later in the century, Golberry, quoted fully by Becker and Martin, gave an idea of the whole Senegambian trade in 1786: slaves, 4,560,000 F; gum arabic, 3,000,000 F; gold, 94,000 F; other, 451,000 F.

It seems clear that slaves were the biggest part of the trade, for the total for both the English and French reached 8,000.[37] Gum arabic played an increasing part in trade with Senegambia and particularly the Senegal river basin region. Gum production well exceeded 10,000 quintals per year, and its gradually increasing use in the textile industry explains the fact that England, France, and Holland entered into a real gum arabic war between 1720 and 1760. But, paradoxically, gum arabic could not take the place of the slave trade, because it was entirely monopolized by the Moors of Mauritania. The result of this was the profitable integration of the Maures into the Atlantic trade. Yet they were the ones who at the end of the seventeenth century had reacted violently against Saint-Louis' commercial monopoly, which drained all of the trade from the Senegal river basin toward the sea without compensation for Mauritania. With gum arabic, the Maures overcame the seventeenth-century crisis and their new power created a new conflict with the black countries of the River Senegal, who weakened gradually from the effects of the slave trade.

During the first half of the eighteenth century, the French made a considerable effort to direct the Moor caravans toward the trading posts on the River Senegal in order to end the large gum arabic trade that was taking place at the Mauritanian posts of Arguin and Portendick with the English and the Dutch. And so Moor pressure on both sides of the River Senegal was a constant factor in the second half of the eighteenth century. With their raids for their internal need for slaves and also because of the needs of the Atlantic trade, the Moors gradually pushed people south to take refuge on the left bank. This was significant for the Walo kingdom whose capital, Jurbel, was located on the north bank until the seventeenth century and gradually moved over to the south bank, at NDer, on the edge of the Lac de Guiers.

Constant pressure also led to a Torodo revolution in Futa Toro in the 1770s, which fought against the effects of the slave trade and Moor domination. The success of the Torodo revolution then created an atmosphere at Futa Toro that attracted neighboring people. Schmaltz remarked that in 1819 the Isle à Morphil in the Futa was inhabited mostly by people from Walo.[38] Previously, the unstable atmosphere engendered by the trade had brought about the massive departure of Muslims from the Senegambian coast to set up the theocracies of Bundu and Futa Jalon in the interior at the end of the seventeenth century. These new theocracies reached at the beginning against the trade and became places of refuge in the plateau of Futa Jalon where population density was extremely high despite the poor quality of the soil. Although they protected their fellow Muslims inside these theocracies, these countries still turned against weaker peoples hunting humans, the ultimate merchandise of the slave trade (imposed from overseas). The wars conducted against the minorities—Tenda, Konagi, Jola, Balantes, and so on—meant that these people had to flee to the marshes or the hills in order to escape extinction.

In general, the slave trade had the disastrous consequences of diminishing the productive forces and weakening all of the Senegambian societies. From a political aspect, fragmentation of the large mainland countries of the preceding period resulted from rebellion attempts by the provincial chiefs. Wars of succession, internal political domination by warriors called ceddo (crown slaves), and the internecine wars often fostered by the managers of the European trading stations on the coast contributed greatly to general instability in the area.

Instability, destruction caused by permanent conflict, and natural disasters brought numerous periods of famine that dog the history of Senegambia. First mention of famine on the coast dates from 1639-42, reportedly caused by an infestation of grasshoppers. Then in 1673-77, after the war of the marabouts and the destruction of crops during this conflict, the river region suffered a general famine that Chambonneau described as follows.

> During my voyage in Futa during July 1676, I saw
> whole families who offered themselves to me for
> slaves, as long as they could be fed. They were in
> such dire straits that they were killing each other to
> steal food . . . to such an extent that we could have
> traded more than 600 that year if the boats—and my-
> self the first—had not refused the merchandise.[39]

Toward the middle of the eighteenth century, a drought, complicated by a civil war in Kajor and Bawol, brought about a great
famine that spread from Bissau to Galam, paradoxically limiting
even the slave trade because there was no grain to feed slaves.
Thus, in November 1753, "lack of food prevented Mr. Ansseno from
trading more than 100 captives who were presented to him by kings
of Kajor and Sin who were at war."[40] In fact, beginning in June
1753, famine covered all of Senegambia and the people of Jolof and
of Kajor fled in 1754 to Walo, which was slightly less affected by
the general disaster.

> The certainty of being captured was not enough to pre-
> vent them coming to the only place where there was
> some slight relief from their destitution, and as they
> had no other alternative to death or captivity, it is pre-
> sumed that the trade would not let up until the harvest-
> ing of the small millet, i.e. until the end of September;
> the harvesting of the large millet that is currently tak-
> ing place along our river draws everyone from nearby.[41]

In fact, during this period, it is difficult to decide which was
worse, the natural disasters of drought and grasshoppers or the
slave trade with its procession of civil wars. There was also the
trade itself, which further depleted the self-sufficient economy by
using its foodstuffs to feed the human cargo in the slave depots of
the coast and during the long ocean voyage. So food production, already greatly diminished by instability, was also monopolized by
the Atlantic trade. This loss was in no way compensated for by imports, which still in the eighteenth century were largely made up of
firearms, spirits, cloth, and iron, without counting the cheap jewelry.
Because of this, even more than during the preceding period, commercial exchange during the slave trade era dealt a fatal blow to all
fields of artisanal production and also to interregional trade between
Senegambia and the neighboring countries. Senegambia, weakened
in the interior, was thus traversed by routes that were full of human
cargo leading toward the coast. This great region was powerless
against the readjustments of the European trading demands in the

nineteenth century, with the abolition of the slave trade that would lead directly to the colonial conquest.

SENEGAMBIA IN THE NINETEENTH CENTURY: READJUSTMENTS AFTER THE ATLANTIC TRADE AND THE COLONIAL CONQUEST

From the end of the eighteenth century, there was a gradual transition from the European economy of commercial mercantilism to industrial capitalism, thus leading Europe to look for new forms of domination of precapitalist economies on the periphery. Under the new doctrine of free exchange advocated by industrial England, abolition of the slave trade was inevitable. It had already well played its role in the initial accumulation of capital. Thus, after three centuries of slave trade, black Africa would have a new role: to supply raw materials and agricultural produce to Europe and to buy, in turn, manufactured products from rapidly expanding European industry. But before this permanent integration into an absolute capitalist system, France attempted in Senegambia an agricultural experiment under a simple economic protectorate. Failure of the agricultural campaign, and particularly peanut growing, precipitated the colonial conquest that forcibly imposed economic and political domination to enable France to exploit Senegambian resources.

Agricultural Campaign in the First Half of the Nineteenth Century

At the beginning of the nineteenth century, industrial England forced its European partners to outlaw the slave trade, and, in order to adapt to this new situation, France undertook an agricultural colonization, with Walo at the mouth of the River Senegal as the center of the experiment. Because of a slave revolt in Santo Domingo that had ruined the sugar colonies for France, and particularly because of the advent of industrial capitalism, it became necessary to integrate Africa into the capitalist system as a directly dependent periphery of the European center.[42] At first France had only limited means to implement this objective and began the agricultural colonization of the Walo with the intention of growing cotton, sugar cane, and tobacco. The idea was simply to use the servile humanpower that had previously been transported into the New World over the centuries to work in agriculture on the spot in Africa.

Walo was chosen by Gov. Schmaltz because of the proximity of this kingdom to the trading station of Saint-Louis and also because

this area, which had already been undermined by the slave trade
and Moor domination, was incapable of opposing this policy. Thus
on May 8, 1819, Gov. Schmaltz signed with the brak, Amar Fatim
Mborso, the treaty of Njaw, ceding France land for its agricultural
project. It must be said that the Walo chiefs agreed to sign the
treaty because they had previously been intimidated by the military
uniforms of the Fleuris expedition in 1818, tempted by the promise
of protection against the pillages of the Trarza Moors, and also attracted by the lure of new customs receipts offered in the treaty.
Walo, which became a sort of economic protectorate, averaging
annual customs of 10,358,640 F, suddenly tripled the income of the
aristocracy in power thanks to its alliance with the trading station
of Saint-Louis.

Schmaltz immediately chose Dagana as the center of the agricultural colonization and undertook the construction of a blockhaus
on the banks of the River Senegal to assure protection of the agricultural buildings. The ministry agreed to a credit of 11,223,358 F for
the period 1818-24 to launch the project. Schmaltz's successors,
Baron Roger in particular (from 1822 to 1827), attempted to extend
the crops on a large scale away from the research at Richard Toll,
creating an agricultural and commercial company for this purpose.
But the results from the experimental growing of cotton, tobacco,
and sugar cane were not satisfactory, so that in 1831 France decided
to put an end to this agricultural scheme. Failure of the agricultural
program was due to several factors.

Pressure from neighboring people, Futa and especially the
Trarza Moors, created an unstable situation that did not help the
agricultural campaign. The Moors and Futa Toro both claimed sov-
ereignty over Walo, and France had to negotiate treaties with them
guaranteeing peace along the river; these were never respected.

The agricultural campaign also ran into the problem of land,
which the inhabitants refused to give up despite the agreement with
the aristocracy. In 1827, before the extension of the Saint-Louis
land concessions, the people of Walo systematically broke the dykes
constructed by the French.

It also failed because of difficulties in obtaining labor. Not
only did the Walo-Walo refuse to work in the French concessions,
but also there was practically no humanpower in a country that had
lost its people to three centuries of slave trading. The French had
to resort to a system of contract labor, thus indirectly perpetuating
the slave trade mode. During the colonial period, the institutional
continuity was perpetuated by introducing forced labor.

Lastly, the agricultural campaign failed because of resistance
by the traditional merchant class of Saint-Louis. The small traders
of Saint-Louis and the slave traders had opposed the economic revo-

lution inherent in the agricultural colonization scheme, because they were worried that they would be eliminated with the advent of the big financial and industrial capital.

Failure of the agricultural campaign brought about speculation in gum arabic and also in illegal slave trading, through the middle of the nineteenth century.

Above all, this was a failure of the economic protectorate, by which the French had wanted to exploit the country by paying customs to the aristocracy. Learning from this failure, France decided on a policy of conquest to be realized when and as the means became available. Walo was thus annexed in 1855, and it became the principal support base for France's future colonial empire in West Africa. Meanwhile, however, after the failure of the agricultural campaign in 1831, Senegambia went through a long period of transition before becoming the first French area conquered at the end of the nineteenth century. The transition was marked by a deep crisis in Senegambian societies, because of attempts to restructure internal politics and economics after the end of the slave trade and also because of the reluctance of the colonial economy to look for new paths. The triumph of legitimate trading went along with armed conquest, thus increasing the troubles of this region before it was permanently integrated to an active capitalist system under colonial control.

During the first half of the nineteenth century, the gum arabic trade represented three-quarters of the exports from Senegal, which totaled 1,643,632 F in 1825 and comprised: beeswax, 88,425 F; leather, 255,894 F; ivory, 32,848 F; gum arabic, 12,227,029 F.[43]

When agriculture failed, the gum arabic trade took top place and encouraged the return of wild speculation. Toward 1830, a real gum arabic fever took hold of the population of Saint-Louis. "Gum arabic has become the safeguard of Senegalese industry and trade: it wants exclusivity and any other idea for enriching Senegal is a heresy."[44] In fact, trade as a whole suffered from the uncertainty of whether the policy should be to have exclusivity or free trade. This period of commercial uncertainty corresponds to the period of transition from a trading station economy to a colonial economy. This transition was dominated economically by the growing importance of peanuts in commerce during the second half of the nineteenth century and also by the political and military conflicts unleashed by the colonial conquest.

Advent of Peanut Growing and the Colonial Conquest

Following the decline of the slave trade and the general commercial crisis in Senegambia, peanuts became the "miracle" product to get out of the impasse. The Portuguese introduced peanuts in the fifteenth century to meet new demands from European industry for lubricants and soap. From that time, production in Gambia increased from 47 tonnes (200 pounds) in 1845 to 11,095 tonnes (133,113 pounds) in 1865. The French in Senegal rapidly overtook the British with exports that went from 1.2 tons in 1840 to 22,500 tons in 1870. Thus the combined production of Senegal and Gambia had rapidly reached 60,000 tons by 1889. From then on, the future of Senegambia was linked in a sort of economic fatalism to the growing of peanuts. Viewed by its promotors at the beginning as a means of saving the colony of Senegal, the new product disrupted all the trade routes and aggravated social tensions. In sum, it produced the major transformations that were manifest during the period of consolidation of legitimate trade in the years 1870 to 1890.[45]

The Senegambian peasant would henceforth be in direct contact with the outside, and he would have as partners the European business manager and the African or mulatto intermediary in the context of a monetary economy. But the peasant who would produce the export crop did not have time to assert his economic and political independence vis-à-vis the former aristocracy. From the beginning, expansion of the peanut crop created a major contradiction between the French or English economic interests on the one hand and those of the aristocracies in power on the other. The prime desire of the aristocracies to control and benefit from the new profits of the peasant world in growing peanuts and to restrict the demands of French and English interests, which became more and more excessive, hastened the armed conflict that led to colonial conquest. And so it was that the pillaging of the Ceddo and the necessity of restoring general peace in order to grow peanuts was used as a pretext, throughout the second half of the nineteenth century, for the conquest of the various Senegambian kingdoms.

The conquest was generally violent, and military victory over individual kingdoms came, with some notable exceptions, fairly quickly. The French and English did not encounter an organized Senegambia-wide coalition capable of fighting the invader. Despite their fierce desire to resist, one by one the Senegambian kingdoms were defeated, revealing their main weakness: geopolitical fragmentation.

The wars of conquest and introduction of the peanut economy would immediately, and for a long time, have a considerable influence on the evolution of the region of the Senegal river basin. The whole of the basin was ravaged continuously by the conquest wars from 1855 to 1890. Nevertheless, the central Wolof region was easily able to recover because of the expansion of the peanut crop, whereas the Senegal river valley lost its commercial vitality for a long time and, up to the present day, has no new economic alternative.

The Casamance and the Upper Senegal-Niger River were conquered later than the central Senegambia and in a more gradual way
that did not generate large-scale migration, because the conquest
was at the village level. Moreover, these regions were underpopulated and had limited economic interest during the precolonial period.
They were not exploited immediately after the conquest. In any
case, famine spread with the wars of conquest because of scorched
earth tactics and also because the retreat of entire populations
from one area to another became the most active form of resistance
that the Senegambian kingdoms made against colonial conquest.
Thus the people and armies, in great number, could not always find
the necessary food nor the time to grow crops in the regions where
they took refuge.

The Wolof kingdom of the Walo, at the mouth of the River
Senegal, was particularly affected by the wars of conquest that ravaged the country and by the exodus of the whole population toward
neighboring Kajor. Gov. Faidherbe discovered at great cost soon
after his arrival in 1854 that the Senegambian kingdoms could be
beaten on the battlefield, but they refused to submit to the conqueror
by fleeing en masse. And so the French, equipped with modern re-
peating rifles and their means of rapid communications, could very
easily beat the Moor, Wolof, and Tukulor armies, which were
equipped only with muskets and horses. But for reasons of health,
the French army had to evacuate the conquered land immediately,
and so the people who had evacuated several weeks before were able
to return. When Faidherbe decided to impose French domination
once and for all over the Senegal river basin, he ordered his troops
to recruit mercenaries to burn the granaries in the villages, destroy
the crops in the fields, and steal the herds. This desolated the
whole region, reducing the nomadic and sedentary people to complete destitution. Following the successive emigration of the Walo-
Walo toward Kajor, Faidherbe attempted to use the right of pursuit
to return the people to the fold. Thus in May 1858, he undertook to
punish the village of Niomre, Kajor, for giving asylum to Sidia, a
hostile from Walo, and during the course of this expedition he burned
20 villages along his way.[46] Despite all these efforts, many Walo-
Walo remained permanently in the Kajor peanut basin. The delta
stagnated economically when they did not repeople it, so that today
it has been declared a pioneer zone and has ceded to a development
agency, the Société Agricole pour l'Exploitation du Delta du Fleuve
Sénégal (SAED).

The Wolof kingdoms of Kajor and the Serer kingdoms of Sin
and Salum were not invaded until 1859 to 1861. However, they were
constantly attacked from then until 1865 and after 1880. The agricultural crisis that was provoked by these military campaigns was
aggravated by a grasshopper infestation that generated a major

famine during the 1860s. In 1871, the French defeat in the Franco-Prussian War led to colonial retrenchment. Kajor, which had been annexed in 1865 but refused to submit, was again allowed official independence. The people rapidly returned to the area and actively developed exports of peanuts. But, in 1879, the new French governor decided to dominate this region economically and politically by constructing a railroad from Saint-Louis to Dakar through central Kajor. The railroad was to link these two administrative centers, to facilitate the movement of troops for conquest and pacification, and also to facilitate transportation of peanuts for French commercial profit. The railroad was constructed between 1882 and 1886, despite fierce opposition from the damel Lat Jor. Construction work therefore had to be protected by troops, and no offensive expedition was taken until the railroad was completed. But as soon as the railroad was operational, in October 1886, both Damel Lat Jor and the new damel, Samba Laobe, were killed by French troops, even though the latter had ostensibly shown his support for France.[47] From then onward, French merchants and their Lebanese agents settled permanently in the various small towns along the railway line to buy peanuts directly from the peasants, thereby eliminating the former Wolof and Moor traders. From the beginning, the indigenous merchants were excluded from peanut marketing, long the only wealth of Senegal, which was maintained as a French monopoly.

Meanwhile, the British, while not undertaking an aggressive campaign of conquest, managed to carve out a colonial domain on the banks of the navigable portion of the River Gambia. Rulers such as Ma Ba and his successors in Salum, who came in conflict with the French, were offered protection by the British. Because most of the kingdoms along the river fell into both French and British areas of activity, a border was negotiated by treaty in 1890, effectively partitioning them into competing colonial political and commercial spheres.

Futa Toro in the middle valley of the Senegal and the Soninke kingdoms in the Upper River were first attacked in 1850, at the same time as Walo. The last campaigns of conquest in the river area occurred after the "pacification" of the Wolof and Serer kingdoms between 1888 and 1891. But already the river basin was experiencing a progressive decline, due to the economic transformation brought by the peanut crop in the Wolof kingdoms. Most of the young people had left Futa Toro in the 1850s to follow the armies of holy war leader, al-Hajj Umar Tal, in the Upper Senegal-Niger area. The opposition of the Futa Toro to the colonial conquest was all the more fierce because the inhabitants, deeply Muslim and long engaged in trade, had no other economic alternative capable of evoking their adhesion to the colonial order. An impressive number of

Futankes went to their deaths in the wars of al-Hajj Umar or in the campaigns against the French. Some settled permanently in present-day Mali, while a considerable number attempted to return to Futa Toro in 1890 after the fall of Segu and Nioro. Very few Futankes who had participated in the Umarian exode (fergo) survived, because they were met on their return by the last campaigns of conquest in Futa Toro. Also, an economic crisis was provoked by the introduction of colonial domination, as former agricultural systems stagnated and offered the people no prospects of economic development.[48] From the beginning of colonization, this zone became the first to have emigration directed toward the urban centers of Kaolack, Dakar, and the towns along the railroad in the peanut basin. This long tradition of emigration of the productive population profoundly altered the social structures of this area, and the process was made worse by the incompatibility of colonial policy with the former social organization.[49]

The Upper Senegal-Niger area was first ravaged by the wars of al-Hajj Umar and then by those of the French conquest. The railroad here also played a crucial role, because the Kayes-Bamako line, constructed between 1883 and 1886, replaced all the former commercial routes and encouraged a French monopoly trade to the detriment of the Soninke and Mandinka merchants. The railroad was also used to transport the troops who finally completed the conquest of the region. As in Futa Toro, the Soninkes had a long tradition of trading. But the colonial conquest offered them no alternatives to traditional agriculture or emigration toward developed areas on the coast and in the peanut basin. This region became very early on the one of great emigration. To this very day, it remains the region of greatest emigration in Senegal, and the Soninke account for the majority of migrant workers in France.[50]

Because of its relative economic and political importance before the colonial era, the Casamance was the last region to be conquered. French infiltration took place slowly between 1900 and 1920, although the River Casamance and certain commercial stations were occupied earlier. The kingdoms of Musa Molo and Fode Kaba, which were the large organized countries there, were conquered in 1905. But in the rest of the Casamance, because of the existence of village democracies, the conquest took very long, as the resistance had to be squelched village by village. The villagers would constantly evacuate the entire region at the announcement of a French expedition and would return after the danger.

When a head tax payable in French currency was imposed after World War I, the people began to flee long distances and settled particularly in Gambia. There again the limited economy of the colonial period led gradually to the people emigrating toward the coastal towns and the peanut basin.[51]

Thus, at the beginning of the twentieth century, all armed resistance had been overcome by the French and British in their separate spheres; each imposed its economic and political domination throughout the colonial period. The present economic and political situation of Senegambia is, in many regards, the result and the continuation of dependence forged by colonization.

CONCLUSION

In order to understand all of the transformations involved in the progressive integration of the Senegambia into the capitalists' system and to find solutions to the number one problem of dependency, it is important to understand the steps in this process beginning in the fifteenth century. It was, in fact, during this long period of mercantile colonialism, which extended from the seventeenth through the beginning of the nineteenth century, that the relationships of dependency between Senegambia and European countries developed. The slave trade, due to its depredatory character, played an important role in the regression of productivity and was thus the source of economic and social stagnation that preceded the conquest. The conquest was intended to correct the destructive effects of the slave trade and to permit, in the context of colonization, a better system of exploitation adapted to the new needs of the center.

For Senegambia, colonization began with the development of peanuts, which were to become an important factor in the progressive dependence of peasants vis-à-vis the world market. The peanut economy inspired the migration of the population of the interior toward the coast, and, at the same time, the colonial partition not only destroyed the unity of this vast Senegambian region, but it also robbed it of its autonomy. In order to recover, Senegambia will have to overcome these artificial borders and perhaps turn its back to the ocean.

NOTES

1. See Bibliography.
2. Philip Curtin, Economic Change in Precolonial Africa: Senegambia in the Era of the Slave Trade (Madison: University of Wisconsin Press, 1975).
3. Yves Person, "Senegambia," Proceedings of a colloquium at the University of Aberdeen, April 1974, pp. 7-8.

4. Jean Boulègue, "La Sénégambie du milieu du XVème au début du XVIIème siècle," Ph.D. dissertation, IIIe cycle, Paris, 1968, p. 177.

5. A. Teixeira da Mota, "Un document nouveau pour l'histoire des Peuls au Sénégal pendant les XVème et XVIème siècles," Boletim cultural da Guiné Portuguesa 96 (1969): 814.

6. Claude Meillassoux, Femmes, greniers et capitaux (Paris: Maspero, 1975), p. 59.

7. Ibid., p. 61.

8. Curtin, Economic Change, p. 74.

9. Ibid., p. 77.

10. Ibid., p. 68.

11. Abdoulaye Bara Diop, "La tenure foncière en milieu rural Wolof," Notes africaines 118 (April 1968): 50.

12. Pathe Diagne, Pouvoir politique traditionnel en Afrique occidentale (Paris: Presence Africaine, 1967), Introduction, pp. 9-31.

13. Curtin, Economic Change, p. 202. We will see the reasons for this reservation on slave trade figures.

14. Vitorino Magalhaes Godinho, "Economics of the Portuguese Empire in the XVth and XVIth Centuries," SEVPEN (Paris, 1969). Page 185 says that the Arguin trading station reported an annual average of 4,709 gold doubloons between 1499 and 1501. One ship took away 2,000 gold doubloons in 1513.

15. Ibid., pp. 199-200, 203.

16. In Gambia, the Portuguese bought from 5,000 to 6,000 gold doubloons per year from 1496 onward. Later, when the Kuntaur and Gambia River trade was leased out from 1510 to 1517, the lessee paid the Crown 45,400 reais per year. The Lisbon mint register listed the king's account for May 12, 1532, at 5,000 cruzados and 35 grains (ibid., pp. 202-3). Walter Rodney tells us that in 1551 a certain Captain de Santiago traded nearly 20 pounds of gold at Kuntaur, while a source in 1581 evaluated gold from Gambia at from 10,000 to 12,000 cruzados for that year. Finally, we must not forget that part of the gold from Senegambia (Bambuk-Bure) was sold on the coast of Sierra Leone to the extent of from 12,000 to 20,000 doubloons and even further along on the Gold Coast, where annual production during these first 20 years of the sixteenth century exceeded 410 kgs or more than 100,000 cruzados; Walter Rodney, A History of the Upper Guinea Coast, 1545-1800 (New York: Oxford University Press, 1970), p. 153.

17. Godinho, "Economics of the Portuguese Empire," p. 217.

18. N. I. de Moraes, "La campagne négrière du Sam-Antonio-e-as-Almas (1670)," Bulletin de l'institut fondamental d'afrique noire, ser. B, 40 (1978): 708-17.

19. Rodney, A History of the Upper Guinea Coast, p. 161.

20. Curtin, Economic Change, p. 177.

21. Godinho, "Economics of the Portuguese Empire," p. 185.

22. Rodney, A History of the Upper Guinea Coast, pp. 95, 98.

23. J. Boulègue, "Relation du port du fleuve Sénégal de João Barbosa par João Baptista Lavanha, c. 1600," Bull. IFAN 24, ser. B, 3-4 (1967): 509.

24. Rodney, A History of the Upper Guinea Coast, p. 72.

25. Le Maire, Voyages du sieur Lemaire aux îles Canaries, au Cap Vert, au Senegal, et en Gambie (Paris: 1695), p. 68.

26. Boulègue, "La Sénégambie du milieu," p. 212.

27. Ibid., p. 244.

28. Person, "Senegambia," p. 16.

29. Boubacar Barry, Le royaume du Waalo (Paris: Maspero, 1972), pp. 135-59.

30. Abdoulaye Ly, La compagnie du Sénégal de 1673 à 1696 (Paris: Presence Africaine, 1958), p. 35.

31. Curtin, Economic Change, p. 162.

32. Ibid., p. 164

33. Ibid.

34. J. Suret-Canale, "La Sénégambie à l'ère de la traite," Revue canadienne des études africaines 11 (1977): 125-34.

35. Charles Becker and Victor Martin, "La sénégambie à l'époque de la traite des esclaves," Société française d'histoire d'outre-mer 235 (1977): 220.

36. Archives Nationales de France (ANF), Col. C 67, April 23, 1723.

37. Charles Becker and Victor Martin, "Memoire Donnet" (mimeograph, 1974), p. 81.

38. Archives Nationales du Sénégal, 3B4 (Saint-Louis, September 4, 1819), replies by Schmaltz to Melay.

39. Carson I. A. Ritchie, "Deux textes sur le Sénégal, 1673-1677," Bull. IFAN ser. B, 30 (January 1968): 352.

40. ANF, Col. C614, November 25, 1753.

41. Ibid.

42. Samir Amin, "Preface," in Le royaume du Waalo, ed. Boubacar Barry (Paris: Masperso, 1972), p. 22.

43. Ibid., p. 93.

44. Georges Hardy, La mise en valeur du Sénégal de 1817 à 1854 (Paris: Larose, 1921), p. 255.

45. Figures given by Mohamed Mbodj, "The Economic Aspects of the Transition Phase (1870-1895) in the Southern Part of the Senegalese Peanut Basin," unpublished memoir, History Department, University of Dakar, 1979.

46. Archives Nationales de France, Section Outre-mer (ANF-OM) Sénégal I, 43, Saint-Louis, May 13, 1858. Correspondence from Faidherbe.

47. For more details on the conquest of Kajor, see Lucie Gallistel Colvin, "Kajor and Its Diplomatic Relations with Saint-Louis of Senegal, 1763-1861," Ph.D. dissertation, Columbia University, 1972.

48. For more details on the conquest of the Futa Toro, see David Robinson, Chiefs and Clerics: the History of Abdul Bokar Kan and Futa Toro, 1853-1891 (New York: Oxford University Press, 1976).

49. Abdoulaye Bara Diop, Société toucouleur et migration (Dakar: IFAN, 1965).

50. Adrian Adams, Le long voyage des gens du fleuve (Paris: Maspero, 1977).

51. For the conquest of the Casamance, see Christian Roche, Conquête et résistance des peuples de la Casamance (Dakar: Nouvelles éditions africaines, 1976).

3

LABOR AND MIGRATION IN COLONIAL SENEGAMBIA

Lucie Gallistel Colvin

The imposition of colonial rule changed every aspect of population mobility in the Senegambia. It reduced and gradually eliminated some of the traditional forms of mobility that had developed: the movement of traders, particularly long-distance traders, the overland slave trade, and the migration incident to precolonial warfare. The imposition of new political borders and elimination of the old ones changed the geographic configuration of migration. The military and economic conquest of the area itself set off major new migratory patterns, flight from "pacification" zones, head tax enforcement, and military and/or forced labor recruitment. Then, as colonial rule was gradually solidified, new forms of labor were introduced and the preexisting occupational structure was radically altered. Many of the former ruling classes and their dependents and retainers were uprooted and fled locally in search of new leaders, identities, and/or occupations. The imposition of a head tax payable in cash and the recruitment of forced labor early in the colonial period led whole villages to flee, across the Gambia/Senegal border if possible. The introduction of cash cropping of peanuts together with cash taxation early in the twentieth century produced a movement of colonization along an expanding peanut frontier, which continues to this day.

New forms of seasonal labor migration also accompanied this change. Client farmers from the hinterland (nawetan) were imported for the rainy season, and Senegambian farmers themselves began to migrate during the dry season (noran) in search of cash income from petty trade, salaried work, or domestic service.

Colonial cities began to experience a rapid acceleration of what had already been a colonial pattern of dry season commercial migration, that is, during the peanut harvesting and marketing

season, farmers tended to congregate and trade in larger and
larger numbers in railroad towns where they brought their produce
to market. The early twentieth century also saw the implantation
of the first colonial cities and the beginnings of the ever-accelerating
process of urbanization. The geographic configuration of the
Senegambia as a migratory and economic region changed radically.
Maps 3.1-3.4 illustrate the expansion of Senegambia as an area
attracting migrants up to a peak in the 1950s followed by a marked
retraction since that time. Maps 3.5-3.8 explore the changing
migratory flows within the region as each of the new border areas
became an area of outmigration, losing population, and as new
areas of growth emerged along the railroad lines and in the colonial
cities. They also illustrate the movement of the peanut frontier,
south and then eastward, in response to more favorable climatic
conditions and the railroad penetration, as well as to political en-
couragements.

BORDERS

The most important new borders introduced by colonial rule
were those affecting the two major rivers, which had been the area's
lifeline, the Senegal and Gambia. Both of these were imposed before the conquest or early in the process of conquest. Gov. Faidherbe
(1854-61, 1863-65) first enunciated the policy that Moors should
live north of the Senegal River and blacks south of it in the 1850s.
Like his predecessors from the 1830s on, he saw Moors as commercial and cultural competitors of the French in the Senegambia,
whose links with the black countries of the area had to be broken in
order to impose French domination. Eventually, the lack of colonial
development potential in Mauritania led administrators to rule it
separately as a military dependency, while the black areas south of
the river were incorporated in two more intensively colonized
areas, the Colony (Saint-Louis, Dakar, Rufisque, and Goree) and
Protectorate (rural areas) of Senegal. The capital of both Mauritania and Senegal throughout the colonial period was at Saint-Louis,
which facilitated some coordination and made the impact of border
status on the river region less influential during the colonial period
than afterward.

The imposition of British-French territorial frontiers along
the navigable portion of the Gambia River had much more immediate
consequences. This frontier was agreed upon in 1889, before the
hinterland had been conquered by either party. During subsequent
military campaigns and, later, the introduction of the head tax in
the hinterland, people on either side of the border took advantage of

the frontier in order to escape whichever coercive policy they were currently subject to, that is, those on the French side fled toward the British; those on the British fled toward the French. Since French military and economic measures were generally more intense and severe, the net flow in the 1910s and 1920s was into the Gambia. Variations of this pattern persisted throughout the colonial period in response to rural policies in either area and continue into the present day in both local and national policies. Merchants on the Gambia who originally shared the same hinterland markets with those on the Senegal River but who got a much smaller territorial cut in the scramble of the conquest had an interest in maintaining those markets by keeping import taxation low. Since the early colonial period, import taxes and hence the prices of imported goods in the Gambia have been substantially lower than those in Senegal. As import duties are a major source of revenue for both colonial and postcolonial governments, this has led to bitter recriminations. The border also permits peasants who owe debts to either private traders or government marketing organizations on either side of the border to move across the border and escape those debts. When marketing policies differ, this may also contribute to border hopping as, for instance, during the 1960s when Gambians were paid cash on the spot for their peanut crop while the government marketing system in Senegal offered only redemption certificates.

The imposition of the French-Portuguese frontier on Portuguese Guinea came later and had much less impact on the region either in terms of migration or of economic activity. Because Portuguese economic activity remained at a low level and because the area had been one of outmigration even in the precolonial period, it has remained an economic backwater, sending population into surrounding areas but not at a rate that troubles its neighbors. The only time that this outmigration reached substantial proportions was during the wars of independence from 1963 on, and even then Senegal and Gambia accepted the large numbers of refugees with good grace, hospitality, and remarkable efficiency. Most of those refugees settled among related ethnic populations in the relatively sparsely populated Casamance and were integrated into the local economy quite smoothly. Some have gone back since the coming of independence and the end of the war, but it is unlikely that the majority will. On the contrary, the 1976 Senegalese census shows that well over half of the foreign-born exiles now claim to be Senegalese. Bissau is still economically retarded compared with the areas into which the refugees have moved, which, together with demonstrated reluctance to return, leads us to believe that the major portion of these refugees will become permanent residents of Senegal and Gambia.

The imposition of French/French administrative frontiers distinguishing the Soudan (today Mali) and Guinea from Senegal was essentially for administrative convenience, because the entire area could not be administered from a single headquarters. It did, however, reflect earlier economic regional patterns. During the latter eighteenth and the nineteenth centuries, Guinea had been gradually drawn out of the Senegambian economic region and toward the coastal trade in Sierra Leone, Liberia, and what is now the Conakry area, thus acquiring a distinct geographic identity. And the French military district of Soudan corresponded closely to the economic region that had been centered on the old Mali empire and that was still held together by trade routes frequented by Mandinka/Soninke traders. As French colonial merchants took over the trade that had been carried on by North Africans and Sudanic traders, the transsaharan trade came to an end. The middle Niger then became an economic backwater, sending trade and people toward three different coastal regions. In the colonial era, the directions were toward Senegal, toward the Gold Coast, and from eastern Mali toward Hausaland, or northern Nigeria.

CHANGING FORMS OF LABOR AND OCCUPATIONAL DISTRIBUTION

Colonial rule completely transformed patterns of labor and occupational distribution in Senegambian societies, particularly in the centralized and highly stratified societies of Tukulor, Wolof, Soninke, and Mandinka lying between the Senegal and Gambia river basins. The top and bottom were most immediately and radically affected. The ruling elite were eliminated by the conquest itself, as most of their jobs ceased to exist and they were coiffed by French and British administrators. Only a few were enlisted as indirect rulers, and they were no longer rulers in the proper sense but junior administrators. The only leisured occupation in the traditional social structure then became that of Muslim clergyman (marabout) and, indeed, many former ruling families either became marabouts or allied with one. The occupation of warrior had been reserved for nobles and slaves in the precolonial period. When conquest eliminated their armies, some opted to fight for the French or British and others allied themselves with the clergy. For those of slave origin, the choice was not always voluntary. Early in the colonial military history, slaves were bought, told that they were no longer slaves, and then involuntarily enlisted in the army for 20-year terms. They became the equivalent of indentured warriors and very few ever were able to claim their freedom. Later, by the turn of the century, warriors and laborers for government buildings, railroads, and port facilities were recruited by the French in large numbers. Local slave-owning aristocrats responsible for "procuring" recruits were not asked whether these were slaves.

Many of those of caste origin who had served as praise singers, diplomatic liaisons, social historians, blacksmiths, cobblers, weavers, and carvers to the nobility also found themselves without occupational security as a result of the conquest. Early recruits to the colonial educational system and migrants to the cities in search of whatever employment they might find came disporportionately from these dispossessed groups.

The ruling classes and castes were numerically small but influential groups. Slaves, on the other hand, are estimated to have constituted at least half of the population in the Wolof, Serer, Tukulor, Soninke, and Mandinka areas. Emancipation forced an immediate choice only on those who served the kings and nobility directly. Others remained in their earlier situations. However, in the 1920s and 1930s, as it became apparent that emancipation was real and offered real opportunities, these groups had an interest in leaving their masters either to colonize the peanut basin, to attach themselves to a marabout (often both), or to go into the cities to look for a new future.

In the new colonial social structure, race, education, and income level replaced birth as determinants of social status. The new recruits into the French educational system moved into positions of influence and prosperity, whether they had come from the top or bottom of the old social structure. Their rural cousins who stayed in the traditional system tended to see their former status distinctions effaced by the colonial situation and move toward a single common social status of peasants. Birth, of course, continued to count, as it still does today. But its implications often are separate from, and sometimes directly in conflict with, the status one is ascribed or achieves in the new system. A village chief of noble birth has frequently watched the slave and caste families attached to his family leave for the city and return as educated government officials contemptuous of "peasants" like him.

A new form of status ascription by ethnicity has also emerged as a result of colonial rule. Each ethnic group traditionally considers itself superior in its own home territory. However, the new urban context has produced an ethnic ranking in which the occupations generally filled by particular ethnic groups correspond in rank to the status ascribed to the different ethnic groups themselves. This tendency may be viewed as negative by modern policy makers because it conflicts with the idea of equal opportunity. However, it is an important factor to bear in mind when deciding migration policy.

Many nations have discovered, to their dismay, that important economic functions simply do not get taken care of if the migrant groups that formerly filled those functions are inhibited from migrating.

NEW TYPES OF MOBILITY

The new types of migration brought by colonialism, colonization of the peanut frontier, seasonal migration, dry-season trade, and clustering around administrative centers were all adaptations of preexisting patterns. It was their scale and the gradual penetration of the logic of a cash economy that made them different from their predecessors. Peanut production for cash sale began in the central Wolof area in the 1840s, well before the onset of colonial conquest. It was spreading rapidly and probably would have continued to expand even without colonial encouragement, because people of all ranks wanted the cloth, guns, ammunition, alcohol, rice, and meat they could buy with the income. However, early in the colonial period, the administrations resolved to force people into the cash economy as rapidly as possible through the imposition of a cash head tax. This obliged every family to either grow peanuts, sell some major capital item, earn cash trading in the dry season, or work for the Europeans. Politically it extended the implications of the conquest down to the household level. It forced Africans to recognize European political authority and relieved the European home economy of the burden of colonial armies and administrators.

On the rapidly expanding peanut frontiers, particularly along the railroad lines, the first farmers to arrive where land was plentiful and labor scarce (most of whom were Wolof) recruited strange farmers, often from great distances, to work as nawetan. Most of these were Bambara, Fulbe, Serer, and eastern (Malian) Mandinka. The institutional framework that allowed local farmers to receive and integrate these strange farmers into the local economy was an adaptation of the Wolof apprenticeship called surga, which has counterparts in several other Senegambian societies. The surga system involved apprenticing single adult young men to farmers outside their own family, usually not far from home. For a period ranging from a few to as many as 15 years, these young men worked land owned by their master, learned the techniques of good farming, and established the independence and dowry necessary to procure themselves wives.

After the Dakar to Bamako railroad was completed in 1923, nawetan-yi came from farther away (the Kayes and Bamako regions and even Upper Volta) into the Saloum area of the peanut basin under the tutelage of Wolof farmers. French administrators saw such an advantage in increased production through this system that they began actively recruiting Bambara nawetan-yi and transporting them for free on the railroad. During the peak from 1934 to 1962, great masses of nawetan-yi came in annually, from 30,000 to 70,000 per year.[1]

Dry season migration, the so-called norani, has deep roots in Senegambian history and probably an important economic role to play for the foreseeable future. Because of the sharp seasonal variation in rainfall, most of the agricultural population of Senegambia is necessarily underemployed or unemployed in rural areas for from four to six months of the year. Most of the arable land of the Senegambia is on plains, not in river valleys, and is amenable only to the rainfall agriculture. In those areas, the first harvest of early millet comes in September and all of the crops have generally been harvested by December. In the precolonial period, once the harvest was in and repairs had been made on the compound and stockyard and the wells had either been redug or new ones dug, men were free to travel during that subsequent dry season. That was the period when people traded, visited family, went to stay with marabouts for study, held political meetings, and nearly all wars took place. During the colonial period, the seasonality of war disappeared. Senegambians who were recruited into World Wars I and II served several years in a row, year-round, and generally far away from home.

On the other hand, the greater security of physical safety gradually developed after World War I, making travel an option for much larger numbers, and the imposition of the cash tax made it virtually an obligation. The options for dry-season migrants became trade or wage labor. As Jacques Faye mentions in Chapter 6, wage remuneration was gradually introduced into the agricultural sector for migrant groups who came to help thresh the peanut harvest. But, otherwise, it was primarily available in the cities or wherever there were concentrations of French. The population of towns along the railroad—Thiès, Kaolack, Dakar, Tivaouane, Louga, Bamako—doubled or tripled during the dry season as farmers came to town to either spend the income they had gained from their crops, seek training in a trade, look for educational opportunities for their children, visit a marabout, or sell or buy livestock.

A permanent urban population gradually evolved, fed by both seasonal migrants of all ages in search of opportunity and young men of an age to apprentice themselves who decided they could earn a dowry more rapidly in the city than in the countryside. Only a tiny proportion of early urban population was educated and brought into the cities through the educational system. This is because the educational system was designed to train a limited number of clerical workers for the emerging colonial administration and economy. However, it is important to know that, even from the very beginning, virtually everyone who did attend the colonial school system through at least the elementary years became an urban resident.

Unlike the Western experience in which rapid urbanization was accompanied by industrialization, colonial cities had very few productive roles into which migrants could be integrated. In the larger economic system into which they fed, colonial cities had no productive economic function. They were administrative centers, commercial and transportation centers; the industrial function was reserved for the European cities that supplied them with manufactured products. Cheap labor was appreciated by the colonial administrators and merchants, but very little of it was actually needed. The roles that were available were almost entirely in service occupations; errand work in the administration and commerce, and domestic service. Inevitably, the migrants themselves were blamed for the parasitic nature of the city and for the fact that no productive role could be foreseen for them. By the 1930s, there were repeated complaints that a useless swell of illiterate migrants was fleeing productive roles in agriculture to become nonproductive in the cities. This complaint has continued to be echoed to the present day.

THE CHANGING GEOGRAPHIC CONFIGURATION
OF MIGRATION

During the midcolonial period, Senegal and Ghana were the two most dynamic poles of attraction for migrant labor throughout West Africa. They were followed closely by lesser poles of attraction in Nigeria and Sierra Leone. In each case, the pattern of migration is clearly related to the early and intensive penetration of the cash economy. The colonial Nigerian economy was more dynamic than either of the two great regions of attraction. Its lesser place as a destination for external migrants seems to be due to its greater size and to the much greater density of its original population, so that migration patterns that elsewhere appear as international migration appear in Nigeria as internal migration.

Map 3.1 illustrates the nineteenth century West African commercial regions upon which colonialism was superimposed, including the Senegambia, and the trade routes that linked them together. It is clear from the map that the once predominant and attractive commercial regions of the Niger river basin and of Hausaland had already dwindled in importance by the middle of the nineteenth century and had given way to the coastal regions of Senegambia, Sierra

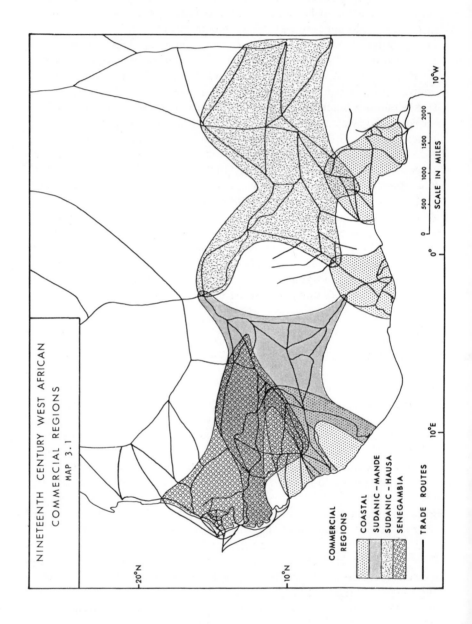

NINETEENTH CENTURY WEST AFRICAN
COMMERCIAL REGIONS
MAP 3.1

COMMERCIAL
REGIONS

COASTAL

SUDANIC – MANDE

SUDANIC – HAUSA

SENEGAMBIA

TRADE ROUTES

20°N

10°N

10°E

0°

10°W

SCALE IN MILES

0   500   1000   1500   2000

Leone, Gold Coast, and what became southern Nigeria. This reflects four centuries of growing importance in trade with Europeans:
first the slave trade and then, in the nineteenth century, the penetration of the so-called "legitimate" trade in oil producing crops
such as peanuts and palm oil and in cocoa and rubber.

Prior to the imposition of colonial frontiers, traders within
any one of those regions were able to trade with Europeans from at
least two and usually from three different nations, because there
were trading posts in each area belonging to two or three different
European nations. Depending on the competitive situation, African
traders could choose their markets. In the scramble for colonial
control of West Africa, the borders of those regions became important in deciding the pattern of the conquest. Each European
power sought to monopolize the area in which it was trading. The
French tried to monopolize Senegal but ended up ceding a portion
to the British on the Gambia and to the Portuguese in Bissau so
that, in fact, three colonial powers tapped into the Senegambian
commercial hinterland (see Maps 3.1 and 3.2). Similarly, Britain
and France each tapped into the Sierra Leonian commercial region.
While the British were able to take the core of the Gold Coast region
by eliminating Dutch and Danish competition at the end of the nineteenth century, the Germans on the Togolese side and the French
on the Ivory Coast side each gained access and were able to tap
into that region. The region that became Southern Nigeria similarly
was nearly monopolized by the British, but again the Germans
tapped in on the Cameroon side and the French on the Dahomey side.
By contrast, African traders no longer had a choice of European
markets unless they happened to live close to a border. African
merchants were in any case excluded from the middle and upper
ranks of colonial commerce, which were monopolized through a
series of customs and financial and credit maneuvers by Europeans
and Levantines.

The strategists of the conquest also dreamed of recreating
the historic importance of the Sudanic interior, using either the
river valleys or the transsudanic and transsaharan railways. In
fact, neither plan ever proved viable, and, instead, dendritic regional economies were installed, which, like great drainage systems, evacuated products from the interior and provided the first
leg of distribution networks for manufactured imports from Europe.[2]
Most of the railroads that were constructed directly replaced preexisting trade routes. This is the case, for example, for the
Bamako to Dakar railroad, the railroad connecting Conakry with
the interior, the Gold Coast triangle, and the railroads from northern Nigeria to the coast (see Maps 3.1 and 3.2). Others tried to
make up for the lack of access to precolonial trade routes by tapping

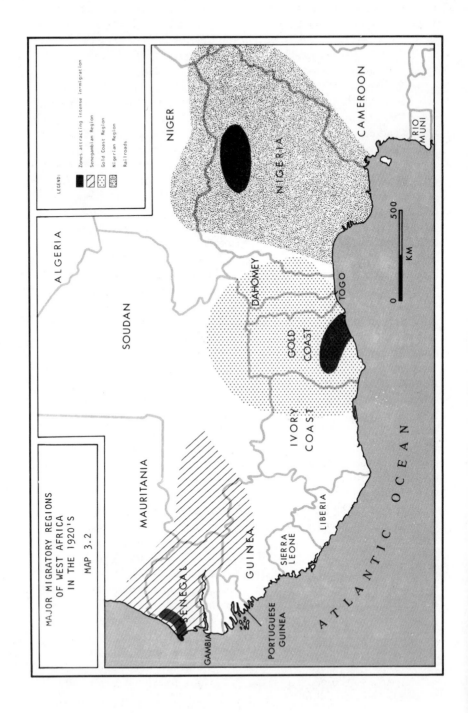

MAJOR MIGRATORY REGIONS
OF WEST AFRICA
IN THE 1920'S

MAP 3.2

LEGEND:

Zones attracting intense in-migration

Senegambian Region

Gold Coast Region

Nigerian Region

Railroads

into a known system in the interior. The Togolese railroad is a
good example of this, where the Germans, not having been established in precolonial commerce, had ended up with a peripheral
territory with no trade routes running through it. The Germans
therefore built a railroad from the coast into the interior, where
they could touch the main trade route linking Hausaland with the
cola producing areas of the Ashanti hinterland in the Gold Coast.
The railroad line linking Abidjan with Bobo Dioulasso is another
case in point. It also was built in an area that had had very little
trade in the precolonial period and stretched into a new economic
hinterland in Upper Volta. On the way, it tapped into the main
trade route linking the upper Niger with the Ashanti hinterland via
Kong. The railroad, however, carried very little trade until the
port of Abidjan was created in 1950 and political circumstances
allowed Abidjan to expand its economy as the Gold Coast declined
(see Maps 3.2 and 3.3).

Senegal's attraction during the colonial period was due, in
part, to its role as administrative capital of all of French West
Africa. This meant that not only the government but also troop
recruitment, educational recruitment, and access to commercial
and administrative employment were centered in Dakar. As self-
government began to be discussed for French West Africa, in the
1950s, the Senegalese deputies, Leopold Senghor and Lamine Gueyè
tried very hard to preserve the unity of the federation and Senegal's
role in it. The French, however, preferred to see their West
African colonies achieve self-government as smaller states, keeping the administrative borders that had been established during the
colonial period. The competitive rivalry of Ivory Coast's Houphouet-
Boigny and a general tendency toward particularism in the newly
enfranchised areas of French West Africa defeated Senegalese attempts to preserve unity.

Since independence, Ivory Coast's economy has grown much
more rapidly than either Senegal's or Ghana's, and the sphere from
which it attracts migrants has grown at the expense of both areas.
This is illustrated in comparing Maps 3.3 and 3.4.

Maps 3.5 to 3.8 illustrate the changing migratory flows within
the Senegambia region during the colonial period and can, in turn,
be compared with Maps 6.1, 6.2, and 6.3 in Chapter 6, which show
the more recent situation. The earliest and most intensive areas
of outmigration are all along political frontiers, most notably the
Senegal river valley. But notice that all political frontiers tend to
lose population. This was also the case in the precolonial era,
when the borders between countries were marked by deserted
forests, allowed to grow to mark the border and to preserve the
political integrity of the separate kingdoms. The colonial areas of

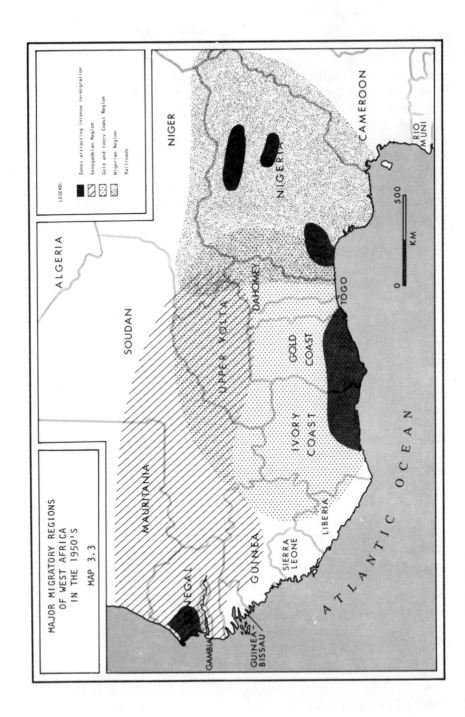

MAJOR MIGRATORY REGIONS
OF WEST AFRICA
IN THE 1950'S

MAP 3.3

LEGEND:

Zones attracting intense in-migration

Senegambian Region

Gold and Ivory Coast Region

Nigerian Region

Railroads

ALGERIA

SOUDAN

NIGER

CAMEROON

RIO MUNI

MAURITANIA

SENEGAL

GAMBIA

GUINEA-BISSAU

GUINEA

SIERRA LEONE

LIBERIA

IVORY COAST

GOLD COAST

UPPER VOLTA

DAHOMEY

TOGO

NIGERIA

ATLANTIC OCEAN

0   500

KM

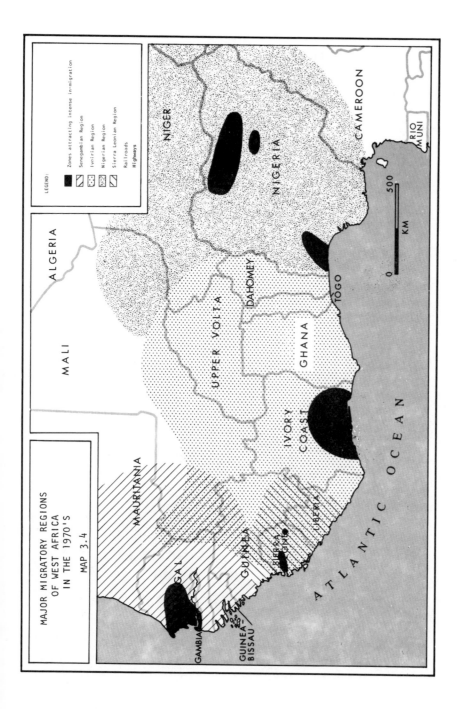

MAJOR MIGRATORY REGIONS
OF WEST AFRICA
IN THE 1970'S

MAP 3.4

LEGEND:

Zones attracting intense in-migration

Senegambian Region

Ivoirian Region

Nigerian Region

Sierra Leonian Region

Railroads

Highways

ALGERIA

MALI

MAURITANIA

SENEGAL

GAMBIA

GUINEA
BISSAU

GUINEA

SIERRA
LEONE

LIBERIA

IVORY
COAST

GHANA

UPPER VOLTA

DAHOMEY

TOGO

NIGER

NIGERIA

CAMEROON

RIO
MUNI

ATLANTIC OCEAN

500

0

KM

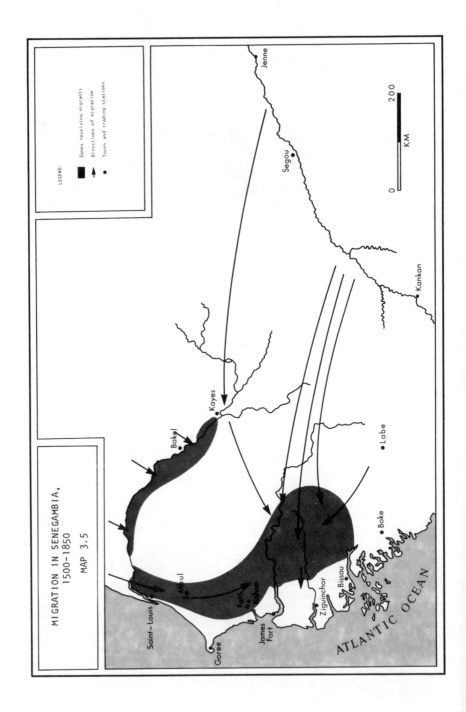

MIGRATION IN SENEGAMBIA,
1500-1850

MAP 3.5

LEGEND:

■ Zones receiving migrants

▲ Directions of migration

● Towns and trading stations

Jenne

Segou

Kankan

Kayes

Bakel

Labe

Boke

Saint-Louis

Kaol

Fatik
Kahon

Ziguinchor

Bissau

Goree

James
Fort

ATLANTIC OCEAN

0   200

KM

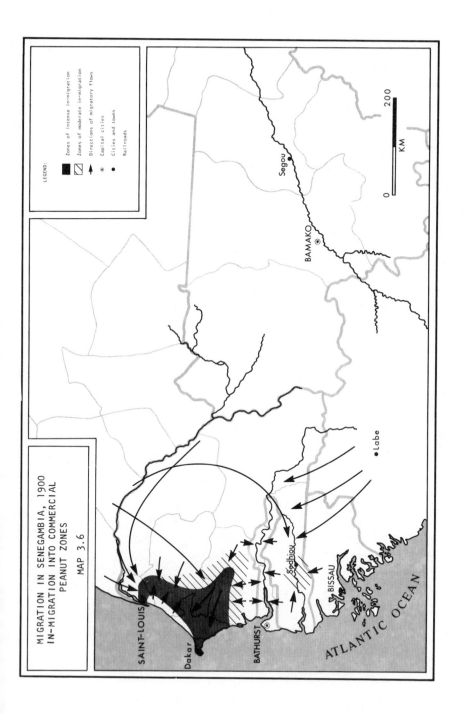

MIGRATION IN SENEGAMBIA, 1900
IN-MIGRATION INTO COMMERCIAL
PEANUT ZONES

MAP 3.6

LEGEND:

Zones of intense in-migration
Zones of moderate in-migration
Directions of migratory flows
Capital cities
Cities and towns
Railroads

SAINT-LOUIS

Dakar

BATHURST

Sedhiou

BISSAU

Labe

Segou

BAMAKO

ATLANTIC OCEAN

KM

0   200

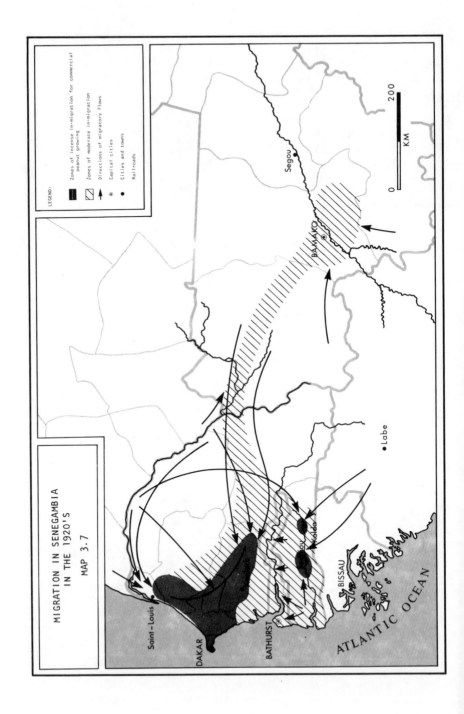

MIGRATION IN SENEGAMBIA
IN THE 1920'S

MAP 3.7

LEGEND:

Zones of intense in-migration for commercial peanut growing

Zones of moderate in-migration

Directions of migratory flows

Capital cities

Cities and towns

Railroads

Saint-Louis

DAKAR

BATHURST

BISSAU

Kolda

Segou

BAMAKO

Labe

ATLANTIC OCEAN

0   200

KM

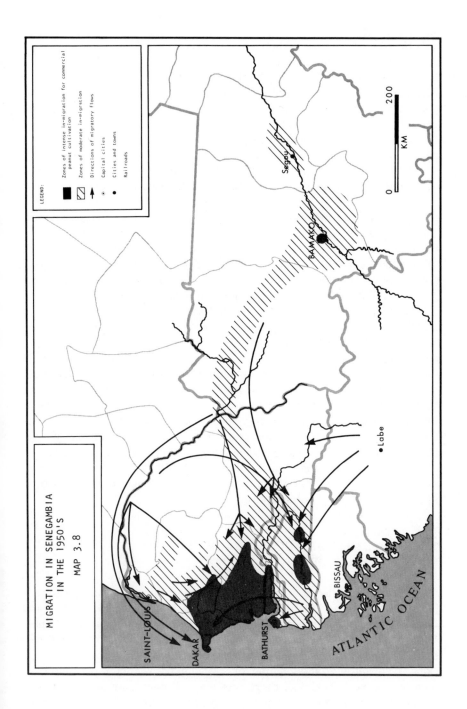

MIGRATION IN SENEGAMBIA
IN THE 1950'S
MAP 3.8

LEGEND:

■ Zones of intense in-migration for commercial peanut cultivation
▨ Zones of moderate in-migration
↑ Directions of migratory flows
⊙ • Capital cities
• Cities and towns
Railroads

200

KM

0

SAINT-LOUIS

DAKAR

BATHURST

BISSAU

Segou

BAMAKO

Labe

ATLANTIC OCEAN

inmigration are primarily the peanut basin and the railroad cities.
The primacy of Dakar emerges very early in the colonial period and
accelerates over time. The Gambia, as an area of relatively fertile
agricultural land and less coercive policy toward rural residents,
has a continuous inflow of agricultural population. On the other
hand, migrants from Gambia as well as from other areas of the
Senegambia to urban areas tend to go to Dakar or the railroad cities
rather than to the capital of the Gambia itself, at that time called
Bathurst. At the beginning of the colonial period, the core of the
peanut basin was between Louga and Tivaouane.

The peanut basin expanded gradually southward and eastward
as colonial rule opened up a formerly fragmented hilly area just
inland from Cape Verde, and the Dakar-Bamako railroad cut a path
to the east. The movement was almost entirely on the part of Wolof
Bambara; Serer and Tukulor served as client farmers but rarely
became founder-settlers gaining land tenure. Wolof migrants moved
all around the Serer and occupied the entire area east and south of
the Serer homeland, thus cutting off expansion of the Serer territory.
As the period of rapid population growth began to affect both Serer
and Wolof in the 1920s and 1930s, this confined the Serer to a very
small area, producing the present overpopulated area around Fatik.
Throughout the 1940s and 1950s, the old peanut basin remained
economically active and viable, even though young people were moving out to colonize on the southern and eastern frontiers. Since the
drought of the late 1960s and the early 1970s, much of this area has
become nonviable and is being abandoned. The area around Louga
is being abandoned by both young and old and appears to be suffering
the encroachment of the desert (see Chapter 6). In the 1960s, yields
in the newer southern and eastern areas of the peanut basin were
already substantially above, sometimes double, those of the old
peanut basin.[3] But only with the onset of the drought did population
in the northern area actually diminish.

THE CONTEMPORARY ECONOMIC GEOGRAPHY
OF THE SENEGAMBIA

The hierarchy of city size in the Senegambia is closely related
to cities' functions, as illustrated in Table 3.1. The most important
functions are port facilities and administration. Bathurst and Saint-
Louis were the major ports in the precolonial period. Smaller subsidiary ports were Rufisque and several villages along the Petite
Cote, Georgetown, and Ziguinchor. At one point during the nineteenth century gum trade, there was a small port near present-day
Nouakchott called Port Etienne, but by the later nineteenth century

it was very little used. Bathurst was by far the best natural port
from the point of view of ease of access. The port at Saint-Louis
has always been blocked by a very dangerous sandbar crossed by a
high surf at the mouth of the Senegal River next to the island on
which the town is built. Bathurst, however, saw its trade routes
to the interior cut off by political frontiers and the French Dakar to
Bamako railroad, which carefully bypassed the Gambia. Alongside
the construction of the railroad came the simultaneous construction
of good port facilities at Dakar, making it the primary port for the
entire Senegambia region. Most of the shipping in the area goes
into Dakar and is subsequently redistributed along the road and
railroad network that feeds Dakar. This is, as yet, a radial transportation network, that is, a series of spokes that all feed toward
the single center at Dakar in a semicircular pattern. This radial
pattern is normally the first stage in the development of a transportation network, to be followed by one or more arcs or circles
connecting the spokes at a given distance from the center. The
Mbour to Thiès to Touba to Louga paved roads can be seen as one
arc in this process, and the second, wider arc is now being paved
from Ziguinchor to Velingara to Tambacounda to Bakel and along
the Senegal River to Saint-Louis.

Administrative functions have been nationalized since independence, producing several subpoles of attraction in each of the
national capitals and feeder nodes in each of the regional capitals.
The headquarters of each of the major commercial firms, banks,
and industrial firms is generally in or near Dakar, with outposts
in outlying cities. Because of Dakar's historic role as an administrative center, this is also true of international agencies, such as the
United Nations and the World Bank, and of European, American,
and Arab bilateral development programs, which tend to have their
headquarters in Dakar and lesser offices in outlying countries. In
each of these administrative networks, recruitment for employment
and decision making tend to be centralized in Dakar. The flows of
goods (directions of trade), flows of migrants, and directions and
volumes of currency transactions follow this same pattern. Goods
flow from the hinterland into and through Dakar and from France
and, to a lesser extent, other Western countries through Dakar into
the rest of the Senegambia.[4]

TABLE 3.1

Hierarchy of Urban Functions and Size in the Senegambia

Functions	Cities in Order of Size							
	Dakar	Bamako	Nouakchott	Thiès	Kaolack	Banjul-Kombo Saint-Louis	Saint-Louis	Ziguinchor
Population 1976	798,000	404,000	135,000	117,300	106,900	99,400	88,400	72,700
National capital	x	x	x			x		
Provincial capital	x	x	x	x	x	x	x	x
Port								
Volume in	1,636	none	375	none	none	n.a.	1.6	71.5
Volume out	766	n.a.	none		14.9	120.7	6.4	6.3
Railroad								
Diesel locomotives	33	1	none	33	n.a.	none	n.a.	none
Freight volume	679	n.a.		679	51	none	36	none
Airport	International	International	International	National	National	International	National	National
Passengers in	221,667	n.a.	16,281	n.a.	n.a.	44,616	n.a.	n.a.
Passengers out	219,396	n.a.	16,439	n.a.	n.a.	n.a.	n.a.	n.a.
Freight in	4,187 tons	n.a.	750 tons	n.a.	n.a.	n.a.	n.a.	n.a.
Freight out	8,964 tons	n.a.	312.8 tons	n.a.	n.a.	n.a.	n.a.	n.a.
Telephones								
Trunk lines	10,969	n.a.	3	845	938	n.a.	696	633
Secondary lines	20,455	n.a.	n.a.	1,544	508	n.a.	447	322

Commerce							
Wholesale	x	x	x	x	x	x	x
Retail	x	x	x	x	x	x	x
Volume of business	918.3	21.1	7.9	6.6	n.a.	1.3	4.2
Banks	7	6	2	4	4	2	n.a.
Educational institutions							
Universities	x				x		x
Professional colleges	x		x	x	x	x	x
Teachers	x	x	x	x	x	x	x
Secondary schools	x	x	x	x	x	x	x
Paved roads (major routes)	5	2	3	4	2	2	1
Hospitals	4	1	1	1	1	1	1
Industry jobs	21,217	n.a. (3,200 in all Mauritania, including construction and utilities)	1,855	729	2,145 (6,866, including construction and utilities)	1,958	424

Sources: For port information, Sénégal en chiffres, 1978 ed., p. 204 (figures for 1976 are in thousands of tons); Atlas de l'aménagement du territoire, p. 54 (figures for 1972–73 are in thousands of tons); for telephones, Sénégal en chiffres; for volume of business, Senegalese figures from Sénégal en chiffres, 1978 ed., converted to U.S. currency at $1–240 cfa, for 1974; Central Statistics Division, Banjul, "External Trade Statutes of the Gambia" (1975–76); for Banjul industry jobs, Central Statistics Division, Banjul, "Quarterly Survey of Employees and Earnings" (June 1978); Mauritanian statistics from Direction de la statistique, Nouakchott (freight volumes are for 1976, in thousands of metric tons. Commercial volume is for 1978, converted at $1–43 ougiyas).

NOTES

1. Vanhaeverbeke, passim.

2. See Allen Howard, "The Relevance of Spatial Analysis for African Economic History: the Sierra Leone Guinea System," Journal of African History 17 (1976): 365-88.

3. See World Bank mission estimates.

4. These centralization and flow patterns are reflected in Senegal, Atlas National (1977), Maps 37, 38 (peanut production); 39 (cooperatives); 44 (industries); 45 (interior communications); 46 (commercial infrastructure); and 47 (flows of produce and merchandise).

II
COUNTRY STUDIES

4

SENEGAL
Lucie Gallistel Colvin

The port of Dakar and outreaching railroad lines have served the entire Senegambia as a focus of import-export trade as well as an administrative center since their creation in the early twentieth century. The agricultural area, known as the peanut basin, stretching on either side of the two main railroad lines leading out from Dakar, has experienced the earliest and most intense penetration of the cash economy. In this respect, Dakar and peanut basin show a more mature economic and demographic picture than the other countries of the Senegambia.

Yet the outlying regions of Senegal show a statistical, economic, and sociological picture much more like that of the outlying countries of Mauritania, Mali, Guinea Bissau, and northern Guinea Conakry than like the central Senegalese regions of Cape Verde and Thiès. In many ways they have been worse off than the independent peripheral countries, because of their direct dependence on Dakar. Their administration until recently could not generate independent development plans. In 1973, the administrative reform initiated the idea of development planning from below, but it is only gradually being introduced in the Casamance and has not yet been introduced in the other two outlying provinces, the Fleuve and Senegal Oriental. The three peripheral provinces were, therefore, throughout the colonial period and the first ten years of independence, areas with low population growth and minimal economic development. The Fleuve region, which had been economically dynamic and central in the precolonial period, responded to colonial neglect with a high rate of outmigration beginning very early and swelling continuously. The other two regions had been relatively sparsely populated and isolated in the precolonial period and remained stagnant demographically as well as economically throughout the period from 1900 to 1970.

In the second decade of independence, the 1970s, attention has suddenly turned to each of these regions. This is directly related to the mature state of the cash economy and the peanut basin in Dakar and the strains that it is experiencing. The drought stimulated a long dormant determination to realize the economic potential of the Senegal river valley with irrigated agriculture, navigation, and hydroelectric power. The expansion of the peanut basin frontier of settlement and the growth of the new cotton frontier into Senegal Oriental have stimulated government interest in that region's agricultural potential and raised the question of how much arable land remains. The same considerations have turned attention to the agricultural and absorptive capacity of the Casamance. The drought stimulated awareness of the fact that this sparsely populated region has a much more regular and abundant rainfall than the existing peanut basin.

The very maturity of the Senegalese economy and population should serve as a warning to Senegal as well as to the rest of the Senegambia as to what will not work. The growth in the modern sector of the Senegalese economy in infrastructure and import-export trade, in education, and in urban amenities is visible and attractive, an apparent sign of success. Yet the demographic picture emerging from the not yet completely published 1976 census and the strains already visible in the economic situation reveal economic and demographic dead ends in the immediate future. Senegal is a classic case of growth without development.

The sources for a demographic picture of Senegal are extremely rich at the regional level, with a multitude of special studies of each of the demographical variables, particularly fertility, mortality, and migration. The 1976 national census, which was the first complete census of the population, also has the potential for very detailed analysis of regional populations in the six regions for which the raw data have been published. The data are not tallied or analyzed, however, and the only national data available at this point are gross regional and capital city totals. The 1970-71 sample census has also been only partially analyzed and published. The 1960-61 sample census was published in the form of a thesis in demography by Paul Verrière. Senegal is also rich in historical colonial censuses, although most of them are of only French posts and their surrounding populations, that is, only of urban areas. However, there is a fairly complete census conducted on the national level in 1933, the results of which, in manuscript form, are available in the archives of Senegal.

Existing studies of migratory patterns and trends in Senegal are all based on 1971 or earlier data. Among the most recent are a statistical analysis (deliberately excluding interpretation) of the 1971 data on migration published as part of the World Bank Organization for Economic Cooperation and Development (OECD) West African Migration Study and articles in the new National Atlas of Senegal and in Daryl Forde and Samir Amin's work Drought and Migration in the Sahel.[1] Particular aspects of the migratory picture, including urbanization and the migration of specific ethnic groups, have also been singled out for special study. Among the important works on urbanization are a World Bank staff working paper, Urban Growth and Economic Development in the Sahel, and two volumes on Dakar, Dakar Métropole Ouest-Africaine by Assane Seck and Dakar en devenir. The earliest and most wide-reaching streams of migration from the Fleuve area, those of the Tukulor and Soninke, have been the subject of full-length studies, and specific aspects of migration of other groups have been the subject of shorter studies.[2] This study is the first to explore the 1976 census data and its implications. It is also the first to relate individual migratory patterns of particular zones within the region to one another and to the economic history of the region as a whole.

The total population of Senegal was probably less than one million in 1900 and had been either stagnant or growing very slowly during the preceding four centuries. It may even have declined slightly, and certainly did in some areas of the country in the last half of the nineteenth century, as the depredations of the colonial conquest set off both famine and outmigration in their wake. By 1933, the first time at which we have a complete census, the population was listed as 1,608,416 sujets française (residents of the Protectorate) and a total urban population (in the Colony) of 148,126. See Figure 4.1 and Table 4.1. By that time, the first attempt to control epidemic disease in the areas had begun to be implemented, mortality began to decline, and the population began to grow faster. In the 1960-61 sample survey, the population was estimated at 3,118,800, which represents an average annual growth of 2.1 percent from 1933 to then. The author of the 1960-61 census, Paul Verrière, calculated the current growth rate at 2.2 percent per year, and this was used for planning and projections during the 1960s. The 1970-71 sample census revealed a population of 3,956,616, at which point the growth rate was recalculated as 2.4 percent per year. The 1976 census shows a population of 5,085,791, some 600,000 more than had been anticipated based on previous growth projections. It implies that the population of Senegal has in fact been growing at a rate of 3.2 percent per year since 1960, only 0.14 percent of which is due to net immigration.

New national birth and death rates have not yet been published, and special studies reveal a wide variety of fertility and mortality from one region to another. However, the one continuing long study

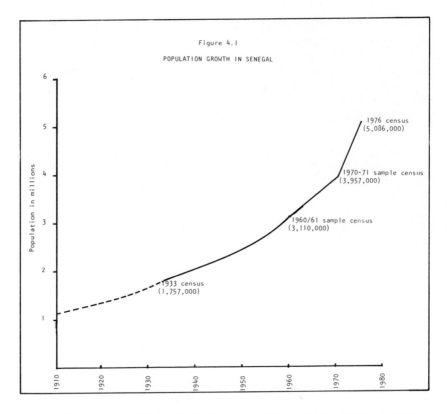

Figure 4.1

POPULATION GROWTH IN SENEGAL

Sources: Archives de l'Afrique occidentale française, 22G6; Paul Verrière, Senegal, Bureau nationale de recensement, Enquête démographique nationale, 1970-71, 4 vols; "Recensement général de la population d'avril 1976, résultats provisoires."

of mortality in Senegal indicates a clear reduction in mortality over the last two decades.[3] Thus, we may hypothesize that mortality has declined substantially and fertility increased slightly, as elsewhere in the region over the last decades. Both censuses and special studies tend to measure only chronic mortality, whereas the chief historical determinant of overall long-term population growth is major mortality crises related to epidemics, drought, and warfare. It is these that have gradually been controlled in twentieth-century Senegambia. The wars of conquest in the 1880s and 1890s brought the last major war-related mortality crisis. Epidemic disease began to be controlled in the 1930s, with first bovine pest and later human sleeping sickness, smallpox, and, most recently, measles eliminated as major killers. The last major killing drought was in 1911-19; in

TABLE 4.1

Population Growth in Senegal by Region, 1960–76

Region	Sample Survey 1960/61	Average Annual Growth 1961–71 (in percent)	Sample Survey 1970/71	Average Annual Growth 1971–76 (in percent)	National Census 4/1976	Overall Average Annual Growth 1961–76 (in percent)
Cap-Vert	443,600	4.7	698,947	7.1	984,660	5.5
Thiés	409,700	3.1	556,031	4.7	698,994	3.6
Diourbel	503,000	2.4	635,205	5.8	842,850*	3.5
Sine-Saloum	727,100	1.1	813,512	4.4	1,007,736	2.2
Fleuve	354,400	1.2	389,991	6.3	528,473	2.9
Casamance	529,800	1.6	618,682	3.5	736,527	2.2
Senegal Oriental	151,200	5.0	245,148	3.1	286,148	4.3
All Senegal	3,118,800	2.4	3,957,516	5.1	5,085,388	3.2

*This figure includes the population of the newly created Louga Region, formerly part of Diourbel.

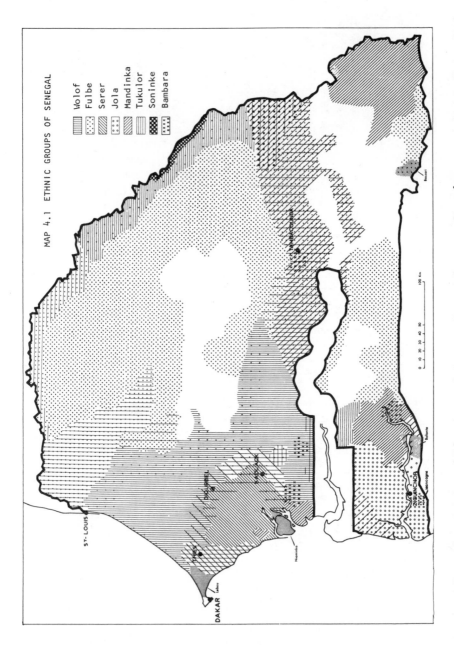

MAP 4.1 ETHNIC GROUPS OF SENEGAL

Wolof
Fulbe
Serer
Jola
Mandinka
Tukulor
Soninke
Bambara

ST-LOUIS

DAKAR
THIÈS

DIOURBEL
KAOLACK

ZIGUINCHOR

Source: Senegal, Ministry of Planning and Cooperation, Atlas pour l'aménagement du territoire (Dakar: Nouvelles éditions africaines, 1977).

the 1970s, food relief, migration, and organized fasting seem to
have saved most of the people, if not their animals.[4] The data imply a sudden spurt of growth since 1971. In fact, the 1971-76 increase represents an average annual growth rate of 5.1 percent, a
figure so high that most demographers prefer to believe that the
1970-71 sample survey involved substantial underenumeration. It
is for this reason that we averaged the growth rate back to 1960 and
arrived at the rate of 3.2 percent. However, the widespread indications throughout the western Sahel that the growth rate is in fact
accelerating in the 1970s suggests that the 1960s represent a growth
rate below 3.2 percent and the 1970s a growth rate above 3.2 percent. A detailed analysis of the as yet unpublished age structure of
the population region by region may help resolve the dilemma of
when and why this acceleration of the natural growth rate began.

Four major types of migration are found in Senegal, each related to a particular set of localized socioeconomic circumstances.
The outstanding trend is toward urbanization. A second tendency is
settlement on an expanding cash-crop frontier, the peanut basin
since the early twentieth century and more recently an expanding
cotton basin. The third major type is seasonal migration, which
has four subvarieties: pastoral transhumance, rainy season client
farming, dry season migration in search of a cash income, and
seasonal migration of harvest and craft workers. The fourth tendency affects only the northernmost section of Senegal, where desertification is obliging the sedentary population to leave the old exhausted
lands of the northern peanut basin and the formerly nomadic population of the arid ferlo zone to sedenterize quite rapidly. The overseas migration of Soninke and some Tukulor workers to France is a
unique situation affecting at present only a small localized area of
the Upper River. This immigration is at present statistically small.
There were an estimated 21,000 Senegalese in France in 1973, almost all from the Fleuve.[5] However, because migration throughout
the area involved essentially a search for cash incomes, and because of the enormous inequalities in cash incomes between Europe
and Africa, we hypothesize that this stream will grow rapidly and
that increasingly coercive measures will be employed to control it,
but it will have very little statistical impact.

URBAN GROWTH

Urban growth, like overall population growth in Senegal, began
slowly in the period before 1920 and has been accelerating. The first
jump came with the decision to make Saint-Louis the base for the
conquest in 1855. Until that time it seems that Saint-Louis had grown

slowly and none of the other towns of Senegal had had a population of more than 5,000. The census of Saint-Louis in 1838 showed a population of 11,909 and in 1845 of 12,130; by 1867 it had jumped to 14,845. [6]

When Dakar was made the capital of French West Africa, it too began to grow, from a village of 1,600 in 1878, to 23,500 in 1904, and to 34,400 in 1923. [7] During the Depression, the price of peanuts was down sharply and the first great swell of refugees from the suddenly nonviable cash crop economy came into Dakar. The population jumped to 92,600 in 1936 and to 132,000 in 1945 at the end of World War II. Table 4.2 shows the growth of Dakar and the regional capitals from 1955 to 1976. The total urban population of Senegal went from about 250,000 in 1933, which was equivalent to 13.5 percent of the population, to an estimated 842,000 in 1965, equivalent to 24.7 percent of the population, and to an estimated 1.6 to 1.8 million in 1976, equivalent to 31-35 percent of the population. [8] The growth in the overall urban population averaged 3.9 percent per year between 1933 and 1965 and 5.5 percent per year between 1955 and 1976. Natural increase is slightly higher in urban than in rural areas, partly because of better health and economic conditions and partly because children born to migrants once settled in the city count among the urban born. Therefore we may estimate that about 2 percent of the urban growth rate is due directly to migration and 3.5 percent to natural increase.

Variations in the size of individual cities from one enumeration to the next suggest that local economic circumstances have a substantial effect on the temporary distribution of the urban population among cities but that the overall rate of growth of the urban population has been remarkably constant. It has only experienced spurts in the face of major crises of national or international scope, including the Depression and, most recently, the Sahelian drought.

The outstanding feature of urban growth in Senegal as illustrated in Table 4.2 is that the majority of the urban population as well as most of the growth is concentrated in Dakar. From 1955 to 1976, Dakar grew at an average annual rate of 6.1 percent while the regional capitals grew at an average rate of 4.7 percent. The overwhelming pace of this growth can be appreciated if it is compared with what was considered uncontrollable urban growth in industrializing cities of Europe and America. There cities in the 200,000 range might double their population in 50 years. Dakar's population has multiplied three and a half times in 21 years.

Table 3.1 in the previous chapter indicates some characteristics of the primacy of Dakar in terms of the hierarchy of urban functions in the Senegambia as well as of size. The hinterland served by Dakar's port corresponds exactly to the Senegambia as we have

TABLE 4.2

Urban Growth in Senegal, 1955-76

	Dakar	Thiès	Kaolack	Saint-Louis	Ziguinchor	Diourbel	Louga	Tambacounda	Total of Regional Capitals, Excluding Louga	Total Excluding Dakar and Louga
1955	230,600	42,500	46,600	39,100	22,400	20,600	—	4,600	406,400	175,800
Average yearly increase, 1955–61	23,967	4,440	3,827	1,623	1,240	1,327	—	979	37,403	13,436
Annual average growth, 1955–61 (in percent)	8.4	8.4	6.9	3.8	4.9	5.6	—	14.7	7.6	6.4
1961	374,400	69,140	69,560	48,840	29,840	28,560	—	10,478	630,818	256,418
Average yearly increase, 1961–71	16,046	2,165	2,668	3,236	1,587	745	—	1,128	27,575	11,529
Annual average growth, 1961–71 (in percent)	4.0	3.1	3.7	5.8	4.8	2.6	—	8.5	4.6	4.2
1971	534,857	90,788	96,238	81,204	45,712	36,010	35,670	21,760	906,569	371,712
Average yearly increase, 1970–72/3	32,457	1,945	2,591	3,466	1,632	670	2,312	1,300	44,061	11,604
Annual average growth, 1970–72/3 (in percent)	5.8	2.1	2.6	4.1	3.5	1.8	6.2	5.7	4.8	3.1
1972–73	616,000	95,652	102,715	89,868	49,793	37,685	41,451	25,009	1,016,722	400,722
Average yearly increase, 1972/3–76	55,391	6,570	1,268	-444	6,949	3,919	-1,936	41	71,760	18,305
Annual average growth, 1972/3–76 (in percent)	8.2	6.4	1.2	-0.5	12.2	9.4	-4.9	0.2	6.7	4.3
1976	798,792	117,333	106,899	88,404	72,726	50,618	35,063	25,147	1,259,919	461,127
Average yearly increase, 1955–76	27,317	3,598	2,899	2,370	2,419	1,443	4	988	41,035	13,689
Annual average growth, 1955–76 (in percent)	6.1	5.0	4.0	4.0	5.8	4.4	—	8.4	5.5	4.7

Sources: Senegal, Bureau National de Recensement, "Résultats provisoires du recensement général de la population d'avril 1976," mimeographed, Dakar, 1976; Senegal, Ministry of Planning and Cooperation, Atlas pour l'aménagement du territoire (Dakar: Nouvelles éditions africaines, 1977).

defined it. The next largest port at Banjul handles only 16 percent of Dakar's volume. The other Senegalese ports of Kaolack, Ziguinchor, and Saint-Louis and the wharf at Nouakchott have less than 1 percent of Dakar's volume. The port of Dakar is linked to 1,500 kilometers of railroad track on two major axes going to Saint-Louis and Bamako. It is also linked to four major axes of paved roads, linking it with Nouakchott, Linguère via Diourbel, Kaolack and Kaffrine, and the trans-Gambia to Ziguinchor and Banjul. In contrast, Nouakchott is served by only one paved road coming in from the north (Akjoujt) and linking it to the south with Saint-Louis and Dakar. Banjul has a paved road linking it with the trans-Gambia at Mansakonko and (after taking the ferry to Barra) another linking it with Kaolack and Dakar. Kaolack is the only other city serving as a major crossroads. It is linked with paved roads to Dakar, Kaffrine, the trans-Gambia to Ziguinchor, and the spur to Banjul. Bamako has two major paved roads, one leading northwest to Sagou and Mopti and the other southeast to Sikasso.

Dakar's university is also the only one in the area and so draws students from the entire area. There are professional colleges, teachers colleges, and secondary schools in several of the other major cities including Bamako, Nouakchott, Saint-Louis, and Ziguinchor. Dakar is headquarters for seven banks; Kaolack, Ziguinchor, Bamako, and Nouakchott are served by four each.

Dakar uses 94,000 kilowatts of the slightly more than 100,000 used in the entire country. Telephone communications show 73.5 percent of the principal lines and 89.5 percent of the secondary lines concentrated in Dakar and in Cape Verde.

Industry accounts for 27,769 jobs in Senegal, which is 45 percent of the total, and 76 percent of those jobs are on Cap Vert. It also offers substantial seasonal employment, ranging from 19,000 in the peak season to 16,500 in the low season in 1974.[9] One and a half percent of the industrial jobs are available in the Casamance, 1.2 percent in Diourbel region, 0.04 percent in Senegal Oriental, 2.75 percent in Sine-Saloum, and 7.4 percent in the Fleuve region. There are four hospitals in Dakar, two in Bamako, and one each in Thiès, Kaolack, Saint-Louis, Ziguinchor, Diourbel, Banjul, Nouakchott, and Segou. New hospitals are under construction in Tambacounda and Louga. Difficult cases, requiring laboratory tests or surgery, from all four countries are referred to Dakar.

DROUGHT AND THE URBAN GROWTH SPURT

The drought that ravaged both livestock and agriculture throughout the Sahel in the early 1970s sent many of its rural victims flocking to the cities. In the cities located in the true arid Sahel, such as Nouakchott and Bamako, this swelling was immediately visible and urgent. In Senegal, most of which lies in a Sudanic vegetation zone where agriculture rather than pastoralism is the predominant occupation, urban-rural relationships are more complex and less visible. Many local observers believed that the drought had not expanded urban populations in Senegal or that, if it had, the effect was temporary. The unusually complete urban census data on Senegalese cities large and small during that period forces us to question that conclusion. It suggests that the drought did indeed swell urban populations, beginning in the earliest phase with the small outlying cities, then progressing by steps to the regional capitals and finally to Dakar. It suggests that most of the decrease in population in the outlying cities and regional capitals, after the return of more normal climatic conditions, was due not to a return to the farm but to a continued journey toward Dakar.

The drought hit earlier in Senegal than in central areas of the Sahel and was nearly five years old before international food shipments began to arrive in 1973. A comparison of the figures from the sample urban census taken by the Aménagement du territoire service in 1972-73 with the national sample census of 1971 indicates that it was the small outlying cities that were first affected by an influx of refugees (see Table 4.3). Remarkable rates of growth are visible in Tivaouane, Bakel, Bignona, Tambacounda, Kolda, Louga, and Saint-Louis. In 1974, the Bureau central d'études pour l'équipement d'outre-mer (BCEOM) conducted another census of the interior cities of Senegal. By this time, several of the smaller outlying cities, with a minimum of economic opportunity and in which food relief was not readily available (it was distributed in rural areas), show either a sharp reduction in growth or an actual decline. These include Tivaouane, Bakel, and Tambacounda. The larger secondary cities were by this time receiving a substantial influx, as the figures for Thiès, Diourbel, Saint-Louis, Louga, and Ziguinchor reflect. Probably this influx was also being felt in Dakar at this time, although no enumeration was made. By the time of the April 1976 census, after three years of mixed but generally better harvests, the population of Dakar had jumped substantially, reflecting an 8.2 percent growth rate over the previous five years. With the exception of Casamance, the secondary cities of Senegal had, in the meantime, either lost population or flowed to a low rate of growth. Since natural increase would account for about a 3.2-3.5 percent increase in the population, any figure below that probably reflects outmigration from those cities.

TABLE 4.3

Drought and Urban Growth in Senegal

	Dakar (Cap Vert)	Thiès (Thiès)	Tivaoune	Kaolack (Sine-Saloum)	Diourbel (Diourbel)	Mbacke	Louga
Population 1971	582,958	90,788	20,409	96,238	36,010	20,065	35,670
Average yearly increase 1971-72/73	18,356	2,702	2,182	3,598	930	2,267	3,212
Annual growth rate, 1971-72/73 (in percent)	3.1	2.9	10.3	3.7	2.6	10.8	8.7
Population 1972/73	616,000	95,652	24,337	102,715	37,685	24,146	41,451
Average yearly increase 1972/73-74	—	10,448	-638	2,986	12,440	446	4,011
Annual growth rate, 1972/73-74 (in percent)	—	10.6	-2.6	2.9	30.7	1.8	9.5
Population 1974	—	111,324	23,380	107,194	56,345	24,815	47,468
Average yearly increase 1974-76	55,391	3,338	-3,349	-164	-3,182	124	-6,892
Annual growth rate, 1974-76 (in percent)	8.2[b]	3.0	-15.3	-0.2	-5.8	0.5	-15.5
Population 1976	798,792	117,333	17,351	106,899	50,618	25,039	35,063
Overall average yearly increase 1971-76	42,320	5,205	-600	2,090	2,864	975	-119
Overall annual growth rate 1971-76 (in percent)	6.4	5.2	-3.1	2.1	6.9	4.4	-0.3
Net increase 1971-76	215,834	26,545	-3,058	10,661	14,608	4,974	-607
Percent increase 1971-76	37.0	29.0	-15.0	11.0	41.0	25.0	-2.0

[a]Rate 1971-74.

[b]Rate 1972/3-76.

Sources: Senegal, Bureau National de Recensement, Enquete démographique nationale, second passage, Dec. 1970-May 1971; Senegal, Direction de l'aménagement du territoire, sample survey; BCEOM, cited in Senegal Atlas national, p. 120; Senegal, Bureau National de Recensement, "Résultats provisoires du recensement general de la population d'avril 1976," mimeographed, Dakar, 1976.

Saint-Louis (Fleuve)	Bakel	Ziguinchor	Bignona	Kolda	Tambacounda (Senegal Oriental)	Total
81,204	4,203	45,772	10,275	16,137	21,760	1,061,489
4,813	—	2,234	766	1,784	1,855	—
5.8	—	4.8	7.2	10.6	8.2	—
89,868	—	49,793	11,654	19,349	25,099	—
6,917	631	9,575	—	2,373	-4,280	—
23.2	13.0[a]	18.4	—	11.9	-17.9	—
100,244	6,285	64,155	—	22,908	18,679	—
-6,578	30	4,762	874	-2,003	3,593	—
-6.7	0.5	7.2	6.9	-9.1	18.0	—
88,404	6,339	72,726	14,537	19,302	25,147	1,377,550
1,412	419	5,285	836	621	664	61,972
1.7	8.4	9.5	7.0	3.6	2.9	5.2
7,200	2,136	26,954	4,262	3,165	3,387	316,061
9.0	51.0	59.0	41.0	20.0	16.0	30.0

Ziguinchor and Bianona in the lower Casamance are the only secondary cities that show a sustained high rate of growth. The opening of the trans-Gambia highway, the bridge across the Casamance River, and the accelerated pace of development projects in the province will probably continue this trend.

Dakar's population growth, which had slowed both in terms of absolute numbers and in terms of rate of growth during the mid-1960s, increased sharply in the aftermath of the drought, from 16,000 to 18,000 net average yearly growth to 55,400 average yearly growth and a rate of 8.2 percent per year between 1972-73 and 1976. Field work in connection with this study by Fatou Sow suggests that the suburban low-income neighborhoods of Yombole, Khar Yalla, Thiaroye, and Hann expanded rapidly at this time and, tentatively, that growth there has fallen off since 1976. The high rates of unemployment, low incomes, and poor living conditions that she also found suggest that the city had not yet managed to accommodate this influx of migrants. This may be serving as a temporary restraint on migration to Dakar. The global statistics, however, indicate that such temporary halts in the urban immigration to particular cities do not slow the overall trend toward urbanization. On the contrary, the accelerating rate of growth of the overall population and expansion of the cash economy imply that the high rate of urbanization will continue or increase.

ZONAL PATTERNS OF MIGRATION WITHIN SENEGAL

The mapping of Senegal according to the types of migratory patterns found in local areas shows that migration trends closely reflect the character and health of the local economy from the point of view of the household economics of rural residents. Areas with high rates of outmigration generally show one or more of the following characteristics: geopolitical peripherality; absolute economic decline; relative economic decline in comparison with other areas; a higher mortality rate than other areas; soil exhaustion and/or agricultural overpopulation; sedentarization of nomads; lack of water, paved road, and marketing infrastructure. The first areas to attract modern (colonial) migrants were the center cities and the central rural areas—now both are overcrowded and they have joined the peripheral hinterland areas as zones of outmigration. The areas of the old peanut basin close to Dakar experience a stepwise migration, with a high rural exodus of locally born residents replaced by a high influx of migrants from farther out areas who fill in the labor gap created by the absent migrants. This secondary influx of seasonal and temporary labor, in an already heavily populated area, tends to result in less permanent settlement than the other major trends. Jacques Faye in Chapter 6 and Fatou Sow in Chapter 9 show that the receiving zones, rural and urban, have expanded on the fringes of former receiving areas.

The oldest area of high outmigration in Senegal is the Senegal river basin, as has been noted in the historical section. More recently, the lower and middle Casamance have shown the same tendency. While rate of departure in relation to local population density are highest in these border provinces, the major portion of actual numbers of migrants in the rural exodus comes from the more densely populated groundnut basin immediately east of Dakar, from a population long involved in the cash economy. Finally, there is a small area in the north of Senegal, a part of the ferlo stretching from the south bank of the river toward Louga which is gradually being abandoned by its inhabitants, both herders and farmers, due to desertification.

INTERNATIONAL IMMIGRATION

Two streams of international migrants flow into Senegal, a small but influential one at the top of the socioeconomic-educational structure and a larger one of farmers, herders, and laborers at the bottom. The 1976 census of Senegal shows an estimated 20,000 residents born overseas, and from 325,000 to 335,000 born in other, mainly neighboring, countries of Africa. Thus about 7 percent of the total population of Senegal is foreign-born (11 percent in the Gambia).

Non-African residents of Senegal are heavily concentrated in the Cap Vert region (Dakar-Rufisque), where they totaled 17,554 in the 1976 census, equal to 1.9 percent of the total population. More than 60 percent of the overseas-born were French (1.2 of the 1.9 percent), another 24 percent were Lebanese, and the rest were from diverse European, American, and Asian countries.[10]

Guineans predominated among African immigrants, comprising an estimated 126,365 or 36 percent of the total. Bissauans were the next largest group with 70,995, followed by Mauritanians (43,938), Malians (26,401), and Gambians (9,424) (see Table 4.4). There are, of course, also Senegalese citizens resident in each of the preceding countries, although they are believed to be very few in every country except the Gambia. Comparison of Gambian and Senegalese census data shows an ongoing population exchange, in which Gambian immigrants to Senegal outnumbered Senegalese in the Gambia 33,000 to 21,000 in the 1960s, but the reverse is true today (27,000 Senegalese in Gambia compared with 9,000 Gambians

TABLE 4.4

Foreign-Born Africans in Senegal by Region of Residence, 1971 and 1976

Region of Residence	Country of Origin											
	Gambia		Guinea		Guinea Bissau		Mali		Mauritania		Others	
	1971	1976	1971	1976	1971	1976	1971	1976	1971	1976	1971	1976
Cap-Vert	1,680	2,331	15,604	60,210	2,386	11,774	6,235	11,044	7,243	18,609	4,829	32,239
Casamance	15,881	4,933	12,260	20,438	71,470	60,410	1,074	1,780	355	1,202	162	4,790
Diourbel	0	9	519	334	59	34	568	245	2,140	625	120	1,847
(+ Louga)		23		360		9		37		1,782		1,390
Fleuve	46	e10	398	e461	193	e223	648	e750	7,346	e15,000	380	e440
Senegal Oriental	6,611	1,398	12,055	20,748	71	175	4,256	3,748	2,020	3,164	244	5,923
Sine-Saloum	8,657	554	14,816	20,006	255	220	6,737	9,958	1,896	4,181	6,478	14,914
Thiès	406	172	1,168	3,808	339	341	1,596	1,054	2,242	3,240	699	3,302
All Senegal	33,281	9,430	56,820	126,365	74,773	73,186	21,114	28,616	23,242	47,803	12,912	64,845

Note: Estimates are preceded by the letter "e."

Sources: 1971 figures are based on analysis of unpublished 1970/71 census data; calculations by K. C. Zachariah and N. K. Nair, "Senegal: Patterns of Internal and International Migration in Recent Years," in Demographic Aspects of Migration in West Africa, OECD/World Bank, 1978. The 1976 figures for foreign born are calculated by taking the foreign nationals in each region divided by a factor representing the foreign nationals as a portion of total foreign-born Africans in each region (see Table 4.5). The foreign-born statistics are not yet available by country of origin. This technique assumes that African immigrants from each country of origin are equally likely to claim Senegalese nationality. In 1976, 68.4 percent of all foreign-born Africans in Senegal claimed to have acquired Senegalese nationality. To the extent that this is untrue, the "Country of Origin" figures may be slightly differently distributed within each region.

98

TABLE 4.5

African Immigrants to Senegal Claiming Senegalese Nationality
versus Nationality of Origin

Administrative Region of Residence	Claiming Foreign Nationality	Proportion (in percent)	Foreign-Born Claiming Senegalese Nationality	Total Foreign-Born Africans
Cap Vert	36,926	27.11	99,262	136,188
Casamance	31,577	33.75	61,980	93,557
Diourbel	1,454	47.15	1,630	3,084
Louga	780	21.65	2,822	3,602
Senegal Oriental	12,822	36.47	22,340	35,162
Sine-Saloum	16,724	33.56	33,108	49,832
Thiès	4,998	41.94	6,919	11,917
Total	105,281	31.6	228,061 (68.4 percent)	333,342

Sources: Senegal, Bureau national du recensement, "Recensement général de la population d'avril 1976," vols. for Casamance, Thiès, Diourbel, Senegal Oriental, Sine-Saloum, and Louga, mimeographed, Dakar, 1978–79; unpublished data for Cap Vert.

99

in Senegal). [11] All of the other Senegambian countries show essentially one-way flows toward Senegal and Gambia.

An astonishingly high proportion of foreign-born Africans in Senegal claim Senegalese citizenship: 68.4 percent overall in the 1976 census, only a tiny proportion of whom have completed legal formalities for naturalization. In part this reflects fear of repatriation, in part the local advantages of citizenship. Although Senegal has never forcibly repatriated immigrants, other West African countries have, either in response to xenophobia at home (notably Ghana in 1969-70) or mother country request (Gambia to Guinea in 1973). Immigrants are aware of the other examples and very sensitive to xenophobia, which they experience from isolated individuals in the Senegambia despite generally very liberal laws and traditions of hospitality.

As the government permeates rural areas in the form of development agencies, land reform, local government reform, cooperative organization, and the providing of employment and educational opportunities, preferential treatment is increasingly accorded citizens of Senegal. Immigrants, who are rarely distinguishable from Senegalese by ethnicity, can easily claim Senegalese nationality during a census. With greater difficulty, but in increasing numbers, they purchase black-market identity cards and/or assimilate Senegalese customs and speech. The end of the war in Bissau in 1974 and the entente between Guinea and the other Senegambian countries at Monrovia in 1978 have enticed some, but only a small proportion, of the total refugees home. The overwhelming tendency is for emigration to become permanent.

HISTORICAL OVERVIEW: MIGRATION
AND PUBLIC POLICY IN SENEGAL

During the colonial conquest, the French authorities needed and wanted to uproot people from their traditional society. On the cultural plane, it was the only means by which they could be "assimilated" to French civilization. In the economic sphere, it was the only means by which they could be brought into the expanding French-dominated cash economy. In the political domain, it was a necessary part of the process of dismantling the precolonial African governments and obliging new subjects and citizens to transfer their allegiance to France.

The earliest colonial policies designed to implement this logic were the imposition of a head tax—which began as areas were conquered, usually within 10-20 years after the initial invasions—and the imposition of forced labor. Both of these policies resulted in

substantial outmigration. Those who refused to pay the tax or contribute labor were obliged to migrate to evade their implementation,
and those who agreed were obliged to migrate to fulfill them. A recent study of military recruitment and labor mobility in French West
Africa 1923-46 has shown absentee rates of more than 20 percent
as a means of evasion throughout Senegal, with the exception of the
Casamance and the area immediately around Saint-Louis.[12] The
gradual freeing of slaves in Senegambia in the early colonial period,
while ostensibly for humanitarian reasons, also had the desired
consequence of moving substantial portions of them physically and
culturally out of the domains of their patrons and into the European-
dominated political-economic sphere. Estimates of local proportions of slaves in the population in the nineteenth century ranged
from one-third to three-quarters, which means emancipation affected a major portion of the population.

Economic and Marketing Policy

Government revenues in the colonial period were derived almost entirely from the import-export economy. This was a logical
extension of the transition from precolonial trading stations to a
colonial territorial empire based on commerce. The Metropole insisted throughout the period prior to World War II that local colonial
budgets be supported by local revenues. In Senegal, this meant that
the only way the government could sustain and enhance its activities
was by expanding the peanut basin as rapidly as possible.
Peasantization has been defined as the process of extension of
urban control over rural areas.[13] The relationship between the government and the countryside and farmers during the colonial period
has to be understood as an extension of this European process, in its
unique colonial context. The farmer-migrant moved out of his ascribed status in the traditional society (which had consistently produced a marketable agricultural surplus) into the role of unit of
labor. At first, his individual rewards were—in economic terms—
substantially above those he could experience in the traditional sector.[14] The deteriorating terms of exchange between 1890 and 1941,
and even more rapidly after World War II, brought him into the permanent cycle of debt and dependence that continues today. Now,
whether he produces a cash crop or not, he is a peasant in a "subsistence" economy (see Table 4.6).
The nationalization of peanut marketing, one of the first decisions of the new government at independence, was intended to re-
lease peasants from this cycle of indebtedness to colonial merchants
and dependence on fluctuating world market prices. To eliminate

the abuses of private colonial commerce and facilitate administration of the new structures, the Office de commercialisation de l'Arachide (ICA) (from 1967 on, in conjunction with the Office nationale de la coopération et de l'assistance pour le développement [ONCAD]) was given a monopoly of groundnut marketing. Rural cooperatives were instituted, and a national system of agricultural credit, extension services, and cooperative administration was installed. To stabilize peasant incomes, it was decided that the new system would offer peasants a guaranteed fixed price. When world market prices were above that price, the margin would be kept and used to stabilize producer prices when the world market was low.

TABLE 4.6

A Comparison of the Average Hourly Salaries of the
Senegalese Peasant, Dakar Laborer, and French Laborer
(in francs)

Year(s)	Dakar Laborer	French Laborer	Senegalese Peasant	Peasant in Sine-Saloum
1890	0.12	0.26	0.28	0.28
1919-21	0.33	1.67	0.90	0.50
1922-26	0.55	2.47	1.40	1.38
1927-31	0.66	3.30	1.30	1.70
1932-36	0.78	3.97	0.80	1.00
1937-41	0.90	5.90	1.30	1.37

Sources: Mohamed Mbodj, "Le Sénégal et la dépendence—le cas du Sine-Saloum et de l'arachide, 1887-1940," unpublished paper, History Department seminar, University of Dakar, April 14, 1979; figures for Sine-Saloum peasant calculated by A. Vanhaeverbeke, Remunération de travail et commerce extérieur (Louvain: Université catholique de Louvain, 1970).

In practice, there were a number of other considerations facing the new government. Among them were the need to provide rice for a politically weighty urban population and the need to finance its own operations. In fact, therefore, producer prices were set well below world market prices and have remained there ever since, despite some recent raises. The profits have not been retained in an autonomous fund, but they have been used to finance the operations of the government marketing system itself as well as in general revenues and in support of artificially low domestic prices for rice, wheat, sugar, and oil. Producer prices for locally grown millet, sorghum, and paddy rice have also been kept low, deliberately below the level that would encourage farmers to shift from peanut cultivation to millet. Most millet and paddy rice are therefore grown for home consumption and/or exchanged outside the government network, not given to the government for marketing.[15]

The peasants, that is, peanut basin farmers, responded with a minor revolt in 1968-69, known as the Malaise Paysan (peasant unrest). At a time when world prices had shot up sharply due to a disaster with the Nigerian crop, the Senegalese producers' price was staying constant. Peasants also complained that they were paid not in cash but in credit slips, redeemable only at the end of the dry season and only after debts had been deducted. The importance of a cash income early in the dry season to facilitate further earnings during the dry season is an important consideration in rural household economics. Peasant protest took the form of refusal to pay debts, smuggling of the crop into the Gambia to be sold for cash, mass reversion to planting millet instead of groundnuts, and various manipulations of the cooperative system. In retrospect, those years were the beginning of the big drought, but no one could foresee it at that time. The government responded by gradually raising the producer price for groundnuts year by year and by agreeing to pay cash for the harvest. During the drought years, in the most severely afflicted areas it forgave peasant debts. However, the government marketing of the harvest still is delayed until the end of the dry season, and peasant indebtedness remains a chronic problem. Producer prices are still quite low, particularly for food grains, and mutual suspicion between government and peasants is high.

Centralization

The policy of centralization has contributed both to the rate of urbanization overall and to the pattern of primacy for Dakar and other regional capitals. A system of centralized decision making, government appointments, party structure, and education, health, and economic planning was inherited from the colonial governments and felt as a continuing necessity by the new governments in order to build coherent nations. This pattern has already been illustrated in Table 3.1 (Chapter 3). France had evolved a similar system at home and applied it directly to the colonies. Britain, although lacking such a centralized system at home, nevertheless instituted it in the colonies for administrative convenience. And most leaders of

new nations argued convincingly in the 1960s that centralization was
the only means to both create a modern nation out of disparate traditional cultures and to bring about the economic development that
was sought. An unwanted and largely unanticipated consequence of
this policy of centralization was the attraction of unmanageable population concentrations at the center.

Perhaps the best illustration of this problem is in the educational system. The French West African system was geographically centralized with only primary schools available in the villages.
Secondary schools were introduced in Saint-Louis, Goree, and Dakar
and only later extended to the regional capitals. The sole university
was inaugurated in Dakar in 1958, immediately before independence.
A second university is now under construction near Saint-Louis.
Children from rural areas, as they moved up in the educational system, moved to schools closer and closer to Dakar. And the earliest
urban migrants' children have had the advantage of privileged access
to the system. Thus educational and socioeconomic mobility im-
plied movement toward the center, and educational advantage became
the basis of a new urban class structure.

The steps left untraveled in one generation are typically wished
for in the next. So that, regardless where one student leaves the
system, he hopes for his children to have at least the same opportunity as he, if not more. Once people leave the educational system
and enter employment, they want to live where their children will
have the best opportunity for education.

This is the major factor inhibiting trained personnel from
working in the rural areas, particularly the outlying rural areas or
those not served by paved roads to the capital. Table 4.7, showing
the centralization of skilled humanpower, illustrates the problem.
Of the 64,035 Senegalese employed males aged 20-59 with secondary
school education or more, 44,294 had chosen to live on Cap Vert, a
total of 69 percent. A similar percentage of the employed males
with some university or college education—4,348 of 6,374—chose to
live on Cap Vert. The statistics for Senegal Oriental particularly
illustrate the problem of finding skilled humanpower willing to work
on rural development projects. All of the 157 educated employed
males in that region were under 35 years old, at which age very few
of them would normally have school-age children. (Average male
age at first marriage is about 30.) Educated personnel obliged to
work in the outlying regions frequently commute to Dakar, either
because of their work or because they leave their families there.
This is sometimes necessary for their work, but is also disruptive
of it.

TABLE 4.7

Centralization of Skilled Humanpower in Senegal

Region	Resident Senegalese Men Aged 20-59 Years	Employed Males Aged 20-59 Years with Secondary or More Education	Per 1,000 Males Aged 20-59 Years	Employed Males Aged 20-59 Years with University or College Education	Per 1,000 Males Aged 20-59 Years
Cap Vert	182,556	44,294	242.0	4,348	24.0
Thiès	123,719	8,412	67.9	582	4.7
Casamance	135,086	5,764	42.0	512	3.8
Sine-Saloum	192,408	3,527	18.3	576	3.0
Louga	77,231	1,469	19.0	269	3.5
Diourbel	82,073	412	5.0	84	1.0
Senegal Oriental	54,484	157 (all under 35)	29.0	3 (all under 35)	0.2
Total Senegal, excluding Fleuve	847,557	64,035	75.6	6,374	7.5

Source: Calculated from 1976 census tables 2-4-A and 3-01-A for each region. Data for the Fleuve region are not yet available.

Educational Policy

Independent Senegal inherited the core of the educational system of colonial French West Africa and has increased enrollment without altering its basic structure or orientation. Administration as well as location of schools is centralized. Planning, personnel, enrollment, and curriculum decisions are made in Dakar for the entire country. The Ministry of National Education is responsible for elementary and secondary schools and the Ministry of Higher Education governs the university, professional, and technical schools.

French is the language of instruction at all levels, and the basic goal is to produce an elite of graduates comparable to those in France. Since independence, this assimilationist heritage has received increasing rather than decreasing emphasis. The ideal has been modified to allow Africanization of the curriculum content in primary schools and, to a lesser extent, in secondary and postsecondary schools. And the products have changed slightly. In the colonial period, the system graduated clerks, interpreters, teachers, lower-level civil servants, and chiefs. Since independence, the products have become bureaucrats and teachers, with only a sprinkling of other professionals. Forty-four percent of the licences (bachelor's degrees) granted by the University of Dakar from its inception in 1958 through 1968 (109 of 245) were in law and economics, the direct line to civil service. Many of the 80 graduates in humanities and 56 in sciences also found administrative jobs in the government, little related to their fields of specialty. Efforts to develop a technical education to provide the skills necessary for Senegal's economic development have been frustrated by resistance among students, parents, educators, politicians, and French advisors. As of 1968, only 1,069 students were enrolled in technical lycées, about 3 percent of the total secondary school enrollment of 33,847.[16]

The politically, socially, and economically most problematic school age population is neither the majority who never attend nor the less than 1 percent who graduate from high school, but the from 20 to 30 percent of a population cohort who receive only part of an elitist education. They drop out or fail the competitive examination system and enter the job market with a contempt for manual labor but with few skills. They swell the ranks of the urban unemployed, partially alienated from but still dependent upon the traditional kinship network. The modern sector has few places for them. This has created pressure to reduce the failure ratio in the secondary school entrance examination and baccalauréat and to guarantee places at the university for all who obtain the baccalauréat. But the government has resisted on the grounds it should not train people faster than it can create jobs. It was estimated in 1966 that of 171,000 in a given age group:

Educational Level	Number	Percent of Total
Never attend school	120,000	70.0
Attend Quranic school only	15,000	8.8
Enter primary school	36,000	21.0
Do not finish	20,000	—
Obtain Certificate of Primary Studies	16,000	—
Enter secondary school	5,000	2.9
Do not finish	3,000	—
Obtain Brevet	2,000	—
Enter high school	1,100	0.6
Do not finish	650	—
Obtain baccalauréat	450	—
Obtain a University diploma (licence)[17]	70	0.04

Overall enrollment in Senegalese schools has more than tripled since independence, from 143,000 to about 500,000, but the school-age population has grown at nearly the same rate. The U.N. Economic and Social Council (UNESCO) estimates that the rate of scholarisation at the primary level crept from 16.6 percent in 1960 to 28.4 percent in 1972 and, by 1985, may reach 31.3 percent. These figures, however, were based on pre-1976 estimates of the total school-age population and hence were overly optimistic.

Health Policy

Health care is another area in which logical, humane, and well-intentioned policies have had unexpected and awkward demographic consequences for the country. Colonial health care had two aspects, an elite system in the cities offering health care as close as possible to the standards in France to French residents and some urban Africans plus an epidemic control policy for the entire rural French West Africa. The government of Senegal's approach has been to try to extend the elite health care system to as many residents of the capital and of outlying cities as possible while continuing epidemic control at a maintenance level. Hospitals, which were found only in Dakar and Saint-Louis at independence, have been built or are under construction in the other regional capitals and at N Diome and Ourossagni. A nationwide public health service has also been instituted, along with a maternity and child welfare service and a school medical service. Each prefecture has a dispensary, usually staffed by a doctor and a midwife, comprising separate outpatient and inpatient facilities, a maternity ward, and a hygiene unit. Each subprefecture has an aid-post staffed by a male nurse.

It remains true, however, that more and better health care is available in Dakar than elsewhere in the country. There are three major hospitals in Dakar, a psychiatric center, a blood transfusion center, and numerous private clinics in addition to the standard nationwide institutions. In 1975, there was one doctor for every 4,188 persons in Dakar, while in the rest of the country the ratio ranged from one to 23,113 (in the Fleuve) to one to 82,656 (Diourbel region). [18] The availability of superior health care in Dakar and to a lesser extent in regional capitals is the second major reason given by educated Senegalese for preferring to live in the capital.

Demographic studies of mortality suggest that a combination of epidemic control, safe water supply, health education, and hygiene have the greatest effect on reducing mortality, far greater than that offered by the western system of hospitals and doctors. As a result of epidemic interventions on a West-Africa-wide scale, mortality has been declining steadily since 1920. The U.S. Agency for International Development (AID) financed smallpox and measles vaccination campaign in the late 1960s was one of the last major efforts in this area.

These campaigns can in fact be credited with the reduction in mortality that is responsible for the present population explosion. The problem with them is that they usually have been temporary campaigns, with a sweeping scope but very brief presence in the area and with the sole purpose of reducing mortality. This single-mindedness of purpose is still found in programs such as the maternal and child health care programs that focus on disease and mortality to the exclusion of overall family and economic health. Such selective programs assure the survival of dependent members of the family, without attending to either the health or the economic ability of the working adults to support them. There are visible strains on families as well as national economics and governments produced by the resulting young population. Only in the past year has the government of Senegal recognized this problem and moved to make family planning programs available to the population. They need to accompany water supply, health care, and economic development programs throughout the rural areas to have any measurable impact.

Migration Policy

Senegal's current policy concerning migration is one of the most open in the world. In keeping with its own traditions of cosmopolitanism, tolerance, and hospitality, the land borders are generally loosely patrolled and an identity card is sufficient for access. Periodically, the borders have been closed with either Mali or

Guinea, but even then people pass around, sometimes even through, border points quite freely (see Chapter 7).

Immigration from overseas has been more closely controlled since independence, in order to assure Senegalization of skilled jobs. Since 1973, expatriates also have been required to have an employment permit if they are recruited locally for employment, and a tax is imposed on firms using expatriate workers. The number of French cooperants, mainly teachers, has been reduced from about 20,000 per year in the 1960s to the current level of 800. These policies seem to have had some success. The 1976 census shows a total of 16,830 overseas residents of Cap Vert, down from an estimated 60,000 to 70,000 at independence in 1960.

Senegal's policy on emigration of its citizens is completely open across land borders and subject to exit-visa control for overseas emigration. The exit-visa system does not seem to have been used to prevent emigration from Senegal, except when such control may be requested by other countries, notably France. It also prevents the departure of those who owe obligations to the government or who have no visible means of survival abroad, and thus are potential wards of the state. It is part of the series of bureaucratic obstacles that has to be confronted by potential migrant workers to France. It eliminates adventurers who lack contacts in France, but not those with either friends or jobs awaiting them.

Currently, the government of Senegal's main concern in the area of migration policy is stemming the rural exodus. Like much of the international community of development experts, it places its hopes for this stabilization on rural development. While it is not clear exactly which improvements or amenities in rural areas are most likely to stabilize the population, it has become customary to list an effect on the rural exodus as a goal of virtually every rural development project. The fallacy of this logic is that no known combination of interventions can raise agricultural productivity to levels competitive with industrial productivity. It will be argued here that rural development, while absolutely necessary, will not solve the problem of the relationship between people, production, and consumption in Senegal over either the short, medium, or long term.

This is because, first, the expanding agricultural frontier, where many of Senegal's development planners hope future population growth will be absorbed, is disappearing very rapidly. Settlers from the presently overpopulated areas of the peanut basin form only a small proportion of the new settlers. The great majority of the arable land in Upper Casamance and Senegal Oriental will be already occupied before any program to reverse this tendency or any expansion of the existing Terres Neuves resettlement project could take effect.

Existing rural development projects offer even less hope. First of all, they are small, rarely getting past the pilot stage. Secondly, the population that does cluster around successful projects comes mainly from farther outlying and less sparsely populated agricultural areas, not from the more densely populated areas already intensely involved in the cash economy. The scale of rural development projects and the number that are extended from the pilot phase to general programs of rural development will have to be vastly increased before they have any demographic impact. Then they will help by stabilizing as large a proportion as possible of the rural population on the land, not, however, by stopping the rural exodus.

Another consideration is that most modernization of agriculture aims at improving productivity per person through the introduction of labor-saving devices such as oxen traction plowing and harvest equipment. This improved productivity per person is essential to development, but it reduces the number of active people per square kilometer needed on the land.

Even rural development cannot focus exclusively on the rural areas because secondary outlying cities are needed for rural development to take place. This need is explored in a recent World Bank paper, "Urban growth and economic development in the Sahel." This is strongly supported by our study of the economic circumstances and motivations that move migrants in Senegal. The sharp seasonality of the climate and agriculture for most of Senegal's farmers is a key factor, for the majority can farm only in the rainy season. Once the harvest is in and for the rest of the dry season, farmers who stay in the village have very few productive opportunities. This sets off a seasonal search for money. At present, money may be found in a variety of activities and services, very few of which are directly productive. Secondary cities are needed primarily to provide productive opportunities for cash incomes closer to home, away from the region's central pole. Secondly, they are needed to provide the services and facilities that farmers need and the amenities without which skilled Senegalese development experts will not stay in rural areas.

The final reason that rural development alone is insufficient is that demographic growth has already outstripped both economic development and the absorptive capacity of the land. The children are already born who, as active adults with children and grandchildren of their own, will provide more than the foreseeable needed agricultural labor force on all the arable land of Senegal. Senegambians are currently producing an agricultural surplus, as indeed they have in the past. They can probably continue to produce enough to feed, clothe, house, and supply their wants, but not through rural development alone. Labor-intensive industrialization must be a major thrust in the future, providing productive employment for urban populations and local consumption needs.

NOTES

1. (New York: Oxford University Press, 1978).

2. Important works on urbanization: No. 315 (1979); Seck (Dakar: IFAN, 1970); Dakar en devenier, eds. M. Sankale, L. V. Thomas, and P. Fougeyrollas (Paris: Presence africaine, 1968). Migration: Adrian Adams, Le long voyage des gens du Fleuve (Paris: Maspero, 1977); Abdoulaye Bara Diop, Société toucouleur et migration (Dakar: IFAN, 1965); Cahiers de l'ORSTOM 12 (1975), entire issue on migration in Senegal, and 8 (1971), entire issue on the Colloque sur la demographie africaine.

3. Pierre Cantrelle of the Office de Recherche Scientifique et Technique de l'Outre-Mer, personal communication, July 1980.

4. See J. C. Caldwell, The Sahelian Famine and Its Demographic Consequences (Washington, D.C.: American Council on Education, December 1975).

5. M. Abdela de la Rivière, "The Soninke of Mali and Their Emigration to France," Etudes maliennes 7 (1973): 1-12.

6. Charles Becker and Victor Martin, "Le Sénégal centre-ouest et son évolution démographique: Sine-Saloum-Bawol pays de l'ouest," Part 1, mimeographed, July 1978, pp. I.3, I.4.

7. Sankale, Thomas, and Fougeyrollas, Dakar en devenier, p. 80. See also Map 13.1, p. 273.

8. Senegal, Atlas National (1933); J. Hossenlop, "Trends in Urban Development in 14 Black African States and Madagascar, with Projections up to 1985," Cahiers de l'ORSTOM 8 (1971); and Senegal, Bureau national de recensement, "Résultats provisoires du recensement général de la population d'avril 1976," mimeographed, Dakar, 1976.

9. S. Berniard, Le Sénégal en chiffres, 1978 ed. (Dakar: Société africaine d'éditions, 1979), p. 70.

10. Unpublished data, 1976 census. Note that "Lebanese" in local parlance comprises natives of Syria and Morocco as well as of Lebanon and that many long-term "Lebanese" and some French residents have taken out dual citizenship, excluding them from counts of foreign nationals.

11. See Tables 4.4 and 12.4, the latter in Chapter 12.

12. Myron J. Echenberg, "Military Recruitment and Labor Mobility in French West Africa, 1923-1946," paper presented to the African Studies Association annual meeting, Philadelphia, Nov. 3-6, 1976.

13. Thesis elaborated in V. Gordon Childe, What Happened in History (Baltimore: Penguin, 1964).

14. Mohamed Mbodj, "Le Sénégal et la dépendence—le cas du Sine-Saloum et de l'arachide, 1887-1940," unpublished paper, History Department seminar, University of Dakar, April 14, 1979.

15. See price data in Klaus de Jonge, Jos van der Klei, Henk Beilink, and Jan Rockland Storm, "Sénégal: Projet d'une recherche multidisciplinaire sur les facteurs socio-économiques favorisant la migration en Basse Casamance et sur ses conséquences pour le lieu de départ. Rapport provisoire," mimeographed, Leiden, October 1976; CILSS-Club du Sahel Working Group on Marketing, Price Policy and Storage, Marketing, Price Policy and Storage of Food Grains in the Sahel: A Survey, 2 vols. (Ann Arbor: University of Michigan, Center for Research on Economic Development, 1977).

16. "Mouvements de population et systèmes d'éducation dans les pays sahelo-soudaniens (Haute-Volta, Mali, Mauritanie, Niger, Sénégal, Tchad)," unpublished, mimeographed proceedings of the UNESCO colloquium, Dakar, May 26–June 7, 1975.

17. J. L. Balans, C. Coulon, and A. Ricard, eds., Problèmes et perspectives de l'éducation dans un état du tiers-monde: le cas du Sénégal (Bordeaux: Centre d'études d'Afrique noire, 1972).

18. U.S. Walter Reed Army Hospital, "Health Data Publications: Republic of Senegal," unpublished report no. 26, Washington, D.C., June 1965; see Sénégal en chiffres, 1978.

5

NORTHERN SENEGAL

Cheikh Ba

PREFACE

The area of Senegal north and east of Louga, including the Fleuve region and the northern part of the Louga region, comprises three major ecological zones, each with its own migratory patterns. The agriculturally rich middle and upper river valley opens below Richard Toll into the sandy plains of the delta, where pastoralism and fishing traditionally predominated. Extending south from the river bank is the semi-arid Ferlo zone, where, despite irregular rainfall, millet was cultivated in combination with herding.

Migration from the river valley has been the subject of numerous studies, the history of which is reviewed by Cheikh Ba in this chapter. The current situation of the river valley is being studied by a Senegal River Basin Development Organization (OMVS) socioeconomic team, the Gannett Flemming team, some representatives of the Afro-American Scholars Council, and the Stanford Rice Project. To avoid duplication of efforts, this chapter limits itself to some general comments on the relationship of migratory patterns in the Fleuve region to developments elsewhere in Senegal and to some comments on the potential impact of the OMVS dam and other development plans on the migratory situation of the river and of Senegambia as a whole.

The 1976 census shows a rate of population growth in the Fleuve region as a whole that, for the first time since 1855, is higher than the growth rate for the rest of Senegal. However, until the volume of detailed statistics for the region is published, we will not know whether this represents an influx of drought victims from the collapsing rural economy of northern Senegal and Mauritania or, in a more positive light, reflects the development of the Société

d'Aménagement et d'Exploitation des Terres du Delta (SAED), the
Richard Toll sugar project, the renewed investment in Saint-Louis,
and/or the success of the irrigated perimeters in the upper and
middle valleys. One of the questions posed when this research
project was originally formulated was what effect the tradition of
outmigration in the Senegal river valley might have on the proposed
OMVS development. Given that localized labor shortages already
inhibited the development of irrigated perimeters in some areas,
would the OMVS irrigation plans face the same problem of labor
supply? The existing studies of the ecology of the upper and middle
river valleys had shown that in Soninke and Tukulor villages with
high rates of outmigration of males, there is an increased labor
burden for children, women, and old people left in the village.
Some of the missing male labor force is replaced by hired migrant
labor from the farther hinterland. But low morale and inadequate
labor at the time of planting and harvest still result in the planting
of inadequate plots. There has also been a lack of humanpower for
heavy projects. It may be noted that this situation still exists, and,
in fact, there is evidence that the migration to France is tending
to extend over longer and longer periods so that men up to the ages
of 60-65 remain overseas.

A U.N. International Labour Office (ILO) humanpower analysis
of OMVS labor needs had also predicted quantitative labor shortages
for irrigated plots on the Senegalese side of the river by 1985, to
be complemented by a humanpower surplus on the Mauritanian
side.[1] The politics of distributing capital-intensive plots in Senegal
to Mauritanian citizens appeared so delicate, if not improbable,
that the team also explored this situation further.

We concluded that unless the plot size is increased substantially above the half hectare per household proposed, labor shortages will indeed be a problem, not because of population sparsity
but because the plots will be uneconomic for households. On the
other hand, if plots are distributed on the basis of total family
membership, or if they are larger in size than the half hectare proposed, the anticipated population growth should adequately assure
a labor supply. This is particularly true since the prediction of a
shortage was predicated on the assumption that 5,000 hectares per
year would be opened up during 1975-85. Since we are already well
into that period and only about 1,000 hectares per year have been
developed,[2] a much longer period should be anticipated before
completion. During that period, population growth will more than
keep pace with labor needs.

In fact, labor surplus is the problem here as in the Senegambian economy as a whole. Where labor shortages occur in a
situation of overall surplus, they are usually localized and related

to organizational inadequacies. Because of the magnitude of the organizational problems posed by the OMVS river valley development plans, shortages are indeed likely to occur at least temporarily and locally.

Three major elements in the current plans have a potential for causing serious labor shortages: poor timing between dam construction, flood regulation, and the coordination of new land tenure and working arrangements may make the traditional economy nonviable and drive people away before new positions are viable in OMVS projects, emigration to France, where incomes will continue to vastly exceed any projection for OMVS participants, may continue to drain the active men, leaving dispirited communities in which absolute numbers of workers are adequate but community organization lacks dynamism, economic provisions for labor in the present plans are based on peanut-basin peasant incomes, which are largely irrelevant. Actually, they must take onto account alternative opportunities available through emigration to the city—Dakar, Rosso, Saint-Louis, and Kaolack—as well as local household economic circumstances. Given that the Senegambia as a whole already has a serious labor surplus, particularly in the cities, it is very important that the OMVS development projects be closely monitored to assure as much absorption of the local active population and as little displacement as possible.

Irrigation as it is presently being implemented is addressing the interests of farming and hurting the livestock sector. The Diama salt-intrusion dam at the mouth of the river, now under construction, will do the same to fishing. The livestock sector is referred to in the OMVS master plan, but nothing is actually being done to protect herders' interests as the new irrigation projects eliminate the grazing and transit rights they once had. SAED, for instance, constructed dikes along a large section of the delta in order to prevent salt intrusion and reclaim the lands for agriculture. Even though the irrigated farming is not yet working, the dikes have made a desert of what used to be grazing land immediately behind them. A very detailed analysis of the use of the river valley by pastoralists, both in their transhumance patterns and their importation of meat to the Dara, Louga, and Dakar markets from Mauritania, is available.[3] Yet it is not being used by the local developers. The pastoralists' use of the valley is seasonal and appears transitory to the development project managers on the spot in the river basin. If a serious dislocation of both the pastoralists' livelihoods and the meat supply of Senegal is to be avoided, local managers need a more immediate appreciation of the herders' needs and how these can be reconciled with those of irrigated agriculture. The herds used to pasture on the stubble in the fields after

the grain harvests in the walo lands of the river valley and the delta.
When irrigation equipment and ditches are installed and/or immediate successive crops are planted, the animals are no longer welcome. Sometimes even their passage across the river is blocked
by development, and no alternative is provided. Development plans
ultimately call for the cultivation of forage crops on the irrigated
lands, but the present pastoral economy does not leave the herders
enough cash margin to purchase forage, so development engineers
would rather grow rice. This chapter shows what is happening to
some of the Senegalese pastoralists forced out of this area and
obliged to settle along the Louga-Dara road.

Labor recruitment experience also indicates that SAED has
little trouble attracting workers, but that a large proportion of them
come from outside the river valley. Since the techniques and structural arrangements for farming with SAED are radically different
from those found in the river valley, SAED finds it at least as easy
if not easier to train outsiders who are already "dépaysé" (uprooted).
Some of those settlers are from the Casamance where they have
the advantage of familiarity with rice cultivation, others are former fishermen, nomads, and/or rainfall farmers. Almost none
are former urban residents. If the development of irrigation in the
middle and upper valleys proceeds at the rapid pace needed for
food production in the country and foreseen in the plan, then the
temptation will surely be to do as SAED has done and use an outside,
already uprooted, labor force. Where risk is high and returns are
very low in such a new enterprise, it is easier to get cooperation
from an uprooted mass of individuals than from a local population
with existing social institutions and vested interests still intact.
However, the likely consequence is an additional contribution to
the already swollen urban unemployed. This is because those who
are recruited for the rural labor force come from the less developed rural areas in general, while the established tradition for the
uprooted of the Senegal river valley is to move to Dakar, Kaolack,
or even France.

The following steps in the OMVS development plan seem most
likely to produce substantial uprooting. First, during the initial
phase after the Diama and Manantali dams have both been completed,
an artificial flood will be created in order to keep watering the
walo (flood plain) lands on which flood recession agriculture is traditionally practiced. This is planned as a mitigating technique, to
ease the sharpness of the transition from traditional agriculture.
However, experience with other dams has shown that artificial
floods provide the water but not the fertility carried by natural
alluvial flooding. Therefore, the fertility of the walo lands can be
expected to decline during that period. Also, the fresh fish supply

will be drastically reduced during this period, according to the Gannett Flemming Study. That study noted that fresh fish is a small proportion of the overall volume of fish available, most of which comes from the ocean. However, it did not address the problem of access. Freshwater fish are accessible to individual families along the river valley through the subsistence economy or local exchange. The cash supply, on the other hand, is so limited that these same families will almost certainly not have access to officially marketed fish imported from Saint-Louis.

The most socially and economically disruptive phase of the OMVS transformation will come gradually as the walo flood recession lands, which are the core of the existing system of land tenure and the social structure built upon it, are lost and replaced by government-developed irrigated plots. Government policy is already officially opposed to the hierarchical caste system found among the Tukulor and, to a lesser extent, among the Soninke, in which former slaves and low caste persons have limited access to the best land and must fulfill customary obligations to their patrons. The Law on the National Domain, a 1964 land reform law, has not yet been implemented in the Fleuve, but it is scheduled to be applied there during the same time as the OMVS developments. That law provides for four classifications, one of two of which might theoretically be applied to the river valley lands, with quite different results. It may either be declared a "pioneer zone," in which case title to the land is vested in the development agency assigned to develop it (the SAED model) or it may be classed as traditional farm land, in which case title accrues to any farmer who cultivates the land two years in a row and is not heritable or saleable. Implementation of either system of land tenure would break the link between the family and the land, which is one of the major factors holding young people in rural areas. As they go through the difficult period of entering adulthood and establishing their own family, the prospect of inheriting established family interests and improvements in the area is one major incentive for them to maintain good relations with their own family and to stay on the land.

In the absence of fixed family ties to the land, the factor that becomes crucial in influencing the viability of irrigated farming from the point of view of settlers and, on the other side, from the point of view of the development agency and the national economy is the balance between plot size, individual income, and productivity. Because of their labor surplus economies, the OMVS countries have planned for a half hectare per household as the optimum plot size. Niger office experience, confirmed by SAED's, suggests that this is too small to enable the farmers to both pay the cost of the irrigated agriculture and realize a minimal income. The

Niger Office and SAED both found that with plots too small, farmers are unable to realize enough profit to pay back water charges and their debts to the company for seed, equipment, and fertilizer. Workers are also unreliable because they leave to work at other employment instead of planting a second or a third crop. They may produce just enough rice to consume themselves, and not enough to pay back the company.

The Niger Office finally found its productivity and its demand for plots up only when it began allocating at the rate of one irrigated hectare per active member of the family (ages 8-55). Operation Riz-Segou, also in Mali, has had to allocate 1.5 hectares per family member, including children. With a national average household size of six, this represents 18 times the land/person ratio proposed for the OMVS. If the OMVS irrigated perimeters should be forced to adopt such an allocation policy, they would absorb only one-eighteenth of the humanpower currently anticipated. Alternatively, the countries involved may have to plan to keep relatively small plot sizes and subsidize the capital investment in irrigation and water charges. This might cost less over the short and medium term than subsidizing the same surplus population as urban un-employed.

INTRODUCTION

In the last decade, the drought phenomenon has inspired a wave of studies and research on arid areas of Africa. This has given rise to a movement of new thinking on the Sahel. The region studied in this chapter is part of this movement. It covers the alluvial valley of the Senegal River and the area southward of this to a line between Ndande and Bakel. It encompasses the administrative regions of the Fleuve and of Louga and the Touba-Mbacke area (Region of Diourbel) of 73,320 square kilometers, which is 37 percent of the total area of Senegal.

This vast area is on the Atlantic at the western extreme of the Sahelian zone of West Africa. The Senegal river basin is the biggest "water hole" or oasis in this part of Africa. Very early on, it drew many people, both black and white. Since then, these people have lived in a situation very conducive to migration.

Continuous migration is almost traditional and one of the specific characteristics of northern Senegal. From the beginning, it was the people's way of counteracting poor local environment. This applied notably to the herders. Pastoral movements are above all a means to make the best seasonal use of a meager supply of water and pasture lands. This pastoral migration is a permanent geographic characteristic of this part of Senegal. From early times, Islam has also been an important factor in migration in the Senegal river basin. But migration is laden with history inasmuch as it may be considered a consequence of people coping with their local and outside environments.

Commercial activity in the Senegal river basin, and later the development of cash crops such as peanuts, brought a new aspect to this already ancient migratory tradition. To the traditional pastoral type of migration were added seasonal or continuous movements begun and continued by the overland trade on both sides of the Senegal River. Later, that is to say during the colonial period, introduction of a cash economy and the opening up toward outlying areas accelerated these processes and offered opportunity for an ever-increasing number of agents.

Commercialization of the peanut crop in its turn began a new migratory process. Until then, the river basin had drawn people either from the north, from the Nigero-Senegalese Sudan, or from the center of Senegal (see Map 5.1). With the growth of the peanut economy on the plains to the south, the river valley became a point of emigration. The fundamental reason for this movement was that the economic activities gravitated toward Cap Vert and the peanut basin.

The whole of northern Senegal thus acted as the kind of place from which people, particularly the dynamic ones, were taken in by urban centers and the peanut crop regions. Thus the migration was north-south and could be interpreted as resulting from a break in equilibrium. A demographic imbalance developed in the river basin: the population density (from around 20 to 40 inhabitants per square kilometer depending on the area in question) was no longer bearable. The ecological balance in the Jeri rainfall agricultural zone (the part of the Senegal river basin that did not flood) also broke down, resources needed for large herds of cattle becoming scarcer and scarcer.

In the 1960s, these imbalances increased as there was a growing, if irregular, decrease in available resources with regard to agriculture, animal raising, fishing, and fruit picking.

From this time onward, migration took a new turn. It came to include all the elements of the population. Whereas those who had traditionally traveled tended to stay put, those who had previously stayed in place became involved in migrations that were more intensive, more extended, and included more people. This happened more rapidly in the Fleuve than in the rest of the region because the lack of amenities were such that there was no alternative to leaving, even in the long term.

MAP 5.1

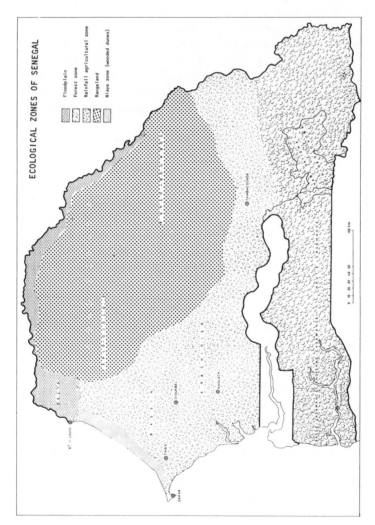

ECOLOGICAL ZONES OF SENEGAL

Floodplain
Forest zone
Rainfall agricultural zone
Rangeland
Niaye zone (wooded dunes)

Source: Government of the Republic of Senegal, Ministry of Planning and Cooperation, Direction de l'Aménagement du territoire, Atlas pour l'aménagement du territoire (Dakar: Nouvelles éditions africaines, 1977).

120

The current socioeconomic development issue in Senegal is one of rehabilitating this old agricultural and animal-raising region. In fact, massive emigration, and, above all, repeated catastrophes related to drought these last few years have showed not only that this region lags behind the others, but also that its natural potential could enable it to play a positive role in the life of the nation.

In addition to this national role, there is now an international one because of the many projects and programs under the aegis of the OMVS.

Thus, in view of all this future geography, one wonders what path migration trends might take. Of course, the reply will depend not only on the way the environment will develop and change, but even more so on the solutions found by the various social groups or administrative agents.

After defining the issue of present and anticipated regional migration and patterns, this chapter will attempt to evaluate regional migratory situations and then to draw up some future prospects from the connection between changes in environment and migration.

REGIONAL MIGRATION IN NORTHERN SENEGAL

Present State of Work on Migration

In the past, migration studies on northern Senegal have greatly varied in type and in the location with which they deal. They have, above all, been centered on the Senegal river basin and, to a lesser degree, on the arid Ferlo zone. They are not interrelated since the aims of their authors and the areas studied have differed. This lack of overall survey of the region has almost always led to an ethnic perspective of migration (for example, as in the case of the Tukulor or the Soninke).

Chronologically, four distinct phases can be seen: before 1958, from 1958 to 1963, from 1964 to 1970, and after 1970. Before 1958, the work was mainly done by or under the aegis of the Mission d'Amenagement du Senegal (MAS). It was at the end of the 1950s that social studies and research revealed the existence of emigration from the middle and lower basin and in the lower Ferlo. These studies were conducted by the socioeconomic mission of Senegal (MISOES) of MAS and by researchers from the (French) Office of Overseas Technical and Scientific Research (ORSTOM). One might cite geographers such as Ph. Grenier (1956/57), Jeanne Audiger (1957), and the team that worked on the Senegalese Sahel under the direction of P. Grosmaire (1957), the MISOES survey (1957/58).

The first years of internal autonomy and political independence (1958-63) marked the beginning of a second phase. This was dominated by sociological studies more directly centered on migration and on demography. There were studies of the middle valley (J. L. Boutilliers and others 1962; MAS-1960), of the Tukulor (Abdoulaye Bara Diop from the Institut fondamental d'Afrique noire (IFAN): Yaya Wane from the Centre national de recherche scientifique (CNRS), and on the Senegal river basin (U.N. Mission 1963; Cheret 1960). During this phase was launched the idea of an overall migration policy based on facts established by research on the Tukulor in particular.

The third phase (1964-70) included work on effective resettlement policies and on social studies of integrated development. Studies done either by or under the auspices of the Company to Develop the Delta (SAED: Cros 1965; government notes and technical studies, specialists' reports), the large amount of documentation compiled by the Inter-State Committee and then by the Organisation des états riverains du Sénégal (OERS) (see the index of the OMVS Data Center in Saint-Louis), detailed geographical studies (F. Ravault 1964; C. L. Blanc 1964), and various reports made by the students of the National School of Applied Economics (ENEA) all contributed to information on migration in the north of Senegal.

In the 1970s, new prospects opened up. The drought produced a large amount of literature and increased knowledge of the spatial, ecological, demographic, economic, and historic order of regional migration (see the general bibliography on the Sahel). Individual studies were done by the Programme de formation pour l'environnement et le développement appliqué (ENDA), by ORSTOM (Cahiers de l'ORSTOM), and by more or less independent researchers or specialists.

During this last phase, the OMVS also conducted numerous studies and research. Studies were done by the countries and by specialists with bilateral and multinational aid and development organizations for the Senegalese government. There was a lot of this kind of work done, and its usefulness varied greatly so far as analysis of the migratory phenomenon was concerned.

Lastly, international emigration was studied in relation to local migration patterns, including the size of the problems both at the place of origin and at the place of destination (F. Kane and Lericollais 1975; Adrian Adams 1977; A. Dubresson 1975).

Themes and Hypotheses

The lack of common aim is the weakness of all these previous studies. Of course, this kind of study rarely lends itself to this.

Our present project introduces three new dimensions in the study of migration—two spatiofunctional dimensions: migration in relation to future development of the Senegal river basin.

So we have an issue that can be subdivided into the following four main points: historic migration, contemporary patterns, environmental changes, and conclusion.

HISTORIC MIGRATION PATTERNS IN NORTHERN SENEGAL

Originally, migration was a solution to an adverse natural environment, particularly an unreliable supply of water and food. Then it was a solution either to lasting conditions such as the deterioration of interchange between the north and central-Atlantic Senegal (the peanut basin, Cap Vert) or to transitory conditions such as the Sahelian-type drought.

The brevity of the rainy season, combined with irregular seasonal and annual rainfall, limits the opportunities for the high-yield agriculture and productive animal raising.

As an example, rainfall calculated over a period of 30 years for the whole of the principal stations in the region (Sagna/Basse Augustine, 1976) is shown in Table 5.1.

One of the very first consequences of so little rain is the limited potential for growing foodstuffs in the region, despite the fact that there is food produced during the season the river is low. This is because of the irregularity of the flow of the Senegal River. It is an allogenic river that loses a good part of its water as soon as it enters the semi-arid Sahelo-Saharian zone, which encompasses the whole northern edge of our region.

Another consequence is the traditional pastoral migration, commonly called transhumance, that is, a way to use outside resources. The Moor and Fulbe migrations fall into this category.

This innate situation is maintained today, despite the development of a monetary economy, because economic activities are oriented around the peanut basin and Cap Vert. Thus there has been a kind of deterioration in the economic and demographic exchange between northern Senegal and central-Atlantic Senegal (peanut basin, Niayes, Cap Vert).

TABLE 5.1

Rainfall, 1944-73
(in m/m)

Station	Normal Rains 1944-73	Average Annual Maximum (year)	Average Annual Minimum (year)
Saint-Louis	314.98	513.0 (1969)	152.1 (1972)
ndr	30.0	48.0 (1950)	12.0 (1972)
Podor	304.0	793.4 (1955)	109.7 (1972)
ndr	28.0	49.0 (1955)	15.0 (1972)
Matam	463.75	713.8 (1950)	175.0 (1972)
ndr	38.0	53.0 (1950)	29.0 (1972)
Linguère	491.0	679.0 (1969)	245.4 (1972)
ndr	42.0	52.0	23.0 (1972)

ndr—number of days of rain per year.

In 1974/75, in terms of cash crops, our region produced none of the cotton in Senegal, 11 percent of the peanuts, 11 percent of the rice, and 9.1 percent of the vegetables and fruit. [4]

Emigration toward Dakar therefore remains the largest flow. For example, in 1973, M. Vernière assessed the migration patterns Dakar from nine provinces (that is, the seven administrative regions in Senegal, neighboring countries, and the rest of the world). The percentage of emigrants from the Fleuve region follows: before 1940, 16-20 percent; 1940-49, 16-20 percent; 1950-59, 26-30 percent; 1960-69, 31-40 percent. [5]

Emigration extends to the whole region: the Senegal river basin, the old peanut producing area around Louga, and western Ferlo. But the largest outward migration recorded in the Senegal river basin was the Tukulor from the middle valley, the Soninke from the upper valley, and the Wolof from the walo (lower valley and delta).

The MISOES study (1957-58) showed that 20 percent of the Fleuve's population left for good. Also, permanent migration became more pronounced than seasonal migration.

According to Abdoulaye B. Diop, by 1965, 70,000 Tukulor had emigrated from the Futa (1959/60), or more than a quarter of the

Tukulor population in the river basin. The Tukulor emigration was essentially directed toward urban centers (86 percent of the total migrants).

The 1960/61 demographic survey revealed that the absent population was assessed at 19 percent for the Fleuve region and at 22.3 percent for the Louga-Diourbel region. The main emigration of Fleuve migrants was toward Cap Vert (51 percent of the total migrants) and of those from Louga-Diourbel (50 percent) was toward the Sine-Saloum. Around 1970 in Dakar, 23.8 percent and 17.5 percent of the total immigrant population came from the regions of Diourbel and the Fleuve respectively.

Demographic exchange conditions thus rapidly deteriorated for northern Senegal. This meant above all a relative decrease in the active population. In the cattle business, for example, the Moors (from Senegal as well as Mauritania) remained a key gauge to activity in Senegal in general. We saw with Santoir (1975) that this population, while decreasing in our region, increased considerably in the towns of central-Atlantic Senegal. Out of a sample of 2,068 Moors from the two sides of the river basin, 1,500 went to Dakar, 358 to Kaolack, and 84 to Thiès, whereas only 346 were scattered over the whole of the seven administrative regions of Senegal (not including 207 immigrants in Saint-Louis and 113 unspecified). The general census of the Mauritanian population (Ministry of Planning and Mines Central Census Bureau, 1977) showed that there were 40,000 Mauritanians in Senegal.

When Dakar was made the capital of Senegal and Nouakchott of Mauritania in 1958, where previously Saint-Louis was the combined capital, there was a sizable effect on the activities of the Fleuve region.

CURRENT MIGRATION CHARACTERISTICS
AND CONDITIONS

The Senegal river basin has obvious potential because of the river. On the other hand, there is not enough rainfall, and, in general, agricultural development depends on surface water. It is a zone of emigration, rural exodus, and local migration at one and the same time.

Rural Migration to Lands under Development

This revolves around irrigation works that have already been constructed or are underway, from the delta up to the region of

Bakel. Two migratory flows of different size intermingle: the flow toward the established projects and the flow to areas neighboring the developed lands.

The flow of people toward the irrigated areas comprised the colonization movements of the delta, of the region of Dagana, of the region between Nanga and Gede in the department of Podor, and the perimeters in the department of Matam and Bakel.

Migration toward the delta began in 1965 with the SAED land development called the "30,000 hectares" operation. This was an organized resettlement program to develop 30,000 hectares of reclaimed land in the channels of the Senegal river delta. In the first phase, the settlers brought from the department of Dagana and Podor were established in the colonized villages: notably the villages of Bundum and Kassak, which had drainage channels. This organized migration included Fulbe herders as well as Wolof and Tukulor peasants. But from the 1970s onward, the resettlement scheme was abandoned because of technical and social problems raised by the project and also because of a change in SAED policy.

And so preference was given to small perimeters, village-scale irrigation schemes. This did not delay extensive migratory movement toward the new villages. Migrants came from both walo villages and jeri villages or camps. (Walo is a flood plain of the river valley, and the jeri or dry land is above and outside the flood plain.)

The same situation is happening at the present time in the development of irrigated perimeters upstream between Dagana and Bakel.

The Dagana channel, for example, involves the Dagana inhabitants (40 percent of the farmers) and the neighboring villages, Gaye (32 percent) and Bokhole (18 percent) in particular.[6]

Further upriver, the pockets at Nanga and Gede-chantier (department of Podor) are also important immigration and polarization points for rice growers. Gede-chantier has about 800 inhabitants and Nanga about 600.

The general result of these strong movements is an increase in requests for land, which has led to the land being divided up (lots of from only 1 to 5 ares per family) and an artificial overpopulation.

The flow of people outside the perimeters is composed particularly of Moor and Fulbe herders.

In the delta and lower valley, for example, not only seasonal migration but also the living conditions have undergone many changes. Irrigation means that people do not have to go so far for water, and it eliminates the reason for migrating.

With the Fulbe, for example, their dry-season camps, as do those for the wet season, tend to be installed along the so-called

Jeri Road (linking Saint-Louis and Matam). Thus the families are
often subdivided: one part takes care of animals seeking pasture on
the jeri; another looks after both the other animals and the small
plots of irrigated rice. These rice-growers cum animal-raisers
are on the increase throughout the whole of the delta and the lower
valley. This must not be forgotten when looking for a link between
agriculture and animal raising.

"Traditional" Rural Migration of Farmers and Herders

This migration is more outward than inward, particularly with
the Wolof and Tukulor. We will discuss the case of the Soninke so
far as international migration is concerned.
Pastoral migration goes both ways: immigration of herders
from the jeri in the dry season and emigration of Walwalbe herds-
men (inhabitants of the walo) toward the jeri at the height of the wet
season.
Similarly, outmigration occurs in the lower valley, more precisely in the region of the walo. Traditionally, the people of this
region emigrate in the dry season toward urban centers such as
Saint-Louis and the towns of the peanut basin. This traditional migration includes women as well as men. Like most of the Serer or
Jola women, they find temporary domestic work. The Tukulor
emigration affects practically all the villages of the middle valley.
The rural areas to which the Tukulor migrants go are more
spread out. Among the largest seem to be the peanut basin, eastern
Senegal, and particularly the Casamance. For example, the village
of Madina Gonasse and its satellite villages are important immigration points for numerous Tukulor families from the middle valley
of the Senegal River. Madina Gonasse is a pioneer agricultural
village in the Upper Casamance that was developed from 1935 onward by a Tukulor marabout who came from the Mauritanian bank
of the River Senegal: al-Hajj Cerno Mamadu Saydu Ba. This village now has more than 6,000 inhabitants.

Rural Exodus and International Migration

These two forms of migration are the ones that have been
studied the most in the river basin. They notably affect Tukulor and
Soninke.
The Soninke generally go to Europe, particularly France.
For example, F. Kane and H. Lericollais estimated Soninke immi-
grants (from Senegal, Mauritania, and Mali) in France at between

40,000 and 50,000 out of a total from 60,000 to 70,000 African workers in France. In the arrondissement of Ololdou (department of Bakel), 40.1 percent of the Soninke population were temporary emigrants, of which 36.6 percent were in France.[7]

The peopling of the river basin's towns is relatively slow. Saint-Louis, the regional capital is, however, the exception. At the present time, it has about 90,000 inhabitants, whereas it had 75,000 in 1968 and 48,500 in 1961, when the capital of Senegal was transferred to Dakar and that of Mauritania to Nouakchott. Also, Dagana, which was losing people during the development of the peanut basin, has regained a relatively large growth rhythm. From 0.8 percent in 1950, the growth rate at the present time is 6 percent, of which only about 2.5 percent to 3 percent is due to natural growth.

According to Ba (1976), from an emigration rate of 1.2 percent per year in 1960, the town now has an immigration rate of 4 percent per year. Its growth is helped by installation of the delta-irrigated perimeters and by the expansion of agroindustries in Richard Toll where many of its inhabitants work.

Permanent migration toward other towns in the valley is less in evidence. Podor, Matam, and Bakel are in fact only stepping points toward more dynamic centers in Senegal or elsewhere.

The alluvial valley of the River Senegal is thus a very dynamic emigration center. However, emigration is developing there while there are numerous internal movements that are as yet not clearly assessed, most of which are linked to current environmental changes. Labor migration is certain to increase. The way it evolves will depend on a certain number of factors, including land development work, improved living conditions (particularly urban), and general demoeconomic conditions between the north and the rest of Senegal.

In the forest and pastoral zone, natural resources and economic and human potential are more limited than in the valley. This underpopulated zone has no water courses and has an even lower rainfall (about 400 m/m per year) than the valley. There is still a lot of space available, waiting to be better incorporated into the socioeconomic development of the Senegal River.

Internal rural migration here is already more important, larger but less diversified than in the valley. There is migration toward the bore-hole wells and the related settlement of the herders, traditional rural seasonal migration, and, lastly, interregional type migration.

The Attraction of Bore-Hole Wells and Settlement of Herders

In view of the fact that most of the deep wells were bored after World War II, the movement toward them is, of course, a recent one. Their original use was twofold: to supply water for cattle and to encourage the nomadic Fulbe herders to settle in one place.

Deep wells have thus become the keystone to organizing seasonal pastoral migration. More than the seasonal water points, these wells have progressively become settlement points for Wolof farmers as well as local herders.

Since the years of drought, the deep wells have attracted more and more people. Many families from the valley area have thus settled around the deep wells in the department of Linguère. These immigrants are known by the general and descriptive term of "egge-egge" (the wanderers).

The deep wells are at the same time polarization points of migratory resahelization movements for people coming from the peanut basin. These are generally Fulbe herders who have been edged out, or even forced out, of the peanut crop regions controlled by Wolof and the Murid Brotherhood, in the regions of Diourbel, the Sine-Saloum, and Louga.

And so both the water itself and the land around the deep wells attract the nomadic herders to settle.

More and more people will settle in wider and wider areas around the deep wells in the forest and pastoral zone. Increasing population in places such as Dara, Labgar, Gassan, and Velingara-Ferlo, which are all in the department of Linguère, is a good illustration of this. For example, between 1958 and 1972, population increased as follows:

	1958	1972
Linguère	2,250	6,430
Barkeji	467	818
Gassan	759	645
Velingara	256	335
Linde	182	224
Ceel	213	322
Labgar	195	277

Linguère should have had 7,500 inhabitants by 1973 and 7,890 by 1976.[8]

At the same time, we must point out a diversification in the ethnic order of the population. Thus at Velingara we note in 1972 an ethnic clustering in wards Moor I and II, Canor (Fulbe), Dialal (Fulbe), Lawbe, and Wolof. Fulbe groups have increased in number much faster than the others.

On the other hand, at Gassan and Linde, Fulbe have decreased as Wolof have increased. For example, at Gassan, there were 393 Fulbe in 1958 and only 121 in 1972, and there are barely 100 of them at the present time, whereas for the same period Wolof increased from 146 to 358 and now number more than 400.

We must not forget that the water sources are "life-saving" centers for many families haunted by drought for several years. The consequences of having more people and herds around the deep wells poses problems and can be grave and ambiguous from an ecological perspective (overuse, deterioration of the environment, and so on) as well as from the socioeconomic perspective (amount of water from the wells, real uses of a well, permanence of the herders, choice of production methods for developing the land).

Traditional Seasonal Rural Migration

We can mention this briefly here as it is generally well known. There is pastoral seasonal migration within the area (short distance transhumance of the Fulbe groups) and external seasonal migration (Fulbe migration toward the Sudanic regions and the south or toward the Senegal river basin). The latter is now centered along the main roads and toward the towns of the peanut basin, because of the women selling milk and seasonal work for adult males.

The agropastoral zone is more urbanized and is better connected to the centers of activity in the River Senegal than the others. The attraction of towns is strongest here. Louga, Kebemer, Touba, Mbake, and Bawol draw the most people. However, it connects with the old peanut basin and also has considerable centrifugal movement.

Two principle migratory flows dominate the zone: movement toward the Sahelian zone (or resahelization) and movement toward the towns.

Resahelization

We have already mentioned the Fulbe herders who settle around the deep wells of the forest-pastoral zone. Thus the agropastoral zone serves as a place of outward migration, but this is

not uniform. The arrondissements of Daru Musti, Sagata, and
Ndam are the main outward points, mainly because of Murid pressure and lack of arable land. This lack is due to high concentrations
of population around Touba and to the peanut crop system that deteriorates the soil.

This last reason also explains the fact that Wolof farmers are
gradually working their way toward the bore-holes in the department
of Linguère. This movement is essentially due to the action of
marabouts, either Murid or Tijan.

The axes of these movements are mainly the upper valley of
the Sin and the upper basins of the Ferlo and Salum Rivers. The
main impact points remain the water sources (deep wells and dried-
up river beds, which have more unused soil).

The infrastructure provided for herders serves as "support
points" for these farmers who were driven by their need for fertile
land and money and forced to settle in a still poor environment, despite the fact that there were incessant conflicts with the Fulbe
herders who were more or less masters of the invaded area.

Although this movement is still small and well spread out,
the most visible result is a series of big gaps in peanut growing in
the forest-pastoral zone, in the east from Linguère out to Tambacounda.

"Rural and Urban" Migration

One result of this is a notable growth in urban centers in the
zone, even though there is a sizable migration toward the Cap Vert
and the Salum zones of the peanut basin. Local towns are stepping
stones, and this is one of the reasons for the slow growth in relation to towns such as Dakar or Thiès.

For example, from 1958 to 1976, for the principal towns of
the zone the increase has been as follows:[9]

	1958	1964	1970/71	1976
Louga	14,608	17,600	35,670	35,063
Kebemer	3,500	4,200	5,121	6,746
Mbacke	7,350	9,100	20,065	25,039

For all three departments of Louga, Kebemer, and Mbacke,
in 1976 the urban population represents 15 percent of the total population. This is low, but officially the towns have been reduced to
three for all three departments. These figures have been collected
and compiled in the same manner for all places and show a definite
rapid increase between 1958 and 1970, particularly for Louga and

Mbacke. The rate of growth of these two towns is from 8.1 percent and 10.4 percent respectively between 1960 and 1973. During the 1970s, when there was drought and long-distance emigration, the population remained unchanged. One of the reasons for Louga's figures may be the difference in accuracy between the survey by poll of 1970/71 and the census of 1976.

Despite economic stagnation, rural exodus is the principal factor in urban growth. The current urban growth of Tuba, the Murid capital, should be mentioned. Unfortunately, we do not yet have viable figures to establish it, but it has been very visible. We will return to this in a study now in process.

MIGRATION AND ENVIRONMENTAL CHANGES:
FUTURE PROSPECTS

Here we will touch briefly on the strategy or strategies (local, regional, and national) of action for medium- and long-term migrations.

The main change in the future will be to the water system, for the towns and rural areas, for animal raising, agriculture, power, and industrial development, and, finally, for shipping and fishing. Irrigation from the River Senegal will be the mainstay of land development.

Despite its limitations, development has some advantages, notably: harnessing the water supply with dams, setting up basic levels for rural incomes that may be easily increased, and finally regularizing and revamping the local humanpower market.

Above all, this means to bend or even reverse current migratory trends, essentially to change from an external migration into an increased intraregional migration viewed as an integrated regional development factor.

The plan of action for migration lies ultimately in a development strategy for the territory, which is the only way to make the best use of northern Senegal and the rest of the country and to change the current migratory pattern of the region. To achieve this aim there can be three areas for further study.

Action on the Flow toward Northern Senegal

There should not be a resettlement policy, but rather a rationalization of current migratory trends. The south-north flow would then be oriented toward the areas that can support the people best, particularly those receiving most development, in the river basin as well as in the forest and pastoral and agropastoral zones.

Stabilizing Regional Geographic Movement

In a creative approach, the problem is not to clog the land by riveting groups of people to precise areas, but rather to create a regional migration dynamic.

We have seen above that migration existed before what is known as the drought. The latter has only aggravated and amplified the former. The question of migration is one of income, employment, and short journeys, therefore a question of what the region has to offer.

Geographic movement can be stabilized with a good balance of needs (land and water above all, foodstuffs, work opportunities, amenities, and aid) between developed areas (irrigated or not) and undeveloped areas; towns and the country (the towns in the north thus being perceived as points of industrial decentralization and of useful urban hierarchization); different production methods: agriculture, animal raising, fishing, industries, tourism, business.

Although this kind of action, which considers the varied geography of the area, is more difficult to achieve, it ensures a better future than the "technical" solutions generally proposed. Irrigation and harnessing of water in general are necessary, but they are insufficient or even powerless against hidden socioeconomic trends.

International Migrations

Future demographic exchange between Senegal and the river countries (Mali, Mauritania, and Guinea) depends to a great extent on the concept of the border in the Senegal River Basin Development. Present crossborder migration activity leaves this in no doubt.

CONCLUSION

This study on regional migration is limited because of lack of statistical support. Nevertheless, it attempts to focus on regional migratory trends and particularly their geographic significance.

Correlation between migration, ethnic group, and production methods make up the basis of the migratory network in northern Senegal. It has also been the basis of past studies on demographic and economic relations between this region and the rest of Senegal, if not "western Sudan."

Traditional socioeconomic systems that have allowed traditional migration will be greatly changed. The first years in the 1970s certainly revealed this with the drought.

Future studies should emphasize these migratory trends and their consequences, in particular the reshaping of rural and urban populations and solutions to policies for migration, rural development, and a regional system for natural resources. It is solely on this basis that the new regional migratory network will be best appreciated.

RESUME

Because of its location in "western Sudan" and its place in the precolonial and colonial economic history of Senegal, northern Senegal has been, and remains a region of migration.

The size, pattern, geographic interpretation, and problems of migration vary according to the ethnoprofessional groups concerned (Tukulor, Wolof, Soninke, Fulbe, and Moor) and also according to the geography of the region (river basin, forest-pastoral, and agropastoral zones).

The drought of the 1970s and the development undertaken in these different zones have, to a greater or lesser extent, upset much of this traditional migratory schema.

The plan of action for this current and future regional migration lies in a development policy for the territory that establishes a system of natural resources based on harnessing the water of the Senegal river basin.

NOTES

1. Gabriel Féral, annex to "Migration and Employment in Senegal; An Introductory Report," World Bank confidential report no. 1302-SE, Sept. 24, 1976.

2. Field mission to SAED (Delta) and Dagana irrigated perimeters, January and March 1978.

3. See the work of C. J. Santoir, summarized in Senegal, Atlas National, Map 41, p. 99.

4. Senegal, Direction de la statistique, "Situation économique du Sénégal, Dakar, 1976.

5. Marc Vernière, "Voluntarisme d'état et spontanéisme populaire dans l'urbanisation du tiers-monde" (Paris: Ecole pratique des hautes études and CNRS, 1973).

6. Alioune Ba, "Aménagement hydroagricole et études socio-économiques de la Cuvette de Dagana," unpublished memoir, Faculté des lettres et sciences sociales, Geographie Dakar, 1976).

7. Cahiers de l'ORSTOM 12 (1975).

8. P. Metge, Le peuplement du territoire (Dakar: Ministry of Planning and Development, 1966); Senegal, Direction de la statistique, "Situation économique du Sénégal," Dakar, 1972 and 1976.

9. Senegal, Direction de la statistique, "Situation économique du Sénégal," Dakar, 1958, 1964, 1971, and 1976.

6

ZONAL APPROACH TO MIGRATION IN THE SENEGALESE PEANUT BASIN

Jacques Faye

INTRODUCTION

Originally this study had two objectives. The first was to make a quantitative analysis of migratory movements in the peanut basin of Senegal in each of the four administrative regions involved, and, if possible, department by department, from data collected during the 1976 demographic census in Senegal. Numerous partial studies on migratory phenomena and village monographs have been conducted by different organizations in recent years and were to be used for the better interpretation of this global data and lead to a good understanding of migratory phenomena. Unfortunately, data from the 1976 census are still not available. This objective therefore had to be temporarily abandoned. The second objective was to establish and to test a geographical approach to migratory movements. For example, we know that until at least the 1950s the whole peanut area had incoming seasonal migrants for the peanut harvest and threshing, and it would be worthwhile to assess the areas still affected by these migrations geographically. Of course, from detailed studies of certain zones and from village monographs, we know that this type of migration continues to occur in the east and south of the peanut basin whereas it has disappeared in the west and north of the basin.[1] But no survey has traced the respective limits of these different zones.

Moreover, we know that the various types of migrations do not occur with the same pattern everywhere in the peanut basin. In some parts of this basin, there are dry-season migrations toward the towns as well as rainy-season migrations toward the east of the territory. In other parts, there are both rainy season in-migration and outmigration. So there are some zones in which there are inward migrations and some in which there are both inward and outward migrations. A survey on the spatial limits of the different types of migrations and combinations of migrations would lead to our ultimate aim of delineating and mapping the migratory patterns in the peanut basin.

The third objective was to test a simple survey method that could be used by research assistants as well as by qualified researchers. Although good survey methods and techniques for studying migratory phenomena do exist, these are often complicated and difficult to apply under some circumstances. Let us take an example: for a large agricultural region, it could be useful and even necessary for a development project or a master development plan or a regional plan to know the principal regional migratory patterns. Generally, there are geographic monographs with data on the types of migrations, the reasons for them, and their statistical magnitude.

Often the problem for the developer and planner is to extrapolate data from a small area and apply them to a much larger or nearby area. Few areas are completely homogeneous. In our opinion, the idea is to be able to "zone" the region; that is, to map it into different zones according to the types of migrations, their patterns, and their development.

Over and above the fact that migrations generally reflect a given economic evolution and are therefore good economic indicators, this kind of mapping will enable better clarification and definitions.

METHODOLOGY

The method used was to poll a certain number of villages. This technique had been pretested. Our postulate was that from a simple interview with the village chiefs it would be possible to gather data on the types of migrations in the village, their relative size, their evolution, and inward and outward migration sites, and the ethnic composition of the migrations. In our opinion, these elements suffice to differentiate various migratory dynamics and to delineate the corresponding zones.

For this we had to ensure that enough villages were chosen and that they were well spread out over the whole of the peanut basin. We could use one of two sampling methods. (1) Pick at random a certain percentage of villages in the peanut basin. If the sample is big enough, this should ensure that the villages to be surveyed are spread out over a wide enough area. (2) Superimpose a grid on a map of the regions in question and pick the villages from this. Villages nearest the intersecting horizontal and vertical lines would be chosen. This technique would underrepresent the densely populated areas and overrepresent the underpopulated ones. But in relation to the objective, which is to place the data on a map, it is an advantage because an even spread of the surveyed villages is essential.

This method has two advantages. It is easier to choose the villages, and they are more evenly distributed. Also it avoids making a mistake by picking the wrong village because it has the same name as another. If by chance a village has disappeared, the researchers can right away choose the second nearest village to survey.

Therefore we chose this second sampling method. We used the map of Senegal to the scale of 1/200,000.[2] This map was already marked out in squares, and we used this grid in choosing the villages. After calculation, we realized that this grid represented a sampling of about one-twentieth, which was what we had decided for our survey, taking into account the means and time available. In this way, we picked 140 villages to survey. Later, when we compiled the data, we kept only 116 survey sheets. The remainder were villages that were not surveyed, villages that no longer existed, questionnaires that had been incorrectly filled in, villages where most people were nomadic, or villages where the people were from an ethnic group that was very minor in the survey area and followed a different migratory behavior from the dominant ethnic groups (for example, Fulbe villages in Serer country).

THE PEANUT BASIN

Around the middle of the nineteenth century, the French introduced peanuts into Senegal as a cash crop. First they were grown along the railroad that was under construction and in the areas on either side of the Gambia and Sine-Saloum Rivers, and then they spread into areas further from the communication network. So peanuts were first grown between Dakar and Saint-Louis (because of the railway line of the same name) and then along the railway line joining Senegal to what is now called Mali (see Maps 3.5-3.8).

The part of Senegal where peanut cultivation predominates is called the peanut basin, but, as one can see, it is difficult to define this area as it changes. Over the years, it has spread not only toward the south and east, but, within the last few decades, also more and more to the northeast.

Usually the peanut basin is considered to cover the administrative regions of Louga, Diourbel, Thiès, and the Sine-Saloum, which together make about 64,093 square kilometers, or about one-third of the area of Senegal (196,722 square kilometers). However, the peanut area does not correspond exactly to these administrative boundaries. It goes much further eastward into the department of Tambacounda. To the northeast, more than half the department of Linguère is excluded as are the coastal part of the Niayes and the western part of the department of Thiès and the Saloum Islands in the department of Foundiougne.

Some figures will show the significance of the peanut basin to the Senegalese economy. Its population is 2,549,680, or 50 percent of the total population of Senegal.

Region	Official Population	Population Density (per sq. km.)
Thiès	693,994	105.9
Sine-Saloum	1,007,736	42.09
Diourbel	425,113	25.12
Louga	417,737	—
Total	2,549,580	39.79
Senegal	5,035,388	25.35

Of 25,000 sq. kms. of land cultivated in 1972, 71 percent was within the peanut basin.

The two main agricultural products in Senegal are millet and peanuts. In any given year, millet production in the peanut basin is around three-fourths of the national production, and millet is by far the number one food crop in Senegal.

In 1975-76, there was a record production of peanuts (1,444,100 tons), but in 1972-73 there were only 570,000 tons. The Senegalese economy depends heavily on peanuts. It is the primary export, representing an average of 40 percent of Senegal's export income.[3]

The area surveyed covered the administrative regions of Thiès, Louga, Diourbel, and Sine-Saloum, but we eliminated the vegetable and fruit area in the region of Thiès, west of the line Popenguine-Thiès-Mont-Tolland; the coastal zone of Niayes, approximately the perimeter of the Niayes reforestation project; the Saloum Islands; and the zone northeast of a line Nguernaal (near Louga)-Dara-Linguère-Tief-Bamianol, that is, northeast of the department of Linguère.

This decision was made while the survey was underway, as most of the villages were found to be abandoned; either the people were moving to another pasturage with their animals or had left permanently. Therefore a total of 116 villages were surveyed.

QUESTIONNAIRE

We have already stated that the survey should be uncompli-
cated, and therefore the questionnaire needed to be simple. The
migration types involved follow.

Nawetanat is seasonal work migration from one rural zone to
another in the rainy season. The nawetan is a seasonal worker who
goes into a village in the rainy season and asks the chef de carré
(head of a ward within a village) to give him board and lodging and
lend him a parcel of land to cultivate and money to buy seed and
fertilizer in exchange for four days' work per week. We have called
the outward migrants nawetaani and the inward ones nawetaansi.

Firdu are migrants who move at the end of the rainy season.
The firdus are almost exclusively people from the Fuladu in the
Casamance (which gives them their name), and they come to the
peanut basin from November to March to harvest and thresh the
peanuts. They are paid by the number of sacks of peanuts. Now
that the picking is mechanized, they only do the threshing, but in
the Sine-Saloum, at least, since 1977 they have been paid according to the size of the peanut mound collected.

Noorani (noor is dry season) are dry season migrations to
look for work or to learn a trade. It could be a migration from a
rural zone to an urban or semiurban one. We have kept only this
latter kind, which is by far the largest.

Toxu and santian are permanent migrations; we have only retained information on the migration from one rural zone to another.
Outward migrations are toxu and inward santian.

We omitted some types of migration on purpose because they
were statistically insignificant at the village level: the mbindaan is
a rainy season migrant like the nawetaan, but different from him in
that he cultivates for himself a field lent by a villager and is lodged
and fed by a chef de carré to whom he pays a prearranged sum.
This has become extremely rare. The salaried agricultural worker,
who is paid to work full time all rainy season in his employer's
field, is a very recent phenomenon and is also very rare. Permanent migration to the towns is exceptional and does not occur at any
specific time but is a gradual process over a long period.

THE QUESTIONS

For each type of migration, we asked questions on whether it
took place, its present development (decreasing, disappearing, increasing), family status of migrants (young bachelors, married
people, chef de carré, unmarried women, and so forth), ethnic

groups, inward and outward migration points, size of one type of migration in relation to others. Some subsidiary questions on the statistical number of migrants this year, and so on, were added to facilitate assessment of the other data.

EXECUTION OF THE SURVEY

The survey was conducted in March by two researchers and lasted three weeks. In order to obtain the most accurate data, the researchers were assigned to interview the village heads, and, when possible, other people from the village. In practice, for administrative reasons, the interviews were carried out in the company of the president of the rural community, which improved the quality of the data collected.

ANALYSIS OF DATA

This work is not as simple as one would think. Unless one is constant with a crude mapping that adds little to what is already known, the collected data need meticulous adjustment.

Let us take the example of inmigration. The reply to the question, "Are there any nawetans who come into the village?" enables the inward migration points to be put on the map. This mapping is crude. There could be a small zone without nawetans. So one must try to find out why. The village surveyed might be populated by an ethnic group that is minor in the survey zone and not have any inmigrants, for example, the case of a village of Fulbe herders in a Wolof zone. The reverse could be true; there might be nawetans in a zone that is not an inmigration zone. This might be the case of a Serer district in a Wolof village, with the Serers receiving nawetans from their homelands. There might also be an error in the data transcript that does not correspond with the other replies. And so the map must be adjusted. But the most difficult part is to record the slight variations in the different types of migrations: for example, in receiving areas, to differentiate between the zones where the migrants come from distant zones, the zones where this immigration is accompanied by internal migration, and the zones where there is only internal migration. To achieve this differentiation, we reexamined the data department by department. Instead of automatically mapping data on the Firdous for the whole peanut basin, we analyzed the data on all types of migrants department by department. This kind of comparative analysis enabled us to record the slight variations.

DISTRIBUTION OF DIFFERENT MIGRATIONS
IN THE PEANUT BASIN

Rainy Season Inmigration

This inmigration from one rural zone to another rural zone
for the agricultural season still occurs in large parts of the peanut
basin and can divide it into two big zones: a zone located east of the
line Foundiougne-Gossas-Diourbel-Darou Mousti-Sagatta (Djolof)-
Barkedji-Velingara-Bem-Bem, where there are incoming nawetan,
and a zone located west of this line, which has no incoming nawetans,
or at least none any longer. The rainy season inmigration occurs
in this whole eastern and southern part of the peanut basin, and,
from the survey answers given by the heads of the villages, it can
be divided into subzones because the nawetanat does not have the
same pattern everywhere (see Map 6.1).

The Pioneer Zone

This is the east and northeast part of the peanut basin. The
area can be marked by a line from Ndam village (north of Koumpan-
toum and at the border between Sine-Saloum and Senegal Oriental)
toward Malem Hoddar-Mbar-Colobane-Sagatta-Barkedji-Velingara-
Bem-Bem. This is a large inward nawetan zone; all the heads of
villages said that there were many migrants and that they were even
on the increase. ORSTOM studies confirm this.[4] G. Rocheteau
shows that in this zone the use of nawetans is almost indispensible
to the head farmers. It also shows that for large plantations (those
of marabouts and big landowners) there is a specific type of farming that uses the nawetanat.

According to the heads of villages, the immigrants come from
Kayor, Bawol, and Njambour and the majority are young Wolof.
There are also young Serers, particularly from Bawol and occasionally from Sine, practically all over but to a much lesser extent than
the Wolof.

Southern Sine-Saloum

Southern Sine-Saloum is the area to the south of the Koungheul-
Kaolack road (that is, the departments of Foundiougne, Nioro, and
the southern part of Kaffrine). Although seasonal inmigration is
less than in the pioneer zone, it is still significant, particularly in
the west around the arrondissements of Sokone, Keur Madiabel, and
Wack Ngouna and in the east to the south of Koungheul. The people

MAP 6.1

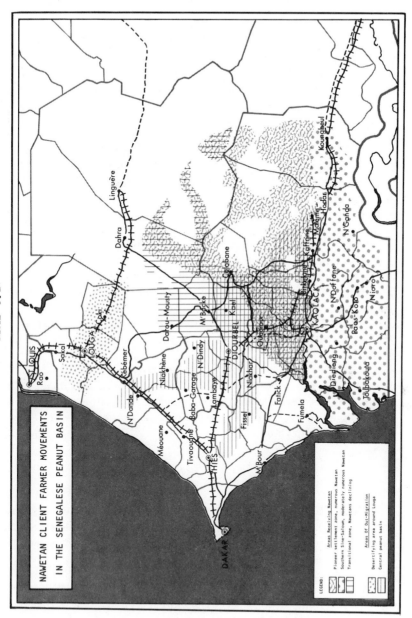

NAWETAN CLIENT FARMER MOVEMENTS
IN THE SENEGALESE PEANUT BASIN

LEGEND:

Areas Receiving Nawetan
Pioneer settlement zone, numerous Nawetan
Southern Sine-Saloum, moderately numerous Nawetan
Transitional zone, Nawetans declining

Areas Of Out-Migration
Desertifying area around Louga
Central peanut basin

interviewed had conflicting statements on the increase or decrease of the number of nawetans. According to Monnier's study, this follows the hypothesis that the subzone could be divided into three parts: a western part including the arrondissements of Sokone, Keur Madiabel, and Wack Ngouna, which still has many incoming migrants; an eastern part to the south of Koungheul up to around Pate Tiangaye, where the use of nawetans is determined by the agricultural cultivations; and the central part (between the transgambian road and Pate Tiangaye), where there are still many nawetans but they are decidedly decreasing.[5] In Saloum, the pattern of the nawetanat is unusual. Nearly everywhere the Bambara, Sarakole, and even Turka from Upper Volta, which were the most numerous in the 1950s and even a little later, have been replaced by the nawetans from Guinea. These Fulbe from Futa Jallon are not, moreover, exactly seasonal immigrants because they do not return to Guinea each year. Most stay put for several years or spend the dry season in the city. They are supported by the many Guinean nationals who have succeeded in setting themselves up permanently as chef de carré in villages and who have often obtained a high social status as storekeepers, charcoal makers, and so on.

There are other nawetans, but these are less numerous: Bambara from Mali in the department of Foundiougne and to the south of Kaolack in the former province of Laphem, that is, where there are some Bambara villages and communities; Serer nawetans from Sine are noted around Ndoffane, where there are a certain number of Serer villages.

Finally, throughout this southern region exists an internal migration from village to village, over quite short distances. It is composed uniquely of young bachelors whose basic motive is to seek a marriage dowry. On the other hand, the survey does not show any inmigration from Gambia.

The Northern Part

This includes the arrondissements of Gandiaye, Ouadiour, Kahone, the southern part of the arrondissement of Kologane, the departments of Mbacke and Diourbel, and the southeast of the arrondissement of Darou Mousti.

This part is above all a transition zone between the west of the peanut basin, which no longer has seasonal incoming migrants, and the pioneer zone, which does. The survey gives even more approximate lines for these than for the others. The nawetans seem to be decreasing clearly except in the eastern part and seem to come from the same regions as the nawetan going into the pioneer zone, that is, the majority are Wolof from Bawol and Kayor and Serer from Bawol and Sine.

SEASONAL INMIGRATION AT THE END
OF THE RAINY SEASON: FIRDUS

The drought during the 1977 "rainy" season doubtless affected the replies in that the firdus heard of the bad agricultural season, fewer than usual came, and those who did come remained for a shorter period of time, since the peasants had fewer peanuts to thresh. The replies from the heads of villages seemed to show a decrease for this reason.

Those replies justify cutting the peanut basin into two zones: one that has incoming firdus each year to thresh the peanuts and another that no longer uses seasonal workers (see Map 6.2). Minor variations, however, are lost in such a division. This absence of variation is also due to the type of migration. If we compare the seasonal inmigration of the firdus with that of the nawetan, we can deduce that the first type of migration is less susceptible to farm constraints than the nawetan. The former's aim is to fill in a lack of humanpower for a particular work (peanut threshing) for which there is no other alternative, whereas the use of nawetan aims to fill a structural lack of available family humanpower. The nawetans are therefore greatly affected both by restrictions on the use of the land and also by the possibility of mechanization. On the other hand, the firdus are more susceptible to the effects of drought than are the nawetan.

Variations in demographic density do not influence the firdus migrations so much as the nawetans, and it is difficult to show concise differences between the zones with the survey method used.

Even the firdus statistics given by the heads of village do not show an increase in the number of firdus going from the western Sine-Saloum region toward the less densely populated east. Yet everyone stated that this number continued to decrease, particularly with the drought of recent years. In the department of Fatick, where the firdus no longer go, people relate their disappearance to the 1972 drought.

Inmigration Zone of the Firdus

The firdus occur in the east, northeast, and south of the peanut basin, that is, the whole of the Sine-Saloum region except the department of Fatick, or, roughly, the department of Mbacke, the

MAP 6.2

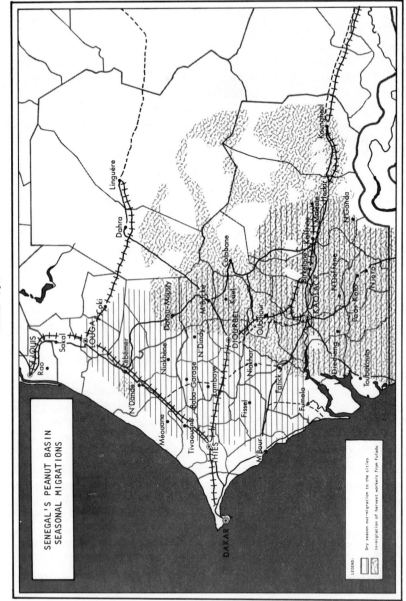

SENEGAL'S PEANUT BASIN
SEASONAL MIGRATIONS

LEGEND:

Dry season out-migration to the cities

Immigration of harvest workers from Fuladu

DAKAR

ST. LOUIS
Rao
Sakal
LOUGA
Kébémer
N'Diambe
Méouane
Tivaouane
THIÈS
M'Bour
Bobo-Garage
Sambaye
Niankène
N'Dandé
Sokh
Dahra
Linguére
Darou-Mousty
M'Backé
Fissel
Nickhar
Kael
DIOURBEL
Ouadiour
Fatick
Fimela
Colobane
Diakhao
N'Dinar
Birkelane
Malème-
Hadar
KAOLACK
N'Doffene
Guinguinéo
Diakhao
Toubakouta
Diedieng
Paos-Oto
NIORO
N'Ganda
Kounghéul

146

south of the arrondissement of Darou Mousti, and the whole of the pioneer zone in the south of the department of Linguère. Notice also on the map a little spot of firdus immigration in the west to the south of Kebemer, around the village of Ndande. Except for this spot, one can see that the firdus immigration zone corresponds more or less to the nawetan immigration zone. [6]

The Western Zone of the Peanut Basin

Sine, the regions of Thiès and Louga, and the department of Bambey use practically no firdus for threshing peanuts. Available humanpower is able to thresh the small quantity produced.

Seasonal Rainy Season Emigration

The southern and eastern part of the peanut basin is a zone of inward seasonal migrants, and, with the exception of some Fulbe from Guinea who have slipped into the south of the Sine-Saloum and who tend to have made this a migration zone exclusive to themselves, the usual seasonal migrants found in other regions of Senegal and even in Mali and Upper Volta—Sarakhole from Upper Senegal, Bambara from Mali and Upper Volta—are almost finished. They are still found in southern Sine-Saloum, but their migration no longer seems necessary for growing peanuts in this region.

Seasonal inmigration in the peanut basin tends to be developing essentially into an internal migration between different zones of the basin. We have discussed the seasonal migrant receiving zone. Its delineation and division into subzones seems easier and clearer as a result of the replies to our survey. Transferring the replies onto a map immediately shows several regions (see Map 6.3).

Southern Sine-Saloum

This area has been previously defined. It also corresponds to a subzone of intervillage migrations. These are young people who leave their villages to go and spend the rainy season in not-too-distant villages. There are not many of them, and virtually none toward the east (Nganda, S. Koundheul).

Gossas-Kahone-Birkelane Zone

This zone includes the department of Gossas except the northern part of the arrondissement of Colobane, the part of the arron-

MAP 6.3

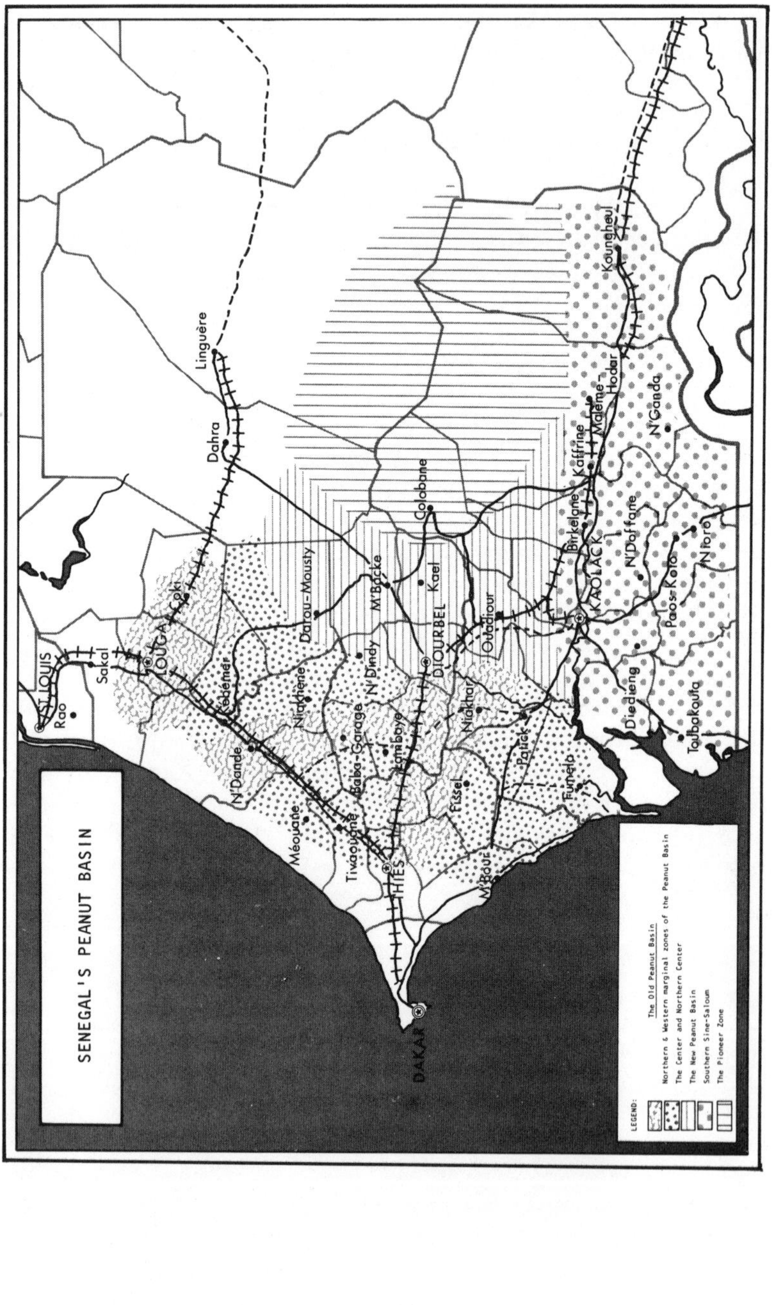

SENEGAL'S PEANUT BASIN

Rao
St. LOUIS
Sakal
Linguère
Dahra
Golobne
Koungheul
Hobar
NGaida
Malème
Kaffrine
Birkelane
KAOLACK
NDoffane
Paos Koto
Nioro
Toubakouta
Diagane
Ndiobène
LOUGA
Yeoumbeul
Darou-Mousty
M'Backe
Koel
DIOURBEL
Ndiokhal
Ouadiour
Niakhene
Babo-Garage
N'Dandy
Djilor
Fissel
Fimela
Popkine
N'Diande
Méoulane
Tiwaoune
THIES
M'Baous

DAKAR

148

dissement of Birkelane north of the Kaolack-Kaffrine road, the northern part of Kaffrine and the arrondissement of Gandiaye. This is a zone that has seasonal inmigrants and also has young bachelors leaving as nawetans in the rainy season for the east, to the pioneer zone that spreads well beyond the limits of the Sine-Saloum toward the west and to the northern part of the department of Tambacounda in Senegal Oriental. For most of the villages, these outmigrations seem to be a relatively recent phenomenon,[7] but they will probably increase.

Center of the Peanut Basin

This encompasses the region of Diourbel, the arrondissements of Medina Dakhar and Niakhene (department of Tivouane), south of the arrondissement of Ndande (department of Kebemer), the arrondissements of Diakhao Niakhar and Tattaguine (department of Fatick in the Sine-Saloum), and the arrondissements of Noto and Fissel in the region of Thiès. These administrative districts include the Wolof who live in Mouride country and the Serer from Bawol and Sine. So far as the Wolof are concerned, migration applies essentially to young bachelors, whereas for the Serer it has been reported that young married men and even young couples leave together.[8] The places of inmigration are Cassone Touba Boulal, Patakour, Velingara, east of Ndioum Guente, Ribo, Guentepate, Sadio, and Payar in the northeast of the department of Tambacounda. All these villages are located in what we have called the pioneer zone, and Wolof and Serer converge there. However, the Serer of Niakhar, Diakhao, and Fissel also mention the region of the new lands to the south of Koumpetoum, which confirms what we have heard elsewhere. These three arrondissements are the principal recruiting places for the New Lands Resettlement Scheme of Senegal Oriental. A study on the colonization villages of the new lands shows clearly that a sizable seasonal migration flow of Serer toward this zone has been created as a result of this project.[9]

The Zone Around Louga

This zone is quite separate from the other rainy season inmigration zones and encompasses the three arrondissements of Sakal, Mbediene, and Coki. The fact that this zone is apart from the other nawetan regions does not, however, mean that it has different migration modalities. The same social group is involved (young bachelors) as are the same destinations—the east and northeast of the peanut basin.

The Zones without Rainy Season Outmigration

In the western part of the peanut basin, there are zones in which the nawetanat is unknown or practically unknown, according to statements made by the heads of villages. South of the Serer country, the arrondissements of Nguekokh, Thiadiaye, and Fimela used to use nawetans in the past and have now almost completely abandoned them. Between Mekhé and Thiès there is a zone that seems not to use the nawetans.

DRY SEASON MIGRATION TOWARD THE URBAN CENTERS: THE NORAN

The replies to the questionnaire show that almost everywhere dry season outmigration is the peasants' solution to their living conditions in a rural area. The few villages (11) that stated that they did not have residents leaving temporarily for the towns in the dry season are scattered sparsely on the map. We cannot map in the peanut basin the zones with and the zones without dry season migration toward the towns. The only differentiation is in the number of noran and the categories of people concerned.

Quite clearly, the replies show that the noran increase the nearer the area is to Dakar, which is, as expected, the city that attracts the most noran. However, the towns of the peanut basin are not ignored by the noran. If they do not go to the big city of Dakar, the peasants will go to the nearest town. Those from the region of Thiès go to Thiès, Tivouane, Mbour, or Payar. Those from Bawol go to Diourbel, Mbacke, Touba, or Kaolack, and those from Saloum and the departments of Kaffrine and Gossas go to Kaolack, Kaffrine, and Diourbel. Even Banjul is mentioned by the peasants from the arrondissements of Toubacouta and Wack Ngouna. Those from Sine mention Kaolack and Mbour. We see that second to Dakar come all the regional capitals. The secondary department centers are mentioned, but almost always in the villages near them. Should we deduce from this that only the regional capitals are used as stages in the rural exodus?

The majority of the heads of villages stated that the number of noran had increased during the last five years, but a number of them scattered over the whole peanut basin said that the contrary is true.

However, the villages from which people migrate to towns are unanimous in saying that the norans who leave outnumber those who leave as nawetans. Therefore, the urban centers have a stronger attraction for the peasants of the peanut basin than do the eastern pioneer zones. The previously mentioned criteria do not enable clear distinction of a noran in the different zones, whereas the analysis of the family status of those concerned in these migrations shows up this distinction.

Serer Country

The Serer country is not homogeneous and has distinct different behavior all over. The Serer is the predominant group in the departments of Fatick and Mbour and is mixed with the Wolof in the departments of Thiès, Bambey, Diourbel, and Gossas. In addition to single and married young people, young Serer girls also go to the towns in the dry season.

The Center and North of the Peanut Basin

This includes the departments of Louga, Kebemer, Tivouane, Bambey, Diourbel, and Mbacke, which are inhabited by Wolof. Here it is essentially the young single or newly married people who leave for the towns, but just about everywhere the chefs de carré take part in this seasonal movement toward town.

South and East of the Sine-Saloum

Apart from the area inhabited by the Niominka Serer around Foundiougne, seasonal migrations to town would seem to affect practically only the young people, sometimes married but usually single, and more rarely heads of households and ward chiefs.

Although we have no data on it, these statements confirm our observations in the villages of the Saloum and the Kaffrine area. Seasonal outmigration toward the towns is still fairly limited and is due to what seems to be the basic motivation of the young men to learn a trade in town (as tailor, watch-, radio-, and bicycle-repairer, apprentice driver, and so forth), which, in most cases, they return to their villages to practice.

THE MAJOR MIGRATORY ZONES OF THE PEANUT BASIN

The spatial distribution in the peanut basin of the various migration types enables us to plot the migrations there. From the map we notice quite distinct combinations of migration types, and it must be remembered that in reality the differences in migratory behavior are in fact far from being so well defined.

A first outline seems to have to combine the seasonal nawetan migrations and seasonal Fulbe firdu migrations, because the lines we have drawn for these are almost exactly superimposed in the east and southeastern parts of the peanut basin, dividing them into two large parts. We can differentiate several large zones as follows (see Map 6.3).

The New Peanut Basin

The southeastern part of the peanut basin has seasonal in-migrants: nawetans and firdus. This is the zone to the east of the line Foundiougne-Gossas-Diourbel-Darou Mousti-Sagatta. It includes the whole of the Sine-Saloum region except for the department of Fatick, the departments of Diourbel and Mbacke, and the southern half of the department of Linguère. We use the expression New Peanut Basin as opposed to the western part, which we will call by the commonly used expression Old Peanut Basin to bring out the obvious characteristic of this part. However, it is not quite homogeneous. Taking into consideration other elements, we can subdivide it into three parts.

The Pioneer Zone

This is the zone that we have already outlined by studying the seasonal nawetan outmigration. It spreads a long way into the north of the department of Tambacounda. ORSTOM studies show that Mouride colonization is still extremely active there. The Wolof and Serer peasants of the Old Peanut Basin are often under Mouride marabouts, and there continue to be many of these who occupy and cultivate the land. After squeezing its way through innumerable national forests in this part of the territory, what is called the Mouride pioneer front is today located in Payar to the north of the Panal national forest and south of the village of Bem-Bem before the valley of Mboume (at the extreme southwest of the department of Matam). [10]

This colonization of ferlo, like the New Lands, has brought to the village a strong migration movement of nawetans coming from the same regions as the santian (settlers) and Fulbe firdus coming from Senegal Oriental, Guinea Bissau, and Guinea Conakry.

This pioneer zone does not have an internal or external seasonal migration with other zones, and the dry season outmigration
to the towns only applies to a tiny proportion of the population. We
can therefore say that it is really a zone of incoming santian,
nawetans, and firdus.

Today, the number of nawetans has greatly diminished. Bambara, Sarakhole, and Voltaic nawetans come now only in limited
numbers, and they have, in large part, been replaced by the Fulbe
nawetans from Guinea who, as indicated previously, make up the
floating population that spends the rainy season in the villages and
the dry season in the towns, doubtless creating a new form of migration.[11]

The southern Sine-Saloum, therefore, is characterized by a
nawetan migration that is still large but decreasing and composed
mainly of Guinean immigrants and young people from the area, by
a firdu immigration coming from Senegal Oriental and the two
Guineas, which only lasts from the beginning of November to February, and by a dry season outmigration toward the towns, which
now only concerns the young men who are not yet emancipated and
who in principle return to the village at the end of the dry season.

Thus, compared with the pioneer zone, southern Sine-Saloum
is no longer a settlement zone, but it continues to attract inhabitants
of other rural regions. Before independence, it used to draw people
from as far away as Upper Volta, but now it does not attract from
such a distance. However, even if these migrations are diminishing,
so far as the firdu migrations are concerned, they are still indispensable to the peanut cultivation in this zone.

Lastly, people from this part are attracted more and more to
the towns, although for the time being this is not very significant.
Population density of this zone remains quite good compared with
other regions of the peanut basin, but statistics show a certain saturation. J. P. Dubois gives a density for this zone that varies between 15 and 20 inhabitants per square kilometer to the south of
Koungheul, between 30 and 50 inhabitants per square kilometer for
the rest, and between 50 and 75 inhabitants per square kilometer
for the arrondissements of Ndiadieng and Ndoffane south of Kaolack.[12]
J. Monnier also places the density in the arrondissements of Nganda
between 50 and 70 inhabitants per square kilometer.[13] According to
the map of population density in the peanut basin established by J. P.
Dubois, this density of from 50 to 75 inhabitants per square kilometer
is found in the departments of Diourbel, Mbacke, Tivouane, and
north of that of Fatick, which are usually considered to be overpopulated.[14]

THE CENTRAL AND NORTH-CENTRAL
PEANUT BASIN

A third zone can be outlined in what we have called the New Peanut Basin. This is all of the area located to the west of the pioneer zone, west of the line Malem Hoddar-Mbar-Colobane-Sagatta (Djoloff), including the arrondissement of Birkelane north of the Kaolack-Koungheul road, the department of Gossas except northern Colobane, the department of Mbacke, part of that of Diourbel, and the south of the arrondissement of Darou Mousti. Between the two world wars this was the area that was colonized and under peanut cultivation. P. Pélissier placed the eastern limit of the peanut cultivation in 1920 along the line Kaolack-Diourbel-Sagatta (department of Kebemer).[15] From 1934 onward, the colonial administration organized the colonization of land east of Gossas and north of Kaffrine in what was called the "New Lands" for the first time.

J. P. Dubois, who has studied this zone north of Kaffrine, pointed out that the population seems to have been completely stabilized at the beginning of the 1960s.[16] The northern part of this zone, that is, the land around Mbacke and Touba, was stabilized earlier from the point of view of settlement.[17]

The answers given by the heads of village enable us to give the characteristics of this zone. It has both incoming and departing seasonal migrants. In the rainy season, it has incoming young Wolof from Kayor and Bawol and a lesser number of young Serer from Bawol, Dieghem, and Sine, each group settling into villages occupied by people from their own ethnic group.[18] Some Fulbe from Guinea are also found, but, as Dubois says, "Now the nawetans are essentially Senegalese originating from the old western regions." Use of firdu humanpower is still necessary here for threshing the peanuts, and these continue to come, if in diminishing numbers, as shown by the replies to the questionnaire.

However, there is a growing number of young people moving toward the pioneer zone and Senegal Oriental during the rainy season. This area does not escape its young people being attracted by the towns. So what characterizes this region of the peanut basin is the fact that all seasonal migrations occur simultaneously. But these migrations are not of the same strength: seasonal migrations toward the towns or villages are on the increase whereas seasonal nawetan and firdu migrations from other villages and rural zones are on the decrease.

THE OLD PEANUT BASIN

On the map, some zones are marked as being only seasonal outmigration zones toward the towns and toward the fields. There is a very clear zone around the town of Louga, made up of the arrondissements of Mbediene and Coki, and there is an area that stretches along both sides of the Dakar-Diourbel railway line with a circle around Thiès, including the arrondissements of Noto, Thienabal, and north to that of Fissel, the department of Bambey, the arrondissements of Medina-Ndakhar, and the southern part of that of Ndande, north of the arrondissements of Niakhar and Diakhao.

If we have faith in the replies from the heads of villages, there are now only two kinds of seasonal migrations: young people leaving for the new peanut lands to the east in the rainy season, which includes particularly young bachelors but also young married men and sometimes even young couples;[19] the massive exodus of young bachelors, married men, and also young girls (in the case of the Serer) in the dry season toward the towns seeking temporary work. This exodus continues to increase and has for a long time been necessary for this area, particularly for the Serer country, which has a population density of more than 100 inhabitants per square kilometer in some zones, notably around Niakhar and Diakhao. These zones no longer attract nawetans nor many firdus.

In their survey, made in 1975 in the villages of Got (department of Thiès), Ndiamsil Sessene (department of Bambey), and Layabe (department of Diourbel arrondissement of Ndingy), Ramond and Fall showed that at Got there were 13 nawetans out of a population of 264, at Ndiamsil one out of 305, and at Layabe two out of 380. They deduced from this that "comparatively speaking, the number of nawetans for this zone is low and has little bearing on the annual crop."[20]

In fact, the local economy is too weak to sustain their needs. They therefore have to go elsewhere to augment their incomes. A. Lericollais wrote, as far back as 1966, on the subject of emigration in the village of Sob (arrondissement of Niakhar): "The Serer from the Sine makes only a small contribution to the seasonal work force (in the pioneer zone) . . ., the (migratory) flow towards the towns is expanding."[21] This evolution heralded the present migratory situation in the western part of the peanut basin.

WESTERN AND NORTHERN BORDER ZONES OF THE PEANUT BASIN

There is a third large part of the peanut basin, from the migratory viewpoint, and it is made up of three zones. One constitutes the department of Mbour and the south of the department of Fatick. This covers a large part of Serer country. Another, to the north of Thiès, is composed of the arrondissements of Pambal, Méouane (department of Tivouane), and Thiénaba (department of Thiès) and west of the arrondissements of Baba Garage, Lambaye, and Ngoye (department of Bambey). The third zone is composed of the north of the arrondissement of Ndande (arrondissement of Sagatta and the north of that of Darou Mousti, department of Kebemer).

These three zones were among the first to cultivate peanuts, and they now seem to have just one type of seasonal migration, the exodus toward the towns, essentially to Dakar, in the dry season. Everywhere the heads of villages stated that a great mass of people left as norans, young single and married men, sometimes household heads, and young girls (in the case of the Serer). The nawetanat no longer figures as an alternative to overpopulation for these people.

Of course, the nearness of towns like Dakar and, to a lesser degree, Thiès, plays a big part in this. But there is also the important factor of being so far away, and permanent settling into an agricultural life in the eastern rural zones no longer attracts them. There is also the potential opportunity in a city of a high income for the urban migrant if he is able to find employment for some weeks or months in town. Also, in this part of the peanut basin, one can rightly say that each peasant has a more or less close relative settled in town.

CONCLUSION

We should, of course, point out some reservations on the survey method used, particularly on the filtering of facts that we did to eliminate discrepancies. A good knowledge of the survey area is necessary for this work.

On the other hand, using quantitative data of the various migrations would not have shown any of the fine variations explored here. But the spatial interpretation of the data is only worthwhile if the migratory combinations observed can be statistically reduced, otherwise it is of no practical use (for planning, development, and so forth).

With these reservations, the spatial representations of the migratory phenomena in the peanut basin lead us to differentiate three large areas in which the seasonal migrations interrelate differently.

One is made up of the eastern and southern parts, where the seasonal nawetan and firdu influxes are large and are still necessary to peanut cultivation because neither the demographic density

nor agricultural mechanization are at a high enough level to be able
to do without them. Only in the eastern part has this density become
great enough for total control over use of the land, and this has led
to a seasonal outmigration, both rural (within the same area region)
and toward the towns. This explains the subdivision into three zones.
Taken as a whole, this area nevertheless has an evident unity.

Another area is one that is not homogeneous but that basically
spreads along the Thiès-Diourbel line and that still has a seasonal
outmigration toward the east of the peanut basin. The predominant
movement is dry season outmigration toward urban areas. Overpopulation takes too much out of the land and has resulted in there
not being enough produced from the land to fulfill the needs of the
people. This is particularly so since the economy is based on peanuts, which is why it is called the Old Peanut Basin.

The final area is another western area, which is now a border
zone in relation to the rest of the peanut basin. For the people of
this zone, there is now only one way to escape the failing peanut
economy; that is the rural exodus. And the first stage toward this
is, of course, temporary departure in the dry season.

Even if this delineation seems arbitrary, from the study of
seasonal migrations two observations have been verified.

The first is a shift of the peanut cultivation toward the east
and the resulting shift of migration patterns. However, on examin-
ing the map, we see that this movement is not uninterrupted. At a
certain point, the New Lands of the east seem to be too far away.
There the nawetan disappear progressively where the noran gradually increase until they are the only seasonal migration. Contrary to
the national policy of developing the territory in order to alleviate
the overpopulated departments of the peanut basin by favoring and
organizing migrations toward the underpopulated regions of the west
of Senegal Oriental and Upper Casamance, it is seen that more and
more migrations toward these rural regions are yielding to an urban
migration.[22]

The second is that the massive inward migration of Guineans
to the east and south of the basin has increased the rural population
everywhere. This enormously reduces the potential for the Serer
and Wolof from the departments of the Old Peanut Basin to settle in
a territory that is still underpopulated. In view of the situation in
their own country, the Guinean migrants are a much more flexible
and "attractive" source of humanpower for the large- and medium-
sized agricultural plantations that still need extra workers for the
peanut crop. Today these Guineans have an effective network set up
because of the families that are already settled in the existing villages.

And so it seems that the limit has been reached in the system of peanut economy that grew by moving toward the east and south, wearing out the land and bringing with it people from impoverished and overpopulated areas. We have seen that the pioneer edges of the east occupied at the present time are less and less propitious for growing peanuts. We should, therefore, expect a growing reorientation of the migratory flow toward the towns.

Are there any technical or economic solutions to enable present production areas to develop and support the denser populations? At the present time, the reply is "no," because the agricultural techniques proposed to the peasants (cultivation equipment, traction animals, fertilizers, and so on) and improved agricultural productions would require larger investments and larger areas for cultivation. It may or may not, therefore, be desirable to use these methods—for they will clearly increase the rural exodus.

NOTES

1. J. P. Dubois, "Les sérères et la question des terres neuves au Sénégal," Cahiers de ORSTOM 12 (1975): 81-120. See the many fieldwork reports of the students of the National School of Applied Economics, ENEA, Dakar.

2. This squared map was done by the National Geographic Institute from aerial surveys dating from the 1950s, but the squares from which we worked were added on by land surveys done in 1970.

3. See S. Berniard, Le Sénégal en chiffres, 1978 ed. (Dakar: Société africaine d'édition, 1979).

4. See G. Rocheteau, "Pionniers Mourides au Sénégal: Colonisation des terres neuves et transformations d'une économie paysanne," Cahiers de l'ORSTOM 12 (1975): 19-53; G. Rocheteau, "Société Wolof et mobilité," Cahiers de l'ORSTOM 12 (1975): 3-18; J. P. Dubois, "L'Emigration des sérères vers la zone arachidière orientale: Contribution à l'étude de la colonisation agricole des terres neuves au Sénégal" (Dakar: ORSTOM, May 1971); and Dubois, "Les sérères et la question des terres neuves."

5. J. Monnier, in "Le travail dans l'exploitation agricole sénégalaise," unpublished paper, CNRA, Bambey, 1974, divides the south Sine-Saloum, as we do, in three parts: an eastern part, a western part, and a central part (Nganda and south of Birkelane), which would have had a much greater demographic density than the other two parts. This would be the reason for these differences.

This hypothesis seems to be confirmed by the as yet unpublished demographic surveys we conducted in 13 villages of the rural community of Sali (south of Koungheul) and in two villages of the rural community of Kayemor, as well as by the survey by Amadou Hadj, "Les inoculations agricoles et les problèmes démographiques dans le sud Saloum: Etude de cas dans la communauté rurale de Keur Saloum Diane" (Dakar: IDEP, February 1977).

6. During this 1978-79 season, we saw firdus in the departments of Thiès and Bambey.

7. Some put this as being since the 1972-73 drought, which was the worst year for the peasants of the peanut basin.

8. See J. Cattin and J. Faye, "Projet Terres Neuves II: Rapport sur le suivi agro-socio-économique de la campagne 1976-77," mimeographed, ISPA-CNPA, Bambey, May 1978. Out of 268 nawetans, 19 were listed as having come with their wives, and, out of 267 nawetans, 61 were married men.

9. Ibid. In two colonization villages surveyed, Serer nawetans constituted 36 percent and 46 percent of the active population. G. Rocheteau's study, "Société wolof et mobilité," pp. 8-9, seems to indirectly confirm this division between the seasonal emigration zone around Louga and that of Bawol. Maps show the different migratory steps of the migrants established in the villages of Darou Ndiaye (Colobane) and Khelkam Diagna.

10. Can we still talk about a Mouride pioneer front? We no longer notice a regular advance toward the east as described by Paul Pélissier in Les Paysans du Senegal (St. Yrieux: Fabrèque, 1966), but there is a scattered and extremely slow movement. Toward the east in the department of Linguère and toward the southeast (the northern part of the department of Tambacounda), the Mouride colonists encounter strong stumbling blocks: very low and erratic rainfall in the department of Linguère, which does not meet the water needs of the peanut crop, and, almost everywhere, the water table is practically out of reach by traditional well-digging methods, so that deep wells must be bored. The many national forests hamper movement and accentuate the problems because between them there are no longer vast expanses that can be cleared for cultivation as in the 1950s. There is very strong pressure to free national parks as a result. According to government officials in the department of Tambacounda, Mouride marabouts are requesting about 500,000 hectares of land be cleared for cultivation. Even if this advance continues, it is likely to come across another block. In the northwest of the department of Tambacounda, there is a similar colonization movement from the followers of the marabout from Medina Gounass, which is progressing toward the north beyond the line Malem-Niani-Sinthiou Maleme.

11. The principal reason for this is the situation in Guinea and the relationship between that country and Senegal. The closing of the frontier has prevented people from returning regularly to Guinea.

12. Dubois, "Les Sérères et la question des terres neuves," Figure 2.

13. J. Monnier, C. Ramond, and R. Cadot, "Etude des systèmes techniques de production pour le Sine-Saloum et est (systéme 8-12 ha)," unpublished paper, IEMVT and CNRA, Bambey, June 1974).

14. IDEM map drawn according to statistics from the list of villages, 1972.

15. Pélissier, Les paysans.

16. Dubois, "Les Sérères et la question des terres neuves," and "L'Emigration des Sérères."

17. Touba was established by Cheikh Amadou Bamba at the end of the nineteenth century.

18. Dubois, "Les Sérères et la question des terres neuves," gives for 1968 an average of from 1,000 to 2,000 Serer nawetans for an autochthonous Serer population of about 6,000 people. This number is very high because the author's survey zone is in what we have called the pioneer zone, around Dioum Guente.

19. In 1977 and 1976, respectively, the heads of the village of Got (department of Thiès) and Ndiemane (department of Bambey) told us that because there was not enough land to cultivate, most of the young married men were forced to leave, and some took their wives. The head of the village of Ndiamane gave the additional information that it was the younger brothers who had to leave because the older brothers had priority to the land. This concerned Serer villages.

20. See C. Ramond, M. Fall, and T. M. Diop, "Moyen terme Sahel: Main d'oeuvre et moyens de production en terre, matérial et chaptel de traction des terroirs de Got-Ndiamsil Sessene-Layabe," mimeographed, CNRA, Bambey, March 1976.

21. A. Léricollais, "SOB, étude géographique d'un terroir sérère (Sénégal)," Atlas des structures agraires au sud du Sahara 7 (1972).

22. Without doubt, the colonization of the New Lands of Senegal Oriental, begun in 1972, has enjoyed, despite all its inadequacies, a lot of success so far as the Serer peasants from the Sine are concerned. But this is just a drop in the ocean and will in no way be able to balance the overpopulated departments of the peanut basin. Personally, we believe that the present people in Senegal Oriental and Upper Casamance have a claim on almost all the cultivable land.

7

REGIONAL MIGRATIONS IN SOUTHEASTERN SENEGAL, INTERNAL AND INTERNATIONAL

Moussa Soumah

Studies of migratory movements in West Africa have multiplied rapidly in recent years, especially concerning those regions
most disturbed by the unbalancing effects of colonial development.[1]
In Senegal such migrations affect particularly the so-called "peripheral" administrative regions, including the Upper Casamance
and southern Senegal Oriental, areas that are the subject of this
chapter. There, in the southeast part of the country, two characteristic migratory patterns have been identified: seasonal labor
migrations originating from within the region itself and directed
toward other regions in Senegal and international migrations, which
involve crossing two major borders in both directions. One border
extends 500 kilometers east-west, separating Senegal from two
neighbors, Guinea Conakry and Guinea Bissau. The other border,
serving as the line of demarcation between the Gambian enclave
and the Upper Casamance, extends from the Pata Forest to the
Kantora Forest, northwest of the confluence of the Gambian and
Koulountou rivers.

Both migratory patterns are well-known in Senegal. Therefore, this study investigates the impact these migrations might
have on the habitation patterns and land use in the region.

Our research, which was of necessity limited, was conducted
during two separate weeks spent in the field, the first time from
December 23-30, 1977, and the second time from March 24-31,
1978. It primarily involved Upper Casamance, with particular
attention paid to the department of Kolda. Organized on the basis
of very simple questionnaires,[2] direct investigations involved 30
village centers in Kolda's "cotton belt," located on two major axes
that meet in the center of the town of Kolda: the Kolda-Medina
Yorofoula axis, which runs northward into Bansang, in the Gambia;

the Kolda-Dabo-Velingara axis, which winds northeast to the old federal road from Tambacounda to Koundara; and direct investigations also involved the city of Kolda and its immediate surroundings: Faraba, Saré Kémo, and Gada Para, among other communities within the new extensions of the city. These new communities seem to be able to accommodate recently settled immigrants. Kolda itself was chosen because its location on the Tambacounda-Ziguinchor axis, so vital to the southeast, renders the city and its environs a principal economic center for Upper Casamance. This capital of the Fouladou has experienced even greater economic vigor since the opening in 1974 of the renowned "Southern Route," with its 200 kilometers of paved road.

We worked with a team of hal pulaaren (pular speakers), originally from Futa Jallon as were the majority of people surveyed. (Hal pularen comprises two major ethnic groups who share the pular language, Fulbe and Tukulor. Other terms for Fulbe include Pël, Peulh from the Wolof, and Fula, from the Mandinka.) This linguistic ability enabled productive exchanges to take place between team members and farmers. Although there were cases of reticence (in Missira Mamabou, district of Dabo), there were also instances when the ease of communication provoked revealing debates, such as in Dioulaye, district of Dioulacolon.[3]

This research project received considerable support from the staff of the Company for the Development of Textile Fibers (SODIFITEX), active in the sectors of Dabo and Medina Yorofoula. They not only graciously furnished statistical information, but often provided contacts without which interviews with seasonal workers would not have been possible. In addition, most village chiefs willingly shared their own fiscal censuses that, despite some gaps, made possible a reasonable estimation of the number of seasonal migrants on the tax rolls and of the number of former migrants, seasonal or nonseasonal, who had decided to settle, and the duration of their stay.

Bibliographical material must complement those direct sources, which are both limited and difficult to utilize quickly. There is very little material concerning Upper Casamance. There are more reports by experts commissioned by development organizations or ministries than there is university-based research. Numerous small monographs (diaries of trainees from large national schools) offer some diversification.

THE GEOGRAPHICAL FRAMEWORK

The southeast region encompasses the eastern part of Casamance plus slightly more than one-third of Senegal Oriental

(Eastern Senegal), and it is part of that vast portion of the country classified as "peripheral" in relation to Senegal Occidental (Western Senegal). It covers Lower Casamance and slightly more than one-third of Senegal Oriental, or about 50,942 square kilometers. It is a geographic region whose mountains relieve the characteristically flat landscape of Senegal. The northern foothills of the Mali Range (1,538 kilometers at Mt. Lour) extend into southern Senegal Oriental, forming a line of low hills (average height of 800 meters) very similar to those dominating the Koureñiaki and lower Tiokoye river basins, west of the Gambia River. Whereas the average elevation further north is 150 meters,[4] the ring of buttes at Kédougou reaches heights of from 300 to 400 meters. On the other hand, Upper Casamance, like the rest of Senegal, is relatively flat.

The climate of the southeastern region is as unusual as its topography. The annual rainfall of this region corresponds to that of the "Sudano-Guinean": an average of from 1,000 to 2,000 millimeters annually (see Map 7.1), spread out rather evenly over the five months of the rainy season (June-October). This rainfall average could be considered to be a "safety factor" in that the regions of the Fuladu[5] and Upper Casamance have enough water to sustain rainfed crops even in periods of severe drought. Naturally, annual variations in rainfall or fluctuations in the distribution of rain during the five rainy months can negatively affect the growth of these crops (cotton, for example, may take up to 100 days).

However, this unreliability is mitigated by the relatively early onset of the rainy season at the end of May and the long duration of the season into October when, at times, there is appreciable rain. This condition has been documented by two stations in the cotton bowl, which measured monthly rainfall during the years 1931-60, in millimeters, based on the 1963 meteorological standards of the Agency for the Security of Air Navigation (ASECNA).

	Vélingara	Tambacounda
May	28.1	19.8
June	137.2	130.9
July	223.6	288.8
August	327.5	288.8
September	275.8	231.2
October	98.1	70.0
November	7.2	2.3

In fact, the "somewhat mountainous tendencies" noted in the extreme southeastern part of this region[6] do not substantially affect the major climatic features of that region. Among these, rainfall

MAP 7.1

Rainfall in Senegal: Annual Averages and Average Number of Days, 1931–60

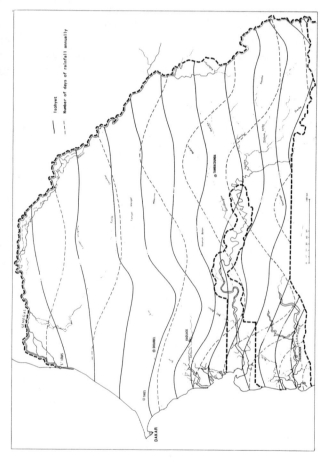

Source: Senegal, Ministry of Planning and Cooperation, Atlas pour l'aménagement du territoire (Dakar: Nouvelles éditions africaines, 1977).

levels receive the most attention, in a country severely tested by drought in these last few years.

In that same respect, Senegal is also distinguished by its soil resources, marked by predominantly tropical ferrous soils. These are regional soils that may normally develop in a Sudanic climate (700-1,200 millimeters of rain). In some cases, because their upper surfaces are leached, the soils are given the name sols beiges (beige soils). They are known to be poor in organic matter and to have limited fertility.

Through Upper Casamance, with the exception of the Anabé basin where hydromorphic soils are found, ferrous, leached tropical soils with concretions predominate. They may develop into soil with a very hard topsoil. They extend eastward and to the northeast (Tambacounda) into rather large expanses of consistently gravelly soils resting on ferruginous, hardened surfaces. The southeastern extremity, which consists mainly of the department of Kédougou, reveals a mixture of several soil types, in which the ferruginous, tropical soils that are leached in spots and have concretions or are of a hardpan nature predominate.

In short, the physical features of the southeast region reveal interesting possibilities within the context of the mainly agricultural economy. However, the limited fertility of the soils and the advancing "bowlisation" may cause some reservation—if only to question seriously the idea that there is an abundance of vacant land—the fact remains that, despite its unpredictability, the high rainfall is a major advantage in the development of this region, especially since macroscopic agricultural development alternatives clearly favor rainfed agriculture.

LAND USE AND POPULATION DISTRIBUTION

Southeast Senegal is sparsely populated and settled. The four departments included in this region occupy 50,932 square kilometers, slightly more than 25 percent of Senegal. According to the last national census, 420,896 people,[7] or approximately 8.27 percent of the total population, inhabit this vast area. The average density is eight inhabitants per square kilometer.

The Upper Casamance shows approximately 15 inhabitants per square kilometer. One area of relative density is located between Kolda and Vélingara, along the two major routes joining these large towns: Kolda-Fafakourou-Badion-Vélingara and Kolda-Daba-Dounkane-Vélingara (this branch is presently little used). Another population concentration exists in the southern part of the department of Kolda, along the tributaries of the Casamance River.

From Bantankountouyel to Salikeñie along the Guinea Bissau border runs a network of moderately large villages (300-700 inhabitants), which thins out perceptibly as one moves east toward Vélingara. Even further along toward Tambacounda, the villages become even more dispersed, a pattern consistent with the Upper Gambia.

The departments of Kédougou and Tambacounda have a population density of five inhabitants per square kilometer, the lowest in Senegal. Despite population increases over the years (between 1964 and 1976 the population of Upper Casamance rose from 96,800 to 225,289, a 7.1 percent growth rate, and the populations of the departments of Kédougou and Tambacounda rose from 118,700 to 195,607, a 6 percent growth rate), the region still suffers from an underpopulation that retards rapid development.

Certain factors, apart from mortality and emigration, account for the demographic depression of this region. For example, health and sanitary conditions are poor. The people suffer from such diseases as tripanosomiasis, onchocerciasis, leprosy, and the Guinea Worm, especially in localities with poor water supplies. In the department of Kédougou, all of these diseases are endemic.[8] Even insufficient seasonal rainfall exacerbates this problem for the populations.

Such "hygienic vulnerability" stems from a general deterioration of the region in relation to Western Senegal, which benefited much more from development by the French colonizers.[9] That development, which was based mainly on the groundnut economy, only affected those zones near the sea or those accessible by natural routes (such as the Senegal and Casamance river valleys), thus resulting in a disequilibrium detrimental to entire regions. The southeast, for example, definitely evolved into a disadvantaged back country and a source of humanpower for the groundnut basin.

Thus, the humanpower needs of the groundnut economy (harvesting, threshing, and so on) were easily satisfied by the seasonal movements of populations coming from the distant fringes of "useful Senegal," inside as well as outside the country's borders. This navetanat (a Wolof word for migrations during the rainy season) was even more active because groundnut cultivation in Senegal Oriental began rather late. Thus it is appropriate to emphasize the impact of this migratory movement on the working population of Upper Casamance, especially during the 1920s and 1930s.[10] Evidently, it is very difficult to make a viable census of these labor movements, as of the well-known migrations (and their effects) of the Firdou of Upper Casamance, in order to measure their impact on the depopulation of the area. It appears, nevertheless, that a significant portion settle permanently in the area where they go to work.

In the same line of thought, it may be surmised that the southeastern region, which has difficulty retaining its own working population, has only been able to serve as a passage zone to the groundnut basin for most of those migrants coming from Guinea Conakry and Mali. [11]

In fact, the development efforts in the area since independence, designed to reintegrate it with the rest of the country, and the sociopolitical and economic turmoil during the same period in the two neighboring Guinea republics have combined to see this area evolve from a transit zone to a receiving area for migrants.

The biggest interest such an evolution has is that it is likely to favorably influence the development prospects for the southeast. At any rate, in the end these results could probably help to cushion the shortage of the working age population, which is seriously handicapping the region. In any case, they will at least constitute significant aid to the attempt at organized repopulation, which does not seem to be obtaining the results expected by its promoters.

MIGRATORY MOVEMENTS

Internal Migrations

Internal migrations essentially consist of population movements from other regions toward the east and south of Senegal.

When organized, [12] these internal migrations have an important objective: a balanced redistribution of the population between the groundnut triangle and the eastern "enclaves." In that respect, it is not superfluous to emphasize the fact that the groundnut basin still remains the mainstay of the Senegalese economy. [13] The historical and political circumstances of its organization in the Senegalese economy are known well enough that they need not be reiterated here. The results of efforts to diversify during the 1960s (and particularly beginning with the Second Plan) still fall below what is needed to diminish the "domination" of the groundnut. We agree with the World Bank's theory of a noticeable decrease of the groundnut in the added value of the agricultural sector, from 56.9 percent to 42.5 percent (current prices) during the decade of 1971/80. [14]

However, concurrent with the continued attempts to diversify, it was necessary to make important investments in improving the conditions for groundnut production. It is incontestable that the modernization of agricultural techniques, the promotion of animal traction, the regular distribution of selected varieties of seed, and the utilization of chemical fertilizers have had a definitely positive effect on the yields, even if, in the last analysis, their growth remains at the mercy of the rainfall factor. It may therefore be surmised that the strategy for agricultural development, which has been in operation for more than a decade now, is ruled by the search for solutions to problems that incite the continuation and intensification of the groundnut operation.

The overpopulation of the groundnut bowl is one of the most preoccupying of these problems. In fact, this part of "useful Senegal" holds the highest records of rural density, reaching as high as, and even exceeding, 100 inhabitants per square kilometer; this is clearly above the saturation level judged to be supportable for rural Senegal.[15] But the relative abundance of cultivable lands lying fallow has historically provided the outlet for this problem, which became inseparable from widespread groundnut cultivation speculation. Thus, the "New Lands" settlement project, based on the historic Murid pioneer front, once again allowed the decongestion of the "old groundnut lands" of Sine. The beginnings of expansion of the groundnut bowl toward the Saloum interior go back to the period between the two world wars. The relatively modest operation for expansion was mostly an administrative answer, more or less effective, for the overpopulation problem in the Sine area.[16]

The recent "Project Koumpentoum-Maka" operation, which initially allowed the transfer of 300 families from the Sine, has a similar objective: opening up the old, used-up bowl through organized migration, moving some of the surplus population from the "groundnut triangle" and settling it in the "New Lands." Naturally, the expected result for the receiving area is growth of its active population, an influx of already "trained" workers who, at least, have a deep, well-formed experience of groundnut speculations. In addition, it seems that their installment in the receiving areas does not run up against any land tenure obstacles, and, for the moment, has incited no social rejection whatsoever.[17]

However, it is rather difficult to discern just how favorable the economic basis of the current operation (largely based on the groundnut) actually is to the regional complementarity between midwestern and eastern Senegal. In this regard, one might perhaps fear that the operation may be reduced to a supportive demographic role in the expansion of the groundnut basin into the lands of the Upper Gambia and the Fuladu.

In the end, the high cost of this project, with its double strategy of relieving the load and repopulating, risks becoming a decisive argument in favor of spontaneous migrations, internal and/or international.

We are particularly interested in the spontaneous international migrations, which most often borrow the form of such old

migration movements as that of the famous navetanat, but in an
apparently new politicoeconomic context.

International Migrations

Today, these migrations take place within a large expanse of
territory, which, for the most part, corresponds to the departure
zone for nawetans during the peak of the expanding groundnut economy in the 1930s-50s. The territory encompasses southeast and
eastern Senegal, northeastern Guinea Bissau, northwestern Guinea
Conakry, and part of western Mali. This area can be called the
Upper Gambia Faleme Migratory Basin (see Map. 7.2).

The portions of these four countries, with overlapping political boundaries formed in colonial days, constitute a regional geographical unity characterized by common physical and human characteristics.

In fact, only because of colonial influence was the Faleme
made a line of demarcation between the eastern and northern part
of Senegal Oriental (from Tambacounda to Bakel), for one part,
and the region of the Malian Upper Senegal (Kayes region), on the
other. The same was done with southern Senegal Oriental (around
Kédougou) and the Fuladu, on the one hand, and the northern part
of Futa Jallon, on the other. Furthermore, such big ethnic groups
as the Fulbe (from Pita to Kolda) and the Mandinkas clearly dominate this region[18] and so constitute another basic element of unity,
which runs counter to the artificial cleavage caused by national
boundary lines.

Another common characteristic of the territories comprising
this region is their marginal nature, as compared with the economic
centers on or near the coast from Conakry to Dakar, passing
through Fria, Boke, Bissau, and Banjul, and with terminals of an
old penetration route, such as Bamako on the Dakar-Niger line.

The most important consequence of this situation is the general state of deterioration observed in this region, despite more
and more promising possibilities, especially iron from the Faleme.
Organization of the cash economy made this region a giant "drainage basin" of products and people, to the benefit of the groundnut
basin. Because of this, at the time of political independence, the
region had a minimum of infrastructure, reduced to what little
communication there was in the Tambacounda-Bamako branch of
the Dakar-Niger railroad line and a road network strictly limited
to the axes of a seasonal evacuation for groundnut depots (Kayes,
Tambacounda, Vélingara, Kolda). Having only an embryonic urban
development, these routes served as simple relays for the big

MAP 7.2

The Upper Gambia/Faleme Migratory Basin

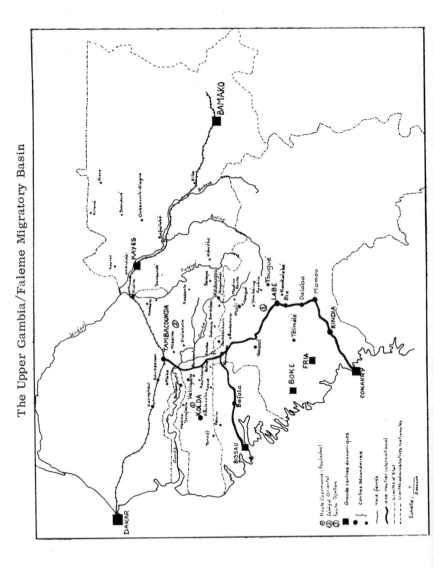

market centers (Kaolack, Thiès, and so on) toward which they assured the passage of seasonal laborers from nearby territories.

This region has always been a stage for great migratory movements, which have undeniably influenced the settlement of Senegal Oriental and the Fouladou region.[19]

But, it is the international migrations of the seasonal workers, which were activated and organized by colonial administration, that had considerable impact on the region. This is how the term nawetanat became the term used to designate those seasonal migrations, a name now adopted by several writers.[20]

In its old form, from the end of World War I until 1961 when Senegal officially suppressed it, the nawetanat was a migration movement systematically organized as an indispensable expansion of the groundnut economy. Quite naturally, the labor was solicited from populations in the marginal regions of the "Upper Gambia" area, which gradually opened up the cash economy. Although available statistics have to be used with reservations, it is clear that the largest groups of nawetanes were coming from Malian Upper Senegal (Kayes, Bafoulabe, Kita, Nioro) and from the Futa Jallon area of Guinea.

One would be correct to pinpoint the search for money as one of the basic motivations of those populations so very interested in the "trip to Senegal."

Furthermore, one of the measures frequently implemented by the colonial administration to stimulate migration was the offer of manufactured products, notably cloth. Manipulations of the price of the groundnut were also important; for nawetanat promoters, it was clear that the workers were coming to the peanut basin in search of cold cash, which had become necessary to satisfy their many needs, taxes first of all.

Moreover, depending upon the situation, the government did not hesitate to substitute outright labor requisitioning for incentives, as was done during World War II.

But, in reality, from the 1950s on, the "free nawetanat" would predominate, develop, and survive attempts at suppression during the independence period. Today, the nawetanat is one of the main currents of migration between southeast Senegal and neighboring countries, particularly Guinea Conakry.

Whether in its old form of incited or organized cash-crop migration or in its present form of spontaneous migration, the nawetanat can evolve into permanent settlement, either directly or following a relatively long intermediate phase of multiple-year migrations. Fluctuations in the West African political and economic situation can strongly influence the migrants' tendency to install themselves for a long time, if not permanently. Such a situation has been considerably reinforced among the Guinean immigrants in Senegal in the last two decades.

In fact, Draconian measures of surveillance of the northern Guinean border by the militia and army, which were especially reinforced from 1970-71 until the frontier reopened in 1978, never succeeded in seriously stopping the illegal immigration of Guineans into Senegal, through Senegal Oriental and Upper Casamance.

Futa Jallon is the main departure point, just as it was during the old trading days, before Senegal nationalized peanut marketing in 1960-61. The Guinean regions of Tougue, Labe, Telimele, and Mali supply the biggest contingents, to which are added small Diakhanke groups coming from Gaoual, Koumbia, and Touba (according to field investigations in the Kolda cotton belt, December 1977).

The imbalance resulting from the recent boom of mining enclaves in coastal Guinea has helped speed up the geographic mobility of the populations from the interior, especially from the Futa Jallon, toward the coast and the big economic centers of the nearby countries: Senegal, the Gambia, Mali, Ivory Coast, Sierra Leone, and Liberia. "The absence of short-term development prospects, the chronic shortage of every kind of product, galloping inflation and generalized smuggling were adequate to make the farmers decide to fall back on self-sufficiency or to migrate."[21]

The Guinean migrant takes the road to Senegal in search of real or imagined possibilities of a job in the country or in the city and whatever financial gains may be offered him. In the tradition of voyagers to Senegal, the Fouladou especially has the reputation of being a "holy land." From the answers we collected from about 50 seasonal workers in Medina Yorofula and Dabo (December 1977-March 1979), we learned the following. By coming to Senegal, they have high hopes of saving up a little store of money by cultivating groundnuts or cotton; 70 percent chose to come directly to Upper Casamance, 25 percent came only after making a fruitless tour for prospects around the Gambia and the groundnut bowl, and 5 percent gave indefinite answers. In reply to a question about how they use their earnings, 60 percent said they plan to return immediately (after selling their yield) in order to bring back home (manufactured) products and the remainder of their money, 15 percent hope to open a little business in Kolda or elsewhere while waiting for the next farming season, and 25 percent gave indefinite answers.

In summary, as during the period of the trade nawetanat, the people still continue to cross the northern foothills of the Futa Jallon in order to answer the call of the groundnut and cotton in Fuladu. In other words, they come in search of cold cash. In that respect, Upper Casamance has relatively adequate welcoming facilities for the job seekers.

THE ECONOMIC PERSPECTIVE

For lack of other basic activities (industrialization is essentially limited to two cotton-ginning plants), the development of Upper Casamance in the last 15 years has depended on the expansion of cash cropping through the modernization and intensification of groundnuts, on one hand, and the expansion of cotton, on the other.

From Kolda to Vélingara, the Fouladou has provided the groundnut with an area most advantageous for its expansion. Weather conditions on the whole are clearly more reliable than in the north or west, even during periods of great drought. The abundance of fallow land suits well the soil needs of the groundnuts. Thus, the groundnut is well-represented among the dry crops cultivated on plateau land.

At the socioeconomic level, the growth of the groundnut as the main cash crop found very favorable terrain in a region with an essentially food-crop economy.[22]

Despite these favorable conditions, groundnut expansion has fallen short of the production capacity of the Fouladou. The handicap of Upper Casamance's relative isolation has not only slowed down the pace but also limited its capacity for land transformation and use. The network of medium-sized villages engendered by the colonial trading economy is not to be found here, as it is along the railroad line or the main axes of the groundnut bowl. Even the old river ports planted along the Casamance-Tankanto-Escale, Diana Ba-Diana Malari are still modest groups of villages that are only very timidly opening up to urbanization. Therefore, Kolda and Vélingara remain the only true urban centers in all of Upper Casamance, probably more because of the functions they serve than their physical features. Thus, these two towns serve as poles to a scattering of towns of various sizes, which have served and still serve as a support of the geographical organization of the groundnut economy. Very often, the bigger villages regroup along the main evacuation routes. These are the "trade points," which are now village centers spread out among the farming villages. They are connected by a loose network of paths that are useful only seasonally. In short, until cotton was introduced in 1963, Upper Casamance had only one very limited program, which centered around slowly expanding groundnut speculation.

Beginning with the Second Plan (1965-69), which envisioned for Fuladu the "introduction or development of some new crops via local development projects with specialized staff," rainfed cotton together with the traditional cereals were to contribute to the expansion of commercial farming. Within a few years, it was thus possible to create a cotton basin, which covered the departments of

Kolda, Vélingara, and Tambacounda (in Senegal Oriental).[23] On
the whole, results have been satisfactory. Combined with the results obtained from other crops during the same period, including
the groundnut, these results can be taken as a start for the economic expansion of Upper Casamance, however limited it may be.
At any rate, while waiting for these agricultural programs to reach
their maximum effectiveness,[24] they have given Upper Casamance
a relative economic dynamism that has made it one of the main receiving areas for rural immigrants coming from the two republics
of Guinea.

THE SOCIAL PERSPECTIVE

The insignificance of the political boundaries for the populations belonging to the same ethnocultural group was quite apparent
in the answers we received (see Migration Questionnaire at the end
of this chapter). Crossing the border (rather dangerous in the past
few years, until its recent reopening) is part of the regular movements that individuals or groups may make, regardless of the state
of relations between countries, just as much for family reasons as
for motives stemming from a poor economic situation.
In addition, general working conditions for the seasonal workers are still affected by very well-established social relations
which have been in effect since the times of the trade nawetanat.
The nawetans are bound in the contractual status of a sourga (the
Wolof equivalent of nawetan, believed to be the institutional model
from which nawetan/host relations are based), in which they lend
their labor for from three to four days out of seven in exchange for
provision by the jatigi (Wolof word for host or patron) of food, tools,
and so on. In the district of Medina Yorofoula, the rate is 3.5
days; it is three days in the district of Dioulacolon. This variation
in rates for the sourga from one section to another (and probably
from one season to another) is the consequence of the free nature
of the nawetanat, no longer directly controlled by the governments.
Working conditions are determined by the parties concerned,
that is, the sourga and the djatigi. But beyond material interests,
the sourga is assured of feeling at home in the Fuladu, with his
relatives (in a broad sense), whether they are from Futa Jallon or
Ngabu. Furthermore, it is this very parentage, real or professed
for the occasion, which is sealed by a common heritage to the
larger group of hal pularen, the context for negotiations about
working conditions.[25] So the immigrant is welcomed by the entire
village, which is related to the djatigi. And, according to the responses of the newly arrived nawetans in Dioulaye and Dinguiraye

MAP 7.3

International Migration from Guinea to Senegal

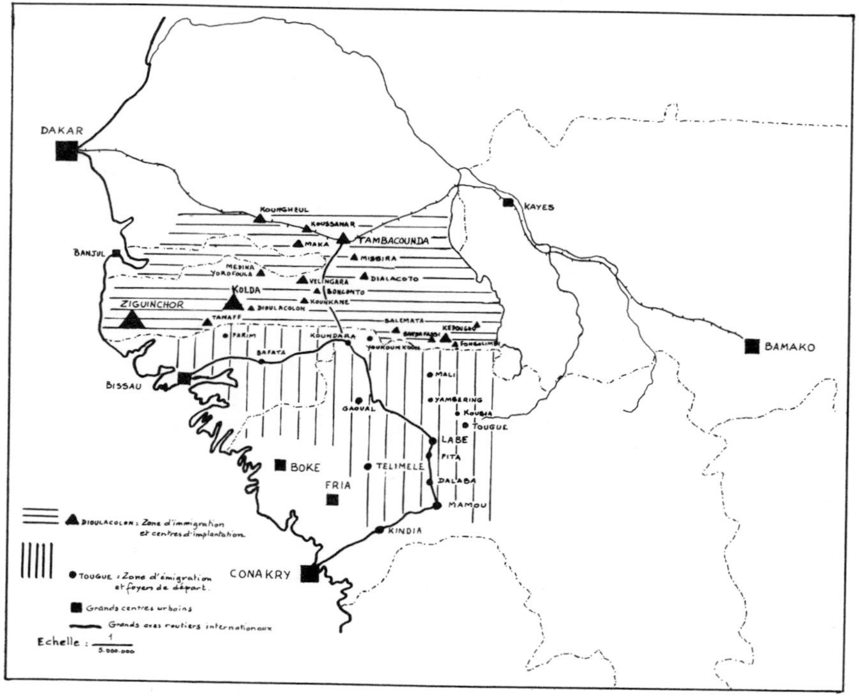

(Medina-Yorofula district), this welcome is even more reassuring when the djatigi, even if he may have been born in Senegal, has been able to keep in touch with that part of the family living on the other side of the border in Guinea. Obviously, when these nawetans decide in favor of a long or permanent stay, they deliberately refuse to declare themselves foreigners. This attitude is often a serious obstacle to attempts to make a statistical evaluation of the migrations. As the matter now stands, one cannot hope to depend on statistics provided by the country from which the immigrants depart. Thus only general estimates may be made. [26]

Immigrants who pass through Senegal Oriental (Tambacounda-Kedougou) and Upper Casamance (Vélingara-Kolda) have three means of transportation for making their move: trains, trucks or automobiles, or on foot.

The train is the mode for those coming from Malian Upper Senegal and Guinea. Guineans taking the train from Bamako follow the migratory axis and are only slightly interested in southeastern Senegal. They are headed for Dakar or the other big Senegalese stations.

Trucks or automobiles, relatively active as a type of transportation just before and after the countries attained independence, have seen many ups and downs in the past 15 years because of the instability of Senegalese-Guinean diplomatic and political relations and Guinea Bissau's liberation war. In fact, strict, constant surveillance of the border at the Guinean outlet of the international routes (Koundara, Samballo, Youkounkoun), as well as the authoritarian settlement project in Koundara, notably of the "rejects" from Conakry and other large towns (in the program for the control of rural exodus), have seriously hindered road connections between Senegal and Guinea Conakry. Recent revival of those connections[27] after nearly 10 years of suspension should allow recording of border crossings in both directions.

However, we are most interested in the last decade, during which Guineans crossing into Senegal on the southeast border have mainly traveled on foot. Such movements indicate that these migrants wish to escape any sort of control, from departure to arrival, until they are safely ensconced in a relative's home in the first Senegalese frontier town. To accomplish this feat, they take to paths outside of the guarded sectors, sometimes with the effective but costly help of experienced passers who go through a complicated network that is difficult to trace.

So, the old nawetanat trade route (Pita-Labe-Kifaya-Koundare-Medina Gonasse-Tambacounda), easily closed out by the army, the military, or the national guard, has been replaced by a secret route composed of detours and traversed by Air Baape,[28] often at night,

along with all of the dangers inherent in such an adventure. Once
the crossing is made, the migrant is almost impossible to catch;
in Kedougou or Kolda, a "Diallo" with Guinean nationality differs
very little from a "Diallo" with Senegalese nationality. Because of
this, any kind of registration of such travelers, which would permit a statistical evaluation of Guinean immigration into southeast
Senegal, is still a big problem, especially since any official control
of the nawetanat was stopped in 1963.

Under such conditions, we attempted to observe the effects of
the migratory trend in the settlement areas. We chose the northern part of the department of Kolda because its relatively low human
population affords great possibilities for settlement of migrants,
if only in the context of the cotton expansion program, and because
the migrants who chose long-term or permanent settlement have a
tendency to go beyond the immediate vicinity of the Guinean border.

From censuses taken in Medina Yorofoula (departmental
capital) and Dinguiraye (central village and collection and marketing point for cotton), a relatively large number of seasonal workers among the taxable workers, about 30-40 percent for the 1977-78
season, and a relatively large number of recently settled Guinean
migrants were observed.

For the village of Dinguiraye, for example, we polled the
populations of 40 neighborhoods made up of Fulbe from Futa Jallon
and Diakhankes, all of whom came from Guinea. They represented
approximately one quarter of the village's population and had settled recently. Only three neighborhood heads out of ten had been
in their locality more than ten years. In the table below, the first
six neighborhoods belong to the Fulbe group and the other four to
the Diakhanke. Most of the heads, in turn, have access to seasonal
workers hired for labor during the rainy season.

Neighborhoods	Residents	Seasonal Workers	Length of Stay of the Neighborhood Head in the Neighborhood (in years)
1	5	3	40
2	9	—	6
3	2	—	20
4	3	1	4
5	3	3	3
6	10	—	3
7	3	2	6
8	7	5	20
9	4	4	6
10	2	2	6

Similar, quickly executed investigations have allowed us to pinpoint 25 cases of recent settlement (June 1977) of Guinean immigrants with their families in Dioulayet, a district of Dioulacolon.

In Farabe, Sare Kemo, and Gada Para, which are towns located in the outskirts of Kolda, we registered 15 new homes that had been established a year before (1976-77).

It appears that the reinforcement of surveillance on the Guinean side of the border as of 1 970 has increased both seasonal and nonseasonal immigrants' tendency to settle down, so as not to be obliged to run the risk of return to Guinea (use of firearms by the militia). Political troubles during late 1970 made any individual who tries to cross over into Guinea from the bordering states, especially Senegal, suspect.

CONCLUSION

The recent rise of the two big cash crops have made Upper Casamance and, secondarily, Senegal Oriental immigration regions for the populations in the northern fringes of the neighboring countries, Guinea Conakry and Guinea Bissau.

At present, a statistical evaluation of this migratory current is out of the question; an official silence maintained on both sides of the border risks keeping such statistics secret for many more years to come. The fact is that there is a general flow of Guineans migrating into Senegal, a situation that has very visibly been on the rise during the past decade, although some people are trying to prove the contrary.

In its seasonal form, this movement seems to prolong the trade nawetanat (officially suppressed) as an outside supplier of the main labor force to satisfy the demand created by the expansion of cash crops in southeast Senegal. In the receiving areas, these international seasonal migrations are seen as a factor of economic equilibrium, which partially conditions the extent of land to be cultivated, the option of one or two crops (groundnut, cotton); seasonal workers can then mitigate the strains of the double agricultural calendar; and possibilities for increasing incomes; the presence of the seasonal workers creates an availability for certain workers who, with the agreement of the rest of the family group, free themselves to look for prime income. For those concerned, this is not just a hit-or-miss tour, but a move made to find exact information about the rainfall situation and prospects for harvests in the target areas or for monetary gain in the case of the urban centers.

MIGRATION QUESTIONNAIRE

Questionnaire for International Migrations

No.   Date   Interviewer   Village of:
                                          Neighborhood of:

First name, last name _____

Sex_____

Age_____

Family status_____

Relationship (to head of neighborhood)_____

Ethnic group_____

Caste_____

Activities: Main_____
             Secondary_____

Origin (village, town, country)_____

Date of departure from home town_____

Date of arrival in department_____

Where is he staying (did he stay) prior to settling in the village?
_____

Did he travel alone or with a group?_____

Means of travel and itinerary_____

Reasons for leaving home town? Main reason_____
                                Secondary reason_____

Previous activities: Main_____
                      Secondary_____

What does he think of life in the town he migrated to?_____

and his reception? his neighbors? his working conditions?

Does he plan to go back to his home town?_____

After what length of time?_____

In our opinion, this internal, methodical organization of labor labor migrations constitutes one of the factors of the survival of the Firdou movement.

In the final analysis, this immigration, which has the advantage of draining off people from the same ethnic group for the most part, is undeniably a partial solution to the problem of repopulating the "peripheral" regions, even if this is contrary to the organized current from the groundnut "triangle" toward the "New Lands."

Furthermore, in the medium and short run, major operations for development foreseen for this region (SOMIVAC, SODEFITEX) could contribute this immigrant humanpower, whose installation in a rural environment, in principle, doesn't require any special investment.

Finally, it would not be an exaggeration to think that the disenclavement of southeastern Senegal is getting off to a start with the help of attempts to intensify agricultural activity and with the planned improvement of the road network (the southern Ziguinchor-Kolda paved road, presently about 200 kilometers long, has recently reached Vélingara). The effect on interior and international movements would be strengthened if the southeast could pass from the stage of a promising region for raw or processed agricultural products to that of an agroindustrial region (cultivation and full processing of cotton, for example). Such urban centers as Tambacounda, Kolda, and Vélingara would then have enough resources to develop into economic centers capable of counterbalancing the influence of the economic centers in Senegal Occidental. The expansion of regional complements between the midwest and the south would most likely reinforce the tendency of migration from the overpopulated zones in the old groundnut basin toward the southeast.

NOTES

1. See, for example, Michel Aghassian et al., Les migrations africaines—reseaux et processus migratoires (Paris: Maspero, 1976), pp. 43-91. Gérard Remy et al., "Mobilité géographique et immobilisme social: 'un exemple voltaïque'," Revue Tiers Monde 18 (July-September 1977): 617-53.

2. Despite this precaution, it was often difficult and/or inadvisable to use these questionnaires directly. The spontaneous reticence of people being questioned was reinforced by a certain "political" suspiciousness, which is understandable, after all, on the eve of a national election campaign.

3. On December 29, 1977, we took part in a passionate debate (aroused by our team) between a former peasant who had been a seasonal migrant from 1963 through 1971 and had been settled in Dakar since 1972, where he was able to find employment in fishing, and a group of peasants, apparently among the most well-informed of the village. The very long discussion turned on the subtle nuances evoked by phrases such as "rootlessness" and "labor migration."

4. P. Michel, "Les bassins des fleuves Sénégal et Gambie: Etude géomorphologique, dissertation, Strasbourg, Doctorat d'Etat (not equal to a Ph.D.), 1969, pp. 8-11.

5. The phrase "Fuladu region" is used here in its climatic sense, as proposed by Paul Moral in his essay defining a schema of the climatic regions of Senegal: "Le climat du Sénégal," Revue de géographie de l'Afrique occidentale 3 (Dakar, 1966): 26-35. The region he calls Fuladu corresponds exactly to the southeastern area we are considering here. The term is also used by historians for the nineteenth century kingdom by that name.

6. Ibid., p. 34.

7. Senegal, Bureau National de Recensement, "Résultats provisoires du recensement général de la population d'avril 1976," mimeographed, Dakar.

8. See M. Danfakha, "Kédougou, ville originale d'une région enclavée," unpublished memoire de maitrise geography, University of Dakar, 1972. This author correctly emphasizes the determining role played by poor health conditions in the isolation and neglect of the region.

9. P. Metge places the western boundary of this zone along a line from Richard Toll to Ziguinchor. See "Le peuplement du Sénégal," unpublished 1ère partie, Dakar, 1966.

10. Danfakha, "Kédougou," pp. 47-49.

11. J. F. Dupont considers that the function of "official center for the assembly, transit and distribution of seasonal peanut farmers" was one of the determining factors in the growth of the town of Tambacounda. "Tambacounda, capitale du Sénégal oriental," Cahiers d'outre-mer 6 (1964): 208.

12. Clearly there exist spontaneous migratory currents in the direction of the eastern margins of the peanut basin, as shown by J. P. Dubois, "L'émigration des Sérères vers la zone arachidière orientale," Dakar, ORSTOM, 1971.

13. Several authors have attempted to define the shifting and imprecise boundaries of this peanut pole of attraction; see P. Metge, "Le Peuplement," and P. Pélissier, Les paysons du Sénégal, les civilisations agraires du Cayor à la Casamance (St. Yrieux: Fabrèque, 1966), pp. 82-83.

14. World Bank, Sierra Leone, Current Economic Position and Prospects (Washington, D.C.: World Bank, November 27, 1974), pp. 69-71.

15. Samir Amin, Neocolonialism in West Africa (Baltimore: Penguin, 1972).

16. Dubois, "L'Emigration des Sérères," pp. 24-32.

17. M. S. Balde, "Changements sociaux et migration . . . ," pp. 102-64. This author succeeds in identifying the zones in which Guinean immigrants (mainly Fulbe from Futa Jallon) settled in Fuladu, the "liberation villages" settled by former slaves from Futa Jallon and other localities recognizable by their toponomy.

18. IFAN, Ethno-demographic Maps of West Africa (Dakar: IFAN, 1952).

19. See, for example, Senegal, Ministry of Planning and Cooperation, Etude d'un plan de développement régional intégré du Sénégal oriental, 1977, Dakar.

20. Following official Guinean administrative nomenclature.

21. M. S. Balde, "Un cas typique de migration interafricaine: l'immigration des guinéens au Sénégal," in Les migrations africaines, ed. Jean-Loup Amselle (Paris: Maspero, 1976), p. 75. These causes of emigration are still in effect.

22. Pélissier, Les paysons du Sénégal.

23. M. Soumah, "Culture cotonnière et développement régional au Sénégal," Annales de la faculté des lettres et sciences humaines de Dakar 7 (1977): 243-68.

24. It is highly probable that SOMIVAC's intervention may improve the agricultural development perspectives of this region.

25. Conclusion of the debate organized between our team and a group of peasants, including both heads of households and nawetans, with the participation of the SODIFITEX field worker, at Dioulayet in the arrondissement of Dioulacolon, December 9, 1977.

26. Longer, in-depth studies would be necessary to arrive at a statistical evaluation of these international migrations, particularly between Guinea Conakry and Senegal. The cooperation of authorities of both countries would be desirable for the success of such an enterprise. (E.N. Guinea has not taken an official census.)

27. After loosening up in the early months of 1978, road links between Senegal and Guinea opened officially following the reconciliation in Monrovia, March 1978.

28. "Air Baape" means in Pular "over the bushes," an expression not lacking in humor as a description of the travel means adopted by clandestine Guinean immigrants to Senegal.

8

DIOLA WOMEN AND MIGRATION: A CASE STUDY

Alice Hamer

STATEMENT OF THE PROBLEM

Migration has increasingly become one of the most cumbersome contemporary problems in Africa. In Senegal this dilemma is predominantly domestic in nature and falls into three different categories. One concerns the overpopulation of the central groundnut basin. Another concerns the underpopulation of some lands with marked agricultural potential in the southern part of the country. The third category concerns the overpopulation of the Cap Vert region, Dakar in particular. It is the latter two that are directly related to the seasonal migration of Diola women.

The official policy of the Senegalese government since independence has encouraged the decentralization of the industrial sector in Dakar and its outlying areas.[1] In spite of this, industrial growth in this area has become more concentrated, accounting for approximately 85 percent of all Senegal's industry. No doubt this is the primary agent pushing many there in search of employment, contributing to Dakar's soaring 10 percent annual population increase.[2] Population increase has been so rapid that, according to the 1970/71 census, two-thirds of Senegal's urban population is in Dakar alone. Thus the density of Cap Vert is the highest of Senegal's eight regions at 1,540 persons per square kilometer. This compares with that of the second most densely populated region, Thiès, at 94 per square kilometer, and with the least populated area, Senegal Oriental, at 5 per square kilometer.[3] This imbalance in urban-rural distribution has resulted in a parallel economic disequilibrium. National expenditure has necessarily favored the Cap Vert region, at the expense of rural Senegal. This is expressed most clearly by the fact that urban incomes are 14 times higher than rural ones.

One source of stress on the Cap Vert region is the seasonal rural exodus whereby thousands swarm there in the dry months in search of employment. Part of this pilgrimage is made from the Lower Casamance, an area dominated by Diolas who comprise approximately 10 percent of the national population. This sojourn involves men and women. Indeed, women make up about half of the movement. In addition to augmenting pressures on urban centers, this migration has major negative implications for the rural extension. Rice production, the principal agricultural activity of Lower Casamance, is crucial not only to the consumption of that region, but also to that of all Senegal. As Senegal's primary rice-producing region, it must be the focus of development to curb the 200,000 tons of rice imported annually.[4] The government has already recognized the enormous potential of this area that produces the largest national quantity of rice. The rice of the Diola of Lower Casamance, which accounts for three-fourths of all rice produced by Senegal, can be augmented given certain conditions.[5] One important determinant is that the land be given the virtual year-round attention it demands. As the work of the rice field is done predominantly by women, their seasonal absence necessarily weakens production. These are grim realities that must be taken into consideration for urban planning as well as for regional development in Casamance.

REVIEW OF LITERATURE

There are several works on the Casamance as well as a few studies concerning migration as it relates to the region. Louis Vincent Thomas has written the most detailed ethnographic material on the Diola. Good historical and additional ethnographic material on the Diola is further provided in a section of Paul Péllisier's massive study on the peasants of Senegal. Of a more narrow focus are studies such as that of Christian Roche, who did an account of the conquest and resistance of the people of Casamance, 1850-1914. Also relating to a more limited theme is Jean Girard's book focusing on the religious beliefs and practices of the Diola. Historical information on Diolas was recently expanded by the dissertation of Peter Allen Mark, who traced the development of religious conversion among the Boulouf Diola, the subgroup with which this chapter is concerned.

One of the few studies touching on migration in Casamance was published in 1976 by the World Bank. A comprehensive analysis of migration in Senegal, it discusses in particular its disproportionate regional population growth and national employment as it relates to national migration patterns. Another study provides specific

information on the seasonal migration of Lower Casamance itself.
In a thorough demographic study made on the area in 1972, Henk L.
van Loo and Nella Star devote one full chapter to this issue. Included is much heretofore unknown data on female migration. In
addition, there was more recently a special research team of four,
presided over by Klauss de Jonge, that examined in Lower Casamance the issues of migration exclusively. The team, which conducted its research from 1973 to 1975, has at present published
only the preliminary report. When the final report has been completed, it will be the most comprehensive and contemporary account
of migration on the Lower Casamance.

Information on Diola women themselves is wanting. The sole
contributions made are by Olga Linares de Sapir, who concerns herself with Diola women's agricultural techniques.

METHODOLOGY

I chose the village of Thionk Essil for a specific case study.
Thionk, located in the department of Bignona, is the largest village
in Senegal. It is representative of the Boulouf Diola, one of the
three major Diola subgroups. The other major subdivisions are the
Diola Fogny, who also live north of the Casamance River, and the
Diola Kasa, who live south of the river. The Boulouf total 40,000
of the total 220,000 in Lower Casamance. They are, as are the
Fogny, predominantly Muslim. The Kasa region alone is that area
that remains significantly animist.

To conduct a questionnaire in the village, I selected a sample
size of 150 for a population of approximately 6,000. The subjects
were drawn randomly from the census entries kept as records in
the neighboring arrondissement of Tendouck. Two-thirds of those
interviewed were women, as it is a feminine issue. A distribution
was also made according to age to guarantee the widest possible
range of input. The questionnaire conducted in Thionk Essil had
three principal goals: to trace the historical evolution of female
migration, to examine more fully its impact on the rural level, and
to gather data on rural income attributable to seasonal migration.
Village interviews lasted from March to November 1978.

I also conducted interviews in Dakar and Gambia. The goal
of Dakar's questionnaires, conducted May 15–May 31, 1978, was to
gather more data on the urban lifestyles of migrants. The objective behind the interviews in Gambia, June 1–June 5, 1978, was to
highlight historical background through discussions with some of the
earliest migrants there.

FINDINGS

The initial seasonal migration of men as well as women from the Boulouf region is intricately linked with the expansion of European hegemony in Casamance. Prior travel was limited, in part, to the lack of personal security prevalent then. Oral accounts colorfully depict the hazards involved in migration, largely due to the endemic wars over rice fields, as well as to the threat of capture and eventual slavery. Although Thionk Essil did not practice slavery, it took an active part in the slave trade. Indeed, throughout most of the nineteenth century, the slave trade was Thionk's raison d'etre for contacts primarily with the Manding further north. It conducted slave raids in the Kasa area in large canoes, selling the captives either to intermediaries in the Fogny area or directly to the Manding themselves. When the French established their first trading post in Carabane in 1836, they found Thionk actively involved in the slave trade, and its persistent involvement eventually led to a punitive expedition being sent against Thionk in 1860.[6] This initial contact established trading links, which were to develop into concrete trading relations on which seasonal migration would build.

A more direct threat to the travel of Essilians themselves, however, were the maraboutic wars in the late nineteenth century. Although begun in Gambia in 1850, they did not spread to the Diola Fogny areas until 1877-78. These wars only occasionally affected the Boulouf, but their termination was crucial to the safe passage of seasonal migrants.

Accompanying increased security with the European hegemony was expanded trade. The initially most viable commercial transactions between the Manding and Boulouf areas were with rubber, which first emerged as a commercial item in 1879-80. Rubber quickly developed into the principal export item to Europe as its tonnage in exportation of 59 tons in 1883 augmented to a tonnage of 252 between 1896 and 1899.[7] Geographically, Thionk was able to tap one of the main sources of rubber, that situated between Baila and Bignona working its way up lagunes and marigots as far as Thionk. There was also a major source north of Kafountine and one southwest of Ziguinchor. Although rubber was not the principal spark for the seasonal migrations of Thionk, it touched off migrations of two other peoples. One involved the movement southward from Gambia by Akous into the Fogny region. The other was a seasonal movement northward from Portuguese Guinea by a group of Kanjaks from the shores of the Rio Cacheu.[8] Rubber production thrived in these regions until the collapse of the wild rubber market in 1913. Its chief importance for Essilians' migrations is that eventually, especially after the termination of maraboutic wars, several

Essilians ventured to Gambia themselves to circumvent economic loss from the middlemen who came to Thionk for rubber. This strengthened trade ties and regional familiarities soon exploited by seasonal migrants.

The palm kernel was the commercial giant that opened the gateways of seasonal migration. The demand for palm kernels was twofold. Gambians themselves wanted them for consumption and the English exported them for the fabrication of various products in the metropolis at far more favorable profit rates than those offered by the French at Carabane. Diolas had a virtual monopoly on this open market. Mandings, as Muslims, had no skill at mounting trees. Traditionally, animist Diolas were, on the contrary, extremely adept from their centuries of experience in mounting for palm wine.

Seasonal migration in Thionk toward Gambia, by some oral accounts, began even before the 1880s. However, it clearly was at least 1900 before it engaged significant numbers of people. The initial migrations for palm kernel exploitation established patterns that would persist over decades. The mode of travel is one example. Travel was usually done in part by pirogue and in part on foot. Early in the dry season in January, Essilians traveled in small groups by pirogue as far as one of several villages along the marigot in the Fogny region, such as Diouloulou and Kubanank. From there, migrants continued to Gambia by foot—first to Brikama, which served as a focal point for dispersion. The journey consumed one day. But if there was no pirogue available, the march entirely on foot took two days. The journey involved intrigue insofar as Essilians had to travel by night in crossing the border areas to avoid the much feared customs officials. The most arduous part of the journey seems to have been the load migrants had to carry on their heads when walking. People carried a dry season's supply of rice in addition to personal effects atop, including all cooking utensils. But the trip did not involve personal danger, although some early migrants traveled armed with large knives in case personal defense was necessary.

Early destinations chosen also set precedents. From Brikama, Essilians dispersed to several villages in Gambia. The criterion used for selecting a village was its supply of good quality palm trees. Oral accounts explain that this is what accounts for the pattern of residency in numerous villages in Gambia and, later, in Fogny, which border the Atlantic. Three of the villages first chosen by Gambian migrants were Kartung, Gunjur, and Siffo. Later, when Essilians disembarked from their pirogues in Fogny, they sometimes remained there seasonally. Residence in these villages lasted up until the rains began in June-July, after which migrants returned for rice cultivation.

The palm oil fabrication in which seasonal migrants engaged was a time-consuming process. Men and women rose early in the morning to return late at night. As with most labor among the Diola, it involved a sexual demarcation of duties. The men mounted the trees to collect palm kernels, while women transported them to the site of preparation and pilled them for cooking. Palm oil was made outside of the village with which the migrants were associated. Each male migrant from Essil had a guardian, the head of a Manding household in the village outside of which he lodged. Migrants themselves lived in makeshift housing constructed each season. The responsibility of the Manding tutor was to provide food and food preparation for male migrants, a duty specifically designated to the wives of household heads. Female migrants were completely responsible for their own nourishment, the rationale being that it was only the men who mounted the trees for the gifts left behind. As payment, Essilian men divided their gains between the Manding household and his wife(s) or sister(s) who assisted him. Palm oil, which was male property, was shared with the male tutor. Palm kernels, which were female property, were divided between the tutor's wife and the female companion from Thionk. This division in property rights was often to the advantage of women. The potential gains from trade with palm kernels was often much more favorable than the selling of palm oil for local consumption. To profit, however, women had to carry their palm kernels on their heads in large baskets as far as Banjul, where the Compagnie Francaise de l'Afrique Occidentale purchased them. Even when migrants began to seasonally migrate only as far as the Fogny area, they still marched as far as Banjul to trade their palm kernels.

In conjunction with the migration for palm kernels was a seasonal migration in search of two other commodities: oysters and peanuts. Fishing for oysters, a traditional task of Diola women, was unknown to Manding women in spite of the market created for it. There are a few villages where Essilians went expressly to find them, such as Lamin. The attraction to peanut production in Gambia was the more favorable remuneration granted by the government in Gambia in comparison with that of Senegal. The inceptions of these migrations were at least 20 years later than that of palm kernels and on a much smaller scale.

Overlapping with the early stages of palm oil trade was a seasonal migration, on a small scale, southward to Guinea Bissau to tap and sell palm wine. The majority of Essilians engaged in this lodged in Cacheau. There are scattered cases of seasonal sojourns to the Kasa area as well, which had to be bypassed to reach Portuguese Guinea. The men, assisted by their wives in the transport of palm wine and its selling, paid them by either sharing a portion of their wages or by giving them a certain amount of palm wine to sell themselves. It is difficult to establish a fixed date as to its inception. It is possible, however, that it began even earlier than the rubber trade, in which case it is arguable that palm wine was the first legitimate trade commodity of Essil. Although oral accounts confirm its existence between 1900 and 1914, clearly its duration is not likely to have exceeded 1930, as the palm oil trade and increasing Muslim influence in Thionk deterred the once crucially important role of palm wine.

One other source of contact southward with the Kasa area involved a dry season activity not part of prolonged seasonal migration. Before established means of trade were instituted, Thionk Essilians often raided the Kasa for cattle. The adventure took place one day after careful planning by an intimate group. In the thick of night, the group descended southward in a large pirogue armed with medicines to reach the village that approached sleep. This trip was enacted in strictest secrecy and discipline due to the risk of battle and death if caught. A rare form of theft from the Kasa region also was bride stealing, once an acceptable form of bride acquisition.

The female component of Thionk's first seasonal movements was, obviously, not characterized by strong female initiative. Rather, she followed male family members to provide supportive labor. Palm kernel exploitation, the activity establishing perennial seasonal migrations of women, appears to have been conducted by many households, but initially only by men. This was done as a trial run to guarantee both safety and profitability. Oral accounts mark women's initial departure to roughly the 1880s, although their involvement remained sparse until at least the circumcision of Eforsé in 1920. Initially, female migrants to Gambia were almost exclusively married women, a mark of the maturity mandatory for departure. A minimum maturation of males, too, was initially necessary, as before the 1920s all men migrating had to be circumcised. There were occasions, however, when single women migrated seasonally to assist a male family member, usually a brother. The revolutionary implications of single women's departure is indicated by the ritual ceremony before her withdrawal by her parents. As women without children were not allowed in the secret forest, older family members went as the girl's representative to it to ask that the girl return in the same chaste state in which she left. This practice lasted for only the first generation of single migrants. After Islam entered Thionk Essil, it became customary to consult a marabout before departure for a forecast of the potential fruitfulness of the sojourn. The most important point about early female migration is that women were never left alone and were always with parental males.

For several decades following its inception, female migration would continue to be primarily an appendage to that of men, augmented by factors that pushed men and women outward together. One such factor was the consolidation of colonial infrastructure, which stimulated seasonal, temporary, and permanent migrations. Temporary and permanent migration as a source of resistance to imposts is not clearly documented. However, direct refusals to pay them are. Although Faidherbe theoretically established imposts in 1861, as late as the 1890s, Boulouf villages, including Thionk, either ignored or directly refused tax collection efforts. Gradually, however, enforcement became more uniform and the amount augmented. Between 1918 and 1920, the impost was doubled from 5 to 10 francs.[9] This augmentation, principally aimed at stimulating the region's involvement in peanuts as a cash crop, nonetheless stimulated further seasonal migration to Gambia for revenue.

Colonial encroachment introduced some factors that undoubtedly sparked increased temporary and permanent migrations. Among them were forced labor and procedures of impost enforcement. Oral testimonies of the severity with which imposts were often collected are quite uniform. There is the frequent report, for example, of how payment refusal ended in the male head of household being tied nude in the blazing sun in shame and helplessness before his family and neighbors. Whereas these occasions were scattered, that of forced labor was not. Lasting from 1921 to the end of World War II, it was passionately hated. There is one noted case in 1929 when Thionk Essil refused compliance.[10] Men still recount with bitterness how they had to provide even their own food while working for no pay arduously, frequently being flogged as they worked.

These types of injustices were weighed with all other life misfortunes and fortunes carefully by households in the decision making for permanent migration. The factor of ill luck in Thionk Essil played perhaps a greater role in permanent migration initially than did direct monetary incentives. This was underscored by Essilians' belief that ill luck was caused by malevolent forces harnessed in the household adversely affected. Removal from that spatial area would, theoretically, foster an escape from any affliction. Before permanent migration began outside of Thionk, some people even moved around the four quartiers of the village. In every one of the ten villages visited in Gambia, informants cited misfortune as a primary consideration in permanent migration. The most frequently mentioned examples of mischance were child loss (either high child mortality, infertility, or inability to have male children), poor harvest yields, poor health (recurrent or incurable illness), and constant sickness and/or death of animals. Some of the first permanent migrations occurred soon following seasonal migrations, beginning

sometime in the 1890s. If a village had been inhabited seasonally
and conditions were favorable, a man might consider a final move.
Of utmost importance as a consideration was the access to arable
rice fields. Here the Manding's and Fogny's granting of land parcels was crucial. These permanent migrations established vital
networks of information and dwelling possibilities that shaped the
volume and character of seasonal migration. See Map 8.1.

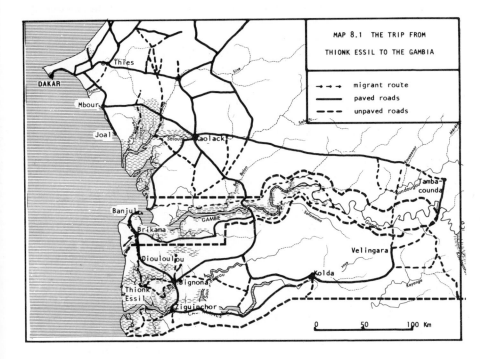

There are several factors beginning in the 1930s that played
a more direct role in the formation of female initiative in migration.
Education was one. Primary schools first opened in Thionk Essil
in 1933. The school masters' initial reports recounted the difficulties encountered in recruiting students. But, in the 1940s, parents
began to favor the education of their male children. School registers,
which reflect the preference for male instruction, show that schools
were in existence in Thionk for 14 years before the first girl was
enrolled. As boys increasingly swelled the school ranks, their role
in the active seasonal labor force declined proportionately. Reflecting the trend of events as well as the educational predicament of
women, at one point one informant succinctly commented, "Anyone
who migrated in the dry season was illiterate." This statement

does not hold, however, for part of the 1950s and thereafter, when education became an important determinant of male migration. Among males, the most educated left for further scholarization or salaried employment involving trade skills.

The withdrawal of men from the labor force set one of the factors conducive to the switch in occupation of women. With the male component of palm oil production diminished, women were obliged to look for various employment alternatives. Gradually, the occupational void was filled by a demand for domestic skills in urban areas. Women from Thionk Essil first worked as maids in the 1930s in Ziguinchor, in Banjul in the 1940s and 1950s, and predominantly in Dakar in the 1960s. Until the end of World War II, there were small numbers only engaged in domestic employment. The primary needed impetus was the expansion in scale of urban and industrial growth, an almost exclusively postwar phenomenon. A corollary to the increasing number of women being drawn into the salaried labor force was the need for maids to take over these wage earners' household duties. Of monumental importance, too, in mounting the number of domestics, was road construction. When the transgambian highway was completed in the early 1950s, easy accessibility to urban centers made it much easier to leave for remunerative activities. Oral reports describe the surge in departures in the 1950s in such a way that even a conservative estimate of its increase would be a minimum of twofold. The sum total of all these factors was that, as girls began to work less and less with male family members, they could leave more and more easily.

Since the 1940s, one of the most important determinants of female migration has been the age-old women's association that has modernized its traditional structure by institutionalizing migration. Since its origin, which dates back at least to the early nineteenth century, it has served primarily as an aid society for women who are victims of high infant mortality. Every woman in the village takes part as a member of one of Thionk Essil's 14 sous quartiers. These groups mobilize when a woman has lost at least three children to place her under its personal care until the woman has given birth and the child has passed its most vulnerable period. When the unfortunate woman conceives for at least the fourth time, the association takes her from her household and places her in that of a more senior member qualified to give her the most attentive care. This guardian, in conjunction with a core subgroup of four or five other experienced women, provides all the detained woman's daily needs: food, clothing, traditional and modern medicines, maraboutic charms, and so on. After the success of the group has been evidenced by the child's acquisition of two years, the mother prepares to return to her husband's household. It has always been an occasion

of celebration, although of late the scale has altered considerably.
Up until the 1940s, these fetes were of moderate expense. But,
gradually, women began to pool their money together for a celebration that they expanded from one to three days and that were enormously expensive. As the returning woman's reentry to her husband's domicile is to symbolize the shedding of her previous misfortune, she is equipped with a new dowry for the fresh and successful marriage about to begin. This includes a bed, a radio, a complete culinary ensemble, and a suitcase of clothes for the woman as
well as her child. The largest expense was and is cloth for every
participating member of the sous quartier. Whereas in the past
women had one new outfit for the celebration, today they have a
minimum of three. Moreover, whereas before there was the expense of feeding the village for one day only, today a group must
feed the entire village for the first day and the sous quartier for the
two days that follow. Today there can be further expenditures by
the returning woman's husband, who likely gives another fete for the
sous quartier on the exact day the woman returns, approximately
one week following the major celebration. And there are additional
expenses that have developed over the years. If, for example, an
Essilian has moved to Banjul or even to Dakar, the association must
rent buses to transport the entire sous quartier of women there for
the homecoming.

From the perspective of rural income, these expenditures are
enormous. To meet them, each member is required to contribute
for each celebration either 10,000, 15,000, or 25,000 cfa, depending on the age of the woman. The more youthful a woman is, the
more she must pay. As the possibilities for revenue in a dry season approaching these figures are practically nil, the women must
migrate. Oral accounts indicate that migrations to satisfy this demand have been significant only since approximately 1960. Since
then, it has been a powerful force pushing married women to urban
centers.

One may add to the causal factors of female migration the important element of the disproportionate growth of consumer demands
and rural revenue. The earliest seasonal migrations had as consumer objectives three principal items: guns, cloth, and animals.
Guns, which seem to have been extremely popular from 1880 to 1890,
were used for hunting, firing as a display of force in circumcision
ceremonies, and assurance of personal safety when carried as an
arm defense in rice fields and when traveling. Cloth and animals
were desired heterosexually. Cloth was used not only for dressing,
but also for the dressing of the dead before burial and ritual exchange
at funeral rites. Animals have always been a symbol of wealth and a
mandatory item of sacrifice at circumcision ceremonies. Gradually,

as exposure widened to more varied commodities, purchasing tastes and habits shifted. The demand for cloth, for example, has augmented tremendously among women since the inception of their seasonal migration. Initially, the shift was largely due to the influx of Islam in the 1920s and 1930s, which emphasized cleanliness and dressing. And, as women traveled more, particularly to urban centers, the importance given to dressing rose. No doubt, it grew weightiest during the 1950s and 1960s with migrations to Dakar and emulation of Wolof women.[11] Considerable expenditure today is on the upkeep of a daily stock of several simple manufactured items for which the women are usually wholly responsible: peanut oil, sugar, soap, kerosene, and matches. Frequently, feminine expenditure is also for transportation, medicine, and school fees for her children.

Ironically, even though the women of Thionk Essil have traditionally cultivated disproportionately more and their responsibilities for food acquisition have been more than those of men, their opportunities for rural revenue are much less. The cultivation of rice in Thionk, its primary agricultural product, is divided along sexual lines as is its distribution. The male component of rice cultivation involves preparation of the rice fields alone. Weeding, planting, fertilizing, and harvesting are feminine duties. But whereas the men in Thionk Essil must provide rice for their households throughout the rainy season alone (approximately three months), each woman must supply rice for herself, her children, and her husband throughout the dry season, which consumes most of the year. This explains the heavy exodus in the drought years of the 1970s. In 1972, the most chronic drought year, 55 percent of all Lower Casamance peasants and 78 percent among the Boulouf had to buy rice.[12]

Yet, in the dead dry season when virtually all rural revenue is earned, the men in Thionk have the possibility of potentially more profitable employment. For example, there is for them construction, fishing, and palm oil. Women's revenues are derived chiefly from the selling of agricultural products. Most frequently, they sell fruits, vegetables, oysters, confections, as well as some artisinal items like baskets and hand brooms. According to one estimate, whereas the average daily wage for individual labor construction in areas surrounding Bignona and Ziguinchor is 300-400 cfa, the mean daily income from market vending fruits and vegetables is 100-200 cfa.[13] Even these possibilities for women have been minimized by the historically difficult problems of transporting their products to the markets in Bignona and Ziguinchor, where potential profit margins are greater.

Historically, Diola women have made minimal personal gain
from the most profitable agricultural product, the peanut. Every
region of Senegal has been dependent on peanut cultivation for the
highest monetary yields from agriculture. This ongoing dependency
in Lower Casamance is reflected by the fact that today the selling of
the peanut accounts for 30 to 40 percent of all rural revenue.[14] However, the profitability of the peanut in Lower Casamance is very disproportionate. Whereas, for example, the Diola in the Mandingized
northeast subregion have made substantial profit, the Diola south of
the Casamance River make minimal gains at best. This may, in
part, explain why the heaviest female migration comes from the
southern area. In Thionk Essil, heavy peanut cultivation, which
became significant in the 1920s, was short-lived. When the drought
came in the early 1930s, farmers were discouraged by their futile
efforts to reimburse the credit given for production supplies by the
government. Peanut cultivation switched from a commercial item
to predominately one of household consumption. But even where and
when peanuts are a plus, the income derived is for male and not
female coffers. As peanuts are classified as a male crop, men receive the direct monetary revenue involved.

For all these reasons, Thionk Essil plays a part in the large
seasonal migration of Lower Casamance. It is estimated that, in
this section of Casamance alone, 33,500 people of a total rural population of 225,000 leave their native village in the dry season. This
accounts for about 15 percent of the total number of inhabitants in
the rainy season.[15] It is a movement of youth. Of all total absentees, 42 percent are single boys and 48 percent single girls.
Married men and women account for 9 and 1 percent respectively
of all seasonal migration. The majority of girls leaving are between the ages of 10 and 19, reducing by 50 percent the female population in this age range in the dry season.[16] These figures indicate
that the age at which girls begin to migrate seasonally in search of
employment is low. In fact, girls in Lower Casamance begin to
leave at an average age of eleven and a half years, migrating seasonally over a period of seven years on the average before returning permanently, usually for reasons of marriage.[17] The motives
of females during their exodus differ significantly from those of
males. Whereas among young men 55 percent leave for seasonal
employment and 30 percent for school, among girls 80 percent seek
temporary employment and only 15 percent leave for school.[18] On
their sojourns to urban centers, girls usually work as maids. Their
most common destination today is Dakar.

Destinations of Urban Female Migrants[19]

Lower Casamance				Other Parts Senegal		
Ziguinchor	Bignona	Other Parts	Total	Dakar	Other Cities	Gambia
9	7	16	32	41	8	18

Concerns over the impact of female migration in Thionk Essil encompass both production and social dimensions. When asked if they found certain aspects of female migration disturbing, approximately 50 percent of all females and 75 percent of the men interviewed responded affirmatively. Their apprehensions reflect firstly a consciousness of the declining rice yields resultant of the tardy return of young girls. Now the average annual time of migration of girls in Lower Casamance is eight months, which eats into planting time. Moreover, about 70 percent of these girls leave again before the month of December when harvest begins. Exploring the quantitative impact of tardy female returns in the rainy season, it was found that in one village, from which only 23 percent of the girls between 10 and 19 migrated, their tardiness caused a decrease of cultivatible surface by more than 10 percent.[20] This figure does not include cultivation loss in some villages, such as Thionk, at which traditional techniques of fertilization have been significantly abandoned.

Period of Return to Village of Groups of Girls
Having Left as Maids[21]
(by month of return, in percent)

	Apr.	May	June	July	Aug.	Sept.	Oct.
Lower Casamance	1	1	15	37	98	98	100

Period of Departure from Village of Groups of Girls
Who Leave for Work as Maids[22]
(by month of departure, in percent)

	July	Aug.	Sept.	Oct.	Nov.	Dec.	Jan.	Feb.	Mar.
Lower Casamance	1	1	2	46	68	83	87	97	100

This area is, furthermore, being hit by an increasing number of girls who do not return at all during the rainy season. In 1972, for example, only 15 percent of all the villages in all of Lower Casamance were fortunate enough to have all the girl migrants return.[23]

Interviews in Thionk Essil reveal that there is another major cause of production loss. Traditional methods of accounting for labor shortage are being weakened by migration. Women's traditional associations, which have always had a second major function as an employable labor group, are increasingly being called upon for service to compensate for the mounting absenteeism. However, at the same time, the labor capacity of the group is being depleted by the exodus of its members. In addition, there are several other dry season activities neglected by seasonal migrants, some of which represent a nutritional loss for households affected: palm oil fabrication, vegetable gardens, fishing for oysters, salt preparation, and searching for cooking wood.

The most acute anxieties in Thionk Essil over feminine migration encompass social parameters. In particular, much of this involves the evolution of social relationships between men and women. When asked if female migration had resulted in changes in this domain, only approximately 15 percent responded negatively. In regard to single people, for example, it is consistently stated that girls no longer want to marry. There are repeated observations concerning the increasing frequency of girls having children before marriage. Indeed, this is a trend in Lower Casamance verified quantitatively. In one village under study it was found that 30 percent of the single girls of age 15 or more had children and that marriage age is being prolonged.[24]

In addition, people give the often expressed sentiment of disappointment with contemporary marriages. Take, for example, the formation of marriage contracts. Heretofore, marriage was an arrangement made by only the parents of both mates. But now, with exposure to different types of marriages, men and women insist on choosing their own partners. Moreover, many complain that exposure to the urban milieu induces an attitudinal change among young girls, which affects their selection of a marriage partner. It is said that they increasingly prefer urban residents and urban life over peasants and country life. They lose their taste for rural work altogether, so that, if and when they return, it is done only half-heartedly. This, in addition to the fact that they meet men from various other villages, accounts for the rise of marriages to partners of other village origins. These liaisons are usually viewed by parents as an unfortunate breech in the continuity of tradition.

Concerns over changing relations between married men and women indicate potentially more negative effects on the household's stability. The migration of married women, which roughly totals 10 to 15 percent of female migration, results in an increasing sense of independence as a result of women's expanded economic role in the family. In scattered cases, it was reported that women nourish their family even during the rainy season. Moreover, on occasion, it was expressed that urban exposure to other men reduces the wife's initial esteem of her husband. Reports of divorce among married migrants are frequent. On isolated occasions, informants cited cases in which married women have either returned to the village pregnant or refused altogether to return to the village. As one woman expressed it, "Migration is dangerous for a married woman because she is exposed to city men that have money regularly, which her husband does not."

The migration of a married woman will likely trigger some upheaval in her household, especially in cases in which the woman is the only wife. If a migrant has a co-wife, it is she who takes over the dry season activities such as salt preparation and wood hunting. In circumstances in which the relationship between wives is not harmonious, it is most often the mother who performs, the sister of the migrant being the next most likely person to take over her activities. But, in single-wife households, even if these tasks are taken over by female relatives, daily household chores may become the burden of the husband. There were numerous reports of men having to engage in cooking, laundry, and child care. No encounters were made with cases whereby men performed female agricultural duties.

Other concerns over the social impact of female migration are related to behavior changes manifested upon their return to the village. Notably, most of those changes are believed to be among single women. Whereas approximately 75 percent of those interviewed noted behavioral differences among unmarried women, only approximately 20 percent noted behavioral differences among married women. When asked for examples, people most often cited the way in which women dress. Having migrated, a woman can often afford to be well-dressed on occasions of village festivals, frequently alternating the variety of colors and styles of cloth. In Thionk Essil, it is clear that clothes serve as a symbolic assimilation into modern Senegalese life. In second position, people cited speaking Wolof as behavioral change, it too expressing exposure to what many villagers see as a more evolved culture. There is a practice rapidly developing in Thionk whereby people employ both to flaunt their urban experience. For the first few days or weeks following the migrant's return, she pays frequent calls on friends and neighbors dressed in some of her best cloth and speaking only Wolof.

When asked if there were any disadvantages to female migration on the village level, approximately 50 percent responded affirmatively. The most frequent illustration was the lack of animation. The festivals of the dry season, it is said, cannot compare with the richness and bloom of former times. In fact, some festivals have

become extinct among women, due, in part, to feminine migration.[25]
Before Thionk Essil's conversion to Islam, which took place approximately 1920-40, there were annual fetes of female wrestling cham-
pionships. These were used as means of separating marriageable
from ineligible girls. In every dry season, there were also celebrations given by certain girls to announce their recent status of
marriage eligibility. As these occasions were accompanied by heavy
palm wine drinking, they were abandoned with the introduction of
Islam. As a substitute, acquisition of maturity gradually became
marked by female circumcision rites. A Manding custom, the first
Essilians circumcised were permanent migrants in Gambia and
Islamic Fogny villages. As early as the mid-1920s, a small delega-
tion went to be circumcised at Thiobon, the earliest convert to Islam
among the Boulouf. The first circumcision rites for women in Thionk
Essil dates back only as far as approximately 1940.

In spite of all concerns expressed, an overwhelming consensus
of more than 90 percent, male and female, believed female migration advantageous to the household. Almost without exception, the
benefits cited are economic. Economic gain is confirmed by the net
returns recorded from household samples. Sixty-five percent of the
households interviewed with migrants absent received money ranging in amounts from 4,000 to 50,000 cfa. Those receiving combinations of money and consumer goods was 45 percent. Recipient households of consumer items only totaled 23 percent. Items received
were various combinations of rice, sugar, and soap. Rice was by
far given most frequently, a fact that underscores the necessity of
supplementary income to furnish essential foodstuffs.[26]

Indeed, the virtual unanimous consensus among informants,
male and female, as to the prestige gained by migrants is attributable to the important economic role female migration plays in the
household. Economic benefits explain, also, why there is little opposition to female migration by affected households. In spite of all
aforementioned concerns, more than 90 percent of those interviewed
stated there was a lack of opposition, financial need being cited almost always as the explanation. Cases of resistance were almost
exclusively with married women. Although no question was directly
posed concerning the imposition of migration on women by their families, there were occasional admissions of parents forcing their
daughters to leave school to seek gainful employment.

Economic gain, however, was not the sole net advantage cited.
A small number of women see it as an opportunity for a valuable exposure to a more elevated way of life, something that means cultural
profit to the village. Capsulizing the additional social dimensions of
migration gains, one woman commented, "Female migration permits
uneducated women to see how the world works while earning money
for her family at the same time."

It is an important point of emphasis that female migration satisfies more than essential household needs for many women. It is very frequently employed to buy luxury items, which, in the case of women, is extra clothes. Although clothes were not quoted as part of household gains, it was my personal observation that it was a powerful motivation factor for migration. Many women as well as men, in fact, rated it as the most important motivation in supplementary discussions. This is most true in the case of women's associations, whose members descend on urban centers expressly to fulfill monetary obligations for festivals. Said one association migrant, "It is an occasion to spend thousands of francs on ourselves alone without having to give one franc to men." This is a dramatic illustration of the strands of consciousness inherent in female migration.

The Dakar interviews serve to illustrate some aspects of urban life for migrants. The 30 women interviewed ranged between the ages of 16 and 34. Twenty-eight were maids. Working as a maid entails a variety of domestic tasks, the number of which depends on the preference of the employer. Duties usually include one or a combination of the following: general cleaning, cooking, laundry, and child care. Working conditions are frequently tediously long and job security low. Approximately one-fifth of those interviewed had kept the same employer for more than a year. Monthly income was dependent on several factors. The city was a determinant, as wages were more elevated in Dakar and Banjul than in Bignona and Ziguinchor. Age was a factor, also, insofar as older women earn more. Experience was a consideration, since the more experienced were better paid. The ethnic background of the employer was an important element. The fact that economic and social status in Senegal tends to correspond with one's ethnic background explains the variation in pay scale. The profitability of households is European, Lebanese, and African. Pay depends, in part, on the responsibilities given to the maid, the best wages being given to those with the greatest obligations. Lastly, income was influenced by the lodging arrangement of the maid. If the woman lives in the household where she works, which is unusual, her wages may decrease. [27]

Urban Lifestyle of Maids in Dakar

	Minimum	Maximum	Average
Hours daily	5	8	7
Number of tasks	1	4	2
Monthly income, in cfa francs	5,000	22,000	13,000

Housing arrangements among those interviewed had little vari-
ance. Most women lived in households in which the head of the
household was a male relative with a base age of 30. But there were
three cases in which those interviewed lived in households shared
by a number of other women, either relatives or friends. Occupants
ranged in age from 13 to 19. The head of the household in these
cases was 18 to 22, and her housing reached high capacity. In one
case, for example, there were 18 women living in a single room.
In such circumstances, women often make arrangements to eat in
other households, making contributions to both domiciles. To help
meet monetary needs and aid savings, many women reported membership in tontines. These serve as savings clubs whereby women
donate a specified amount monthly to collect a bulk sum on a rotat-
ing basis.

RECOMMENDATIONS

The migration of Diola women has, from its inception until
now, been motivated primarily by economic gain. Any viable pro-
posals to impede it in any way must involve economic profits at
least equal to those of present urban migration. The alternatives
open in the village itself are not likely to deter it, although some
aspects of rural development are advisable. Transportation should
be improved, as it will help increase the profit margin for many
women engaged in market gardens. Projects that ease women's
workloads and give them extra earning time, such as rice thrashers,
are also attractive. However, the total economic gain of these ven-
tures is not likely to measure up to urban ones, especially if all
maids were to remain in the village and engage themselves in that
work alone.
As urban economic incentives are not likely to be counterbalanced by rural development, easing the weight off overburdened
urban areas might help. The most frequently quoted request in
Thionk Essil itself contains much potential. The establishment of
factories in nearby urban centers would provide income to migrants
as well as bring them closer to home. The development of factories
that exploit available agricultural items, such as Lower Casamance's
abundant fruits, would be a valuable stimulant to rural revenue. The
development of other facilities that draw people to cities, such as
schools and offices, is a consideration. In short, redistributing
urban populations is the most viable policy alternative.

NOTES

1. Senegal, Ministry of Planning and Cooperation, Atlas pour l'aménagement du territoire (Dakar: Nouvelles éditions africaines, 1977), p. 113.

2. World Bank, Migration and Employment in Senegal: An Introductory Report, Working paper, Washington, D.C., September 24, 1976, p. 30.

3. Ibid., p. 4.

4. Klauss de Jonge, Jos van der Klei, Henk Meilink, and Jan Rockland Storm, "Sénégal: Projet d'une recherche multidisciplinaire sur les facteurs socio-économiques favorisant la migration en Basse Casamance et sur ses conséquences pour le lieu de départ. Rapport provisoire," Leiden, October 1976, p. 98.

5. Olga Linares de Sapir, "Agriculture and Diola Society," in African Food Production Systems, ed. Peter F. M. McLoughlin (Baltimore: Johns Hopkins Press, 1970), p. 198.

6. Peter Mark, "Economic and Religious Change among Diola of Boulouf 1890-1940: Trade and Cash Cropping and Islam in Southwest Senegal," Ph.D. dissertation, Yale University, 1979.

7. Peter Mark, "The Rubber and Palm Produce Trades and the Islamization of the Diola of Boulouf, 1890-1920," Bulletin IFAN, ser. B, 2 (1977): 346.

8. Christian Roche, Conquête et résistance des peuples de Casamance (Dakar: Nouvelles éditions africaines, 1976).

9. Ibid.

10. See Mark, "Economic and Religious Change," chap. 4, for a detailed discussion of resistance among the Boulouf.

11. For a good description of this Wolof emulation, see Solange Falade, "Women of Dakar and the Surrounding Urban Area," in Women of Tropical Africa, ed. Denise Paulme (London: Routledge and Kegan Paul, 1963), pp. 217-29.

12. Henk L. van Loo and Nella J. Star, La Basse Casamance, Sud-Ouest Sénégal: données de bases démographiques et socio-economiques (University of Leyde, July 1973), p. 254.

13. Ibid., p. 152.

14. de Jonge et al., "Sénégal: Projet d'une recherche multi-disciplinaire," p. 37.

15. van Loo and Star, La Basse Casamance, p. 194.

16. Ibid., p. 195.

17. Ibid., pp. 214-16.

18. Ibid., p. 198.

19. Ibid., p. 202.

20. de Jonge et al., "Sénégal: Projet d'une recherche multi-disciplinaire," p. 15.

21. Ibid., p. 212.

22. Ibid., p. 211.

23. Ibid., p. 212.

24. Ibid., p. 16.

25. See Mark, "Economic and Religious Change," for a detailed explanation of the correlation between migration and religious conversion.

26. These figures, which are an agglomeration of returns from male and female migrants, should be considered as approximate gains only. It is assumed that most people understate their real income. Klauss de Jonge estimates that migration revenue represents 10 to 15 percent of total peasant income in Lower Casamance.

27. van Loo and Star, La Basse Casamance, p. 217.

9

MIGRATION TO DAKAR

Fatou Sow

INTRODUCTION: MIGRATION AND THE DROUGHT

Migration is a very old phenomenon in West Africa. It continues to reach peaks, which leads one to believe that the drought of recent years has contributed to the process and exaggerated its effects in the afflicted areas. Some even believe that this has led to a large-scale migratory explosion.

Our research proposed for this multidiscipline study outlined the subject immediately. In the areas afflicted by the most recent drought in West Africa, there is more migration than usual and greater temporary displacement. Can one assume from this that migration is a means to combat drought?

Before the drought, there were sizable regional migrations in Senegal, as witnessed by the great amount of literature on the subject. One of the most current results of migration is the rapid development of small towns. This is followed by the growing urbanization, of Cap Vert in particular. Are we at the present time undergoing a new migratory process hitherto unknown? One would have to elaborate the statistics over the long term in order to be able to establish such a hypothesis.

There is no doubt that these last years of drought in the Sahel have led to a sizable demographic flow. However, this is not a haphazard migratory flow, and one wonders whether the migrants are not seeking a permanent answer to the drought.

It appears rather that the drought served as a catalyst, but was not the original cause of all this migration. Some people apparently fared so badly during the most crucial period of drought that there is a strong numerical correlation between the drought and migration. People fled the countryside for the shanty towns on the edges of the cities. But there were deeper, long-term causes.

It is essential to put this study in a new perspective based on an enquiry into the motives, facts, and real significance of the migration. This led us to pose some preliminary questions: who emigrates, how, and why? For how long? Where does the immigrant stay? What happens to him? What are his long- and short-term plans?

The preliminary results of our enquiry revealed the paradox that, without regular annual census data, there was a lack of visible correlation between the drought in some of the Sahelian countries and the migratory flow. The city of Dakar, where the enquiry to demonstrate the link between the drought and migration was held, barely reveals a larger impact of the drought on the population. A more important migratory movement of Senegal seems to have taken place 15 years previously, and it shows a big structural change that took place at the same time as independence and the new development policy that went with it.

These data contrast strongly with hastily made suggestions that the drought would result in a large-scale increase in migration. It is true that in 1972 and 1973 the official position of numerous Sahelian countries upheld the national opinions that the drought was the cause of all evil. This idea was constantly emphasized in official speeches, articles in the press, and dramatic pictures on television in Africa as well as in the West.

Governments took advantage of the drought in order to request new aid in the form of money as well as foodstuffs. We are well aware of the fraudulent use that is sometimes made of this assistance. One may remember that the military coup d'etat in Niamey in 1974 was justified by the team that then came to power as being a reaction against the wrongdoings of President Hamani Diori's regine. His team had been inundated by outside assistance, whereas he himself had just been in a film to make the Western public aware of the dramatic consequences of lack of rain. He was also head of the Committee of States afflicted by the drought. At a recent trial of the Malien colonels, one of the major reproaches made about one of them concerned the use he made of outside aid for his own personal profit.

The social crisis engendered by the drought was in large part the result of bad political and economic choices made during colonization and after independence. One sees how those choices affected the economic, cultural, and social order. When the drought struck, there was not a sudden catastrophe in 1972, but a progressive worsening starting in 1968. Each year people were more and more deprived and unable to confront it. The drought revealed a certain social, political, and historical evolution. And this history is one of destructive dependence. [1]

From the results of our enquiry, as a permanent organic element of the socioeconomic evolution, migration in Senegal has been affected much more by circumstances than by structural events. Local rural migrations have doubtlessly been subjected most to the unfavorable circumstances. The people seem to have adjusted to this. They have temporarily deserted the affected areas for short periods of time. They have returned to their villages each time that the climatic or material conditions have improved.

On the other hand, traditional migration determined by structured factors have maintained their patterns: intrarural, rural-urban, inter-African, intercontinental. In certain cases the flow has even decreased because of official population-fixing policies. This is the case in the New Lands, in the development of the Senegal river basin, and in the Casamance river basin.

Examination of the migratory phenomenon in Senegal shows very well the political, social, and economic development of the country. Throughout the Dakar study, one can see major stages. In 30 years, migration has seen two high points. These took place well before the drought.

In the 1940s and 1950s, the development of Dakar as an administrative and industrial metropolis of L'Afrique Occidentale Francaise (AOF) needed a sizable labor force. The movements stemmed not only from the Senegalese hinterland, but also from other countries such as the Sudan, Guinea, Dahomey, Togo, Ivory Coast, and so on. One still finds the remnants of communities from these countries that have remained there and settled.

The second period of change due to circumstances occurred around the 1960s. Independence introduced important structural changes: new development policies for rural living, reform of marketing and distribution networks, administrative reform, and so forth. These changes overwhelmed the administrative and economic apparatus. A state bureaucracy expanded to the detriment of numerous activities, particularly commercial ones. This was the beginning of the decline of the towns and of peanut marketing. ONCAD and the Société Nationale de Distribution (SONADIS), in particular, killed the autochthonous trader who would have more difficulty in finding other work than the Lebanese or Syrian or a colonial company. The administration gets the best of the marketing of the peanut harvest.

In the first place, this chapter explains the impact of politics on the migratory movement and also gives information likely to contribute to what is known of the patterns and process of migration. In this respect, it will enable the formation of a more suitable development policy.

MIGRATION TYPOLOGY

It must be pointed out that the question of typology is of considerable interest not only for understanding the migratory process, but particularly for policy formation and for projects that should take into account population movement.

J. L. Amselle, following a certain number of North American and European researchers, reminds us of the broad outlines of the typology most frequently used to classify migration. He has made a close critical analysis of these.[2] They include ancient or archaic migrations, movement of peoples, agricultural migrations, colonization movements, rural migrations, spontaneous migrations, modern migrations, migrations of humanpower, work migrations, urban migrations, and organized, directed, planned, or guided migrations. For our study we needed to define a schema of migrations that attempted to refine these typologies.

The concepts put forward here have been expanded accordingly. They seem to present the facts better for a development strategy in which migrants, particularly in the Sahel, constitute the motor elements. They rejected certain typology terms while stressing others.

As a population distribution process, migration contributes to the socioeconomic whole. Thus each society and economy forges its own migration patterns and structures that differ in space and time. We believe it is of prime importance to distinguish migration that is a result of changed circumstances and that which is structural.

Peasants from Bawol and Kayor, who were previously dedicated to a traditional polyculture, migrated toward the heart of the peanut basin, and later toward the New Lands, and structurally changed the whole local precolonial economy. The space was transformed. Culture and patterns changed. A whole new environment was created. The precolonial economy knew a space-conquest migration: the north-south migration of the river basin (Tekrur), the north-south migration of the Sose-Nominka toward Sin and the Petite Cote, and the east-west migration toward the Atlantic and the trading posts. Quite to the contrary, the sale of the peanut harvest incited a different migratory structure, which translated into a come-and-go, country-town-country movement.

The industrialization of Cap Vert radically changed rural and urban Senegalese life. It has also introduced a structure migration characterized by large and permanent departures from the country and the interior toward an industrial pole in full growth.

This structural break was seen quite clearly between 1950 and 1960, a pivotal period in contemporary Senegalese history. In 1958, the capital was transferred from Saint-Louis to Dakar. This left the former northern city empty. At the same time, it produced a change in the power and economic structures. The 1960 period also marked a new transformation in the migratory process. It will be seen how the country and peanut-marketing towns were abandoned for Dakar and other, secondary, administrative centers.

On the other hand, migration connected with the drought has only increased a preexisting trend. This can be considered as a circumstantial phenomenon or as a circumstantial migration. In general, it was transient.

The distinction between traditional and modern, although this is classic and correct, seems inadequate and ambiguous.

The precolonial economy has produced a migratory schema different from colonial or postcolonial capitalism. In fact, during these periods, the migratory schemas produced splits. Thus the transition from self-sufficient rural and village economy into medieval trading cities has given a distinct significance to the normal migration. There has been a movement from the north toward the south, from the country toward the towns, and so forth. The same phenomenon took place in the colonial period with the attraction the Atlantic coast held.

The contrast between the traditional and modern migrations is interesting. It is not enough to understand the dynamics of successive changes that occurred in the past. This contrast can only be a moment in the structural migration.

The idea of individual and group migration is another real distinction. This includes the movements of individuals caused by reasons varying between looking for work and political exile. It also includes the movement of communities and peoples. The ancient Mandingo migration toward the Petite Cote and those of the Soninke to Paris, of the Mossi toward the south of the Ivory Coast, and the Serer or Jola toward Dakar as a labor force illustrate this.

The migration of nomads to water sources and deep wells can be considered technoeconomic. In the same classification falls the migration connected with shifting slack and burn agriculture.

The notions of spontaneous and organized migrations are equally important for the contemporary economy in order to plan population movements for the distribution of resources and to face and attempt to resolve the problem of under- or overpopulation, of desert encroachment, of abandoned villages, and so on. The migration from Saint-Louis to Dakar, mentioned previously, was organized. So was that of the Libano-Syrians at the beginning of the century, who filled intermediary places in the economy and prevented a national middle class in the countries under French rule.

One can also compare simply spatial or geographical migration with a migration that is spatial but leads to socioeconomic change.

Geographical migration is effectively a simple change in place without a change in the status of the migrant. While a transforming migration implies a change in lifestyle and status, the latter involves a deep transformation. Such is the case of a Bawol-Bawol peasant who comes to the city and becomes a street trader. The one-crop farmer from the peanut basin who changes to growing cotton in Senegal Oriental takes on a more profitable activity under the new circumstances. This transformation is extremely important when considering development projects that require adaptability. The migrant is often obliged to take up an economic position for which he is not generally trained. Thus it is necessary to have a policy of training and education.

The move to the towns often brings with it this transforming migration. The problem is no longer only spatial. We stress this idea of transforming migrations because they seem to us to be worth analyzing.

What do the following three types of migrants have in common? The civil servant or high school graduate from Saint-Louis will leave Saint-Louis for Dakar, either for reasons of education or government. The migration is urban center to urban center and does not involve a big effort. A peasant from Mont Rolland in the Thiès region leaves his village for Dakar with a certificate of primary education. He can no longer live there because he cannot find a salaried job, which his minimal education has led him to expect. The young Serer domestic worker from the Fatick area who has had no education is also obliged to migrate in the dry season. She could equally well have remained in the rural milieu if she had not had economic pressure to leave.

Rural life is such that the town attracts everyone, whatever the immigration type. The solutions to the problems will be different. It is a question of understanding the reasons and the social implications of such migrations and of assessing integration at the various levels of these migrants.

In this way, an analysis of the urban context is made. Migration toward Dakar has an obvious structural dimension. In the 1950s, the industrialization of Cap Vert and the development of peanut growing brought general urban growth. In ten years, the population living in an urban center of more than 10,000 inhabitants increased by 73 percent. It accounted for 30 percent of the total population in 1977, whereas in 1961 it represented only 22 percent. It is estimated that this will reach 40 percent in 1980.[3] Everywhere towns sprang up, stimulated by the peanut marketing. There were secondary sources of migrations. It was a colonial type migration. The capital took the major part, and the trading towns served as backups.

The postcolonial schema after 1960 was characterized by an increase in Dakar's role as the political, economic, and administrative city. The concentration of people became stronger, with the state taking control of the economy. With the disappearance of private peanut marketing and the creation of ONCAD, the rural market towns died. There was no policy to redress the urban balance. A new type of town prefecture was set up to handle the people. And then the town of civil servants (governor, development assistants, prefects, district heads, and various other administrative personnel) replaced the town of peanut traders. The administrative towns developed, and the others decreased with the exception of some that were the centers of big projects (agrobusiness at Richard Toll or Dagana, for example).

MIGRATION TO DAKAR

Urban

The migrant to Dakar can be considered from two viewpoints. He must be placed in relation to the socioeconomic whole, which has changed since independence, and also to a migratory schema deeply affected by the postcolonial political economy.

The socioeconomy was affected three ways. It was dominated by a "socialization," which took over the whole rural economy through the state projects and organizations. The ONCAD cooperatives controlled the peanut production. Société Agricole pour l'Exploitation du Delta du Fleuve Sénégal (SAED), SATEC, and the Société de Développement et de Vulgarisation Agricole (SODEVA) took care of the peasants. Agrobusiness took over the most profitable sectors: BUD-Senegal for market gardening, Compagnie Sucrière Sénégalaise de Mimran, and the Société pour le Développement des Fibres Textiles (SODIFITEX) for cotton. Ranching projects were defined. Fishing, in which the state's hold was less strong, organized cooperatives. The state defined the agricultural colonization on policy: peanut basin, new lands, and so forth. These were the main projects that fashioned production, consumption, and movements of rural life.

It was the end of an intensive industrialization period, polarized on Cap Vert, which affected the migration because of Dakar's attraction. The end of the French West Africa Federation lessened Senegal's influence on the neighboring countries of Mali, Mauritania, and Guinea. The formation of frontiers, even though they were easily crossed, did act as a brake to the flow of humanpower. The migrant tended to find less work and faced unemployment.

The progress of education in the rural areas affected the villages sociologically. They brought up youth who were led at school to expect a future they could not satisfy locally. Youth dreamt of advancement. This led to their massive exodus toward the towns. It accentuated the start of a semi-intellectual subproletariate.

The migratory schema developed. The backup towns for the colonial economy stagnated as Dakar flourished because of the state-controlled "socialist" regime. They no longer had the job opportunities to attract migrants, since the peanut marketing no longer took place there. They yielded their place to new regional submetropolises that were established with administration reform.

Two types of towns were established as poles of attraction: administrative submetropolises, which held the governors, prefects, and so on (one is struck by the recent demographic progress of new administrative centers such as Mbacke and the relative decline of Kaolack at the heart of the peanut trading economy) and centers that harbored mining projects (Taiba) and agricultural projects (Richard Toll, Dagana, Sedhiou, and so on).

Statistics show that, from 1960 on, there was an increase in the migration toward Dakar, which became the focus of political, diplomatic, economic, and cultural power.

The following table shows the growth of the city over nearly 100 years.

Year	Population	Year	Population	Year	Population
1878	1,556	1945	132,000	1972	623,765
1891	8,737	1955	214,000	1973	667,429
1904	18,000	1961	374,000	1974	714,149
1926	33,700	1965	456,999	1975	734,062
1936	92,600	1971	582,958	1976	798,792

The 1970 survey found that 46 percent of Dakar residents had arrived since 1960. The natural growth rate of the city was between 3.7 and 4 percent, the migration rate from 2 to 3 percent; therefore, there was an increase of about 7 percent.

There is no need to give here the history of Dakar, but we must refer to some important dates for the purpose of our study.[4] Before 1800, Cap Vert consisted of a group of fishing villages, which were the heart of the Lebu community. The political influence of this Lebu community is still marked, and they own the major part of this city's land. In 1905, the Government General moved from Goree to the Dakar Plateau. The Lebu population was pushed out, but there are still pockets of them at Mbot, rue Raffenel, Victor Hugo, Carnot,

Assane Ndoye, Felix Faure, and so on. During the plague epidemic of 1915, the government established the Medina to house people leaving the plateau.

The consistent theme in Dakar's growth is successive slum clearances (see Map 9.1). Today, Dakar Plateau remains a European city. After the colonials left, the foreign technical assistants, international officials, diplomats, and expatriate business managers moved into the better residential areas with, here and there, a Senegalese elitist from top government, politics, or business. It must, however, be noted that people of this last sector, outdone only by the Lebanese, are trying more and more to take over the real estate business.

The Lebanese occupy most of the heart of the city. It is the center of commerce. Most of the stores on the main downtown avenues Georges Pompidou and Lamine Gueye belong to this community. They have come a long way from their chawarma stands, which made so much noise during the 1977 electoral campaign. Their territory lies between Avenues Pompidou, Lamine Gueye, and Faidherbe and juts out into the Medina along Avenue Blaise Diagne. It is a district of small storekeepers, overpopulated and badly constructed, which encompasses certain autochthonous pockets such as Mbot.

Most of the Senegalese and Africans spread out from Sandaga Market, where the former European district ends, and extend to Rufisque via Pikine from one shantytown to another. From pockets on the plateau and Rebes, via Société Immobilière du Cap Vert (SICAP) and Habitations à Loyer Modéré (HLM) where they have almost a monopoly, they occupy the Medina, Fass, Gueule Tapee, Grand Dakar, and certain spots of Point E, Bopp, Colobane, Rass mission, Champ de Courses, and so forth. They have a near monopoly on an intermediate outer city band of government subsidized housing, the SICAP and HLM.

Whole districts, former shantytowns and slums, have disappeared: the old Gueule Tapee has been replaced by the new Gueule Tapee where, in 1950, there was the first inexpensive housing in the time of Becher. Alminko, Tiwawoon, Daru xan, Kip Koko, Bay Ley, Waxinan, Angle Mus, Mbod, Bay Gainde, Nimzat, Jamagen, Lamsar, and Kaksaw were also displaced.

It would be interesting to chart intraurban population movements. Individuals are thrown out of overpopulated areas to resettle further out. The Medina was formed in this way in 1915 as were the new Gueule Tapee, HLM at Angle Mousse and Nimzat, and the new industrial zone along the autoroute. The next large-scale operation will be at Rebes and will house the arts center.

MAP 9.1

CAPE VERDE PENINSULA

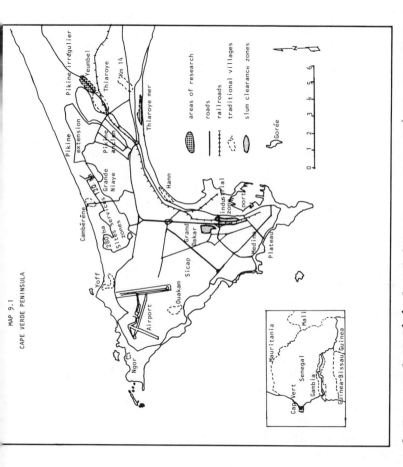

Source: Senegal, Projet Rul-12 Sénégal, L'habitat du grand nombre VI, Sam et Diamagueune-Yeumbel. Habitation et autres équipements (Dakar: IFAN, 1975).

Framework of the Enquiry

The survey was undertaken in greater Dakar, in the nearby suburb of Hann, and at the beginning of the industrial zone. It also included districts a little further away: Diaksaw, Diamagene, Yembel, and Waxinan along the Rufisque road next to the industrial zone after Pikine.

Why were these districts chosen? There were two main reasons. During the last few years, a great number of the poorest slums were torn down. They were replaced by residential developments, industrial zones, and public works. On the whole, they had few or no services. The slums were generally inhabited by migrants with a very mediocre standard of living. We are thinking of Nimzat, Angle Mousse, Waxinan, Diaksaw, and so on. They were inhabited largely by a floating population and were pushed back toward the outskirts and outer suburbs. The relocation of some slum residents was often organized as at Pikine, where the minimum services were supplied to the sites. On the whole, the installation was rudimentary. It constituted what Marc Vernière rightly described as "the pioneer front of natural urbanization."[5] Also, we were interested in two types of areas like Hann and the Yembel area, between Thiaroye and Mbao. The residents picked from these areas came from slum clearance areas of the city, from other areas of the Dakar metropolis, or from the rural or urban interior of Senegal.

Hann

Hann is essentially populated by migrants who have lived in Dakar for quite a long time. The population is heterogeneous and growing, if we may judge by the physical expansion of the area. There is, however, a majority ethnic group in each district, reflecting the migration history. The overpopulated parts burst out so that the districts expanded from time to time.

The type of occupancy varies according to location. There are few here who have title deeds. The government allocation of lots is almost nonexistent. Apart from the industrial installations, we see no trace of government planning or urban development. This little world was created all at once by individuals fleeing the oppression of the city in all its forms: slum clearance, high cost of living, and so on. One could say that there is lamanal law here. The first occupant clears the land and lets it pass on to others. This illegal occupancy in the eyes of the administration finally becomes ratified. All over west Africa there has been an increase in voluntary movement to the edges of the capital cities, particularly since autonomy.

Independence increased it. This corresponds to the development of the structural migration wave defined previously.

The majority of the inhabitants of Hann Plage are from Walo, near Futa. At the beginning, they were employed by the Hann Zoo and Gardens. On retirement, they would have obtained from the colonial administration the right to occupy this land. They were gradually joined by their relatives and friends from their home areas. Despite the present existence of other ethnic groups, they remain the largest. The land there is state land. As we have mentioned, the first occupants redistributed it themselves, largely to members of their own group. Interethnic mixing took place eventually, little by little.

Hann Pecheur is inhabited by Lebu from Thiaroye and the Petite Cote. They came there to fish and returned to their villages in the evening. Gradually they settled there to live for essentially economic reasons—the sea is full of fish and the place is near the city markets. There are other groups: Maures, Jola, Serer, and Lawbe. Their living there used not to be legal, but now the government has recognized it. Hann Pecheur is the oldest district in the area and also the best equipped with community facilities and cement buildings. It has the principal market, the main mosque, the dispensary, and the social center.

Hann Equipe was in the zoo's domain until it was given over to the personnel. They built with their limited means. When the railroad station was constructed, the railroad workers joined them. It is the only district in which the residents have deed titles. The district head must be a former park employee. The district is fairly well-equipped with infrastructures such as water, electricity, and public latrines. There are even septic tanks. The complete primary school is the largest in Hann. The inhabitants dislike the fact that they cannot extend their area because it is surrounded by industrial plants (including the Sibras factory, the new Senegalese printing house, pharmaceutical company, Public Works Laboratory, Société Nationale des Eaux et Electricité du Sénégal [SONEES], and so forth), the railroad, the police department, and so on.

Hann Yenn is divided into Yenn I, Yenn II, and Yenn III and receives the Yenn migrants from the Petite Cote who are involved in fishing. It is an extension of Hann Plage. Situated in the state maritime lands, the housing is illegal. It has very few amenities, no public latrines, and only one public tap. It is surrounded by fishing industries that recruit workers, particularly women.

Hann Montagne covers the largest area and has the densest population. The dominant races are Tukulor and Lebu. There are also communities of Maliens, Guineans, and Voltaics whose delegates help the district head. Here also residence is unofficial. The only ones with title deeds are the industrial plants along the Rufisque road. It is therefore in this area that there are comfortable residences overlooking the beach and the sports clubs (sailing club, and so on).

Hann Marigot was built on a dried-up swamp. Its first residents were seasonal Lebu fishers from Thiaroye and the Petite Cote. They settled at Hann Pecheur because the district was too small for them. No deed titles were given them. Although most of the dwellings were of cement, the public amenities were poor: one sole latrine and a few public taps. The cemetery there is for all the neighboring areas. The second one is at Hann Equipe.

Dalifor is the furthest Hann district from Dakar. It lies between the Rufisque, Camberene, Pikine roads, and the autoroute and dates from about 1950. It is peopled almost entirely by employees of the neighboring agricultural fields, the zoological gardens, and small industries. There are not cement buildings, just shanties. The only water source is a well that the inhabitants dug for themselves. There is no electricity and no public latrine. The only two-class school was built by the residents. The teacher is taken care of by the government.

Yembel

Cap Vert is growing, and the outskirts stretch toward Rufisque. Pikine is the densest and most structured nucleus, but the growth is just as great in the urban fringes, as noted by Vernière.

Yembel began with one Lebu village, which received an increasingly larger migration flow from 1952 onward. The population of Yembel doubled in less than five years and went from 3,368 inhabitants in 1970 to 7,615 in 1975, or more than 14 percent annual increase. This incredible increase is the result of slum clearance in the city of Dakar these last few years. The people earned their living from cultivating the land and raising animals. These two occupations are decreasing in importance.

The Lebu peasants have parcelled out the land and resold it either to people from Dakar or to migrants. Some of their fields were allocated to city dwellers who introduced market gardening, orchards, and animal raising (cattle, chickens, and eggs). It is to be noted that there was not necessarily a deed title with the sale of the land. Much of the land belonged to the state. This sector is mainly occupied illegally, particularly around the Agency for the Security of Air Navigation (ASECNA) and Post Office communications centers, ASECNA Marine Department, and so on. The Pel villagers, who used to live off of their livestock, have relegated it to a secondary activity. There is practically no scrub for grazing.

There is a very strong community of the followers of Iman
Laye, where the lamanal system prevails. This community, most
of whom came from Thiès, were called by the Iman Limamon Laye.
Cramped for space in their compound, they came to settle and have
not stopped growing in number since.

The districts of Waxinan, Diaksaw, and Diamagene have a different occupancy pattern. All the district heads whom we interrogated gave the same cooperative experience. The deed holders all
came from the same unofficial district in Dakar. When, during the
1960s, they were told that they had to move out, they formed a cooperative to purchase land. Here is the experience of Samba Drame,
present delegate of the district of Diamagene.

> I obtained a parcel of land at Ker Baye Gainde in 1958
> and built a hut for my family. Automatically I inte-
> grated into the area. I undertook all the organization
> and participated in the politics until the time when I be-
> came responsible for political work and then became
> the district delegate.
>
> In 1960, it was decided to let us know that the
> district was going to be cleared. At this time, many
> of us did not want to live in Pikine or Guediawaye.
> So, using my political pull, I decided to look for some
> land where our district could be relocated. I contacted
> officials, particularly Lebu, to find some available land.
>
> Thus it was that I was put in contact with the pro-
> prietors of an immense piece of land on the Rufisque
> road. I was shown two pieces, one of 7 hectares and
> 20 ares for the price of 5,307,750 cfa, the other of 4
> hectares for 2,800,000 cfa. I did not have enough
> money to pay this amount myself and held a meeting
> with all the people in my district. I told them of what
> steps I had undertaken and proposed that we establish
> a cooperative. It was the first in Dakar. In joining
> the cooperative, each member had to agree to pay a
> monthly sum of 4,000 cfs or 2,000 cfa for a whole
> year. Once the required sum had been paid, each
> head of family became the owner of a parcel of land
> and holder of an individual deed title. In fact, these
> two pieces of land, which made up the present area of
> Diamagene, had title deed numbers 7798 and 9993. We
> obtained the support of the public authorities.
>
> Out of 998 household heads in Baye Gainde, only
> 454 replied to my appeal, paid their money, and moved
> house with me. After an agreement with the Department

of Urban Planning, access roads were cleared and 454
parcels were laid out and distributed.

This same process of centralized collection of money at the
heart of a buyers' cooperative took place at Tiwawon. Diaksaw and
Lamsar grew up from the same cooperative, founded in 1963. They
bought the land from a Lebanese proprietor.

Thus, from our enquiry, we can affirm that the majority of
these people came from Dakar slums that have been cleared over
the past 20 years. One comes across even the names of former districts in Dakar. Therefore, a good part came from Dakar itself, as
is noticed with an intraurban migration.

These districts cover a big area and offer large land concessions where the modest dwellings are essentially of cement. Although many houses have electricity, not all do, and the water supply is from public taps. Facilities such as schools and dispensary
and social centers are very scarce compared with the population
density.

The Enquiry

The enquiry covered 200 people picked from two districts that
we have designated Zone I (Hann) and Zone II (Yembel) in the following proportions: Zone I, 100 people; Zone II, 100 people, including
38 from Diaksaw, 25 from Diamaguene, 25 from Waxinan, and 12
from Yembel.

The person interrogated had to be the head of a household or
someone with some moral, spiritual, social, or material authority
over the household. The connotation of borom ker (master of the
house) covers this idea quite well. In any case, the people understood very well whom to designate as the person we should question.

The sample of 200 people was spread into 120 men and 80
women, all considered as heads of households.

Of these household heads, 151 were the father or the husband
(81 people) or the mother or wife (70 people). The women's authority over the household is considerable. It is almost as great as the
men's. It is true that in these districts, notably in Hann, women
are paid workers. Many of them work in the fishing sector, either
in the lighter work (such as selling the fish in the markets or drying
and smoking fish) or in the industrial part (canning factories). In
the agricultural sector, they have almost a monopoly on the sale of
flowers along the main boulevards of the capital.

One quarter of the sample, 49 people, were children (42) or
other relatives (7). Other relatives would be a brother, cousin, or

so on, who played a predominant economic or social role in the household. This role was most often economic, with the other family members being under his financial care.

A little more than 50 percent of the people were between 25 and 50 years old, that is, 38 people between 25 and 30, 37 between 31 and 40, and 31 between 41 and 50. Forty-two people were under 25, and 52 were over 50.

Of course, the sample was essentially Senegalese: 187 out of 200, 94 percent. The others were Mauritanian (1), Guinean (5), Malian (1), or Voltaic (1).

The majority ethnic group was Wolof-Lebu (82). The others were Tukulor-Pel (48), Serer (26), from the Casamance (Manjack, Jola) (14), from Senegal Oriental (Konagi, Basari) (1), from the Manding group (Sose, Bambura, Malinke) (16), Soninke, Saraxulle (8), Maure (4), and Mossi (1). It is surprising that only one Maure declared himself as being of Mauritanian nationality. This was a Hassania Maure, still called a white Maure. The others were black Maures who had lived in Dagana and Kayor and claimed Senegalese nationality.

One hundred ninety-five of our subjects were Muslim. The five Christians belonged to the group from the Casamance. We noticed that the followers of the Tijanya brotherhood were the most numerous. They represented 56 percent of the sample, 112 people. The others were Mourides (37), Xadrya (34), followers of Iman Laye (10), and no brotherhood (2). The Laye followers were concentrated at Yembel (7 out of 10).

Of the people interrogated, 76.5 percent (153) were married, 18.5 percent unmarried (37), 2.5 percent widowed, and 2.5 percent divorced. Forty-one percent were polygamous (82 people, 55 of whom were bigamous and 27 polygamous).

Education, Profession, and Employment

The level of education was generally low, but it was higher than the national average. The following table indicates educational levels, number of people, and percentage of people.

No education	58	29.0
Koranic school (no reading or writing of Arabic)	45	22.5
Reading and writing Arabic	30	15.0
Apprenticeship of a trade without schooling	1	0.5
Some years of primary school	26	13.0
Certificate of primary education	13	6.5

Some years of secondary school	21	10.5
BEPC*	3	1.5
Terminal class level	1	0.5
Others	2	1.0
Totals	200	100.0

*Brevet des Etudes du Premier Cycle

This means that 67 percent had not been to French school, which is still the yardstick for education. Few interesting jobs are available to those who lack the imprimatur of a French education. The districts of Hann and Yembel were not unusual in this aspect. These districts were all as underprivileged as each other so far as educational facilities and the quality of education are concerned. The quality of schooling in the home villages of the migrants is barely better. Only 19.5 percent had been to primary school, which is the most common level of education among the Senegalese.

Level of education more or less determines the level of professions and employment.

Hann and Yembel are located in the industrial suburbs. Hann is right in the heart of the industrial zone and Yembel on its outskirts. The work opportunities are therefore relatively high, although for subordinate positions. As an offshoot to this salaried workpower, there is a growth of small jobs due to the urban network and its constant increase.

Thus, almost 36.5 percent of the people sampled were without a profession or were retired, and many of them, as we will see later, came to join these peripheral districts only on retirement. They bought either a parcel of land or a house, unless they built it themselves. Most of them had lived in Dakar. On retiring, the government slum clearance policy of recent years and the high cost of living forced them to leave the center of the capital or nearby districts.

There were five fishermen, all from Hann. The only farmer we interrogated lived in Yembel, right near the fields.

In small commerce, there were 8 with middle-sized trading jobs or boutiquiers and 23 market vendors or people with stalls. These grew from the usual kind of small commerce found in low-income areas.

The neighboring factories did not account for a large number of jobs. Only 47 people, or 23.5 percent of the sample, said they were small employees of business and industry (22), middle personnel, that is, office employees, bookkeepers, and so forth (5), skilled workers or foremen (14), or average workers (6). It is true that the survey did not specify those who worked or did not work in the industrial zone. However, 19 people were classified as service personnel: messengers, watchmen, domestic personnel, and so forth. The only details were that 41 people, or 20.5 percent of the sample, were employed in industry or private business, whereas only 4 worked for the state. Moreover, when interrogated about the location of their work, 68 people, or 34 percent of the sample, affirmed that they worked in the district they lived in (25), in a neighboring district (14), or at the heart of the industrial zone (29).

Among the other professions, there were 12 artisans. These were tailors, jewelers, woodcarvers, weavers, mechanics, and so forth. There was also one policeman. Five marabouts replied positively to the category of "occupations linked with Islam."

Some first conclusions can be made from the data that follow. For our sample, one head of household out of two had a paid occupation. There was very little difference between one district and another. The fact that Hann was in the industrial zone gave it a slight advantage over Yembel and the neighboring districts, but not a great one.

Thus, out of 41 people working in private trade and industry, 27 lived in Hann and 14 in Yembel. Likewise, out of 102 people without a profession or employment, 43 were in Hann and 59 in Yembel. Out of 38 who said they were unemployed, 11 lived in Hann and 27 in Yembel. Out of 74 with permanent work, 41 came from Hann and 33 from Yembel.

From this, it can be deduced that the fact that Hann is in the center of the area does not mean that any more people from there are employed, although it does have a slight advantage in this respect over Yembel.

Data on employment—sector, location, and length of time—are presented in number of people and percent of sample.

Are you
employed by the government	4	2.0
employed in industry or private business	41	20.5
employed by an individual (domestic or agricultural work)	3	1.5
self-employed	50	25.0
without a profession, without employment, or retired	102	51.0
Totals	200	100.0

Main work situation
unemployed, out of work	38	19.0
day workers	10	5.0
permanently employed	73	36.5
seasonally employed	3	1.5
job worker, occasional worker	12	6.0
without profession or retired	64	32.0
Totals	200	100.0

Length of time in present situation

less than one year	7	3.5
1-3 years	16	8.0
3-5 years	16	8.0
5-7 years	14	7.0
7-10 years	10	5.0
more than 10 years	35	17.5
without work, without a profession, or retired	102	51.0
Totals	200	100.0

Income

As often happens with enquiries on income, it is not always easy to obtain replies, and those that are received are not entirely satisfactory. Information on occasional income for the period is misleading so far as the household heads are concerned. It is also difficult to have them assess both their own income, except in the case of the regular monthly employee, and the financial contribution of other members of the household.

Often, any declaration of income is inaccurate unless it is at least partially corrected by a detailed analysis of corresponding expenditures. It is very generally underestimated, and sometimes people try to exaggerate their importance by overestimating their incomes.

In view of these considerations, we thought it worthwhile and prudent to interrogate on details of the type of money coming into the household and from where it came.

Out of 200 people, 96, or 48 percent of the sample, stated they had a fixed monthly income corresponding to a salary. The scale of salaries went from 15,000 to 70,000 cfa per month. Thirty-one, or 15.5 percent, had a quarterly income corresponding to a pension or retirement allowance. The highest was 70,000 cfa and the lowest 14,470 cfa. The average was around 40,000 cfa per quarter.

Other income was spread between daily worker pay (35 or 17.5 percent) and weekly worker pay (5 or 2.5 percent). Thus, 83.5 percent of the sample declared an income, whereas 16.5 percent or 33 people were considered "without income."

The same kind of enquiry, done by NEDECO in 1969[6] and BCEOM in 1971, on the heads of households in illegal districts of the city of Dakar, gave 90 percent of the people with an income and 10 percent without. Even though there was a difference of several years between the enquiries, they show the disparity of income between Dakar and its suburbs. The city offers more potential for income.

To the question "Have you any other income?" 75.5 percent (151 people) replied "no." The 24.5 percent with affirmative replies related to monthly (33), quarterly (15), occasional (4), and daily income (22), income from rent (14), family allowances (10), pension or retirement pay (5), farming (2), and business (1). There were multiple replies. The type and source of income varied for one person.

But, of 200 households, 142 had one or several people apart from the household head who had paid employment, 78 households had one other, 63 had from 2 to 5 other people, and 2 had more than 5 other people. Most were the spouse (64 people), brothers or sisters (43), children (30), parents (25), cousins, nephews, or nieces (23), and more distant relatives (5). All contributed to the household expenses.

We must call attention here to one of the characteristics of African societies. There is not necessarily a correlation between employment or occupation and income. A good number of people receive incomes from a working father, mother, uncle, or other relative, the result of strong family ties in Africa.

Here is a table of the professions of the members of the households who have paid occupations. (The numbers reflect multiple replies.)

Middle-level public workers (teachers, nurses, office workers, bookkeepers, and so on)	14
Farmers and market gardeners	3
Fishers	7
Middle-level business managers, shopkeepers	8
Artisans (tailors, jewelers, woodcarvers, mechanics, weavers)	34
Skilled workers, foremen	17
Average worker	10
Apprentices, agricultural hands	2
Small office and business workers (secretaries, sales representatives, and so on)	42
Market vendors	32
Service personnel (domestic workers, maids, messengers, and so on)	30
Nonclassified (soldiers, police)	9
Others	6
Type of work unknown	30

Migration

In our sample of 200 people, 54 (27 percent) are not migrants. They were born in the capital. This denotes the importance of migration in the formation of these districts, because 73 percent (146 people) came from other regions and countries outside Senegal.

Here are their places of origin.

Cap Vert	15
Fleuve region	26
Thiès region	25
Senegal Oriental region	5
Casamance region	13
Diourbel region	22
Sine-Saloum region	15
Louga region	10
Other African countries	15
Total	146

The greatest number of migrants come from the Fleuve Valley. Abdoulaye Diop pointed out, in 1960, that there are 50,000 of these migrants in Dakar, "representing the second largest ethnic group after the Wolof. Their immigration dates back a long way; in 1926, out of a population of 40,000 people, there were 3,500 Toucouler. The 1955 census found 25,000: 12.4% of the whole of the African population. "[7]

The proximity of the Thiès region makes Dakar its natural outlet. It is not surprising that 25 people were found to come from this region. Then come the migrants from other areas of the peanut basin, Dourbel (22 people), and Sine-Saloum (15).

If we exclude the 15 West African migrants, of whom 7 said they had Senegalese nationality, there remain 131 people of local stock. More than half of them (54 percent, 71 people) were of rural origin. Seventeen came from villages in the Fleuve basin, 15 from Cap Vert villages, 12 from Thiès, 7 from Casamance, 7 from Diourbel, 7 from Louga, and 6 from the Sine-Saloum. The other 60 came from urban origin: 15 from Diourbel, 13 from Thiès, 9 from the Fleuve, 9 from the Sine-Saloum, 6 from Casamance, 5 from Senegal Oriental, and 3 from Louga. Here again we encounter the migration process, the rural exodus to the regional capitals and secondary towns, which are stepping stones toward Dakar. The population growth rate for these towns is not much less than that for Dakar. It is increasing at the rate of between 5 and 7 percent for the regional capitals and of about 4.5 percent for the secondary towns.

The table of migration data is significant. In fact, 123 people (61.5 percent of the total of the sample and 84 percent of the migrants) have been settled in Dakar for more than ten years. The others have lived there for periods of from 8 to 10 years (4 people),

5 to 8 years (7), 3 to 5 years (4), 1 to 3 years (6), and less than one year (2 people). There seems to have been a fresh outbreak of migration between 1970 and 1973. This took place during the drought and seemed small, compared with the structural migration flow.

Occupations in the place of origin, whether rural or urban, are related to the rural tradition. The people we questioned were farmers (65), fishers (8), traders (5), and artisans (3). Few had a salaried job; we counted only one worker and one employee. Thirty-five people who had left the countryside at a very young age were still mostly students of the Koranic school or at French school.

These occupations correspond to those encountered by J. Roch in the study of dry-season economic migrations in the Senegalese peanut basin. Roch stated, "Dry season migration affected numerous peasants who had no education and very little qualifications who came to the capital to compete in the employment market." He mentions four categories of occupations, in which ours are classified: solely agricultural work, predominantly agricultural work with a permanent secondary occupation in the village (artisan, small trade, and so on), rainy season agricultural work and looking for extra income from seasonal exodus or with a secondary occupation in the village even in the dry season, and nonagricultural work in the towns and larger villages (artisans, peddlers, small traders, and so on). [8]

On the whole, the exodus is linked with the search either for extra income or simply for income. The reasons are economic and professional. Out of 200 replies, 72 ascertain this, stating that it is a question of migrations and of humanpower. "My parents cultivated the fields and this brought in nothing."—"I came to Dakar to look for work."—"I came here to learn a trade."—"I came to work."—"I worked with Americans in Kaolack when I arrived from Upper Volta. When they went to Dakar, I followed them."—"I was a seasonal worker. I used to come to Senegal often, then one day I decided to stay here permanently."—"When I finished my military service, I stayed on in Dakar to work."

Samir Amin made a distinction between these work-oriented migrations of people, which "in the new colonization areas led to establishing total, structured and organized societies." [9]

Fifty-five replies gave family reasons. "We joined my father in Dakar."—"I came to be with my husband."—"I got married in Diourbel and followed my husband to Dakar."—"I am with my mother in Dakar."—"For family reasons."

Eighteen people pointed out that they came to Dakar to further their education. For many years, only Dakar and Saint-Louis had primary and secondary school systems. The high schools in the regional capitals are a recent innovation. Technical and professional schools were rare. Another reason was the medical facilities. The quality of these services outside the capital left much to be desired.

The wish to settle in Dakar was relevant. Out of 200 people, 141 (70.5 percent) wanted to settle permanently in the capital. Only 16 wanted to return to their birthplace, whereas another 9 would like to do so under certain conditions: better homes, work, and so on.

The links between Dakar and the other regions remain strong, even if permanent return to the home country is not particularly desired. Thus people return home: regularly, several times per year (32); quite often, one, two, or three times a year (62); rarely, every two, three, four, or five years (14); very rarely, no details given (16); never (22); or say there is no reason to, nor to Dakar (54). The reasons for returning show that migration is irreversible.

For these long-term migrants, returning in the rainy season to plant crops is no longer continued. Only 3 people out of 200 kept to it.

A strong social reason motivates people. Seventy-four percent of the sample (148 people) went to visit relatives or to attend family ceremonies (deaths, baptisms, marriages, and so forth). The religious element can be considered a social principle. The way of life of the brotherhoods is filled with events that frequently bring together the talibes of the community. Religious chants and ziara (massive gatherings to pay homage) are the foci of a distinctive social milieu around the marabout. Twenty-four people in our sample pointed to this occurrence very clearly.

"To carry messages, to take care of personal problems, because of homesickness"—these are the other reasons for returning home.

Dakar Living

Districts such as Hann and Yembel have grown up out of small traditional villages. Dakar's increase in size has led to these districts increasing also.

Sixteen of the people interrogated were born in these districts; 97 out of the 200 had lived there for longer than ten years. This means that 113 people (56.5 percent of the sample) had been residents for a long time. Forty-one people had lived there between 5 and 10 years. Only 46 people (23 percent) had fewer than 5 years of residence, or 3-5 years (19 people), from 1-3 years (17), less than one year (9), and there was one temporary resident. One might think that the heaviest time of arrivals coincided with the establishment of the district between 1960 and 1968 and corresponded to the times of biggest immigration. Thus, when asked why they had come to the district, the replies given gave the real situation.

Sixty-seven people (33.5 percent) came to join their family, relatives, friends, or acquaintances. In fact, generally one emigrates toward the places where one already has connections.

Sixty-two people (31 percent) acquired a personal house. We have seen that some retired people left the center of town to come and settle in the outlying districts such as Hann or Diamaguene and Yembel. So one hears this kind of thing: "I am in my own house."—We bought a house to live in peace with the family."—"Before I rented a house, now I am a homeowner."

Twenty-five people (12.5 percent) came because of slum clearance where they had been. Here there is a clear distinction between Hann and Yembel. Out of 25 people who had been forced out, only two were in Hann. The others were in the Yembel area, which grew considerably with the clearance programs. We should point out that we did not ask a specific question on slum clearance. However, some people who had been forced out of slums gave as their reason for settling in the district the fact that they could own their own houses there.

Other motives for moving were professional (16 people) and economic (lower rent, better or more accessible lifestyle) (11 people).

Twenty-two people had always lived in the district either because they were born there or else because this was their first residence in Dakar. Here we must point out that the spatial mobility of these people is substantial. In fact, only 60 people had never moved house. The others, that is, 140 people (70 percent) had moved at least once (72 people), twice (27), three times (20), four times (12), five or more times (9). The most usual practice was to have changed residences once, a corollary to intraurban migration.

This plan is well-illustrated here. It is twofold. There is a movement from the country toward the urban peripheries. There is a second movement, which here seems to be the largest. It goes toward the center of the city of Dakar. Then, little by little, the extension of the city means people are more or less thrust out to the urban fringes. The projectory of urban dwelling is centripetal rather than centrifugal. The center of Dakar is not really the plateau but the extensions around this plateau.

And so, while 40 people arrived, just before settling into these districts, from the interior of Senegal or elsewhere in Dakar or by direct migration, 134 people (67 percent) had already lived in Dakar in other districts, as illustrated below. The figures are for number of people and percentage of sample.

Dakar plateau	6	4.5
Dakar center (Rebes, Niaye Tioker, Credit Foncier, and so on)	12	1.5

Extension (Medina, Gueule Tapee, Colobane, Fass, Rass Mission, and so on)	18	13.5
Grand-Dakar, Usine Bene Tali, Niari Tali, and so on	19	14.0
HLM-SICAP	2	1.5
Slum clearance districts (Alminki, Angle Mouss, Nimzat, Champ de courses, Bay Gainde, Waxinan, Bay Lay, Diaksaw, Lonsar, Darou Xan, and so on)	46	34.0
Suburbs (Hann, Pikine, Guediawaye, Thiaroye, Grand Yoff, and so on)	41	31.0
Totals	134	100.0

Slum clearance programs (39 people) and moving into one's own house (43 people) were also main reasons given for leaving the district. "We were renting lodging at Gueule Tapee."—"Because of slum clearance."—"We were relocated."—We were forced out because of the building of Lycee Kennedy."—"I had my own house."—"I built my own house."—"I bought a house in the district." People were cleared out of districts to make room for Dakar housing projects such as SICAP, HLM, industrial zone, and so on.

Family ties were very strong. People went to join a relative (25 people). As stated by J. M. Gibbal for Abidjan, one rarely lives on one's own. "Family, village and ethnic ties are still the only real social factors that are strongly adhered to." "I moved house with my uncle."—"My father had bought a house here."—"My brother put me up."—"I joined the family home."—"I am an only son and I prefer to be with my relatives."—"I live with my relatives to help them out."

Bad financial conditions were evident. "Rent was high."—"I didn't have enough money."—"I was only a tenant."

Bad financial conditions mean bad material conditions (13 people), which is the fate of the populous districts of Dakar that have few amenities. "My house was small."—"There wasn't enough room for my family."—"The district was dirty."—"Living conditions were not good. We were often flooded."—"There were no public latrines." One wonders whether these poor conditions improved in the new locations.

In the majority of cases (68 percent), the type of housing is a compound, incorporating several buildings, against only 32 percent with just one building. There is a distinct difference between Hann and Yembel. In Hann, our sample gave 85 compounds with several buildings and 15 with only one. At Yembel, on the other hand, the distribution was more even: 51 compounds with several buildings and 49 with one.

This structure of a multiple-building compound is traditional in agrarian Senegalese societies. As Paul Pélissier described so well, "The main element is what is called the keur. The translation of this as 'family dwelling' and particularly 'house' does not explain its structure and composition well enough because it is made up of buildings of only one room, separate from each other and it includes not only the buildings but also the space between them. One is thus obliged to render it (and not only for the Wolof areas) in the French-African vernacular as 'concession' (compound) or 'carre.'"[10]

In this traditional compound are grouped the same family community, "the dimension . . . and the number of dwellings in it depends on the size of the family it houses."[11] Thus several generations live together in the same area. At the present time, in the towns, the compound system continues. But it can bring together people who don't know each other and are united only because of location.

Of the dwellings occupied, 69.5 percent are made of cement and only 27.5 percent of wood. There are a few cement/wood combinations (2.5 percent) and one straw hut was mentioned. What started as temporary and spontaneous had become permanent. Already, in the spontaneously created districts of Dakar, "in almost all cases (98%) houses were made of wood, not cement, but nor were they made of banco, corrugated iron or other scrap material. In this respect the shanty towns of Dakar are not comparable to the slums or shanty towns so frequently found elsewhere in the world. The housing is generally able to be dismantled; this was the case for more than half those who in the past resettled in the Pikine extension."[12]

As in the unofficial districts just mentioned, from which a large part of our families come, for more than half (53.5 percent) the housing consisted of from one to three rooms; that is, for 9.5 percent one room, for 19.5 percent two rooms, and for 24.5 percent three rooms. We observe here a great discrepancy in the number of rooms: 46.5 percent of the housing had four rooms and more; that is, 16 percent four rooms, 16.5 percent five rooms, and 14 percent more than five rooms. Therefore, the accommodation was quite spacious. It is true that the plots of land were small at Hann where the population is more dense, whereas at Yembel the average was from 150 to 200 square meters.

The report of the Senegal project Rul-12 on the life of the majority in Sam, Diamaguene, and Yeumbeul[13] indicates that the architecture of the buildings conforms to a plan type.[14] Whether they have two or five rooms and whatever dimensions they have, there is the same space plan: a row of rooms opening onto a courtyard between two store rooms.

As also mentioned in the Senegal project Rul-12, water supply is a problem. There are very few private installations since the cost is so expensive in relation to the inhabitants' finances. Over our whole sample, only one person in Hann said he had an individual water faucet, and this was in the courtyard of the compound, not in the house.

The most usual source of water was the public tap. Generally this supplies a distance of $\pm$ 100 meters under the best circumstances. One hundred eighty-five people (92.5 percent) stated they received their water in this way.

There were also wells that were the source of water in the outlying areas too far out for public taps. These were used by 7 percent of the sample.

When there was electricity, it was above all for lighting up the large public roads. Sixty-nine people (34.5 percent of the sample) used it for their own lighting. The others used kerosene lamps (108 people), candles (22 people), and butane gas lamps (1 person).

The discussion of land tenure in the introduction to this chapter indicates the type of land use found in this neighborhood. The introduction gives details of land occupancy. The breakdown of occupancy of the household heads follows, in number of people and percentage of sample.

Proprietors and coproprietors	69	34.5
Tenants and subtenants	27	13.5
Lodgers	104	52.0
Totals	200	100.0

Sixty-nine people (34.5 percent) said they owned their own houses and land. For some parcels of Diamaguene or Yembel and Hann Equipe, the owners, as we have seen, held title deeds. For others, there as well as in Hann, the occupants said they were proprietors. In fact, they got their land free or for some payment. This payment would be in the form of dues that gave them the right to settle in the compound. The same practice is found in other extralegal districts of Dakar.

Out of these 69 people, 34 obtained their land free or by acquisition. The donors were, let us remember, the family, the head of the district or of the community, the employer, or the state. Thirty-three people bought their property, and two obtained it by an exchange. For these 33, 24 were in Yembel and 9 in Hann. This proportion reflects the appropriate property structure of the two districts. The cost of the plots of land was generally less than 200,000 cfa. We should also remember that a certain number of proprietors belonged to purchasing cooperatives in order to acquire their land from individuals or from the state.

One hundred thirty-one people (65.5 percent of the people interrogated) did not own either house or land.

A minority of 27 people (13.5 percent) leased or subleased their houses. They paid rent, generally less than 5,000 cfa. This was the case of 23 people out of the 27. These rents varied between 5,000 and 7,000 cfa for two people. Only one tenant paid rent between 7,000 and 10,000 cfa. It must be noted that this price, which may seem to be modest for the city of Dakar, weighs quite heavily on a family budget with such a low and often irregular income.

More than half the sample (52 percent, 104 people) paid money for their keep to the family. Here we have a good example of the ties in the urban milieu. We have already noted that family and group ties are still extremely strong. The replies confirm this: "I was ill, I was brought to Dakar for medical care. Since in Dakar my brother was making a good living, I thought it worth staying."— "I came to join my older brother."—"I was a seasonal worker. I was always coming to Dakar. Then one day I decided to stay for good. And so the family took me in."—"I moved in with my father."— "I lived with my uncle."—"Most of the heads of family have retired. They live with their children who help them."

It is important to define the relation between the residence and the place of work. In these outlying districts, the place of residence affects the opportunities for work as well as where one works. For everyone with or without a salaried occupation at the time of the enquiry, or 98 people out of 200, only 8 worked in the center of Dakar and another 8 in the outlying districts such as the Medina, the SICAPS, or Point E. All other work was located in the area of enquiry.

To the question, "Is your district far from your place of work?" the replies were: yes, 38 people; no, 60; unemployed, 102.

The center of Dakar holds an attraction for all Dakarois, but this did not hold true here. In this connection, public transportation was only used to a limited extent for getting to work. Fares would add to budgets that were already stretched to the limit. Each Société de Transport en Commun (SOTRAC) bus trip costs 40 cfa.

Out of 98 people with paid work, 15 were not affected because they worked in their own homes: artisans, people with small boutiques, retailers, small-scale mechanics, and so on. Forty-nine people walked to work, whereas 18 took the car rapides (small communal buses), 12 used SOTRAC buses, and only 4 used transportation supplied by their place of work. It must be noted that the car rapides belong to private Senegalese. They run more often on the bus routes and cost a few centimes less than the state SOTRAC buses. These car rapides have regular routes. They serve the outlying districts and link them with the city of Dakar over certain routes. They are not allowed on the plateau.

The place of work seemed to have an effect on where meals were taken. The noon meal was usually taken at home. One had the time to get there. Whether one worked or not, this was the case for 174 people out of 200. The others either brought their lunch and ate it at work (7 people) or at the work's canteen (2 people). Nine went to restaurants or eating places called gargottes (cheap restaurants). In this category fall the people who ate very inexpensive meals prepared by women who came to work sites or to the factory gates. Three people are with relatives or friends, whereas two others went without this meal. The remaining three people ate here and there, without any fixed pattern.

Food supplies, medical care, and education present primordial infrastructure problems for a district. Our interrogees did not hesitate to mention these during group meetings and individually on the questionnaires.

For supplies, each district had its own small market with stalls carrying very basic foods. A bigger market with more variety served several districts. Small boutiques generally held by Moor or Tukulor sold grocery products (milk, rice, sugar, oil, canned goods, fish, and so on), hardware, drugstore items, haberdashery, stationery, and so on. Goods are sold in the smallest amounts, which is what the local inhabitants require. Thus a packet of sugar, a can of tomato paste, a packet of butter, cigarettes, needles, or a liter of oil are broken down. One can buy a quarter liter of oil for 50 cfa (one liter costs 200 cfs), a tablespoonful of tomato paste for 25 cfa, 4 or 5 lumps of sugar for 5 cfa, 2 Camelia cigarettes or a needle for 5 cfa.

The Moors or Tukulors also extend credit. Debts are settled weekly or monthly. Depending on the amount of trust, homemakers would even give them their monthly housekeeping money to keep. They come each morning and take the amount they need for market that day. Thus they are sure they do not waste their budget, and the storekeeper has money for his own stock of goods.

SONADIS is a higher class store that does not sell items in such small amounts, nor does it extend this credit. At an even higher level, there is the large supermarket type store, located in the center of the city. This is directed toward a generally more affluent clientele.

Replies to the question, "Where do you usually buy your monthly food?" suggest that in most cases shopping was done in the same district, at the nearest boutique and market. One went farther afield only rather exceptionally. The big stores drew practically no one. The low level of income did not enable them to shop there regularly. Some replies mentioned a cooperative. It is worth mentioning that there are business cooperatives that supply their employees with

basic products such as rice, milk, oil, and sugar at the same price
as in the large stores. The only advantage is that they are supplied
on credit. But this only applies to salaried workers.

Markets in the center of the capital supplied the suburban
areas with manufactured products and fresh food: fish, meat, fruit,
and, to a lesser degree, vegetables, because this is in the middle
of the market garden area. A reselling system exists toward the
outer suburbs. It means that the prices in these outer places are
much higher. It is therefore worthwhile for consumers to go to
Dakar for big shopping. Since these occasions are rare, they only
affect a small minority.

Supply sources were divided among the people in our sample,
who gave multiple replies, as follows.

The local Maure boutique	163
Local market	105
Local store, SONADIS	32
Company cooperative	18
Store outside the district	17
Market outside the district	14
Dakar markets	12
Big stores (Score, Supermarché)	2
Unspecified	13

Medical facilities in Hann and Yembel are very clearly insufficient. Hann is served by two dispensaries. They are in Hann
Pecheur and Hann Equipe. They hold consultations for all the other
districts.

Yembel has a municipal dispensary with a nurse and a medical
assistant. Very basic care is given there. It covers all of Yembel
and seven nearby villages: Thiaroye Kaw, Thiaroye Gare, Touba
Thiaroye, Guediawaye, Malika, Pikine, and Ker Massar. There
has been a maternity center since 1975. This also covers the large
area of Yembel, Thiaroye Kaw, Malika, Ker Massar, Guediawaye,
Pikine, Thiaroye sur Mer, Diaksao, Diamaguene, and Wakhinane.
As mentioned in Rul-12 report, "Having people come from other localities for care at the Yembel dispensary does not rule out movement in the other direction for treatment of certain illnesses needing
specialist care. On this subject, it must be noted that for treatment
of most of the young children the village goes to the Notre Dame du
Cap Vert dispensary located at the southern entrance to Pikine."[15]
Thus, due to not having appropriate medical care, people go to other
nearby areas or to Dakar, either to private or government centers.
There are no prenatal and baby clinics in the two districts. Works'
dispensaries provide a limited amount of medical care.

Replies to the question, "Where do you take your family for medical treatment when necessary?" give a good picture of the situation of existing medical facilities. Here is a table giving the answers, by number of responses; multiple replies were possible.

Dakar Hospital	131
Local dispensary	129
Local healer, marabout	64
Dispensaries in the center of Dakar	35
Work dispensaries	25
Private doctor	14
Antinatal and baby care clinics in Dakar	4

Dakar hospitals were the most frequently used for medical care. Three hospitals serve the Fann area. The main one, Savorgnan de Brazza Hospital, is the best equipped of them all. It is a military hospital that is still run by the French. The Aristide Le Dantec Hospital and the Fann Psychiatric Hospital are university hospitals. Their excellent medical personnel is made up of hospital interns, doctors, and teaching professors, but equipment is sadly lacking. In this connection, government redevelopment and financing projects have been established these last few years. The Dakar dispensaries and work dispensaries also receive patients, but these are a minority, like those who attend private doctors.

During the last year, our interviewees stated they had consulted a doctor for illness in the following fields: general medicine, 90; gynecology, 19; surgery, 19; pediatrics, 7; others (sight, fractures, mental illness, and so on), 15; or they did not see a doctor, 61.

We must note that 61 people out of 200, or nearly one-third of the sample, did not see any doctor during the whole year. This does not mean that the suburban residents were in good health, but rather that health services were insufficient. More medical visits would come with better facilities.

When ill, people also went to local healers. During the past years, 64 people out of 200 (32 percent) said they had turned to traditional medicine. This applied to children's illnesses, intestinal problems, headaches, and chest aches, as well as to mental illnesses. There is not room here to give in detail the curative or preventive remedies of traditional medicine and pharmacopea. We will just stress that they are still often used for many cases, to the extent that people have more confidence in them than in Western medicine.

Education is one of the most important problems that the migrants in the urban milieu have to solve. Already, in the rural

areas, the increase in primary education is being blamed—rather
than the rural exodus—because it raises the hopes of youth. "School
produces unemployment and migration."[16] The idea that education
is a factor in the progress and improvement of living standards can
sometimes appear illusory. In any case, it has created large consumer needs in African countries. So one faces two problems: that
of the amount of schools and that of the types of schools and kinds of
education.

The facilities are clearly insufficient. Only one primary
school with 14 classes has been operating since 1934 for the whole
Yembel area. It takes students from the neighboring villages:
Yembel, Thiaroye Gare and Kaw, Pikine, Malika, Waxinan, Toube
Thiaroye, Hann, Diaksaw, Diamaguene, Ker Massar, and even
Dakar. The limited number of places cannot meet the demand and
means that parents must either give up the idea of entering their
children there or put them in other schools. For the whole of Hann,
there are only three schools.

Schooling's relation to the social, political, professional, and
cultural organization becomes more and more critical in these suburbs because of the dual educational system. The conventional education is Western, and one notices a deep gap between what is taught
at school and through everyday life. This is aggravated by the fact
that schooling is given in a non-African language and springs from a
different culture.[17]

F. Flis-Zonabend undertook a survey in 1962 at the Delafosse
technical lycee, showing that the majority of students came from the
Dakar area and, to a lesser extent, from the neighboring regions of
Diourbel and Thiès. "The geographical origins determine the inequalities in the opportunities for secondary education and significantly influence how the students adapt to school."[18] Likewise, the
material conditions of a financially insecure life do not favor success at school. We found the following influences on the academic
levels of the children surveyed (multiple replies possible).

No children or none of school age	75
Children of school age not at school	27
Children in school at primary level	77
Children in school at secondary level	22
Children at technical or professional school	5
Children at university	2
Children at Koranic school	12
Children serving apprenticeships	12

As the level of schooling rises, the number of students attending lowers. Only two people had children at university. The obliga-

tory education is, however, fulfilled. Many children of primary school age go to school. Moreover, our survey showed that 141 people (70.5 percent) of the sample who had children of school age did send them to school. When they did not go to school, it was because they were poor students, according to 24 replies. There were no complaints that the school was too far away, nor that it was not worthwhile. In fact, mostly they said there was no room (14 replies), the child was too old (10 replies), first they had to go to Koranic school (9 replies), educational expenses were difficult to meet (5 replies), or that enrollment documents were difficult to obtain (3 replies). A second question on dropping out of school indicated that mediocre grades led to retaking a class, which led to being sent away (46 replies).

To the question, "What career would you like for your children?" many opted for something in the city: middle-level civil servant (10 replies), high government official (37), top-level work in the private sector (12), and office worker (6). No one mentioned a trade, and only seven suggested a manual worker. Here we see the influence of academic teaching to promote the contemporary elite in the guise of the white-collar worker.

Because education is not designed specifically for the African way of life, national officials have been encouraged to look for new formulas. So Senegal has established the enseignement moyen pratique program, to provide vocational training for school leavers. It is not without its own problems. This program tends to seek a solution for the 80 percent who drop out of the Senegalese primary school. An evaluation of the project at this stage would be more than worthwhile. A major criticism is that the practical education does not attempt to change the fundamental education system, which is the root of the problem. It is an effort to patch up the homes. In these set societies of West Africa, totally new perspectives are taking place.

Studies undertaken in West Africa in recent years have often posed the problem of adjusting to city life in terms of those living on the fringes and underintegrated urban growth.[19]

This living on the fringes of town illustrates the relationship between the urban extensions and one city center, which serves as a frame of reference, whereas the idea of underintegrated growth establishes a classification of districts by the poor standards of living.

Marc Vernière proposes "to put these fringe inhabitants in the same category as the two main types of city dwellers: those who are puppets of urbanization policies and are thrown out of the center of town and rehoused in the peripheral areas, and those who, acting for their own reasons, go to settle freely but illegally at the edge of towns, creating an unwieldy urbanization sector."[20]

The migrants studied here no longer have access to the capital. They belong to the impoverished city-dwelling masses who have no other choice than to live on the edges. In the new life they are forging for themselves, they end up creating a semblance of balance in an urban milieu that is itself both already off balance and a cause of imbalance. To the questions posed on the living conditions in these districts and their view of them, the replies have shown this. One must not forget the context in which these districts were formed. They were a chance solution for problems that arose out of a quickly growing urban area: growth, slum clearance, rural exodus, and so on. Also, they have a temporary character, found both at Yembel and Hann, which allows certain change. Marc Vernière has compared, in the Dakar area, the shock of Guediawaye, "a transplanted slum that suffers the effects of shock treatment," with Fass Paillote, which had adapted better to the social transition role between town and village. [21]

Only 16 people out of the 200 said straight out that they did not like their district. They were sorry it did not have adequate facilities such as roads, water, electricity, and others. They did not find it unhealthy or unsafe. At least ten replies formulated these criticisms. Social relationships were bad: no understanding, inquisitive or unpleasant neighbors. It was the second most frequent complaint: "no good neighborliness, unhappy people, cliques"—"no modern amenities"—"poor security, juvenile delinquence"—"no electricity, public tap, or market"—"people have a hard time"—"no amusements"—"many political cliques"—"the neighbors are nosy"—"no market, store, or electricity; we are cut off"—"It is a district which makes one aware of one's social and even political standing. In one word it is a real education for life."

It is surprising that only two replies mentioned unemployment, and yet this was constantly brought up during group meetings.

On the whole, they liked the district. Ninety-two percent of the sample (184 people) said they were satisfied for the following reasons (multiple replies possible).

Calm district, safe	121
Good social relationships with parents and friends	92
A lively, well-located district	27
Own one's own house	22
Used to the district	16
Professional reasons, established clientele, place of work, and so on	17
Other reasons	18

"Yes, the district is calm, the rent is low, and daily expenses are not high because the sea is nearby."—"I get along with everyone."—"I have some clients, and the district is lively."—"I have my relatives, and I'm in peace here."—"I am respected by my neighbors."—" People try to overcome the difficulties of life."—"Sympathy counteracts misery and ignorance."—"I have my own house."—"Peace and harmony"—"I have lived here a long time; I am used to everyone."—"I can satisfy my personal needs."—"My business is going well."—"My husband owns a house."—"Because there are so many people here, everyone mixes well."

Because of the lack of good material conditions, people cling to the close-knit society that the district offers. Good friendships and a good social environment are points that are often mentioned and are indications of social cooperation.

Of our sample, 35.5 percent (68 people) belong to an association that aims to maintain social ties. These are religious (25 people), social (23), political (22), cultural (4), sports (3), and ethnic (3) associations. They meet particularly to attend family and religious ceremonies (28 people), to satisfy any personal problems (23), and to assure good social relationships (16). Some people are activists in political organizations (19 people), and others meet for amusement (6).

The experience of migration from villages and throughout the urban areas consolidates the community feeling for a district. Thus 147 people out of 200 (73.5 percent) would not like to live elsewhere because:

Own their own house	69
Find happiness and good understanding	49
District is peaceful	11
Used to the district	16
Professional reasons	6
District is lively	5
Other reasons (low rent, well-located, and so on)	23

Few people, here again, wanted to move because of poor and unhealthy living conditions. Only seven replies quote the lack of facilities and bad state of the place. In fact, above all, they were looking for their own housing. Twenty-nine replies mentioned this: "If I had a job, I would put in a request for a house."—"The house doesn't belong to me."—"Yea, so long as I had my own house."

They would move to go to find family (six people) or from dislike of the milieu (three people). Only two people wanted to be nearer the town to get work.

The districts chosen follow, with figures for number and percentage of responses.

Do not want to live elsewhere	147	73.5
No specified choice	6	3.0
HLM, SICAP housing	18	9.0
Outer suburbs (Pikine, Hann, Guediawaye Medina, Fass, Gueule Tapee, Colobane)	15	7.5
Plateau	4	2.0
Peripheral districts (Nari Talli, Grand Dakar)	2	1.0
Government projects supplying sites and services	2	1.0
Other towns and villages in Senegal	2	1.0

SICAP and HLM housing is a symbol. It is the dream of the middle and upper-middle class. It is modern living. It's the impossible dream of the underprivileged classes. Pikine and Guediawaye are the new towns for migrants. They do not dream of the plateau much. It is beyond hope.

The desire for community facilities reflects a very real need. They would like dispensaries, maternity centers, pharmacies, and social centers (146 people), schools (129), electricity and public lighting (105), running water and public taps (95), sports and cultural facilities, cinemas, youth centers, sports grounds (68), paved roads (44), public latrines (35), markets and commercial facilities (35), and mosques (21).

CONCLUSION

The study of regional migrations in Senegal shows the size of the migration toward Dakar. It is an ancient phenomenon, which had peaks in 1960 and between 1968 and 1973, and is more than a migration in name only. It has added to the demographic progress of the Dakar metropolis, which has acute growth problems. Small towns are stepping stones in the migration and take some people, but it reduces the movement only a little.

African and international migration contribute also to the growth of Senegal. Foreign immigration of French and Lebano-Syrians is particularly large. Senegal received many French up to independence. It does not seem that they have diminished in number, despite the official statements that want to camouflage the real percentage for political reasons. Also, recent events in Lebanon have increased immigration from that country.

For some decades, Senegal's development has filtered migrants toward the coast, where they have become almost permanent settlers. Among them are Mauritanians, Malians, Guineans, Beninois, Togolese, and so on. Postindependence may have slowed down some seasonal movement, but it does seem to have accentuated the long-term migration of some groups, for example, Guineans toward Upper Casamance and Senegal Oriental.

Internal migration in Senegal is also linked to international emigration. Dakar is a stepping stone to Europe and to other African countries.

Many studies have been made concerning this migration toward Europe, which affects around 70,000 people. Although it is heterogenous, it is very largely dominated by a low-skilled labor force. It has ancient roots in precolonial and colonial Senegal, where the movement was dominated by navigators, sailors, and demobilized soldiers. The migrants work as manual laborers or factory hands in France, Germany, and the low countries.

There remains to be mentioned Senegalese emigration in Africa. It affects nearly 200,000 people throughout the Ivory Coast (50,000 people), Gambia (25,000), Benin (25,000), Mauritania (20,000), Guinea (20,000), and Mali (15,000).[22] They are found in other countries such as Upper Volta, Niger, Gabon, Cameroon, Congo, and Zaire and also Burundi, Kenya, Uganda, and so on. This emigration is rarely one of unskilled workers. It is made up mostly of skilled tradesmen and workers, who supply the middle-level labor that the developing African countries lack: jewelers, masons, painters, woodcarvers, fishers, and so on. More and more higher level personnel (engineers, teachers, doctors, and so on) are evident in this emigration. Senegal has signed agreements with certain countries to send them these different levels of humanpower. Business managers, merchants, and diamond merchants are among those who earn the highest incomes.

The contribution of national emigration to the Senegalese economy is not negligible. Several studies have shown that the Post Offices in Matam and Bakel register several hundreds of million cfa per year in international money orders from these regions. This income supports the families who have stayed in Senegal and gives them means to live. It contributes to improved diet, clothing, and housing. It also finances religious buildings (mosques) and community infrastructures (wells, schools, municipal buildings, and so on). The town of Mbacke in the peanut basin is developing similarly, with contributions from the expatriate Mouride community in West Africa.

Emigrants prepare for their eventual return by investing their remittances in animals, agriculture, and construction. They are not looking to establish industrial enterprises as are the expatriates.[23] In this sense, they neither develop nor transform the economy.

Internal migration, according to statistics, affects about 15 percent of the Senegalese population. Because of the rural production methods modeled on the seasonal cycle, many people are free between seasons. This means that the so-called seasonal migrations of rural people increase. In fact, a good number of these people go to visit relatives (gane) in the city. They used to bring a few products from the country and take back little. Now they no longer bring anything and come to look for income, and some settle for long periods or permanently.

This trip to town is almost classical. The people leave the village for greater Dakar with a longish stop in slums. The slum clearance policy over the last ten years has designed urban sites based on a spatial segregation according to the level of living, income, and insecurity of material conditions. However, in these peripheral districts, people do organize themselves. Older city dwellers welcome the new residents and thus facilitate definite social integration. This does not eliminate the difficulties of settling into the city, because there remain other big problems related to the fast-growing city.

They come up against the institutional vacuum in the big city. Administrative buildings and sociocultural facilities are viewed as alien to the milieu in which they live. In any case, there are not enough of these and they are not suited to the needs of migrants. For them, education, employment, and housing are the important parts of the urban problem.

NOTES

1. See J. Copans, "Images, problématiques et thèmes," in Sechéresses et famines au Sahel, vol. 1 (Paris: Maspero, 1975), p. 62.

2. J. L. Amselle, "Aspects et significations du phénomène migratoire en Afrique," in Les migrations africaines, ed. J. L. Amselle (Paris: Maspero, 1976), p. 12.

3. S. Berniard, Le Sénégal en chiffres: Annuaire statistique du Sénégal, 1976 ed. (Dakar: Société africaine d'édition), p. 9.

4. On Dakar, read Assane Seck, Dakar: Métropole ouest-africaine (Dakar: IFAN, 1970). See also the Dakar study groups under the direction of M. Sankale, L. V. Thomas, and P. Fougeyrollas, Dakar en devenir (Paris: Présence africaine, 1968), p. 517.

5. Marc Vernière, "A propos de la marginalité: Reflexions illustrées par quelques enquêtes en milieu urbain et suburbain africain," Cahiers d'études africaines 51 (1973): 598.

6. "Study on the Dakar Water Supply," Dakar, 1970.

7. Abdoulaye B. Diop, Toucouleur Society and Migration (Dakar: IFAN, 1965), 232 p. 16 fig. 2 maps p. 53 (demographic figures and census of Dakar).

8. J. Roch, "Economic Migrations in the Dry Season in the Senegalese Peanut Basin," Cah. ORSTOM 12 (1975): 55-81.

9. S. Amin and Daryll Forde, eds., Modern Migrations in West Africa (London: Oxford University Press, 1974), p. 3.

10. Paul Pélissier, Peasants of Senegal, Agrarian Civilizations from Cayor to the Casamance (St. Yrieux: Fabréque, 1966), pp. 146-47.

11. Ibid., p. 148.

12. BCEOM, "Aménagement de parcelles assainies et de trames d'accueil à Dakar: Compte rendu d'enquête socio-économique par sondage dans les bidonvilles de Dakar et les quartiers de Pikine-extension," 1972, p. 20.

13. Senegal, Projet Rul-12 Sénégal, L'habitat du grand nombre VI.

14. This report suggested it was due to the fact that it was the masons who decided what plans to use and that they preferred to limit themselves to one well-known plan. One must also realise that the inhabitants themselves judged that this particular plan suited them better than any other, given the technical and financial means available.

15. Senegal, Projet Rul-12, L'habitat du grand nombre, p. 122.

16. "Population-Education-Development in Africa South of the Sahara," Bureau Régional d'Education en Afrique, mimeographed, Dakar, 1971. See particularly Nelson O. Addo, "Rural Exodus in Africa, Role of Education in This Process," pp. 163-87. Jacques Bugnicourt, "Migration, Growth of Shanty Towns and Educational Alternatives," pp. 241-325.

17. Pathé Diagne, "African Languages, Economic and Cultural Development," Notes Africaines 129 (1971): 2-19.

18. F. Flis-Zonabend, Lycée Students of Dakar (Paris: Maspero, 1968), 213 pp. 33.

19. See the special edition of Cahiers d'études africaines, entitled "Villes africaines," 51 (1973), eds. Mouton and Cie; M. Talence, "Urban Growth in Black Africa and Madagascar," vol. 2 (Paris: Editions du CNRS, 1972).

20. Marc Vernière, "A propos de la marginalité," Cahiers d'études africaines 51 (1973): 588.

21. Marc Vernière, L'expulsion des bidonvilles dakarois: bouleversement d'une société urbaine de transition. Leçon d'enquêtes réalisées à Fann Paillote et Guedj Awaye," Psycho pathologie africaine 10 (1974): 321-51.

22. World Bank, "Rapport sur la situation de la migration et de l'emploi au Sénégal," Washington, D.C., mimeographed, June 1976.

23. For example, the fortunes of N. Kebe or D. Mbaye, emigrants, amount to billions of cfa and have been invested mainly in real estate and business.

10

MAURITANIA

Lucie Gallistel Colvin

Mauritania has experienced the most extraordinary demographic changes over the last two decades of any country in the
area. When it entered independence in 1960, it had a sparse population of approximately 970,000, three-quarters of whom were transhumant nomads, herding cattle, sheep, goats, and camels in the
fragile Sahel zone where rainfall is too sparse for agriculture.
The other quarter of the population was primarily engaged in agriculture, in the southern sector of the country where some rainfall
agriculture is possible, particularly in the fertile Senegal river
valley. The two largest cities, Kaedi and Atar, had populations of
about 9,000 each. [1]

Mauritania made rapid economic progress in the first decade
of its independence, followed by the shattering effects of drought and
warfare from 1969 to 1978. Both the progress and the subsequent
turmoil contributed to radical redistribution of the population of the
country. In Mauritania, the great majority of the population now
lives in both a place and a style different from their families' patterns just two decades ago.

The changes show four clear trends, three of which are likely
to be ongoing and one (shifts due to the recently ended war) of which
may be partially temporary. The ongoing trends include rapid
sedentarization of the nomads, urbanization, and a sharp southward
population shift. The population in 1964-65 was 25 percent sedentary
and 75 percent nomadic. In the 1976-77 census, the figures are 65
percent sedentary and 35 percent nomadic, [2] that is, the predominance has exactly reversed in the space of 11.5 years. The second
trend is an extraordinary rate of urbanization. Mauritania has gone
from one of the least urbanized areas of Africa to a fairly substantial rate of urbanization, superior to that of its other Sahelian

neighbors with the exception of Senegal that has a long urban tradition. The third one is a general southward movement of the population into the agricultural zones, particularly the Kaedi and Selibaby areas. As will be seen, this is connected with radical social change in a disruption of the traditional hierarchical class and caste system, as well as with the fragility of the Sahelian ecological zone, revealed by the drought. The last clear tendency in the figures is a flight from the zones affected by the war between Mauritania and Polisario over the former Spanish Sahara. The war zones lost population during that war, which is now in an uneasy truce.

Despite the sparse population, harsh climate, and low level of literacy in Western languages, the statistical and social science literature on Mauritania is relatively good. This is, in large part, due to the work of French geographers, notably Charles Toupet and F. Barbey, as well as the very thorough analysis being done on the 1976 census report.[3] Earlier censuses include one of all towns with more than 1,000 populations in 1961-62 and a sample census of the rural population in 1964-65.[4]

The demographic picture of Mauritania still shows a relatively small total population: 1,407,000 in December 1976, which would mean a population of 1,524,000 three years later in 1979. An additional estimated 110,000 Mauritanian nationals were living abroad in 1976, corresponding to 7.8 percent of the total population. Of these, 61,000 were transhumant in Mali and an estimated 40,000 were in Senegal, of whom some 6,000 were transhumant nomads. An additional 2,000 or more were in the Gambia, and small groups could be found in Guinea Bissau, the Canary Islands, North Africa, and overseas. The number of immigrants from other countries in Mauritania in 1976 is not yet published in the census results. However, field observations would indicate that their number is quite small, a few thousand, including primarily Senegalese and Moroccans, some Guineans, and a few North Africans and Europeans of diverse origin. Thus Mauritania has a substantial net emigration, equivalent to at least 7 percent of the resident population.

The average population density is 1.21 per square kilometer. It ranges from a low in the north, where there are large expanses of virtually unpopulated desert, dotted by oases, to a density of one nomad per square kilometer in the drier zone of the Sahel below the 100 millimeter annual rainfall isohyet, to a density of about four per square kilometer in the densest nomadic zones in the Keur Macene, Rosso, and Boghe departments. See Map 10.1 and Table 10.2. The agricultural zone begins, in general, south of the 350 millimeter isohyet. The population reaches modest densities on the rainfall agricultural plains and intense densities of up to 50 per

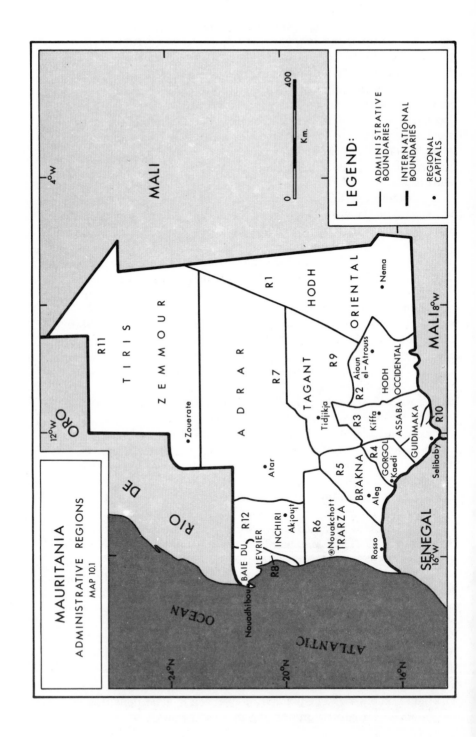

MAURITANIA
ADMINISTRATIVE REGIONS
MAP 10.1

LEGEND:
ADMINISTRATIVE BOUNDARIES
INTERNATIONAL BOUNDARIES
REGIONAL CAPITALS

MALI

RIO DE ORO

12°W

4°W

Km.
0   400

ATLANTIC OCEAN

Nouadhibou

BAIE DU LEVRIER

INCHIRI R12
R8
Akjoujt

TRARZA
R6
⊛Nouakchott

Rosso

TIRIS ZEMMOUR
R11
•Zouerate

ADRAR
•Atar

R5
BRAKNA
Aleg

GORGOL
R4
Kaedi•

R1
HODH ORIENTAL
•Nema

TAGANT
R7
•Tidjikja
R3

R9
Aioun el-Atrouss•
R2
HODH OCCIDENTAL
Kiffa•

ASSABA
GUIDIMAKA
R10
Selibaby•

SENEGAL

MALI

8°W

16°W

24°N

20°N

16°N

246

TABLE 10.1

Population Growth in Mauritania by Region, 1965-77

Region	Population Total January 1, 1977	Population Total 1965	Total Growth Since 1965 (in percent)	Average Annual Growth (in percent)
Nouakchott	134,986	12,300*	+997.4	+23.2
01	205,545	168,900	+21.7	+1.7
02	133,952	87,400	+53.3	+3.8
03	130,517	100,800	+29.5	+2.3
04	150,556	82,000	+84.0	+5.4
05	151,060	123,900	+21.9	+1.7
06	216,735	199,500	+8.6	+0.7
07	55,482	64,700	-14.2	-1.3
08	24,460	10,800	+126.5	+7.4
09	76,608	74,800	+2.4	+0.2
10	87,107	63,400	+37.4	+2.8
11	22,467	15,800	+42.2	+3.1
12	17,567	24,600	-28.6	-2.9
All Mauritania	1,407,042	1,028,900	+36.6	+2.8

*Based on the 1964 census, believed to be an underestimate.

Sources: Mauritania, Direction de la statistique, "Recensement général de la population de la Mauritainie au 1 janvier 1977; France, Secrétariat d'Etat aux Affaires Etrangères, Société d'Etudes pour le Développement Economique et Social, "Enquête démographique en Mauritanie, 1965: Résultats définitifs" (mimeographed, Orleans, France, n.d.); "Seconds résultats provisoires du recensement de la population," Nouakchott.

TABLE 10.2

Mauritanian Population by Region and Nomadic or Sedentary Lifestyle

Region	Nomadic Population*	Sedentary Population	Population Present
Nouakchott		134,986	134,986
1st Region Nema	85,344	71,026	156,370
2nd Region Aiount	64,038	60,100	124,138
3rd Region Aftout	43,136	85,642	128,778
4th Region Kaidi	16,551	133,210	149,761
5th Region Aleg	50,856	100,204	151,060
6th Region Rosso	106,022	109,144	215,166
7th Region Atar	17,791	37,691	55,482
8th Region Nouadhibou	75	24,385	24,460
9th Region Tidjikja	44,095	32,513	76,608
10th Region Selibaby	9,248	74,088	83,336
11th Region Zouerate	742	21,725	22,467
12th Region	7,750	9,817	17,567
Total	445,648	894,531	1,340,179

*Transhumant nomads were counted as present only if they were in whole households and campments.

Source: Mauritania, Direction de la Statistique, "Recensement général de la population de la Mauritainie au 1 Janvier 1977; seconds résultats provisoires," Nouakchott, Table 4.

square kilometer on the rich alluvial flood plain on the north bank
of the Senegal River. The densest concentrations are found in the
fourth (Kaedi) and tenth (Selibaby) regions.

The average annual growth rate of the Mauritanian population
is 2.7 percent, if one accepts the results of the 1964-65 sample
census and the 1976 census. In Mauritania, as in Senegal, Mali, and
Gambia, both the total population and the implicit rate of natural
increase in the 1970 round of censuses was substantially higher than
had been predicted from the 1960 sample censuses. In Mauritania,
as in the other countries, demographers tended to doubt the implicit
increase and assume that the 1964-65 census must have been underestimated. However, when one looks at the generality of this phenomenon, it seems much more likely that, in fact, the death rate
has decreased substantially and the growth rate has actually increased. Moreover, in Mauritania the much higher growth rate
emerges from two independent calculations.[5]

The 1964-65 sample census in Mauritania found an overall
birth rate of 43 per 1,000 and a death rate of 27 per 1,000, yielding
a natural rate of growth of 16 per 1,000 or 1.6 percent per year. If
those rates of growth had been accurate and had continued until December of 1976, one should have found a population of 1,260,000
in Mauritania instead of the 1,407,000 actually counted. In the 1970
census, the estimated birth rate increased from 43 per 1,000 in
1964-65 to 46 per 1,000 in 1976. Meanwhile, the death rate decreased substantially from 27 per 1,000 in 1964-65 to 14 per 1,000
in 1976-77. This would yield a rate of natural increase of 3.2 percent per year. The 2.7 percent average annual growth rate calculated by this means for Mauritania excludes a fairly substantial increase in emigration as has been noted, which implies that the rate
of natural increase is greater than this. Because of emigration,
net growth averages 2.7 percent per year.

The regional distribution of growth was highly uneven, reflecting specific trends and events described in Table 10.1. The seventh
and twelfth regions, which were in the war zone, actually lost population between 1965 and 1977. Nouakchott experienced the spectacu-
lar growth of 997.4 percent; that is, its population multiplied ten
times in 11 years. Nouadhibou also grew extremely fast, which reflects on its regional total. Zouerate experienced growth due to
urbanization and industrialization, followed by a slight decline due
to the war.[6] The northern regions in general saw their growth rates
substantially below that of the national total as the process of
sedentarization also led to a general southward movement of the population. The agricultural area, particularly in the fourth (Kaedi) and
tenth (Selibaby) regions, increased substantially faster than the national average. New villages were founded by freed slaves and other
war and drought refugees, and existing towns swelled.

URBANIZATION

Urbanization cannot be said to have begun in Mauritania until after the attainment of independence in 1963, but since that time it has assumed a pace unmatched in history (see Table 10.3). It has been stimulated by the process of sedentarization of nomads, which was already well under way, and by the creation of a new administrative capital at Nouakchott in 1958 (the colonial capital had been Saint-Louis). The urban population grew apace with the rapidly expanding mineral economy in the prosperous decade of the 1960s. The drought, which began to ravage the rural economy, both pastoral and agricultural, in 1968, thus brought the strongest possible conjunction of so-called push and pull factors, an appearance of great opportunity in the cities combined with life-threatening losses of herds and crops in the countryside. Then the modern sector of the economy ran into serious difficulties, through a combination of problems associated with nationalization of the currency and the mining industry in 1973-74, followed by the war with the Polisario.

The most striking characteristic of urbanization in Mauritania is that it is concentrated overwhelmingly in Nouakchott, an administrative center with very little productive base. People are coming because money and power are concentrated there or because they cannot live in the countryside, not because of any job opportunities. By 1973, it was estimated that there were only approximately 20,000 salaried workers in all of Mauritania, of whom 9,000 were in the public service, 5,400 in the mines, and 4,000 in other private organizations (see Table 10.4).[7] Another 20,000 persons could be considered independently employed in the modern sector, mainly as traders.[8] Very few of the incoming migrants moved into the salaried sector. Instead they sought their opportunities in the informal sector, in commerce, in petty services, in water distribution. It soon became clear that the real opportunity for migrants, as for residents already present in the cities, lay in real estate speculation, an opportunity open to anyone with Mauritanian citizenship. Plots were distributed until very recently without charge to those who could establish a claim. While a speculative real estate market is found in all Mauritanian cities, the situation is much more acute in the capital than anywhere else. The process of building a new capital, beginning in 1958, meant good quality housing was in demand for the diplomatic community, banking officials, officials of new national institutions, and mining company representatives. Since the drought, a plethora of relief distributors and officials of development agencies have further intensified demand.

TABLE 10.3

Urban Growth in Mauritania, 1961–77

Locality	Population January 1, 1977	Population 1961–62	Date	Total Increase (in percent)	Average Annual Growth Rate (in percent)
Nouakchott	134,986	5,807	1961	2,324.5	22.5
Nouadhibou	21,961	5,283	1961	315.7	9.6
Kaedi	20,848	9,197	1962	126.7	5.8
Zouerate	17,474	4,659	1962	321.4*	10.4
Rosso	16,466	4,811	1961	242.3	8.3
Atar	16,326	9,528	1962	71.3	3.8
Kiffa	10,629	4,359	1962	143.8	66.3
Aioun	8,775	4,877	1962	79.5	4.1
Nema	8,232	3,893	1962	111.5	5.3
Boghe	56	5,867	1961	37.3	2.1
Akjoujt	8,044	2,518	1962	219.5	8.3
Tidjikja	7,870	3,661	1962	115.0	5.4
Boutilimit	7,261	2,774	1962	161.8	6.9
Aleg	6,415	1,360	1962	371.7	11.3
Selibaby	5,994	2,737	1962	119.0	5.6
Timbedra	5,317	1,815	1962	192.9	7.7
F'Derick	2,160		1962		
Total	298,814	73,146	1962	302.9	10.1
Industrial and commercial cities	66,105	18,303	1962	261.2	9.3
Other urban centers	105,723	50,298	1962	110.2	5.3
Cities of more than 5,000	304,654	35,682	1961–62	753.8	15.4

*With F'Derick, as in 1962.

Notes: Atar includes Kanawal and Douerate; Aioun excludes Aioun Source; Boghe excludes Toulde, Thienel, and Bakaw; Boutilimit includes Zem-Zem.

Urban population in 1977 constituted 21 percent of the total population of Mauritania (1,407,000).

Urban population in 1961–62 (73,146) constituted 7.5 percent of the total population of Mauritania (970,000).

Source: Mauritania, Direction de la Statistique, "Recensement général de la population de la Mauritainie au 1 Janvier 1977; seconds résultats provisoires."

TABLE 10.4

Employment in Mauritania, 1973

Sector	Men	Women	Total
Traditional			
Pastoralism[a]	210,000	40,000	250,000
Agriculture	60,000	50,000	110,000
Fishing, trading, hunting	2,000	—	2,000
Crafts, traditional	8,000	40,000	48,000
Teaching, traditional	3,000	—	3,000
Transportation, traditional	1,000	—	1,000
Personal domestic, traditional	35,000	42,000	77,000
Total	319,000	172,000	491,000
Modern			
Administration	7,500	1,500	9,000
Fishing	1,000	—	1,000
Mines	5,400	100	5,500
Construction, industry, utilities	3,200	—	3,200
Banks, commerce, insurance	700	300	1,000
Transportation	1,200	—	1,200
Self-employed (including merchants)	20,000	—	20,000
Domestic servants (salaried)	1,100	300	1,400
Total[b]	40,100	2,200	42,300
General total	359,100	174,200	533,300

[a]These figures include 30,000 children younger than 15 years and 15,000 people older than 60 years.

[b]Soldiers are not included, but police officers are. The figures also include 3,500 foreign employees.

Source: Troisième Plan de Développement économique et social.

Measures of the population of Nouakchott allow us to observe its growth from the end of 1961 through 1964, 1975, and 1976. Informal observations and published estimates allow us to guess at two phases in the interval between 1964 and 1975. We therefore inserted a benchmark at 1970 in Table 10.5. The population of 5,867 at the end of 1961 reflects a large village surrounding the French army base at Nouakchott, with only the beginnings of the administrative capital. The next period, 1961-64, saw the active building of the administrative center and the population more than double, to 12,307. After that, it continued to grow but at a more modest rate according to contemporary observations, until the effects of the drought began to be felt, about 1969. One 1970 estimate listed the population as 18,000.[9] Others suggested 20,000. The impact of the drought on the pastoral economies of the Sahel has been explored in detail elsewhere and need not be repeated here. Suffice it to say that the drought began earlier in Mauritania and Senegal than elsewhere in Sahel, in 1968 and 1969 rather than in 1970 or 1971. Also, its impact was much more immediate upon pastoral people than upon farmers because their reserves were on the hoof rather than in granaries. When there was no pasture, the animals stopped giving milk very quickly. In an extremity, herders began to sell off their animals, but then the price of meat plummeted and the capital they realized tided them over only a short while. This cycle was already well under way in Mauritania before relief food supplies began to be imported from the outside. The streets of the cities were swollen with people offering their services in any capacity possible, looking to eat with relatives, or simply begging.

TABLE 10.5

Phases of Growth of Nouakchott, 1961-77

Date of Enumeration	Population	Average Annual Growth (since preceding enumeration, in percent)
End 1961	5,867	—
May 1964	12,307	34.5
Sometime in 1970	18,000	6.5
February 1975	104,054	42.0
December 1976	134,986	15.0

Sources: Mauritania, Direction de la Statistique, "Recensement général de la population de la Mauritainie au 1 Janvier 1977; seconds résultats provisoires," p. 26. Estimate for 1970 from Samir Amin, Neo-Colonialism in West Africa (Baltimore: Penguin, 1972), p. 275.

When external aid began to come in large quantities in 1973, food was given out in the cities of Mauritania rather than in the rural areas. This has to be considered a major contributor to the rate of drought-related migration in that country. By comparison, Senegal was able to organize delivery of food rations in local government areas so that peasants and herders were obliged to stay in their district of administrative allegiance in order to collect their rations. This combination of rural food distribution and a primarily sedentary, as opposed to pastoral, population made the drought-related urban influx considerably smaller in Senegal than in Mauritania. As Table 10.1 shows, during the years of the drought, the population of Nouakchott multiplied several times. It was measured in 1975 at 104,054 people, during a preliminary census in preparation for the official 1976 census. There was a general hope, even optimism, that this influx would gradually be decimated once the rains returned. The two urban censuses conducted, the preliminary census in 1975 and final census in 1976, allow us to observe in Mauritania, better than any place else in the Sahel, exactly where this return to the land did and did not take place and to what extent. It spanned two years of improved rainfall, 1974 and 1975. Some cities did indeed lose population between the 1975 and 1976 censuses, presumably due to an influx of pastoralists from the drought returning to the land. These were Atar, Tidjikja, Kiffa, Aioun, and Nema, all regional capitals in predominantly nomadic zones with little modern economic sector other than their administrative function. The iron-mining city of Zouérate and the copper-mining city of Akjoujt also lost population during that time, but the explanation is believed to be the disruption of the mineral industry and a flight of population due to the war. More important is the fact that Nouakchott, Nouadhibou, and the cities in the southern agricultural belt did not lose population during that period. Nouakchott's growth merely settled down from an astounding 42 percent per year to a still very high pace of 15 percent per year. At the latter rate, it will double only every five years instead of every two. Field observations in September 1978 and October 1979 indicated that a rapid rate of growth continues for Nouakchott.

Urbanization has brought severe social strains in Mauritanian cities, not only because of the rapid rate but also because of the peculiar circumstances that accompanied it. Ironically, the height of the drought coincided with the peak of economic growth and confidence in the modern sector of the economy in Mauritania. A succession of major decisions was taken in 1972-75, which brought social, economic, and, eventually, political change at a very rapid rate. In 1972, Mauritania ended its "special relationship" with France, broke its remaining neocolonial ties, and revised its cooperation agreements so that France essentially became like any other developed country. In 1973, Mauritania left the franc zone and established its own national currency, the ougiya, based on its own reserves of hard currency gained through the mineral industry. In 1974, it nationalized the Mines de Fers Mauritaniennes (MIFERMA), honoring the debts of the iron-mining company and paying off its French stockholders, and, in 1975, it did the same for the copper-mining company, the Société Minière de la Mauritanie (SOMIMA). Had the mining industry continued to prosper for a few years, the currency probably could have held its own. However, world demand for iron dropped off 10 percent in 1975 and, at the same time, the price of copper plummeted. Then, while foreign exchange was down from the mining sector, Mauritania became involved in a very costly war with the Polisario Front over the Tiris El Gharbia region of the former Spanish Sahara.

The war proved far more consequential for Mauritania than the small scale desert guerrilla mop-up campaign that President Ould Daddah seems to have anticipated. At first, the Mauritanian military was able to move in and easily take over the three small towns in the portion of Spanish Sahara that it claimed. However, Mauritania's own mining economy proved very vulnerable. By 1977, the guerrillas were able to disrupt quite easily the railroad carrying iron from Zouérate to Nouadhibou, the lifeline of Mauritania's economy.

The war also increased the role of the military in national politics. In 1975, for the first time, a colonel was brought into the government in the cabinet of ministers.

Gradually, industrial and agricultural development projects were affected even in areas of the country not directly affected by the war. In some cases, it was because the donor country or cooperating country sided with Algeria and Polisario in the war. In other cases, it was simply because, with the government mobilized around war issues, there was not time to carry through development projects. Finally, in 1978, as sabotage brought the iron-mining industry to a halt, the government approached bankruptcy. In July of 1978, Ould Daddah was overthrown by a military coalition in a bloodless coup and replaced as president by Ould Salek. The military government's first action was to negotiate a cease-fire with Polisario.

The continuing tensions in Mauritanian government and society will not be discussed here except as they relate to migration. Drought-related migration and, to a lesser extent, the war-related influx, coming as they did in the context of real modern economic growth potential, have contributed to a radically revised vision of Mauritanian society and its potential future. The traditional economy and society of Mauritania was very highly mobile, which surely contributes to the high rate of mobility today. Both pastoralism and commerce, which were the traditional sources of wealth in the society, required a high rate of mobility. The range of Mauritanian long-distance traders from precolonial times through the present covers the entire Senegambia, as it is defined here, plus Morocco and the Canary Islands. It is still a major source of capital accumulation for migrants coming directly out of the pastoral economy. Most pastoral families have some members engaged in commerce while others are managing the combined herds. Both sides have been affected in the 1970s, the herders by the loss of their animals and the traders by the nationalization of the currency, followed by periodic restrictions of currency movements and exchange. This has not forced people out of long-distance commerce but has often obliged them to stay either in Mauritania or outside of it for extended periods. Those with capital in Mauritania have almost universally invested in real estate and found a much more ready expansion of capital there.

The drought and social reform coming out of the process of modernization have also transformed the social structure of Mauritanian society, producing substantial permanent migration of the lower castes and former slaves and serfs. In the precolonial social structure, political power and control of the large herds was in the hands of Arab warriors (hassaniya). Lesser herds were also maintained by the clerical zwaya and conquered Berber peoples (aznaga). Black serfs (haratin) and domestic slaves (abid) served the Arab and Berber groups as herders and did much of the actual work of tending the animals. The haratin also cultivated grain for their pastoral masters. Their status was different from slaves in that they were not individually owned. They were considered former slaves whose attachment was no longer to individual masters but who retained the collective status of serfs. Craft castes (mallmin) and griots and iggawen (bards and praise singers) were attached as families to particular noble families and provided them with butchers, livestock merchants, blacksmiths, leather workers, weavers, praise singers, messengers, oral historians, and court jesters. The colonial period had already seen the departure of many of the castes for more lucrative opportunities in the cities, notably Dakar, and it had reduced the capacity of the nobles to maintain a large body of dependents. A sharp further erosion in this inherited hierarchial social structure occurred as the result of the drought. The lower groups, being in control of fewer resources, were the first to suffer and the first to flee the effects of the drought. Many went south to establish themselves as farmers; the government generally encouraged them. In 1974, informants report that the government announced the freeing of the slaves, although, since slavery had long been officially illegal, it is not clear what this meant. In 1979 the new military government again announced publicly in the press the freeing of the slaves. The issue was not probed further in this study. Destitute free-born herders, however, who are now settled along the paved roads, have no hesitation in giving this as the major reason that they are unable to return to herding. They say that the former slave herders will not work for wages and that those who belonged to their families have run away. Historical experience here and elsewhere would suggest that this flight from low status in traditional society is an irreversible process.

Analysis of the directions of migration and its rates by points of origin and destination will be possible once the complete results of the census are published. An informal preliminary census tally indicated that the greatest absolute numbers of migrants came to Nouakchott from the most populous regions, that is, the fourth, fifth, and sixth regions. However, the highest rates of outmigration, that is, numbers of migrants in relation to the density of the population of the original province, came from the seventh and twelfth districts, immediately northeast of Nouakchott; the eleventh region in the far north also had a high rate of outmigration. The seventh region, of which Atar is the capital, lost the major French army base in 1973 as a result of the nonrenewal of accords with France, and its administrative function disappeared. As a result, there has been a large outflux of population from there. The twelfth region is the site of the Akjoujt copper mine, and the eleventh region is the site of the Zouérate iron mine. Those provinces have suffered from the combined effects of disruption of the mining sector, war, and drought.

In urban areas, former haratin and abid tend to lodge in the center city. While Nouakchott is in no sense a segregated city, there is a tendency for the Tukulor, Soninke, and former haratin and abid to concentrate in the solid housing of the older, already densely built-up sections of the city, while the former nomads settle in the tent city around the edges. This neighborhood association, in addition to the general process of liberation affecting the haratin and abid, appears to be changing their social alliances. Black Moors have traditionally been culturally Moor Arabic-speaking, which has been a barrier between them and the Tukulor and Soninke populations. In the cities today, however, they are finding a common bond in a newly emerging black consciousness. There is some tension over both urban and rural development issues between blacks and baidani. It enters development strategy as the government is determined to seek "geographically balanced" development. In geopolitical terms, that phrase means investment in the Sahelian area and northern oases, not preference for the naturally more dynamic river basin area. It also accentuates the competition for urban real estate, as the black populations in the center city seem to have had a slight advantage in getting access to lots so long as those lots were being given out freely to all citizens. This competitive real estate situation applies only to the lower levels, as the more valuable property is being accumulated in the hands of the already wealthy, who are mainly well-connected baidani.

POLICY IMPLICATIONS OF MIGRATION IN MAURITANIA

Policy in Mauritania has to focus on the current state of crisis. It is a vast country, most of which is desert, with a small, very rapidly growing, rapidly sedentarizing and urbanizing population. The return of good rainfall, even for many years in a row, will do very little to alter that state of crisis. The rural pastoral economy and the social structure that supported it are collapsing, largely as a result of the recent drought, but also in response to the potential shown in the modern sector. The modern economy has also been seriously disrupted by drought, by economic reforms, and, most importantly, by the war with Polisario. It continues, however, to have substantial potential. The lingering political and socioeconomic instability generated by the events of recent years will make it more difficult to establish a rhythm of economic development comparable to that of the 1960s. Moreover, a recovery of financial stability for the government will not provide any solution to the economic problems of individual migrants.

In the short space of the last ten years, most of the population has changed place of residence and occupation or gone from having an occupation to having none. Finding productive new occupations for both rural and urban Mauritanians should be the highest priority. The proposed OMVS irrigation development in the river valley offers the clearest large bloc of new job opportunities. In the Sahel areas, a return to livestock raising, but with new patterns of labor and perhaps modernized systems of feeding and marketing, will be necessary. The rapid growth of the population means also that a high priority has to be put on food production in the agricultural areas of the south.

None of these will deal, however, with the urban population's needs and demands. The most urgent need is clearly productive employment, the continued development of labor intensive industries. Housing is probably not the priority in Mauritania that it might be elsewhere in the Sahel, as the Mauritanian private sector adapts very quickly to the market. Government-sponsored housing projects would most likely only contribute to the inflationary situation at present. On the contrary, government intervention in this area might be more constructive if it were negative, that is, the gradual phasing out of housing subsidies.

NOTES

1. Mauritania, Direction de la Statistique, "Recensement général de la population de la Mauritainie au 1 Janvier 1977; seconds résultats provisoires," Nouakchott, p. 24. The population of Kaedi was 9,197, of Atar 9,528.

2. A new definition of sedentary (families living with at least one permanent structure) may be causing some exaggeration in the figures, but there is no question that the transformation is real. One in four of the remaining nomads indicated an intention to sedentarize in the immediate future.

3. C. Toupet, La sédentarisation des nomades en Mauritanie centrale sahelienne (Lille: Université III, repr. de thèses, 1977); F. Barbey et al., Atlas régional de l'Afrique de l'Ouest (IFAN and IGN, n.d.).

4. Mauritania, Direction de la statisque, "Recensement."

5. Questions on natality and mortality in the 1976 census yielded rates of 46 percent and 14 percent respectively, which would imply a 3.2 percent rate of natural increase. This is close to the figure derived from comparison of the total population in 1965 with that in 1976: using the formula $P_2 = P_1(1-r)^n$ (1,407,000 + 110,000 emigrants = 1,028,900) $(1-r)^{11.9}$; r = 3.3 percent/yr. Some small allowance must be made for an unknown number of Mauritanian emigrants abroad in 1965.

6. Urban areas were enumerated twice in the course of the 1976 census, once at the end of 1975 and once at the end of 1976. Zourate showed a rapid jump by 1975 and a slight decline in the second round.

7. Samir Amin, Neocolonialism in West Africa (Baltimore: Penguin, 1972), pp. 77-78, estimates that the public service actually employed 12,000 of the 20,000 and the mines only 4,000. Since that time, the copper mines have closed indefinitely and the iron mines intermittently.

8. Ibid., p. 275.

9. Field mission, September 1978.

11

MALI

Lucie Gallistel Colvin

Historically, Mali, like ancient Egypt, was a river valley civilization. Most of its people did and still do live in the river valleys:
the upper and middle Niger and the upper Senegal and its tributaries.
In the premodern period, Mali's wealth was based on the superior
productivity of the flood plains of the valley and on the commerce
that could be carried on its more than 1,500 kilometers of navigable
river at the northern edge of the Sudan, the northernmost of the
transsaharan outlets to the Sudan. Its political unity over a vast
territory and its military power were similarly based on the advantages of river navigability and closeness to the transsaharan trade.
Those aspects of Mali's geography are still very important to the
functioning of its economy and are an essential to an understanding
of its demographic patterns. However, they provide little basis for
a dynamic role in the modern economy. Cheap and fast ocean, railroad, road, and air travel have altered economic advantages for the
foreseeable future in favor of the coastal areas, dooming the old
Niger buckle route from Mopti to Gao to a subsistence role. As a
landlocked country surrounded by colonial commercial drainage networks, Mali has become a commercial hinterland and provider of
humanpower to more dynamic commercial areas of Senegal, Ghana,
and, most recently, Ivory Coast. The Gao region of Mali, in the
east, has a similar coastal orientation toward Nigeria via Niger.
Thus the modern economy of Mali is pulled in three different directions, toward the dynamic economies of Ivory Coast, Senegal, and
Nigeria. So also are the emigrants who move from Mali toward
these areas. They make Mali the second major source of emigrant
labor in West Africa, following only Upper Volta.

Because of the importance of these divergent outward flows in both the economy and migration patterns of Mali, traditional country-wide global statistics for either the economy or the demographic picture of the country are not very useful. What is needed is a region by region, cercle by cercle, and arrondissement by arrondissement statistical picture, coordinated with statistical sketches of surrounding countries. The demographic picture of Mali is drawn from two censuses, a sample census done in 1960-61 and the first complete census, only provisional results of which are published, done in 1976. These are combined with inferences drawn from more detailed monographs, geographic and historical monographs on particular regions, in order to have a more localized picture. Reference is also made to statistics on urbanization kept by SEDES in Orléans, France. Economic statistics come from government publications of current accounts, United Nations compilations of those statistics, and International Bank for Reconstruction and Development working papers with interpretations of the same statistics. In the area of finance, these are supplemented by the Banque Centrale des Etats de L'Afrique de l'Ouest (BCEAO) currency records.

Mali's 1976 census shows a substantially higher total population than had been anticipated by previous census projections and, by inference, an accelerated rate of population growth compared with the period prior to 1960. The total population resident in Mali in 1976 was 5,908,000. In the 1960-61 sample census, the population was estimated at 3,714,500. The natural growth rate had been estimated in 1960 at 2.5 percent per year. But actual growth, not counting emigration, averaged 2.9 percent in the 16-year inter-censal period.[1] Again, as in Mauritania, we hypothesize that the theoretical interannual variation in mortality rates is the best explanation of why cumulative growth exceeds predicted natural increase. The questions on fertility and mortality from which demographers generally estimate natural increase apply only to a single 12-month period, and the precensus year was apparently not average. Fertility and mortality rates have not yet been estimated from the new census. The 1960 estimates yield a birthrate of 55 per 1,000 (58 in urban areas, 54 in rural areas) and a mortality rate of 30 per 1,000 (25 in urban areas, 30 in rural areas), implying 2.5 percent growth. In view of the 2.89 percent measured annual growth between censuses, we may hypothesize that, as elsewhere in the Senegambia, the birthrate has increased slightly the the death rate decreased substantially.

The urban proportion of the population in 1960-61 was 258,900 or 6.9 percent of the total. In 1976, it was 751,380 or 12.4 percent of the total. That means the urban population is growing at an annual average rate of 6.89 percent and that it doubles every 10.7 years.

Mali officially defines urban centers as having more than 10,000 population. In 1960, that included Bamako with 129,300 and Mopti, Sikasso, Segou, and Kayes with a total rural population of 107,600. By 1976, the population of Bamako was 386,492; it had tripled since 1960. The other four cities, Mopti, Sikasso, Segou, and Kayes had a total population of 218,200 or double their original number. In addition, there were at least seven new cities to qualify, which had formerly been listed as towns of 3,000-10,000 or had not been on the list at all. These included Kita, Nioro, Koulikoro, Koutiala, Gao, Tombouctou, and Kati.

Regional growth was highly uneven throughout Mali. The Bamako and Mopti regions grew very rapidly, and the other three regions for which there are both 1976 and 1960-61 statistics (Kayes, Sikasso, and Segou) grew much less rapidly. See Table 11.1.

TABLE 11.1

Regional Population Growth in Mali

Region	1960/61	1976	Percent Increase
Bamako	541,000	1,320,170	144
Mopti	497,500	1,236,172	148
Sikasso	727,700	1,171,861	61
Segou	593,100	984,613	66
Kayes	513,500	871,871	70

Sources: Mali, Service de la Statistique in cooperation with France, Secrétariat d'Etat aux Affaires Etrangères, Institut de la Statistique et des Etudes Economiques (INSEE), "Enquête démographique au Mali, 1960-61" (mimeographed, Orléans: INSEE, 1967); Mali, Bureau National du Recensement (BNR), "Résultats provisoires du recensement national de la population, 1976" (mimeographed, Bamako: BNR, n.d.). Regions not included in the 1960/61 sample survey are not included in this table. The official 1976 totals include legal residents of Mali whether enumerated as present or absent.

Average population density in Mali in 1976 is given as 4.8 people per square kilometer.[2] However, for the country as a whole and for most of the regions of the country, overall population density is a meaningless statistic. Only in the Sikasso and southern Bamako region are fairly dense dispersed agricultural populations possible. Elsewhere the agricultural population is concentrated in the river valleys. In the Kayes region, for instance, which particularly interests us in studying the Senegambia, the overall population density is given as seven people per square kilometer. However, the agricultural populations in the river valley approach 50 per square kilometer, and the northern part of the region has essentially a pastoral population with a very low density. Thus, despite the overall low population density, population pressure on the arable land of the river valleys is a contributor to emigration.

EMIGRATION

Emigration from the buckle of the Niger River is an old tradition in Mali, having begun with the ancient empires as an expansiveness, a reaching into new areas to draw trade into the Niger buckle area. The long-distance trading groups that initiated that penetration in the thirteenth through fifteenth centuries are still the most dynamic migrant groups today. In those centuries, Soninke (called Sorakhole in local reports) traders colonized trade routes from the Niger buckle to the upper Gambia River and south from Jenne to the Akan hinterland in what is now Ghana. They were followed by waves of migrants, settling and developing the agricultural potential of the trading areas, particularly along the Gambia. Trade routes already existed, linking the upper Senegal with the Niger, and these, too, were traveled by Soninke as well as Moor traders. The Mandinka population of the Gambia and Upper Casamance areas originated primarily from this period of heavy colonization.

The Soninke area on the upper Senegal River in the Matam area of Senegal, the Kayes region of Mali, and the Nema region of Mauritania were earliest and hardest hit by the economic dislocations of the colonial era. As the first leg of the eventual Dakar-Bamako railroad was completed in 1886, it supplanted their trade route between Kayes and Bamako. The tradition of young Soninke seeking opportunity in long-distance trade provided the background for their adaptation to the colonial economy. Soninke disproportionately figured among the early sailors on the French merchant marine, urban migrants to Saint-Louis and Dakar, and more recently, migrant laborers in France.

A 1973 study of African immigrants in France listed the total as 70,000 including, in round figures, 35,000 Malians, 21,000 Senegalese, 10,000 Mauritanians, and 5,000 from other countries.[3] In fact, those Malians, Senegalese, and Mauritanians, comprising 66,000 of the 70,000, were almost entirely Soninke from the same homeland that happens to be divided among those three countries. Soninke are also among the most enterprising ethnic groups seeking high-income opportunities in trade or wage labor, wherever they may occur. Thus, in sharp contrast to the majority of the population of the Kayes region, which sends migrants traditionally toward the nearby, cash-crop areas of Senegal, the Soninke are found in faraway Ivory Coast, Nigeria, Gabon, and other areas of Central Africa, as well as in France and Senegal.

The Bambara areas of the Kayes region served as a human-power reservoir for Senegal, historically as well as in the modern period. During the era of the slave trade, this area was the major source of slaves both for Senegalese societies and for export. In the early twentieth century, labor recruitment continued in these areas under colonial rule in a form more efficient and only slightly less coercive than during the slave trade. Young men were enlisted to build the railroad, to cut the first roads, to keep the river navigable, and, during World War I, to serve as military labor supply. In addition, when it was discovered that they came as voluntary apprentice farmers into the peanut-producing areas as clients of landowners in the area, they provided a valuable, expandable work force for peanut production, which the colonial government wished to encourage, and this seasonal labor migration was organized and administered by the colonial government. The seasonal migrant client farmers became known as nawetan, the Wolof word for rainy-season migrant farmers. The cash the nawetan gained from the sale of their crops was reinvested in dry-season trade; that is, they took their incomes, went to the nearest trading station or city, and purchased consumer goods that they distributed in the interior at an additional profit. A substantial proportion of nawetans engaged in this dual-seasonal migratory employment, others returned home, and still others stayed in their adopted villages doing repairs, fencing, and well digging for their patrons. At its peak in the period just before and after World War II, the annual flow of nawetan into the Senegalese peanut basin constituted 60,000-70,000 migrants, 60 percent of them of Soudanese (Malian) origin.

With approaching self-government in 1956, the governments of both Mali and Senegal tried to discourage the nawetan migration—Senegal in order to increase opportunities for its own surplus labor and Mali in order to develop its own cash-crop peanut-growing areas. Nevertheless, the system continues to be very important in the expanding areas of the groundnut basin on the Senegalese frontier and in the Gambia. Regguts estimates suggest that 9,000-11,000 still work annually in Senegal and 33,000 (21 percent of whom are Malian) in the Gambia.[4]

The Dakar to Bamako railroad, particularly the section from Kayes to Bamako that runs through Mali, has been crucial in the development of this migration. The areas along the Kayes to Bamako railroad were the main areas from which nawetan came. Jacques Fouquet's study of the nawetan noted that, in the period from 1934 to 1950, Malians constituted 60 percent of the nawetan in Senegal and that they came predominantly from the circles of Kita, Bafoulabe, Kayes, Nioro du Sahel, Segou, and Bansaro. [5] The railroad line was also the area chosen by Mali for Operation Arachide, its own peanut crop development project in the early 1960s. However, Operation Arachide has had only a small measure of success and the areas in which it was developed continue to be the major sending areas for nawetan to the Senegambian peanut basin. The most recent study of migrant farmers in the Senegambian peanut basin is Swindell's study of Gambian strange farmers (nawetani). It is also the first to provide a measure of their places of origin. It indicates that, by far, the majority of the Malians currently migrating into the Gambia as nawetan come from the Kayes, Bafoulabe, Kita, Bamako, and Bougouni circles. Smaller portions are found from the Nioro and Koulikoro areas and negligible groups from other areas of Mali. The most notable change in the nawetan movement, however, since independence, is that the Malian proportion in the overall total has declined substantially. Internal migrants' proportions, that is, Senegalese and Gambians, have increased, and Guineans have come to predominate among both the seasonal and the permanent immigrants to the frontier areas of the Senegambian peanut basin.

The other aspect of Malian agricultural emigration that has changed substantially since the 1950s is the development of the attraction of the Ivory Coast. Fouquet estimated that 25,000 Malians emigrated from Sikasso and Bougouni circles toward the Gold Coast in the period from 1934 to 1950. Since the construction of the port of Abidjan in 1950, the focus has shifted toward Ivory Coast and the number has multiplied. A 1963 tally of visa requests in Bamako indicates the sweeping change in directions of migrations; by then, 61 percent of all legal emigrants went to the Ivory Coast. Annual estimates are not available for the present period; indeed, annual seasonal migration and return is no longer the general pattern. The common practice today is a temporary migration covering at least several years of a young man's life in which the rainy season is spent farming and the dry season is spent in various other remunerative cash occupations including commerce, well digging, fence building, compound work, and crafts. But the total number of Malians living in Ivory Coast in 1975 was 364,000. By contrast, only 21,000 Malians were estimated to be living in Senegal in 1971.

Emigration tends to be regarded as an economic loss by the country from which migrants go. This is a traditional African assessment and probably an accurate one despite the countervailing argument that migrant remittances of income are important to their families. Since migrants are predominantly males in their most active ages, from 20 to 35 years, they have a serious effect on the age and sex structure of the population in the areas of origin. This is most notable in the Soninke areas in which average male emigration is near 40-50 percent and some villages experience absentee rates of as much as 70 percent of the active male population.[6] In the absence of the men, the work devolves on women, children, and old people and deteriorates in both quantity and quality. Some of it is done by nawetan and nooran from the farther hinterland. Social institutions and organizations also tend to erode, and an atmosphere of deprivation amidst monetary affluence pervades the area. There is evidence that the wages sent home by migrants working in France are quite substantial sources of income, averaging 40 percent of the migrant's salary or about $950 per year. This makes the emigrant area one of the higher income per capita areas of each of the countries concerned. However, the income does not add to local production. The loss of the active hands means a net loss of agricultural produce in the area, and the remittances tend to be spent for nonproductive investments in durable housing, mobilettes, and other consumer goods, rather than for agricultural equipment, fertilizer, water supply or processing, or cottage industry. One reason for this lack of productive reinvestment is that the migrant stays away an increasing number of years, expending his creative energies as well as his labor abroad.

In the context of migrant incomes and remittances, it is important to note that the irrigated perimeters planned for the OMVS river valley development propose to provide a household income of only $425 (100,000 cfa) per year—half of what an individual emigrant saves and remits. Plot sizes would have to be double the proposed one-half hectare size and/or allocated to all adult members of a household in order for that agricultural development to compete as an opportunity for young Soninke males. If plot offerings are enlarged, the population gainfully employed in the project will be correspondingly reduced and income inequalities between irrigation and rainfall farming areas exaggerated. If plot size offerings are not increased, emigration of Soninke will probably accelerate as their lands are converted to irrigation and the plots will be taken by inmigrant farmers from other less advantaged areas.

The economic dilemma posed by emigration from Mali is that it results in capital accumulation through savings (migrant remittances) but not in the necessary further step of productive reinvestment. Therefore, Mali at present counts a gain of income from emigration but a loss of productivity. It also may pose a substantial obstacle to irrigation development in the home area due to family dislocation and opportunities competition that local development cannot match.

URBANIZATION

Urbanization has very similar dynamics for Mali. Mali had a medieval period of urbanization connected with the transsaharan trade, which produced such cosmopolitan centers as Timbuktu, Jenne, and Gao and the nuclei of Segou, San, Bamako, Kankan, Sikasso, Kayes, and Mopti. These cities had long been losing importance to coastal centers, however, by the time colonization introduced a new wave of urbanization. Today, although the cities of Mali have very little productive function, Mali has developed the rate of urbanization that is one of the highest in the world. The pattern whereby the capital city is primate and much more rapidly growing than the rest is not so marked in Mali, partly due to the rival attraction of the primate cities of Abidjan and Dakar. The population of Bamako was measured at 386,492 in the 1976 census, roughly three times its 1960-61 size of 129,300. This represents a 7.1 percent annual rate of growth. The total urban population of Mali (defined as those living in cities with more than 10,000 inhabitants) has grown at an almost identical rate, 6.9 percent per year, which reflects little tendency toward primacy. In addition to the increased demand for housing, schooling, health care, and other social services generated by this high rate of urbanization, the lack of directly productive employment in the towns and cities makes it a clear burden to the national economy.

The 1976 census gives a profile of emigrants, without, however, distinguishing between those who are absent overseas or in another country and those who are absent within Mali. In 1979, only the preliminary results were available, that is, a listing of population by sex, region, circle, and residence status. Residence status means either present, absent, or visitor in the compound enumerated in reference to the day of the census, December 16, 1976. The category of "residents absent" gives an approximation of the emigrant and outmigrant population. The total number of residents absent was 400,005, of whom 237,268 were males and 162,737, females. They constituted 6.6 percent of the total population, 8.1 percent of the male population, and 5.2 percent of the female population. This number is almost certainly an underestimate, as the Malian emigrant population in Ivory Coast alone was estimated at 364,000 in

1975. Many have presumably left Mali long enough to no longer be counted. [7] What is measured by the Malian census is migration within the last six months or year, including some temporary displacement for noneconomic purposes.

A better estimate of total emigration can probably be gained from looking at the Malian-born population of surrounding countries and of France and at the nonlocal population of various areas of Mali. This nonlocal population figure will presumably be published in the final census results; it is not available now. Estimates of the Malian-born population elsewhere include 35,000 in France in 1973, 364,000 in Ivory Coast in 1975, 21,000 in Senegal in 1971, 13,412 in Ghana in 1970, and 6,930 in Gambia in 1974-75. If we assume a conservative 2.2 percent growth rate for the emigrant Malians in France, Ivory Coast, Senegal, and Gambia and a decline (due to economic and political constraints) in Ghana, we would come up with a total of some 452,000 Malians living outside the country in 1976.

It is likely that the number of internal migrants, mainly rural-urban, is roughly equal to the number of emigrants, about 450,000. In 1960-61, 53 percent of the population of Bamako was born elsewhere. While a corresponding figure is not available for the 1976 census, in the face of accelerating urbanization, we must assume that in both Bamako and other cities this proportion has increased. Thus, well over half of the 751,380 Malians living in cities with more than 10,000 in population in 1976 would have been born elsewhere. Not all of those born elsewhere moved directly from rural to urban residence; some were stepwise migrants moving from smaller to larger cities. In 1960-61, 37 percent of the urban population had been born in rural districts.

There is a clear, statistically demonstrable lack of opportunity in the formal sector of the economy, yet it is no inhibition to the rural exodus. In 1974, there were 36,437 salaried jobs in all of Mali, 27,886 in the private sector and 8,551 in the public. The working-aged population was about 3 million.

Very few salaried jobs are taken by rural migrants, and those are mostly at the lower levels of domestic service: guardians, gardeners, and errand runners. The better opportunities in the informal economy are also likely to be monopolized by long-time city residents. A list of the marginal occupations and estimated incomes at which fresh migrants usually start their urban "employment" was made in a 1967 memoir of the Ecole Nationale d'Administration:

> Domestic servant: pounding millet, going to market for cooking supplies, going to herders park to buy milk, sweeping court-yard. Salary 1000 FM/month [usually in addition to some food and/or lodging].

Push cart vendor: earns c. 300 FM/day.

Street vendor: cigarettes, candy, matches, etc., sells c. 200 FM/day; most are Sarakole.

Cola nut vendor: takes in 150 FM/day; most are Sarakole.

Lemonade and baby-glasse vendors: hired by the women who make it.

Vendors of grilled snacks: sell cooked meat and other foods, grilled on their roadside charcoal grill.

Garibous: beggars who try to pass for Koranic talibs (disciples). [Real disciples are often brought to the city to beg by their marabouts, making the distinction difficult.]

Filanis: take dirty laundry to the river and wash it.

Baragninis: people seeking work, who stand around public places waiting to be picked up. [8]

One could add a multitude of similar odd jobs done by migrants, including selling water (carried to the compound), washing and/or "guarding" parked cars, carrying market baskets, and so on. Many pay less than enough to purchase a day's food and involve more work for less income than farming. Food and lodging have to be sought separately, by alternately dropping in on as wide as possible a circle of relatives and friends, by adopting a single established patron, or by sharing expenses and crowded sleeping rooms with other migrants. The only reason that the jobs appeal to the worker is that they yield cash. A young man may never see cash in a rural area, even if some of the family crops are sold for money, since it remains entirely under the father or older brother's control.

Rural migrants need cash for a variety of purposes. Young men typically work to earn their dowry, which will enable them to take a bride, and young women to buy the clothes and jewelry that will attract a prosperous husband. They may also work to help their parents pay debts or taxes or to buy a radio, tools, batteries, bicycles, sewing machines, and other manufactured items important in rural areas. Because of the structural rural unemployment imposed by the dry season on most of the country's farmers, any income in the city is a plus. It takes only a small margin of success to make urban incomes better than rural. This is true of nearly everyone in the dry season and, for young people or low status or landless adults, any time of year.

Rural society is generally hierarchical and authoritarian, whereas national ideals expressed daily on radio broadcasts throughout rural areas encourage the concept of individual dignity and opportunity. The city offers freedom even if it is at the margin of survival. This is important to young people when they reach the age at which they need to establish independent households. Once they have lived with city liberties for a season or two, it becomes increasingly difficult to accept village values and standards. This is particularly true for people with ascribed low status and rigidly defined roles in the village—women, castes, and people of slave origin, who together constitute a large majority of the population. Government leaders in Mali, as elsewhere in Africa, evoke the ideal of a nation founded on modern individuals, unconstrained by caste, status, or sexual discrimination. However, these ideals come in direct conflict with village customs, and much less progress has been made in eliminating them at the village level than in the city. Virtually the only efficacious means available to villagers affected by limited role ascription and discrimination is departure.

Even though the data on absentees are not comprehensive, they do give a general indication of the structure of migratory patterns within the country and a profile of the migrant population. In other words, we assume that it involves a reasonably systematic under-enumeration of emigrants, but, internally, it reflects approximately correct proportions among regions and population groups. The proportion of males to females among absentees was 146 to 100. The resident population, on the other hand, shows only 96 males for every 100 females. The actual sex ratio of emigrants is probably even higher than that indicated, since a substantial proportion of women moving short distances across district lines for the purposes of marriage are included by census definition as absent residents. Using the 1976 data, it is possible to see that emigration varies widely from region to region. The regions sending emigrants to Ivory Coast contribute the greatest amount to the total emigrant flow, with Sikasso contributing 27.6 percent, Mopti 20.3 percent, and Bamako 20.9 percent, while the Segou, Gao, and Kayes regions trailed with 11.2 percent, 10.4 percent, and 9.6 percent of the total emigrant group, respectively.

From the point of view of loss of labor in the agricultural sector, it is also important to look at the male absentee rates in relation to the resident male population of a particular region.[9] In this respect, the ratio of absentees to resident populations is highest in Sikasso, Mopti, Gao, and Bamako, in declining order, at 12.7 percent, 9.0 percent, 8.0 percent, and 7.0 percent, respectively. It declines to 5.8 percent in Segou and 5.7 percent in Kayes regions. No age breakdown of the total population is yet available for the 1976 census, but it is clear from the observed patterns of growth, mortality, and fertility that the age structure will be close to what it was in 1960-61. Specialized studies indicate clearly that the age of migrants is still concentrated in the 20-35 year bracket.

Other tendencies that have been observed but not yet recorded in census data are a shift from seasonal to longer term migration and an increase in the proportion of married migrants accompanied by their wives. They have been observed in the Upper Volta migration study, seem also to be true of Malian immigrants,[10] and may be important considerations in measuring the long-term impact of migratory trends in the area. The earlier seasonal migration to Senegal resulted in little permanent population transfer in relation to the large volume of temporary migrants shipped in and out seasonally. The 21,000 Malian-born residents in Senegal in 1971 is very small in relation to the number of nawetan who made the journey between 1934 and 1960, at the rate of some 32,000 per year. The more recent migrations into Ivory Coast and the peanut frontiers of Senegal and Gambia today seem to be tending toward more permanence as migrants bring their families with them and attempt to acquire land and/or other fixed resources in the area of immigration.

IS RURAL DEVELOPMENT THE CURE FOR THE RURAL EXODUS?

Mali offers an excellent test of the theory that rural development is the best answer to the problems generated by emigration and urbanization. Since independence, the government of Mali has put high priority on agricultural development, realizing that the fertile river valley is one of its best sources of wealth, both traditionally and potentially. The large irrigated land project on the interior delta of the Niger, called the Niger Office, was its main hope, and there were additional projects to extend the cultivation for export of peanuts and cotton as well as the increase in rice and sugar production. Twenty-six percent of initial investment in the 1960-65 five-year plan was aimed at agriculture, versus 16 percent for industry and 14 percent for social services. Forty-three percent was destined for infrastructure, much of that roads and irrigation equipment to facilitate the development of the agricultural sector. The groundnut scheme, "Operation Arachide," can only be termed a failure. Although it did introduce the commercialization of groundnuts in an area along the Kayes-Bamako railroad, total Malian groundnut exports fell continuously from about 50,000 tons of shelled peanuts in 1960 to about 20,000 tons per year by 1970. And the area remained a major source of emigrants to the peanut basin of Gambia and Senegal.

The Niger Office, while from the peasant point of view and, in some respects, from a total economic point of view, is considered more successful, offers no solution to the problems of the rural exodus or population growth. After an initial two years of growth in the Niger Office area in 1961 and 1962, difficulties connected with the socialization of agriculture, the repatriation of Upper Volta colonists who had been recruited during the colonial era, and failures in the economics of cotton production and marketing led to an actual decline in the number of colonists on the Niger Office lands, lasting from 1963 through 1968. From 1969 on, however, the demand for land in the Niger Office has grown steadily. It is clear that both peasants and government see it as an alternative to the rural exodus and that both also see irrigated agriculture as an alternative to the uncertainties of drought. During the drought years, applicants for plots in the Niger project increased to ten times the number available each year.[11] It is also clear that in recent years yearround cultivation of irrigated land has provided peasants with a revenue substantially higher than that available to their neighbors engaged in rainfall agriculture.[12]

Thus, since 1969, the Niger Office has been claiming a greater rate of success. To the peasant, it is successful in that it offers, now with improved marketing and organization, a better income than rainfall agriculture in surrounding areas. From the government's point of view, it is a success in that it offers higher yields per hectare. In this sense, it is an important viable option to the rural exodus for a few peasants. The problem is that it is not a viable option for as many peasants as need employment. Productivity of the land has increased, but the proportion of the total population involved in the productivity has decreased. The population of Mali increased 59 percent from 1960 to 1976 (from 3.7 million to 5.9 million). The population of the Niger Office increased only 31 percent (from 32,000 in 1960 to 42,000 in 1975). More importantly, the Niger Office, even if it had doubled in population instead of increasing by a third, would have had very little measurable impact on the rate of urbanization. The urban population of Mali increased by some 400,000 during the same period. This indicates that, even though the Niger Office is reasonably successful and one of the largest agricultural development projects in all of French West Africa, it is on far too small a scale to have any statistically measurable impact on the rate of urbanization. While the total population involved in the other agricultural development projects is not known and cannot readily be determined, it is known that their total is less than the total population involved in the Niger Office. These figures suggest that the scale of agricultural development projects will have to be greatly increased in the future just to keep up with population growth and that attention must also be paid to introducing productive activities for the urban population.

MIGRATION AND PUBLIC POLICY IN MALI

Public policy makers in Mali have tended, with some justification, to regard all news brought by demographers as bad news. The high birth and death rates, like the major outward flows of migration, portray a difficult situation for years to come. Yet the overall sparsity of population and low level of urbanization have meant a weak market potential for industrialization. Thus, in the abstract, Mali would be in a more favorable politicoeconomic position for industrialization if it had a larger total population, providing greater market opportunities within shorter distances. This has influenced Mali's official political conception of population problems, as has its Islamic heritage, creating pressure against any program of limited population growth on a national scale. Only recently has it instituted a national committee to examine demographic issues. This means that, for the immediate future, the predictions are that the current trends will continue at rates that are difficult for Mali, for plans to cope with social services, and for the economy of the country in its present state. It would take at least two decades for a national system of family planning to have any measurable impact on the rate of population growth, even if one were implemented immediately. This is due to a phenomenon called demographic inertia: essentially, ever-larger population cohorts already born will reach child-bearing age. Since family planning on a national level has not been decided in Mali and there is no nationwide system of health care capable of delivering it if it had, at least a third decade of extremely high population growth must be anticipated.

It is also important for donor countries to recognize that family planning is not politically acceptable on the national level unless there is also some prospect of real economic development. When the prospect is for unrelieved poverty, many would rather be poor and numerous than poor and few.

The high rate of population growth in the rural areas implies that a high priority must continue to be put on agricultural development, seeking increased yields from diminishing per capita resources. On the other hand, it also means that the inevitability of urbanization must be accepted and dealt with. The rural exodus is likely not only to continue, but also to accelerate. This implies rapidly increasing demand for education and health care and urban infrastructure. It must mean also a new emphasis on productivity in the urban economy, on finding productive occupations for urban

residents. So long as the high rates of population growth and a low
rate of economic development continue, outmigration is an unfortunate necessity in the Malian economy. On the household level, outmigration means survival throughout large portions of the rural
areas. On the national level, it means additional foreign-exchange
earnings, however modest. In the case of the Soninke and repatriation of revenues from France, these foreign-exchange earnings offer
a possibility, a source of capital formation and savings, which represent an opportunity for sustained economic growth, provided they
can be directed toward productive reinvestment rather than consumption. In short, the negative aspects of migration patterns are
well-known through long experience in Mali. All efforts to reverse
the major migratory trends have failed and are likely to fail in the
foreseeable future. The best hope is in the area of policies designed
to mitigate the social and economic consequences and to capitalize
on the few opportunities offered by this situation.

INFRASTRUCTURE: TRANSPORTATION
AND COMMUNICATIONS

In many areas, the implications of the migration situation are
that Mali's current development policies are appropriate but not yet
adequate in scale. Transportation and communications comprise
such an area. Mali has been investing heavily, since independence,
in paving roads, in developing electrical capacity, and in irrigation,
all expensive infrastructural improvements that have to be subsidized by foreign aid. Yet, as Mali is a landlocked country, the real
possibility for a more productive future is to develop this network
still further. Unlike Niger or Chad, geography has not doomed Mali
to eternal status as a commercial hinterland and manpower reservoir. The western area of Mali has real potential as a communication center, not just a hinterland.

The Dakar-Bamako railroad has been its lifeline, but, since
independence, Ivory Coast is a still more important axis. Mali
would profit immediately from a rail spur linking Bamako to the
Abidjan-Ouagadougou line at Ferkessedougou. This is already Mali's
most heavily traveled trade route, yet the road is only recently paved
in spots, and maintenance is poor. A rail spur would, of course,
have to be combined with an improvement of the efficiency and capacity of both the port and the railroad within Ivory Coast. Ivory
Coast itself needs, and is willing to invest in, those improvements.
The long mooted agreement with Guinea to build a Bamako to Conakry
railroad and an additional spur connecting Bamako to the existing
railroad from Kankan to Conakry could, in the long term, also be

important. Guinea hopes, in turn, to extend its railroad to the Mount Nimba iron-mining area. Either one of these Malian spurs, and eventually both, would make Bamako a rail entrepot, linking more dynamic seaport areas. The link from Bamako to Ivory Coast would have the most immediate impact because it would link two already growing economies, those of Senegal and Ivory Coast, which currently have substantial commerce with one another by sea. The link with Guinea would open Bamako up to an area rich in mineral resources.

A paved road along the same two axes would also offer an immediate improvement to the development potential of both the rural and the urban areas along it. Again, the completion of two links, one toward Ivory Coast and one toward Senegal, offers much greater potential than a completion of either link alone, because it offers to make Bamako a crossroads between the most productive forest region of Francophone West Africa and the most productive Sahelian region.

Although Senegal currently buys an increasing number of Ivorian imports, chiefly coffee, fruits, fruit products, and light manufactures, only the cola merchants and the art dealers still regularly use the overland route from the forest area of Ivory Coast, north into Bamako, and then west into Senegal. A recent consultant study, prepared by the Louis Berger firm for the government of Bamako and AID and concerning the feasibility of a paved road link between Kayes and Bamako, completely overlooked this regional transportation potential and measured the utility of the road entirely in terms of existing traffic from Kayes to Bamako.[13] This is a myopic approach, characteristic of the hazards involved in planning economic development entirely on a national basis in a Balkanized West Africa. Since it is currently possible to travel from Kayes to Bamako and back only via the railroad, the economy of the region has stagnated and naturally presents little measurable traffic beyond what the railroad can bear. The study's conclusion that the Kayes region is likely to continue to be viable primarily for pastoralism and could make do with upgraded dirt roads is based entirely on the relationship between the region and Bamako. It ignores the historic population density in the area, the cash-crop potential for much of the southern part of Kayes region, and the dynamism of the expanding agricultural economy in peanuts and cotton on the other side of the Senegalese border (to which the Kayes region is still contributing a substantial number of emigrants). The government of Mali knows and has tried to prove through "Operation Arachide" that the Kayes region has the same ultimate potential as the Senegambian groundnut and cotton basin to the west. However, without viable market roads, the area enters a vicious cycle of decline.

Economic history also gives us some perspectives on routes that are attractive but not economically feasible. The transsaharan paved road is a good example. Mali and Algeria have agreed to reestablish the historic link across the Sahara, and this is still attractive to Malian planners for historical as well as political reasons. It gives Mali hope of recovering its advantaged position in the transsaharan trade. The proposed road would connect Gao and Bourem with the Ten Zouaten border post and eventually the Tamanrasid route through Algeria, an extremely long route through once vital but now peripheral desert towns. Mali has been unable to find financing to pave that section of the road, which is understandable. The Bamako-Dakar, Bamako-Courousa-Conakry, and Bamako-Ferkessidougou-Abidjan routes are economically more viable, given the economics of road and rail as opposed to sea transport today. The transsaharan trade and Mali's glorious place in it date from an era when overland routes were the only secure ones for long-distance trade. It is futile to dwell on the geographic arguments of past civilizations, especially when modern patterns offer real potential.

RURAL DEVELOPMENT

Rural development projects represent another area in which scale and quality are needed to keep as much of the rural population as possible in a viable rural situation. The major factors pushing rural residents out of their home villages seem to be lack of cash-income opportunities and lack of a reliable water supply. Both of these can be substantially affected by government policies. The greatest single step that could improve the situation of the rural resident and diminish his need to migrate is an increase in the price to the producer for his crops, both traditional cash crops, such as peanuts and cotton, and food crops, such as rice and millet. Students of West African economies have pointed to the low price to the producer as the cause of inequalities, both internally, between city and countryside, and internationally, between workers in the developed and the less-developed countries. Products produced in the tropics are bought at cheaper prices and marketed at cheaper prices than those produced by Western farmers. Correspondingly, the revenues of European farmers, their hourly incomes, are on a scale far above those of West African farmers. Some of that difference in income is because of greater efficiency, but a substantial portion could be made up by increased African producer prices.

MARKETING, PRICE POLICY, AND TAXATION

The government of Mali, beginning in Modibe Keita's time and again with the military regime that took over after he had failed, recognized the essential exploitation involved in low prices to producers and the vulnerability of Malian farmers to commercial exploitation. In response, the regime organized government monopoly marketing systems by the Office des Produits Agricoles du Mali (OPAM) and the Société Malienne d'Importation et d'Exportation (SOMIEX). While, in conception, the state marketing monopoly for each product or project has the protection of the peasant as its purpose, in practice, the government has found itself in the same position as the colonial economy; that is, its revenues depend too heavily on the exploitation of this sector of the economy. Therefore, it continues to pay low prices to the producers and to take a substantial proportion of government revenues out of the margin between producer prices and world-market prices.

Price policy rests on official, socialist, egalitarian ideals, conceived in terms of protection for the consumer rather than the producer. A complex price situation has resulted, in which there are official producer and consumer prices fixed every six months by a government committee. There are also free market retail prices for virtually every commodity (black market for monopoly items). Official consumer prices are generally below free market prices, as are producer prices.[14] However, since consumers include both rich and poor, while peasant producers are almost all poor, keeping official prices low has had the effect of subsidizing the better off at the expense of the poorest.

Salaries and incomes of all levels of workers are low and inelastic in Mali compared to pay for similar work in Ivory Coast, Senegal, or particularly in developed countries. In face of this, price setters have reasoned that Malians cannot absorb the recent worldwide inflation, especially in food prices. Imported rice, for example, went from 80 Malian Francs (at 200 FM = 100 F cfa = ± $.45) in 1971 to 280 FM/kg in 1975. The government subsidy of consumer prices went, in the same period in Bamako, from 9.3 FM/kg to 178.7 FM/kg, while the producer's price went from 18 FM/kg to 40 FM/kg.[15] By 1975 the consumer's subsidy was seven times the price paid the Malian peasant. As the gap between world prices and official ones increases, the government finds itself unable to carry the cost and is forced to reduce the amount of subsidized food available. Estimates of the proportion of goods selling at official prices, handled by the government monopolies, ranges from 25 percent to 40 percent.[16] As the amount of subsidized food shrinks, pressure to make it available to people with influence increases. Free market urban food supplies also tend to shrink, as there is a scramble for the officially priced food, and many of the poor cannot afford free market prices. In short, in the face of rapid inflation, the consumer subsidization policy is bankrupting the government, reducing overall food supplies, and penalizing rather than protecting the poor.

The disparity between Mali's low producer prices and higher ones in Ivory Coast and Senegal provides incentive to farmers to either smuggle their crops into neighboring countries for sale or migrate there to farm.

In 1974, Mali was paying farmers 18 FM/k ($0.04) for millet when the world market price was more than four times that. In a major 1975 shift, it raised the price to 32 FM/k ($0.07) and simultaneously raised rice to 40 FM/k ($0.09). But Senegalese producers received 32 cfa (64 FM) per kilo of millet and 41.5 cfa (83 FM) per kilo of rice in 1975.

Efficient transportation and marketing of agricultural produce was and still is a major need for agricultural development in Mali. The government was and is the largest organized body in the area capable of developing such a marketing structure. However, the monopoly provisions, designed to make the initial system successful, seem to have deprived its bureaucratic managers of the incentive to develop real commercial efficiency.

Increased marketing efficiency needs to be combined with a system of regularly established increases in the price to the producer, so that, eventually, producer prices will be supported, not driven down, by the government. Only higher prices to the producers will enable peasants to escape from the cycle of debt and dependence in which they have been held since the colonial period.

Not all, or even a substantial portion, of increase in producer prices need be directly reflected in prices to the consumer, particularly of food crops. Some of the difference can be absorbed by reduction in the margin taken by government marketing corporations, OPAM and SOMIEX. To do this, the government would have to reduce personnel and diversify its source of revenues, most probably through progressive income and property taxes. This would be politically difficult. The current marketing system results in what amounts to an invisible, indirect tax on agricultural producers. Because of its indirect pattern and lack of visibility, it is politically feasible as long as most of the people do not understand the practice. Many peasants do, in fact, understand the disadvantage they suffer by it, however, and consider themselves justified in illegally exporting their crops for sale.

The feasibility of transferring some government revenues to progressive income tax would depend on the government's ability to cope with the wealthier urban population and its political pressure. So far, local sentiment among bureaucrats, and perhaps among urban dwellers in general, has focused on the much greater international inequality, which they see reflected daily in the luxurious lifestyle of the locally stationed international elite. Tax policy thus far has recognized the need for austerity by levying heavy duties on luxury imports. This may be more an apparent than a real solution, since, in practice, it has the opposite tendency of encouraging government to expand the import-export trade in order to assure itself revenues. And since the imports must in fact be paid for with corresponding exports of agricultural produce, the burden ultimately returns to the farmer. A system of price supports for producers, storage of surplus, and progressive income and property taxes on the wealthy would offer a better long-term prospect for reduction of inequalities and economic growth.

That producer prices directly affect the amount of a particular crop to be produced has been shown repeatedly in Senegambian and nearby Ivorian economies. The impression among some development planners, that Senegambian farmers are governed more by tradition than by market mechanisms, simply is not historically valid. Sometimes they are kept in less profitable forms of production, such as groundnuts in Senegal, by indebtedness and essentially administrative manipulations. However, there has been a clear response, particularly across border areas, when producer prices are varied from one area to another or one year to another. Depending on price levels, farmers in one area will grow rice while those in another turn to cotton or groundnuts. Raising the price of food crops such as millet also substantially affects the amount sown and the viability of fertilizer purchase. Even when the price is not raised, where the drought decreased the reliability of the groundnut crop, farmers switched en masse to millet in order to ensure their survival.

The mode and timing of payments to farmers for their crops also has a substantial effect on their satisfaction with rural residency. Farmers have shown a clear preference for an early and immediate cash payment. The advantage to the farmer of an early cash payment is substantial. He can then reinvest it in commerce during the dry season or he can have the use of the consumer goods that he buys with it for a longer period of time. Or he may finance for himself a period of apprenticeship in a craft during the dry-season period, which, if he has no income, is essentially a period of underemployment or low productivity.

RURAL DEVELOPMENT PLANNING

Consideration of causes of outmigration also suggests some important goals for the design of rural development plans. To have any restraining effect on the rural exodus, projects must provide cash income. In rainfall agricultural areas, they should also deal with the problem of dry-season unemployment. Both of these may be provided most efficiently in small, nearby, outlying towns rather than in rural villages or capital cities.

Rural development plans will also have to give careful consideration to providing opportunities for young, casted, and slave-origin people and for women, while anticipating resistance and conflict from upholders of the old order. One of the common failings of a well-meaning "democratic" approach, involving consulting "the people" on the design of projects in their area, is that village meetings customarily consist only of adult male heads of households. The planners who consult them, also normally adult male heads of households, rarely take exception to this. The result is often that excluded groups have fewer rights in new projects than they had been able to negotiate over the years in the old system. Malian and donor planners will have to consider carefully how to revise the design, consultation, and decision-making processes to open the way for these excluded groups. It would help if planners themselves were of more diverse origins, ages, and sex.

The problem of water supply has three major aspects: water availability for agriculture (irrigation or garden-plot wells), water for village domestic use, and water for livestock. All three are highly precarious at the present state in Mali, and all three are essential to the stabilization of the rural economy and population. While rural development economists tend to focus on water supply for irrigation and for livestock, the provision of a domestic water supply would probably have the greatest effect on the rural exodus. Although no nationwide survey has been conducted, field observations indicate that a substantial proportion of the rural villages of Mali lack a water supply for drinking and village hygiene from approximately the middle of one dry season to well into the next rainy season. From January or February at some places and March and April in others, wells run dry until June or July when the new rains bring up the water table again. This is a really disagreeable time in village life; it is the hottest season of the year and villagers sometimes have to travel great distances to obtain small supplies of water for drinking. Under these conditions, hygiene deteriorates since water, which is in such scarce supply, is reused or washing cannot be done. This is also a period of high morbidity during which measles, polio, and encephalitis frequently reach epidemic proportions. At the

end of the period comes intense agricultural labor, when the fields
are being prepared and planted and then the first weeding needs to be
done. Understandably, this dry lean time, particularly the months
of March and April, is when rural cousins most frequently visit
their urban relatives. Agricultural productivity could be substantially increased if this interfamily visiting allowed urban relatives,
particularly students, to provide extra agricultural labor at peak
demand times. In fact, the opposite is usually the case, as urban
residents time their visits at low labor demand periods so that
people will have time to visit with them and they will not be asked
to work.

URBAN POLICY

The other side of the migration situation in Mali is the urban
scene. The inescapable conclusion, based on the demographic and
economic statistics previously cited and on the historical experience
of modernization elsewhere in the world, is that every effort that
must be made and is being made in rural development will not alter
the basic direction of urbanization that Mali is currently taking.
Efforts must be made to stabilize the rural economy, but the rural
economy does not have the capacity to absorb the current population
growth. The tendency of most agricultural modernization plans,
including the introduction of mechanization—particularly in the Mali
area of animal-drawn plows—and seeding and harvesting equipment,
is to increase the amount of land that one person can cultivate.
Thus, even projects designed to be labor-intensive generally reduce
the proportion of labor necessary per unit of land area in rural
areas. This is part of the reason why we cannot look to rural development alone to stop urbanization. The economic implication is
that urban employment must grow very much more rapidly than it
has been growing.

Moreover, if the increasing economic dependency of Mali is
ever to be reversed, urban employment must be increasingly productive rather than service- and income-oriented. Mali's initial
attempts at industrialization have been relatively successful. Transformation industries include sugar refining at the Niger Office,
peanut-oil refining at Koulikoro, refrigerated slaughter houses,
and the Baguineta fruit-canning factory. Cotton ginning and the textile industry are also beginning as is tobacco processing and a car-
pet factory. Finished-goods manufacturing has also developed to
replace imports, with a match factory, a small shoe industry, a
cement works, and a metal-goods factory. Productive cottage industries have also sprung up in the urban and small town centers.

These create off-farm employment at a minimal cost-per-job compared to job generating costs in private or government enterprises. Yet neither local governments nor foreign aid agencies have yet found a way to foster their growth without drawing them into a suffocating web of regulation and taxation. Bilateral foreign aid agencies, of which the French Fonds d'Aide et de Coopération (FAC) and the U.S. AID are the largest in Mali, are bound by their own regulations and customs to do most of their purchasing in their own countries. They thus encourage production at home rather than locally.

EDUCATIONAL AND HEALTH POLICY

In Mali, as in Senegal, the formal educational system is geographically centralized, with high school education available only in the large cities, and post-high school training available only in the Grands Ecoles in Bamako. It also operates on a French academic calendar, related originally to French agriculture's peak seasonal labor needs. There is no compelling reason why a school calendar could not be adopted immediately to free Malian pupils and students to help with Malian harvests or other local peak labor. By comparison, the functional literacy program that Mali has adopted reaches farmers in their villages and improves their efficiency in both farming and dry-season occupations, without so directly uprooting them.

All forms of education, like all forms of communications and transportation improvement and most varieties of rural development, probably contribute something to the rural exodus. This is one reason that the overall process is irreversible. It is as true in Mali as in Senegal that every child who enters the educational system at the lowest level multiplies his chances of joining the rural exodus. The system as a whole is still a small contributor to the rural exodus only because only 19 percent of all eight-year-olds ever start school. [17] Thus one must look for types of education that encourage unproductive or premature exodus the least, not at educational alternatives that will actually reverse it.

The criteria for least-urbanizing educational programs are similar throughout the region: geographically decentralized, that is, available in a small city, in a relatively densely populated farming area, or in a rural area itself; teaches skills that can be used directly in that rural area and will provide cash income there; and reaches the population in the migrant age group, 20-30 years old. Notice that the age usually targeted for vocational education is much younger than that, in the 12-16 age range, at which time most students are being flunked out or are otherwise dropping out of the formal educational sector. From the point of view of migration trends and the integration of the trained individual into the economy, lower age-group targeting is entirely inappropriate. Difficult as it is politically, those who drop out or flunk out of the academic educational system would be better left at their young ages to rejoin the family and work back into the family and village economy rather than being accepted immediately as charges of the state, that is, as people in need of additional training. Even if given an additional six months to four years of training at that young age, they still emerge from the system too young to be employed by traditional criteria. Because of the young-age structure of the population, there are also many more of them than of the older age group, so they swell the group of people seeking employment. From the point of view of migration, it would be much more appropriate for vocational educational programs to target the age group 20-35, male and female.

In the general relationship between educational policy and demographic impact, perhaps the greatest potential for long-term improvements would come from an intensified campaign to educate women. Studies throughout the world indicate that the educational level of the mother is the major determinant of fertility. And fertility is the main determinant of the overly youthful population structure, which spurs high migration rates. The following table, from a study of contemporary Ghana, dramatically demonstrates the relationship.

Fertility by Mother's Educational Status
and Urban-Rural Residence
(in numbers of live births)

Educational Status	Total Fertility Ratio		Completed Fertility	
	Urban	Rural	Urban	Rural
No education	5.5	6.4	5.7	6.2
Elementary	5.8	6.9	5.2	5.9
Secondary	2.8	3.4	2.5	1.0
University	4.5	2.5	0.5	—

Source: Gaisie, Dynamics of Population Growth in Ghana (Accra-Tema: Ghana Pub. Corp., 1969), p. 33.

Mali has the most innovative system and, at the same time, the most traditional system of health care of any of the Senegambian countries. Through a national organization of traditional healers, it is attempting to open up communications between scientific medicine, based in the capital, and village health care available through traditional herbalists and marabouts. This may help Mali to avoid the pattern found elsewhere in which modern health care is available primarily in the large cities and to the urban population while the rural population is treated only with epidemic control. At present, epidemic control has benefited from colonial and postcolonial Western-based medical technology. The mortality rate has been substantially reduced. The problem is that the epidemic approach, here as elsewhere, reduces overall mortality without providing a balanced system of health care in rural areas. Thus, while the attack on the greatest killers is both understandable and necessary, without an integrated system of health care it has disastrous demographic results for the family and village populations. The reduction in the mortality rate increases the number of infants who survive, putting an overburden of dependents on the active members of the population in families, villages, and the nation as a whole. Health care projects designed to serve primarily nursing mothers and young children only accentuate the strain on the active population, even though their motivations are thoroughly humane. A balanced health care system should take account of the demographic and economic consequences of its implementation. Otherwise, benefits gained in the area of disease control are lost in the area of nutrition.

The implication of Mali's current demographic picture for health care planning is that health care needs to be available at the mass level and to all sexes and ages. In particular, it needs to be available to the active working population as well as to dependent members of the population. If family planning is adopted as a national program by the new population coordinating committee that Mali has instituted, it is as a component in an integrated system of family health care that it will probably be most acceptable to the population. In this connection, in Mali as elsewhere, family planning is seen as a necessity primarily so that individual families can plan the spacing of their children in relation to their own economic and social situations, not as something the government should impose.

NOTES

1. The actual annual growth rate would have been greater than this because of underestimated emigration. See note 2.
2. Bibi Diawara and Sekou Traore, "Population and Economic Activity in the Transformation of the Rural Sector of Mali: Forces of Inertia and Factors of Change," Les Annales de l'IFORD (Yaounde) 1 (1975).

3. Marie-Therèse Abéla de la Rivière, "The Soninke of Mali and Their Emigration to France," Etudes maliennes 7 (1973): 1-12.

4. A. Vanhaeverbeke, Renumération de travail et commerce extérieur: Essor d'une économique paysanne exportatrice et termes de l'échange de producteurs d'arachides au Sénégal (Louvain: Centre de Recherches de Pays en Développement, Université Catholique de Louvain, Faculté des Sciences Economiques, Sociales et Politiques, 1970); Kenneth Swindell, "A Report on Migrant Farmers in the Gambia," in "Demographic Aspects of Migration in West Africa," eds. K. C. Zachariah and Julien Condé, The Gambia, Annex I, mimeographed, World Bank and OECD, Washington, D.C., 1978.

5. "La traite des arachides dans le pays de Kaolack," Etudes Sénégalaises 8 (Saint-Louis, IFAN, 1958).

6. Francine Kane and André Lericollais, "L'Emigration en pays Soninké," Cahiers de l'ORSTOM 12 (1975): 177-89.

7. The provisional census report does not give definitions for the status of "resident absent," but it is customary in Francophone African censuses to include only those who have been gone more than one month and less than six months or one year.

8. Samabaly, "L'Urbanisation et l'exode rurale," mimeographed student thesis, Bamako, Ecole Nationale d'Administration, 1967.

9. Female agricultural labor is nearly as important to production in most areas as is male, but the data on female absentees are confused by short-distance movements connected with marriage and childbirth. In their present form, they cannot be used for inferences concerning labor supply.

10. The Malian-born population enumerated in Senegal does not include the children of migrants who, being born in Senegal, are, by custom if not by law, considered Senegalese. It nevertheless represents quite a small rate of permanent immigration in relation to the very large rate of seasonal migration from which it derived. By contrast, emigration into the Ivory Coast, Senegal Oriental, and the peanut frontier of Senegal and Gambia today appears to result in a higher rate of permanent settlement.

11. Guimbala Diakite, "Le colonat à l'office du Niger," Mouvements de population et systèmes d'éducation dans les pays sahelo-soudaniens, UNESCO seminar, Dakar, May 26-June 7, 1975.

12. Malick Sène, "Exode rural et insertion de la jeunesse dans les structures socio-économiques du monde rural—zone Operation Riz—Segou," Mouvements de population.

13. Mali, Ministry of Transportation and Public Works, Etude des transports, Bamako-Kayes (n.d., about 1977).

14. CILSS/Club du Sahel Working Group on Marketing, Price Policy and Storage, Marketing, Price Policy and Storage of Food

Grains in the Sahel: A Survey (Ann Arbor, Mich.: Center for Research on Economic Development, 1977), II: Mali Country Study, Diagram 1, p. 13.

    15. Ibid., pp. 18, 19, 24.

    16. Ibid., p. 20.

    17. Malick Sène, "Exode Rural."

12

THE GAMBIA
Lucie Gallistel Colvin

Migration takes on unique aspects in the Gambia because of
the Gambia's unusual historic identity and geographic position in
the Senegambia. It is customary to emphasize the Gambia's smallness (it consists of a band of territory 20-50 kilometers wide and
325 kilometers deep with a land area of 10,400 square kilometers
and a 1973 population of 493,500). See Map 12.1. Ironically, this
smallness reflects not historic weakness but the strength of the
Gambia's position within the Senegambian commercial economy.
The Gambia was attractive to British conquerors at the end of the
nineteenth century because it is the better of the two river systems
of the Senegambia. By controlling the navigable portion of the
Gambia, the British could tap the trade of the entire Senegambia
region and forego the expense of extensive territorial administration. Since the fourteenth century, the Gambia has been attractive
to immigrant farmers, pastoralists, and traders, for many of the
same reasons. With an average of 49 inhabitants per square kilometer, it is one of continental Africa's most densely populated
countries, surpassed only by Rwanda and Burundi (169 per square
kilometer, 142 per square kilometer), Nigeria (72 per square kilometer), and Uganda (52 per square kilometer).[1]

The river is navigable yearround as far as Kaur, nearly 200
kilometers upriver, and seasonally useful portions extend more than
another 200 kilometers upriver. The river banks have offered the
continuing attraction of a regular water supply and trade opportunities, attributes critical to both farmers and pastoralists throughout the region in periods of drought or warfare.

In this context, migration patterns in the Gambia have taken
the form of a regular and ongoing population exchange with Senegal,
the country that surrounds it on three sides. Fluctuations in total

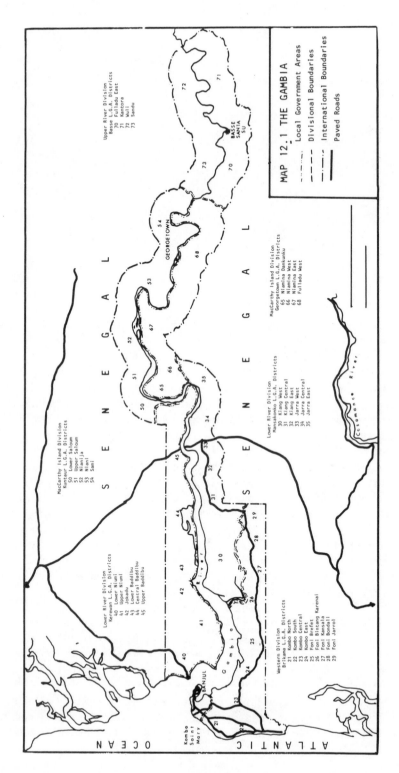

MAP 12.1 THE GAMBIA

······· Local Government Areas
—·—·— Divisional Boundaries
——— International Boundaries
——— Paved Roads

Upper River Division
Basse L.G.A. Districts
70 Fulladu East
71 Kantora
72 Wuli
73 Sandu

MacCarthy Island Division
Georgetown L.G.A. Districts
65 Niamina Dankunku
66 Niamina West
67 Niamina East
68 Fulladu West

Lower River Division
Mansakonko L.G.A. Districts
30 Kiang West
31 Kiang Central
32 Kiang East
33 Jarra West
34 Jarra Central
35 Jarra East

MacCarthy Island Division
Kuntaur L.G.A. Districts
50 Lower Saloum
51 Upper Saloum
52 Nianija
53 Niani
54 Sami

Lower River Division
Kerewan L.G.A. Districts
40 Lower Niumi
41 Upper Niumi
42 Jokadu
43 Lower Baddibu
44 Central Baddibu
45 Upper Baddibu

Western Division
Brikama L.G.A. Districts
21 Kombo North
22 Kombo South
23 Kombo Central
24 Kombo East
25 Foni Brefet
26 Foni Bintang Karenai
27 Foni Kansala
28 Foni Bondali
29 Foni Jarrol

population overlay the pattern of steady growth and are exaggerated by the Gambia's small size. Because political, economic, and natural climatological circumstances can bring rapid influxes and outflows of migrants within this small territory, population growth should be looked at in the context of the entire Senegambia, not merely according to national boundaries. The Gambia's fluctuations can be explained in relation to specific historical development.

Under the combined influences of the Sahelian drought of 1968-73 and the war of liberation in Guinea Bissau from 1961 through 1974, the Gambia has recently had a large influx of migrants. It has also experienced a rapid growth in the number of nawetan from Mali and Guinea Conakry (seasonally migrant client farmers called "strange farmers" in the Gambia). Over the last two decades, as this nawetan system has decreased somewhat in importance in Senegal and has become localized on the expanding frontier, it has increased in usage throughout the Gambia. The 1974-75 study of strange farmers in the Gambia estimated that they totaled 33,000, or nearly 1,000 more than the total number of rural households in the Gambia (32,000 dabadas).[2]

The Gambia is a pole of attraction for Senegambian farmers because of the river valley and for traders because of low tariffs. The attractiveness of the Gambia, both rural and urban, must be explained in terms of household economics, in the context of surrounding economic, political, and climatological events. Both the capital urban area, Banjul-Kombo Saint Mary, and the smaller towns are growing at very rapid rates. The capital area nearly doubled its population between the 1963 and 1973 censuses (from 40,017 to 78,583), growing at a rate of 7 percent per year (see Figure 12.1).

The Gambia has the longest time-series of independent nontax censuses of any country in the region. Beginning with the 1901 census, which showed 90,404 people in the country, there is an irregular pattern of population growth, averaging 2.3 percent annually from 1901 through 1961 and culminating in an apparent 4.6 percent annual increase between the 1963 and 1973 censuses (see Figure 12.2). This jump is subject to varying interpretations. We estimate that 3.6 percent of this growth is real, and close to 3.0 percent of that 3.6 percent is due to natural increase. The other components of the 4.6 percent growth rate would appear to be excessive undercounting in the 1963 census, the return migration of Gambians who had been living in Senegal in the 1960s, and immigration of foreign born into the Gambia. We have an actual count only for the last factor (55,554 foreign born counted in the 1973 Gambian census versus 35,555 counted in the 1963 Gambian census). But even that figure requires reestimation depending upon hypotheses about the other three factors (see Table 12.1).

FIGURE 12.1

Growth of Banjul-Kombo Saint Mary

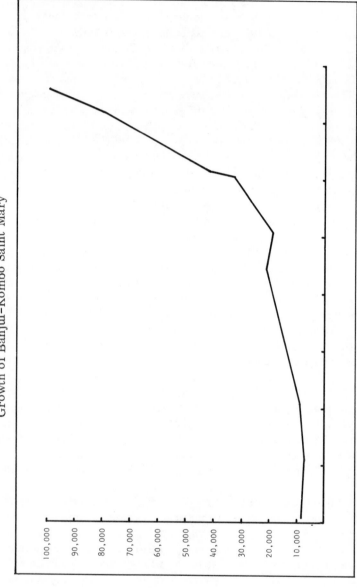

Source: The Gambia, Population Census of the Gambia, 1973, vol. 3 (Banjul: Government Printers, 1976).

FIGURE 12.2

Population Growth in the Gambia

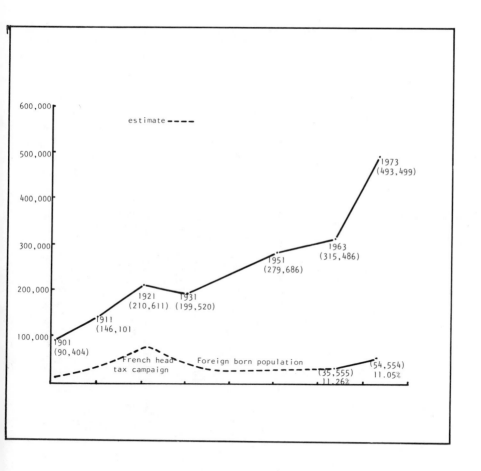

Source: The Gambia, Population Census of the Gambia, 1973, vol. 3 (Banjul: Government Printers, 1976).

TABLE 12.1

Components of 1963–73 Intercensal Growth in the Gambia: Three Hypotheses

Hypothesis 1: Natural increase from 1951 through 1973 averaged a constant 2 percent annually.

Results: Estimated Gambian population in 1963 was 354,709, as opposed to the 315,486 actually counted that year. The difference of 40,000 is attributable partly to Gambians who had emigrated to Senegal and partly to excessive undercounting in the 1963 census.

Components of 4.6 percent intercensal growth rate explained by this hypothesis:

	Number	Percent of Growth	Part of Growth Rate (in percent)
Natural increase	77,700	44	2.0
Gambians returned from Senegal	20,000–25,000	11–14	0.5–0.6
Excess undercounting in 1963 census	15,000–20,000	8–11	0.4–0.5
Foreign immigration	17,000*	9	0.4
Amount of 1963–73 growth explained	134,700	75	3.4
Amount of 1963–73 growth not explained	43,300	25	1.2

Hypothesis 2: Natural increase accelerated from 2 percent annual average from 1951 through 1963 to 3 percent average from 1963 through 1973.

Results: Estimated Gambian population in 1963 was 354,709, as opposed to the 315,486 actually counted. The 40,000 difference is attributable partly to Gambians absent in Senegal and partly to excessive under-enumeration in the 1963 census.

Components of 4.6 percent intercensal growth rate explained by this hypothesis:

	Number	Percent of Growth	Part of Growth Rate (in percent)
Natural increase of Gambians	109,000	61	3.0
Gambians returned from Senegal	20,000–25,000	11–14	0.5–0.6
Excess undercounting in 1963 census	15,000–20,000	8–11	0.4–0.5
Foreign immigration*	17,000	9	0.4
Amount of 1963–73 growth explained	166,000	91	4.4

Hypothesis 3: Natural increase averaged 2.6 percent annually from 1951 through 1973.
Results: Estimated Gambian population in 1963 was 380,573, as opposed to 315,486 actually counted. The 65,000 difference is attributable partly to Gambians absent in Senegal and partly to excessive undercounting in the 1963 census.

Components of 4.6 percent intercensal growth rate explained by this hypothesis:

	Number	Percent of Growth	Part of Growth Rate (in percent)
Natural increase of Gambians	100,000	56	2.6
Gambians returned from Senegal	20,000–25,000	11–14	0.5–0.6
Excess undercounting in 1963 census	35,000–40,000	20–22	0.9–1.0
Foreign immigration	15,000	8	0.4
Amount of 1963–73 growth explained	180,000	100	4.6

*The foreign born are assumed to have been underenumerated at the same rate as the population as a whole in 1963.

During the 1960s, a large Gambian migrant community developed in Senegal, attracted by Senegal's earlier independence (Senegal 1960, Gambia 1965) and by French subsidization of peanut prices, which continued until 1967. By 1970, an estimated 33,000 Gambians were found in Senegal, spread throughout the country in rural as well as urban areas.[3] In fact, nearly half (215,900) were in the Casamance. But marketing policies and drought seriously worsened the situation of peasants in Senegal beginning in 1968-69, provoking a well-known peasant unrest there. This situation may also be responsible for an apparent, as yet unresearched, return migration of Gambian peasants to their homeland. By the 1976 Senegalese census, only 9,400 Gambian-born residents remained in Senegal. Because the dates of the Senegalese and Gambian censuses do not coincide, we cannot know precisely the dimensions of these movements in 1963 and 1973, when the Gambian censuses were taken. But the boom and bust periods in Senegal and Gambia would suggest that the net flow began to be heavily toward Senegal in the 1950s and peaked in 1968-69, thereafter turning sharply toward the Gambia. We have therefore hypothesized that 20,000-25,000 Gambians returned home from Senegal between the 1963 and 1973 censuses.

The number of foreign-born African residents in the Gambia increased from 35,555 (38,000 is adjusted for census undercounting) in 1963 to 54,554 in 1973. But the proportion of the total population that was foreign born stayed nearly the same (11.26 percent in 1963 versus 11.05 percent in 1973). In the 1978 sample survey, the foreign born constituted only 6.84 percent (505/n7,379) of the residents, but this may have been too small a sample to indicate a trend.

The rate of natural increase is perhaps the most important variable for planning and yet the most difficult to ascertain surely. Calculations by accepted demographic methods from census questions on the total births versus number of surviving children of women enumerated, on the survival of parents of each person, and on the age-sex profile of the whole population were made in the 1973 census report. The conclusion was an estimated crude birthrate of 49-50 percent per thousand and a crude death rate of 29-30 percent per thousand, yielding a natural increase of 20 percent per thousand or 2 percent per year.[4]

This low a rate of natural increase cannot, however, explain the long-term pattern of growth found among the Gambian-born population in historic censuses, nor is it consistent with the total regional geographic picture of population growth and international movements in the Senegambian countries. If one smooths out the growth curve shown for historic Gambian censuses since 1951

(Figure 12. 2), the average growth rate from 1901 through 1951 is 2.3 percent, from 1951 through 1973, 2.6 percent. Fluctuations appear in the curve due to varying migratory fluxes and varying quality of the census counts. But the long-term trend is clearly toward accelerating growth, more than 2 percent. And in the combined Senegambian countries, cumulative growth 1960-76 averages 3 percent per year (see Table 13.1), despite the fact that the four countries combined appear to be a slight net exporter of migrants. We have calculated the components of growth between the 1963 and 1973 Gambian censuses according to three different hypotheses concerning the rate of natural increase (see Table 12.1) and concluded that the best explanation is a rate of natural increase that averaged 2.6 percent over the entire period 1951 through 1973 and that is probably higher at the end than at the beginning (that is, now circa 3 percent).

Further research would be required to determine why the cumulative growth shown in both the Gambia and the region as a whole is greater than that predicted from fertility and mortality data. One reason may be that mortality in the region is highly variable from one year to the next (the maximum year exceeded the minimum by about 300 percent in Cantrelle's time-series data for two villages in Sine-Saloum)[5] and that epidemic mortality, not chronic mortality, is what is showing long-term change. The epidemic killers in the region have gradually been reduced or eliminated, beginning with cholera, yellow fever, plague, and smallpox in midcentury, and measles in the late 1960s. Yet decennial census techniques are ill-suited to measuring the demographic effects of epidemics, which have to be studied individually in correlation with all other information available for the years in which they actually occur.

A fairly detailed portrait of migrant communities in the Gambia can be drawn using the results of the 1978 National Migration Survey, conducted by the Gambian Central Statistics Division in collaboration with this study, together with census data. There are also three important specialized studies, the Land Resource Study, conducted by the British Ministry of Overseas Development on behalf of the Gambian Agricultural Ministry; a survey of migrant client farmers, conducted by Kenneth Swindel; and a study of rural-urban migration in the Gambia by Pap J. T. Williams.[6] The main types of migration are: rural-urban (both Gambian and foreign born); rural, of both pioneer settlers and client farmers (Gambian and foreign born); and the sedentarization of pastoralists.

URBANIZATION

Urbanization takes on an unusual agglomerative character in the Gambia, compared with the centralized pattern of urban geography in the Francophone cities. Banjul proper, where the port and government offices are located, is on a tiny spit of land with little room for urban expansion. Accordingly, the outlying villages in Kombo Saint Mary have been transformed into an urban agglomeration. From 1963 to 1973, the population of Banjul proper increased from 27,809 to 39,179. This represents a 3.5 percent annual growth rate, 3 percent of which should be assumed to be natural increase of the urban population. This means only 0.5 percent can be attributed to net inmigration. By contrast the immediately neighboring rural area of Kombo Saint Mary became urbanized and went from a total population of 12,208 in 1963 to 39,404 in 1973, surpassing Banjul itself. That growth rate corresponds to 12.4 percent per year. Again, 3 percent can be attributed to natural population increase, but 9.4 percent must be attributed to immigration. In fact, the largest of these former villages, Serrekunda, which in 1973 still had a population less than half that of Banjul (17,000), appears from field observations to have surpassed Banjul by the present time. Included in the growth of the Bakau/Serrejunda area is some suburbanization of people squeezed out of Banjul by housing shortages and inflation. This suburban sprawl is now extending to the next outlying government area, Brikama, where rural population densities are increasing, household size is increasing, and people seem to be attempting to combine the advantages of farming and urban cash-income opportunities.

Urbanization in the Gambia was confined to the capital area before 1963, but it has clearly been extending to medium-sized and small towns in the last decade and a half. As shown in Table 12.2, the list of towns having more than 1,000 population in 1973 greatly exceeds those listed as having more than 700 in 1963. Towns in the 2,000 to 5,000 range, which all lie outside the Banjul-Kombo Saint Mary-Brikama area, had a combined population of 48,164 in 1973, up from an estimated 29,544 in 1963, representing an average 5 percent annual growth rate.[7]

RURAL-RURAL MIGRATION

Areas of growth (inmigration) and those experiencing outmigration are clearly related to local economic history. The general trend of rural-rural migration is from the upriver provinces toward the west and from the areas with poor road service to those

TABLE 12.2

Population of Gambian Towns, 1963 and 1973

Settlement	District	1973 Population	1963 Population
Banjul		39,476	27,809
Serrekunda[a]	Kombo Saint Mary	25,505	2,081
Brikama	Kombo Central	9,483	4,195
Bakau[b]	Kombo Saint Mary	9,337	3,563
Gunjur	Kombo South	4,677	3,561
Sukuta	Kombo North	3,844	2,504
Farafeni	Upper Baddibu	3,778	1,618
Gambissara	Fulladu East	3,646	1,356
Salikeni	Central Baddibu	3,312	3,899
Basse	Fulladu East	2,899	1,639
Garowal	Kantora	2,855	1,759
Brufut	Kombo North	2,765	1,901
Lamin	Kombo North	2,693	not listed*
Georgetown	Maccarthy Island	2,510	1,592
Aluhunghari	Fulladu East	2,420	1,583
Sabi	Fulladu East	2,257	1,434
Kerewan	Lower Baddibu	2,166	1,647
Sanyang	Kombo South	2,136	1,282
Bansang	Fulladu West	2,109	1,437
Sifo	Kombo South	2,080	1,332
Bajakunda	Wuli	2,017	not listed*
Katchang	Upper Baddibu	1,929	1,646
Njabokunda	Central Baddibu	1,876	not listed*
Kulari	Fulladu East	1,859	1,252
Kaur	Lower Saloum	1,785	1,183
Damfakunda	Fulladu East	1,732	1,340
Kaiaf	Kiang East	1,722	1,294
Dembakunda	Fulladu East	1,686	704
Kuntaur	Niani	1,682	1,356
Diabugu	Sandu	1,634	not listed*
Saba	Lower Baddibu	1,613	1,473
Bambali	Upper Baddibu	1,600	1,360
Sutukoba	Wuli	1,525	not listed*
Konte Kunda Niji	Upper Baddibu	1,524	not listed*
Numuyel	Fulladu East	1,508	733
Koina	Kantora	1,472	1,098
Sara Kunda	Upper Baddibu	1,458	not listed*
Dankunku	Niamina Dankunku	1,456	1,070
Sintet	Foni Jarrol	1,403	not listed*
No Kunda	Upper Baddibu	1,392	1,534

(continued)

Table 12.2, continued

Settlement	District	1973 Population	1963 Population
Jambanjelly	Kombo South	1,326	not listed*
Kartong	Kombo South	1,320	1,184
Tujereng	Kombo South	1,313	1,282
Ngeyen Sanjal	Upper Baddibu	1,302	not listed*
Bwiam	Foni Kansala	1,300	not listed*
Sibanor	Foni Bintang Karanai	1,288	not listed*
Fass	Lower Niumi	1,276	not listed*
Toniataba	Jarra West	1,272	1,013
Soma	Jarra West	1,267	not listed*
Berending	Kombo Central	1,234	not listed*
Sankwia	Jarra West	1,267	not listed*
Barrokunda	Jarra East	1,218	938
Barra	Lower Niumi	1,203	not listed*
Mandinary	Kombo North	1,187	not listed*
Faraba Bantam	Kombo Central	1,186	not listed*
Jahally Medina	Fulladu West	1,186	not listed*
Ndungu Kebbeh	Lower Niumi	1,185	not listed*
Dingiring	Fulladu East	1,147	791
Sutukung	Jarra East	1,145	922
Basori	Kombo Central	1,128	not listed*
Somita	Foni Brefet	1,101	not listed*
Pakalinding	Jarra West	1,080	not listed*
Pakaliba	Jarra East	1,066	not listed*
Bureng	Jarra East	1,054	885
Masembe	Kiang East	1,039	not listed*
Balangarr Ker Ndery	Lower Saloum	1,021	not listed*

*Presumably less than 700 population.

[a]Serrekunda here comprises the planning areas of Serekunda, Latrikunda, part of Jeshwang, Kanifing, and Bundung. This is the area covered by the villages of Latrikunda, Serrekunda, New Jeshwang, Kanifing, Dippa-Kunda, Ibotown, Bundungka Kunda, and Talinding Kunjang.

[b]Bakau here comprises the planning areas of Camaloo and Bakau. This is the area covered by Bakau village, Wasulung Kunda, Cape Point, and the Mile 7 Quarters.

Sources: The Gambia, Population Census of 1973, vol. 1 (Banjul: Government Printers, 1976), Table 4, pp. 16-17 (all towns more than 1,000 population are listed); Population Census, 1963 (Banjul: Government Printers, n.d.), Table 28, p. 66 (all towns more than 700 population are listed).

with paved roads. Soil exhaustion is also a factor, as the old
peanut basin in the Badibus is losing both permanent and client migrants, as is an exhausted area of former peanut-cropping land
immediately outside Banjul in the Brikama area. The other areas
of major outmigration are all upriver.

In areas of outmigration, the proportion of locally born as
opposed to nonlocal members of the population tends to be higher
than in areas receiving migrants. The sex ratio shows a lack of
males, which may range as low as 75 males per 100 females.[8] The
areas most marked by these trends include the Kombo South area of
Kombo Saint Mary, the Foni Bandali district and Foni Jarrol as
well as neighboring areas of the Kiangs and the Jarras, and the
Badibus, Kantori, and Wuli districts of Basse areas. See Map 12.1.

Areas receiving migrants, in contrast, tend to show an excess
of males and a more favorable ratio of active adults to dependent
population.[9] This includes the Banjul-Kombo Saint Mary area first
and foremost, but also the growing groundnut area in the Saloum
districts and Niani and the expanding rice-growing area in Njamina
East.[10] Groundnut cropping is currently intensifying in the lower
river north bank and western divisions, and there is a strong
tendency toward inmigration.

The general pattern is for the establishment of immigrant
households and, in some cases, new villages by men from freeborn
founder-settler families, accompanied by client farmers who are
either Gambians from other provinces and social strata or Senegalese, Guinean, or Malian nawetan (client farmers).[11] Gambians
predominate among the nawetan in the western areas closest to
Banjul while foreign nawetan, particularly from the peripheral countries of Guinea and Mali, predominate in the upriver provinces.[12]

The development of commercial irrigated rice cultivation in
the Georgetown area of the MacCarthy Island division has also attracted immigrants. The pattern in these most rapidly growing
rural areas is not a frontier settlement, since the frontier in that
area has long since disappeared. It is rather of an increasing concentration of population in already populated areas.

There are also areas in which uncleared land is being settled
and cleared by inmigrant populations, generally founder-settlers of
Gambian freeborn origin, accompanied by client farmers, in this
case, generally of foreign origin. These areas include the Nianija,
Niani, and Niamina districts. In these frontier areas, mixed farming tends to be the pattern, with groundnuts, cotton, and occasionally, rice as cash crops, but much of the land in food crops. The
Niaminas also appear to be the main area in which pastoralists are
sedentarizing, as pasture land is given over to agriculture.

CHARACTERISTICS OF MIGRANTS

The foreign-born African population of the Gambia, not surprisingly, is dominated by Senegalese. As indicated, the Gambian-
born population in Senegal sometimes exceeds the Senegalese-born
population in the Gambia. In this population exchange, however,
20,000-30,000 Senegalese constitute a much greater proportion of
the Gambian population of 0.5 million than a similar number of
Gambians in the Senegalese population of 5.1 million. As shown in
Figure 12.3, the Senegalese population in the Gambia increased
from 21,498 in 1963 to 27,177 in 1973. This represents only a 2.4
percent annual growth rate, less than the 3.0 percent natural increase in the region. And, in fact, the Senegalese proportion of
the total foreign-born African community dropped in those years
from 60.5 percent to 48.7 percent. The difference was made up by
much larger increases in the number of Guineans and Malians in
the country. Guineans jumped from 14.8 percent of the total foreign-
born African population in 1963 to 19.5 percent in 1973, and Malians
jumped from 5.4 percent to 10.6 percent. There was also a substantial increase in the Mauritanian immigrant population, although
their numbers were quite small and remain so. The Mauritanian
component in the population jumped from 1.6 percent to 3.6 percent
over the decade. In the 1978 National Sample Survey, the Senegalese proportion had continued to drop (it comprised 44.8 percent of
the sample foreign-born population), while the Guinean proportion
had increased to 22.4 percent and the Mauritanian proportion to
6.3 percent. The Bissauan proportion, which was holding steady
at 13.1 percent in 1973 before the war there ended, appears to have
dropped (in 1978 it constituted only 7.5 percent of the sample). On
the other hand, nearly half of those born in Bissau who are still in
the Gambia now claim to be of Gambian nationality, which may
suggest an intention to remain in the country. A similar or even
stronger tendency is observable in Senegal among Bissauan immigrants.

The responses to questions on citizenship and ethnicity in the
census are an interesting reflection of tendencies toward assimilation. In the 1973 census, only 3,686 (7 percent) of the total 54,554
foreign born claimed to be Gambian nationals. In the 1978 National
Sample Survey on the other hand, 174 (34 percent) of the 505 foreign
born in the sample claimed Gambian nationality (65 percent of
foreign-born Africans in Senegal claimed to be Senegalese). The
proportions of "assimilees" by country of origin showed that, while
more than half of the Senegalese-born living in Gambia claim to
have Gambian nationality and nearly half of the Bissauans similarly
claimed Gambian nationality, none of those from Guinea Conakry

FIGURE 12.3

Foreign-Born Population of the Gambia by Country of Birth

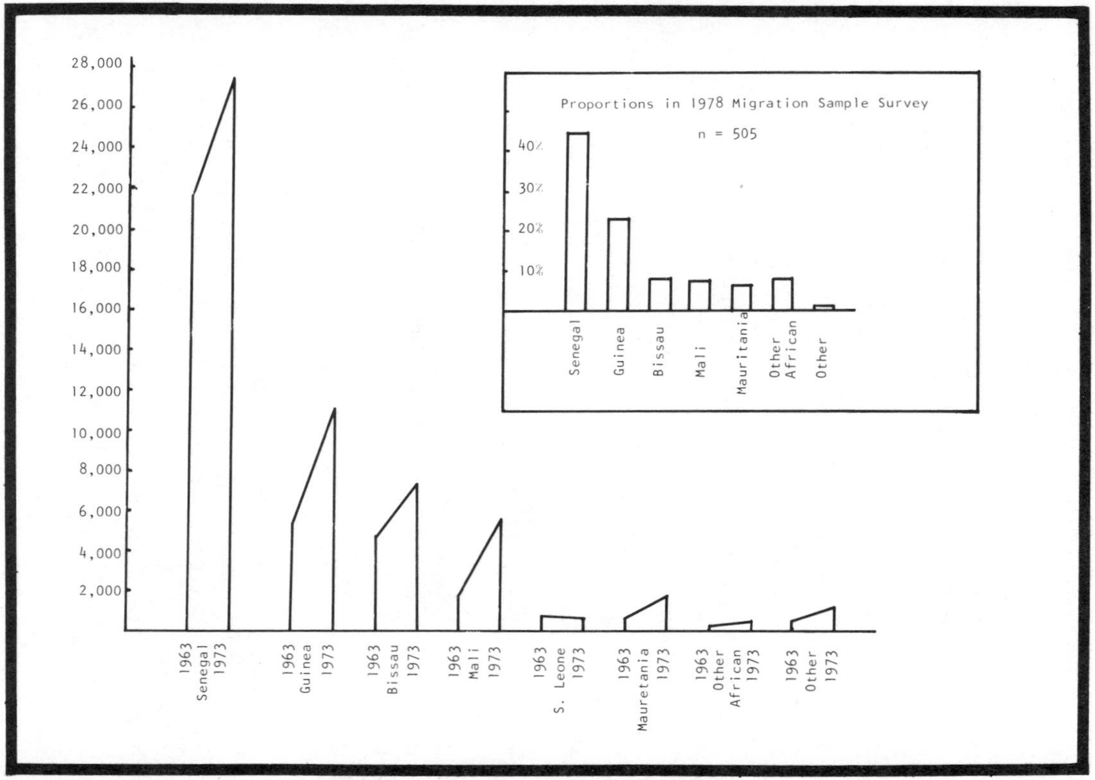

Sources: The Gambia, Population Census of 1973, 1976; Population Census, 1963.

301

and only one (Fulbe) from Mauritania claimed Gambian nationality. Malians fell in between, with 76 percent claiming Malian nationality and 24 percent Gambian. It is possible that an additional proportion of the foreign born has both claimed Gambian nationality and Gambian birth, but it seems to have been small. In the Gambia, legal formalities are required in order to become a naturalized citizen, and only a tiny proportion of those claiming citizenship have completed this process. It appears in both Gambia and Senegal that the advantages accruing to citizenship are increasing, and there is a corresponding tendency to claim citizenship in the country of residence.

The different immigrant communities are spread throughout the Gambia, although there is a notable tendency toward concentration of the foreign-born population in the Banjul-Kombo Saint Mary area. In the 1978 Sample Survey, 22.1 percent of the Senegalese in the Gambia lived in that area and an additional 25.7 percent lived in the neighboring rural, semiurban area of Brikama. In the capital area, 48.6 percent of the Malians and 75 percent of the Mauritanians were found. By contrast, the Guineans and Bissauans tended to be concentrated in rural areas, the Bissauans overwhelming in rural parts of Brikama, while Guineans were more widely distributed through the country.

The 1973 census, which was the first nationalized tabulation of educational level, suggested that the foreign-born African population of the Gambia was slightly less educated than the Gambian population as a whole. The 1978 National Migration Sample Survey, however, suggests that that tendency is diminishing (see Table 12.3).

In it, the educational profile of the foreign-born African population in the Gambia is similar to that of the Gambia as a whole. Of the foreign born in our sample, 88.1 percent had no formal education, against 90.6 percent of the total sample of the Gambia. High school, university, and teacher training graduates were all slightly better represented among the foreign-born population, although the numbers in each case are very small (for example, 2.4 percent of the foreign-born sample population had been to high school, against only 1.4 percent of the total Gambian sample. This represented 12 of the 505 foreign born as compared with 102 of the total 7,379 sample).

In the younger age groups particularly, the foreign-born sample appears to have a higher level of attendance at primary school than the Gambian population as a whole. Only among males aged 15-34 years, when migrant farmers predominate among the immigrant community, does the immigrant community appear to be significantly less educated than the Gambian sample as a whole.

TABLE 12.3

Percent of Gambians and Immigrants Having
Primary Education, 1973 and 1978

	Age Group						
	5-9	10-14	15-19	20-24	25-29	30-34	35+
Males							
1973 Census							
All Gambian							
residents	16.6	30.0	27.8	19.7	11.4	8.1	5.8
Foreign born	9.2	16.0	14.5	10.2	6.2	5.0	4.6
1978 Sample							
All Gambian							
residents	13.5	26.4	7.9	3.8	2.7	0.9	0.9
Foreign born	24.0	24.0	0.0	0.0	2.3	0.0	0.8
Females							
1973 Census							
All Gambian							
residents	9.0	16.0	12.6	7.7	3.6	2.2	2.4
Foreign born	6.0	9.6	7.8	5.7	3.5	3.2	4.0
1978 Sample							
All Gambian							
residents	7.4	13.9	3.4	5.6	0.8	0.0	0.2
Foreign born	25.0	21.7	6.5	5.0	0.0	0.0	0.0
Male, 1978							
Internally							
migrant							
Gambians	24.5	50.0	5.6	4.4	3.4	2.0	3.0
Absent							
Gambians	20.8	23.9	7.6	4.7	4.9	1.5	0.0
Female, 1978							
Internally							
migrant							
Gambians	9.6	13.5	2.3	5.7	1.5	0.0	0.0
Absent							
Gambians	8.2	14.7	4.1	2.7	3.5	0.0	0.0

When one breaks this data down by country of origin, the pattern is much clearer. Migrants coming from the less-developed peripheral countries of the Senegambia, Mauritania, Guinea Conakry, Guinea Bissau, and Mali, are overwhelmingly lacking in formal schooling. On the other hand, the Senegalese immigrants appear to have a slightly larger component of formal education, and the Other African category appears, along with Europe and the Americas, to be represented at the higher end of the educational scale. These groups appear to include a significant proportion of people with imported technical expertise.

The geographic centralization of the educated population in the Gambia is clearly demonstrated by the 1978 National Migration Sample Survey (see Table 12.4). It reflects the overwhelming preference for urban residence, in particular residence in the capital area, among those who have even a minimum of formal education. To a lesser extent, it also reflects the greater accessibility of formal education in the capital area. It shows that the capital, Banjul-Kombo Saint Mary, and the adjoining semiurban area of Brikama hold 55.3 percent of those who had been to primary school and the proportion accelerates rapidly to 100 percent of the university graduates.

TABLE 12.4

Geographic Centralization of Educated Gambians
(1978 National Migration Sample Survey)
(by percentage)

Educational Level	Banjul-Kombo Saint Mary	Banjul-Kombo Saint Mary and Brikama	Rest of the Gambia
None	8.3	16.6	83.4
Primary	33.3	55.3	44.7
Junior secondary	71.4	84.8	15.2
High school	87.2	96.0	4.0
Vocational	75.0	100.0	0.0
Teacher training	45.5	81.9	8.1
University	100.0	—	0.0
Total sample	12.4	21.5	78.5

Source: Gambia, Central Statistics.

The occupational patterns of immigrants into the Gambia show that a majority (59.1 percent) are farmers. This is not so large a majority, as more than 80 percent of the total Gambian population is engaged in agriculture. The international classification of occupations, which we used in this study in order to facilitate international comparisons, is inappropriate to the Gambian economy in that it shows only broad categories and makes no distinction between, for example, traditional blacksmithing and working in a peanut oil factory (both are production) or herding and farming (both are agriculture).

The active population in the sample consisted of 1,688 women and 2,147 men, 48 percent of a rural sample of 7,937. Even though the international classification asks that only people older than 15 years be listed as active, we believed that the labor of youth was visible and probably worth measuring. Therefore, enumerators were instructed to record 5-14 year-olds as active if they had individual plots (if farming) or could be said to do at least half an adult's work. Thus, the total active population listed above includes 636 youth aged 5-14 years, 374 boys (98 percent of whom are farming) and 262 girls (97 percent of whom are farming). Without them, our sample would have shown a 40 percent active population instead of 48 percent.

The primary occupation at the time of the survey was agriculture for 84 percent of the men and 94 percent of the women in the total sample. Among recent migrants (those who had moved across district lines in the last five years), only 71 percent of the men and 59 percent of the women were engaged in agriculture. The next major occupation among migrant men was production (12 percent, versus 1.4 percent of the sedentary men). For women who moved, the second major occupation was homemaking (21.5 percent, versus 0.3 percent of the sedentary women). Each of the other categories is sparsely represented for men and women, stable or migrant (from 0.1 percent nonmigrant professional women to 3.5 percent migrant men in services).

Among international immigrants, farming is somewhat less important, involving only 68 percent of the men older than age 10 (n = 258) and 47 percent of the women (n = 179). Immigrant males were equally divided among employment in sales, services, and production (about 8 percent each), while many immigrant women seem to have moved from farming to homemaking (26 percent). Non-Gambian women are more likely to be found in service occupations (7 percent) than Gambian women (settled 1.9 percent, migrant 3.3 percent). Immigrant professional men, while only a small number (8), comprised a relatively large 3 percent of the immigrant male occupations and 17 percent of all professional men in the sample.

Looking at immigrants according to national origin, we see that 70 percent of the Mauritanian males in the sample are reported to be in sales occupations, which accords with their observed concentration as traders. Immigrants from Guinea Bissau and Conakry are concentrated overwhelmingly in agriculture, 79.1 percent and 84 percent respectively. By contrast, only 60 percent of the Senegalese are in agriculture, and only among Senegalese are a significant proportion engaged in production (crafts and industry). Of the 116 Senegalese, 12 (10.3 percent) were in the production area.

The age profile of migrants, both internal and international, showed that they are primarily young active adults, aged 15 to 40 years. See Figures 12.4 and 12.5. The age pyramid of both internal and international migrants shows a concentration in the 20s, although 15 to 19 year-olds and people in their 30s are also well-represented. The sex ratios and marital status data found among migrant communities suggest that the pattern of single male migration is no longer predominant. Migrants appear to marry at approximately the same ages as the entire sample population, although they are far less likely than their settled counterparts to have children younger than 10 years old.

Male predominance among the migrants is much clearer among the foreign born than among internal migrants. Among the foreign born, the males constitute 60-90 percent of each age group older than 25 years. Women predominate among those listed as migrants in the 15-25 year age groups, but this is overwhelmingly due to migration in order to marry or divorce. Among the single foreign-born migrants from 15 to 24 years old, men outnumber women.

Migration of single young women, however, constitutes a greater component of the migratory labor force than it had in earlier studies of migration. It appears to be an increasing tendency among both internal and foreign (especially Casamancaise) migrants in the Gambia. There is some tendency for migration to be connected with a slightly older age at first marriage for women and with a higher proportion of bachelors throughout the age groups for men. Women, both migrant and nonmigrant, tend to marry between the ages 15-19, and the overwhelming majority are married by the age of 30. Men, on the other hand, tend to marry between 25 and 35.

A separate tally was made of those aged 15 and older who had moved within the last five years (see Figure 12.6). It revealed a highly mobile population, particularly in the active ages. From 25 to 28 percent of each of the age groups 15-40 had moved within the last five years. The percentage only dropped below 20 percent (to 17.3 percent) at ages 40-44. The search for cash employment was by far the predominant motive.

FIGURE 12.4

Age–Sex Profile of Gambian Internal Migrants

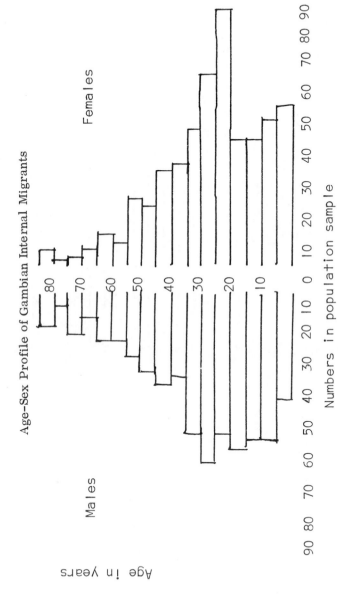

Note: Many of these women have moved relatively short distances in order to marry, and should ideally be counted separately.

Source: 1978 Gambia National Migration Survey. (Internal migrants are defined as those who lived outside their districts of birth in 1978.)

FIGURE 12.5

Age-Sex Profile of Foreign-Born Migrants in the Gambia

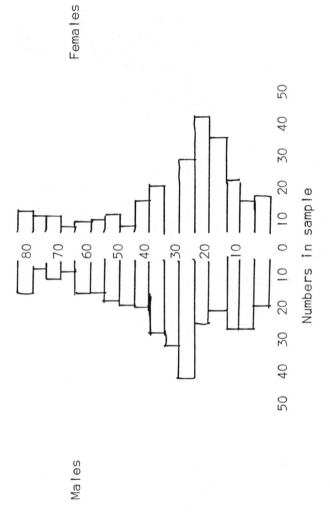

Source: 1978 Gambia National Migration Survey.

FIGURE 12.6

Age-Sex Profile of Recent Migrants in the Gambia

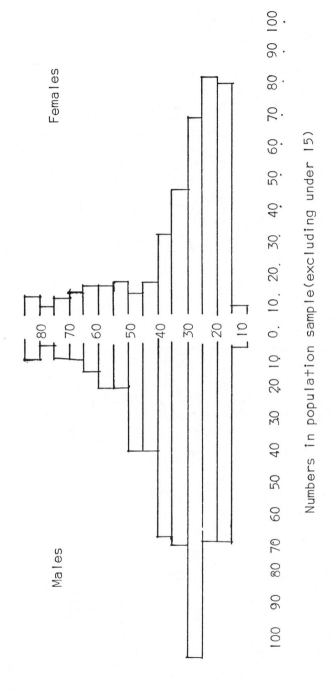

Numbers in population sample(excluding under 15)

Source: 1978 Gambia National Migration Survey. (Recent migrants are defined as those who had had at least one change of residence across district lines in the five years from the rainy season of 1973 through May 1978.)

MIGRATION AND PUBLIC POLICY IN THE GAMBIA

Migration in the Gambia involves the same trends as in the rest of Senegambia; urbanization and a concentration of rural as well as urban population in the capital area. Yet Gambia's port facilities, unique river bank geography, and independent Anglophone political and economic heritage give it a special place in the region. Like neighboring Senegal, it is a pole of attraction for migrants from throughout the area. Like Senegal, it has outlying provinces that are losing population due to their peripherality and neglect and areas of early cash cropping that are now losing population due to strains on the person-land ratio. Also like Senegal, it is receiving a small but steady stream of migrants from the still more peripheral countries of Guinea Conakry, Guinea Bissau, Mali, and Mauritania.

Like the other countries of the Senegambia, Gambia allows free passage across its borders for periods of up to three months on the basis of only an identity card. Only once, in 1974, did the Gambia officially deport aliens, and that was to return Guineans home at their own government's request.

Urban policy is an area still ill-defined in the Gambia. Only recently has its one urban area, the Banjul-Kombo Saint Mary, begun burgeoning in a way that demanded more than an ad hoc approach to urban problems. Urban problems have presented themselves in the light of intense demands for services, transportation from the sprawling workers' suburbs of Serrekunda and neighboring towns, water supply, electrification, and subsidized housing. The real problem in the Gambia, as elsewhere in the region, is a poorly developed productive base for the urban economy. Because urbanization is coming here later than to other areas, the Gambia may have opportunity to foster the development of a productive economic base as it provides for urban services.

Gambia is relatively favored in that the economic base of its main urban area, while small, is more substantial in relation to the population size than in other countries in the region. It is also better distributed geographically, with some decentralization. Moreover, cheap transportation between major economic activities is provided by the navigable river. The port at Banjul and related commercial, storage, and transport are complemented by two major peanut oil mills and an industrial sector in Bakel, Fajara, and Serrekunda. The rapidly growing tourist industry, stretched along the Atlantic beaches off the main Banjul-Serrekunda road, is still largely in expatriate hands. Its negative side effects are already leading Gambian policy makers to search for more productive areas for industrial expansion.

An economic site and services approach to urban housing, water, electrification, and transport demands is already developing as a tradition in the Gambia, and it has excellent potential. The Gambian government has not developed the practice of subsidizing housing and drivers for civil servants to the extent that the Francophone countries have. Facilities and services are, here as in other countries, significantly better in middle-class residential areas than in poor areas. The government, however, has not subsidized housing and transportation for government employees as have the Francophone countries.

The Gambia's Five-Year Plan for Economic and Social Development, 1975/76-1979/80 and its rural development project planning already take into account overall population distribution, rural-urban drift, and youth unemployment. Two of the major remedies it offers, improvement of the rural transportation system and of the rural water supply, are identical to those we have found important throughout the region. The rural development project, however, will be confined to the lower portion of the country. Unless it is extended, it will have no impact on the neglected upper river areas, which are poorly served by transportation and are experiencing economic stagnation and outmigration.

The link between Gambia's place in regional migration patterns and in the regional economy emphasizes the importance of the regional context in developing a plan for Gambian transportation, rural development, and overall economic development. Because of the navigable river, generally more advantageous rainfall patterns, and fertility of the river basin, Gambia could be in a very favorable position in a regionally integrated economic system. The contribution of client "strange farmers" to the productivity of the rural agricultural sector is an example, from a sector very little touched by government intervention or regulation. The 1974 study of strange farmers indicated that there were a total of 33,000 strange farmers in the Gambia. This constituted 12.6 percent of the total Gambian agricultural labor force.[13] Yet the attractiveness of the Gambia to strange farmers is not so much in the land available as in the fact that groundnuts cultivated in the Gambia earn Gambian currency, which can be spent on a better variety and cheaper assortment of consumer goods. These are bought at harvest time and used or traded in the dry season. Thus even Gambian agricultural productivity is substantially dependent on the regional economic differentials that derive from competitive pricing and customs policies between the Gambia, Senegal, Mali, and Guinea.

Gambia's rural development may do relatively well if the competitive attitude between nations within the region persists, yet its industrial development cannot be seriously considered outside of a regional context. It is simply too small to consider production for internal market in more than a few infant industries. Yet, in Gambia as elsewhere in the region, students are entering the wage employment market far faster than jobs are being created in the modern sector. The plan estimates that 38,000 youths will enter the wage job market between 1975 and 1980, while only 6,200 new jobs will have been generated. It is not possible to calculate exactly the proportion of these that are urban-born, but we can estimate that between one-third and one-half are born and raised in urban areas. This means that rural development offers no prospect of productive employment for them. Thus Gambia, like the other Senegambian countries, must look to develop a productive urban economy much more rapidly than it has.

From the point of view of regional transportation planning as well as industrial development, it is very important for the Gambia and Senegal river basins to be examined together. In this respect, it is unfortunate that the OMVS and the OMVG have been constituted as two separate regional organizations. Even though both are devoted to coordinating regional planning, neither has been given a mandate covering the full economic region in which they operate.

NOTES

1. United Nations, UN Demographic Yearbook, 1977 (New York: United Nations), pp. 140-41.

2. A dabada is a cooperative work group, one or more of which comprises a household eating group. More than one such food-sharing household frequently inhabits a single compound.

3. K. C. Zachariah and J. Condé, "Demographic Aspects of Migration in West Africa," mimeographed, World Bank and OECD, June 1978 (uses unpublished 1970 Senegalese Sample Census data).

4. Two earlier studies have used this figure in estimating the components of the 4.6 percent intercensal growth rate: the report of the 1973 census and the World Bank/OECD West African migration study. The Gambian census report, without the benefit of the later Senegalese data showing Gambian return migration, attributed 0.8 percent of the 4.6 percent to immigration on the assumption that the migrants already in Gambia in 1963 had experienced natural increase but had disappeared into the Gambian population and hence were not counted in 1973 (our study of migration would suggest it is much more likely that some went home, to be replaced by others; that is, migrant communities do not behave demographically like stable ones). It was also obliged to assume a

massive 17.5 percent greater undercounting in 1963 than in 1973 (see our hypotheses in Table 12.1, in which the greatest estimated undercount excess amounts to 10 percent of the total population).

The World Bank/OECD study reduced the proportion allotted to foreign immigration from 0.8 to 0.6 percent and lumped return migration of Gambians and census errors together as 2.0 percent of the 4.6 percent.

5. P. Cantrelle's data for Niakhar (Sine area of Senegal) and Paos-Koto near Nioro du Rip, just across the Gambian border, extends from 1963 through 1978. A recent summary is "Variations annuelles de la mortalité de l'enfance en milieu rural au Sénégal (1963-1978)," unpublished paper, ORSTOM, Bondy, December 1979. The best time-series for the Gambia has been done in an area of relatively high mortality by Dr. Ian MacGregor and his colleagues of the Medical Research Council (MRC). See particularly Ian MacGregor, K. Williams, W. Billewica, and R. Holliday, "Mortality in a Rural West African Village (Keneba), with Special Reference to Death Occurring in the first Five Years of Life," MRC laboratories, Fajara, the Gambia.

6. Land Resource Study (Banjul: Ministry of Agriculture and Rural Development, 1977); Kenneth Swindel, "A Report on Migrant Farmers in the Gambia," in "Demographic Aspects of Migration in West Africa," eds. K. C. Zachariah and J. Condé, mimeographed, OECD/World Bank, Washington, D. C., June 1978.

7. The two towns not listed in 1963 had less than 700 population each, so for the purposes of estimation they were assigned a combined 1963 population of 1,000.

8. The Gambia, Population Census of 1973, vol. 3 (Banjul: Government Printers, 1976), Tables 11.14, 11.15, and 11.16.

9. A ratio reflecting the proportion of active to dependent population in each district has been calculated in British Ministry, Land Resource Study, Table 51, p. 250.

10. Ibid., p. 251.

11. Ibid., pp. 276-77.

12. Swindell, "A Report on Migrant Farmers."

13. See the Gambia, Ministry of Economic Planning and Industrial Development, Five-Year Plan for Economic and Social Development, 1975/76-1979/80 (Banjul: 1975), p. 25.

III
POLICY IMPLICATIONS

13

MIGRATION AND PUBLIC POLICY IN THE SENEGAMBIA

Lucie Gallistel Colvin

The countries bordering the Senegal and Gambia river basins, Senegal, Gambia, and parts of Mauritania, Mali, Guinea Bissau, and Guinea Conakry, belong to an historic economic region within which some extraordinary migration patterns are developing. The historically sparse population of the area, which remained stagnant while Europe went through a long period of population growth in the fifteenth through twentieth centuries, has recently entered a growth spurt that is still accelerating in intensity. The 1976 censuses, whose results are still only partially published, allow us to measure and map the dimensions of these population movements historically for the first time. They show that the long expanding agricultural frontier will close within the next decade or two as the sparsely populated peripheral border areas fill up and virgin land is exhausted. Urbanization, after a late and slow start, is proceeding at a pace unequaled in earlier historic waves, and in a context of severely lagging economic growth. Nomads are also sedentarizing at extremely rapid rates, as land and water resources critical to their traditional economy are exhausted by agricultural expansion and the growth of their own herds.

All previous planning for economic development, food needs, labor supplies, and social service demands, as well as for market potential, traffic intensity, and so forth, has consistently underestimated the dimensions of both overall growth and of urbanization in the area. The 1976 census results (in the Gambia, the 1973 census results) will require recalculation of the base statistics for all such estimates. Senegal's population appears to be growing at the rate of 3.3 percent average annual growth as against the 2.4 percent used in previous calculations. Mali's growth rate appears to be 2.9

317

percent per year as against the previous figure of 2.5 percent. Mauritania's rate is calculated at 3.0 percent as a result of the 1976 census, as against the 1.6 percent previously used. And the Gambia's 1963-73 growth rate was measured at 4.6 percent, about 3 percent of which appears to be natural growth. The population of Senegal in 1976 was enumerated at 5.1 million as against the 4.5 million expected. The population of Mali was 6.1 million as compared with the 5.5 million expected. The population of Mauritania was 1.42 million instead of the 1.26 million expected. And the population of the Gambia was 493,000, as compared with the 385,000 that might have been expected. Natural increase in the region as a whole approaches 3.0 percent per year.

TABLE 13.1

Population Growth in the Senegambia by Country, 1960 to 1976

Country	1960/61 (estimates)	1976	Annual Average Growth (in percent)
Senegal	3,109,800	5,085,388	3.1
Mali	3,714,500	5,908,000	2.9
Mauritania	923,100	1,407,042	2.7
Gambia	318,000	548,600 (estimate)	3.5
Regional total	8,065,400	12,949,030[a]	3.0

[a]The figures in this column include a net immigration of 126,000 Guinean, 78,000 Bissauan, and 60,000 non-Senegambian African immigrants in Senegal and Gambia (plus an undetermined number in Mali and Mauritania); they also include perhaps slightly more than 20,000 immigrants from overseas, most of whom are temporary.

The figures exclude a net emigration from the region comprising an estimated 375,000 in Ivory Coast (mostly Malians) and 70,000 migrant workers in France (mostly Soninke from the Upper Senegal River homeland, parts of which are in Mali, Senegal, and Mauritania).

Sources: These figures were calculated from census figures cited in each country chapter, with figures reconciled to common dates by projection at the implicit rate of growth of each country.

The demographic situation in the Senegambia has been substantially influenced by the policies and practices of the colonial
governments in the past and by independent governments over the
last two decades. Policy decisions taken now will similarly affect
the future. The current young population structure and socioeconomic situation virtually guarantee that demographic growth and urbanization will continue for the next 30 years at very high rates,
whether or not family planning is introduced and whether or not
there is economic development. But the local socioeconomic picture in three decades will be radically different, depending upon
what is done now. And the political relationship between the developed and developing nations is likely to be substantially influenced
by the success of present policies and programs.

The demographic dilemma of the area is that, despite the fact
that the actual rates of growth are unmanageable, the total size of
the countries' populations is relatively small. Balkanized colonial
frontiers and earlier centuries of demographic stagnation have made
these countries smaller than their leaders would like, limiting their
diplomatic weight in international politics and their potential for industrialization. Their leaders have therefore wanted the population,
as well as the economy, to grow as rapidly as possible. In the past,
Senegambia had a predominantly agricultural economy, and a growing population was almost always a plus. Every new hand meant new
land that could be brought under cultivation. But because of the un-
balanced way in which the modern cash economy was introduced into
this area under colonialism, rapid population growth in today's context means more dependents and more consumption for both nations
and families. It does not necessarily mean more production. To
keep demographic growth as an advantage in the process of modernization, the countries of the Senegambia need to transform the quest
for cash in every sector of their populations into a quest for productivity.

Government planners should be encouraged to project some
demographic scenarios for their countries in 30 years time, so that
they can focus on imbalances between rates of growth of the population, productivity, and social services. Family planning, over the
medium term (from 10 to 40 years), will mean the difference between
Asian levels of overpopulation and the possibility of balanced produc-
tion/consumption patterns. Yet it alone is neither an immediate
answer nor a long-term panacea. It is not an immediate answer because of clearly foreseeable delays before it can have any nationwide
statistical impact. It is only beginning to be considered as a possibility for government sponsorship in all of the countries concerned
and is still illegal in Senegal and Mauritania. Mali is the only country with a national committee to consider population issues, and the

Gambia is just considering instituting one. Even if government
leaders were to become convinced that family planning was important, which many will not, poor communications and transportation
and the general lack of rural health care delivery would mean many
years before national policy had measurable impact on rural fertility.

There is also a phenomenon known as demographic inertia,
which means essentially that even a decline in fertility to a replace-
ment level would take a subsequent two decades to level off the population growth. This is because current high levels of fertility mean
that the age structure of the population is very young, and each next
youngest cohort in the population is larger than the one ahead of it.
Thus ever larger groups of women enter the child-bearing age. So,
even if they were to have an average of two surviving children or
fewer, there would still be more children born to each cohort than
to the preceding one. Should family planning be widely available immediately, it clearly would help some families and individuals, but
it would be unlikely to have a widespread immediate statistical impact. These are the considerations that have led to the prediction
that there will be a minimum of three decades and possibly many
more during which the populations of this area will grow at very
rapid rates.

In addition to the demographic inertia dilemma, there is the
irony that Senegambian families lack the economic and health security necessary to make family planning viable in their own lives. In
the Senegambia, we may hypothesize that family planning is unlikely
to be widely adopted until mortality is reduced considerably below
its present rate. A large family is the only protection most Senegambians have against a major personal crisis or the possibility of
a lonely and destitute old age. At the present rate of mortality in
the Senegambia, model life tables indicate that in order to have a
90 percent chance of having one son survive to age 25 to provide
support during his parents' old age, a woman must average six live
births. (At current rates, the average woman may have an equal
number of miscarriages and stillbirths.) Three of the six will be
daughters, and only a little more than half of the sons will survive
to age 25. The daughters normally will have married between the
age of 15 and 20 and will have families of their own to support by
the time the mother is in her 40s. The son at 25 will not have married yet, however (average age at first marriage is about 30), and
will begin contributing to his parents' support before he takes a wife
himself. In these socioeconomic circumstances, the goal of having
at least one son survive to age 25 seems eminently rational. Thus
what appears to be in the abstract a very high birthrate is, in fact,
just adequate from the point of view of individual families, given
current mortality and socioeconomic patterns.

Family planning is not a panacea because it has to be accompanied by economic development. Both nations and families have to envisage a new role for themselves in an industrialized economy before they can make a commitment to family planning. It is only one aspect of control over one's life; if one has little control over the other life chances, there is little incentive to control reproduction. Over the short term, in the context of an expanding agricultural frontier and a bleak industrial prospect, both Senegambian nations and families could, and do, reason that there is greater strength in numbers.

Urbanization and sedentarization are also likely to continue at very rapid rates. We have concluded that these trends, like overall population growth, are irreversible and have to be incorporated into development planning rather than wished away. Moreover, they are on a scale and proceeding at a pace that require attention to macroeconomic aspects of policy with a potential for mass effect. These include price policy, tax structure, and a reorientation of economic goals toward production rather than exchange. The scale of the anticipated population growth means that a continuation of the present small development project approach with no change in the existing economic structure is hopelessly inadequate. On the other hand, feasible changes in policy in a wide variety of areas offer the possibility of both improving the economic/demographic structure themselves and of making it possible for development projects to work.

GEOGRAPHY

The geography of migration in the Senegambia shows a highly centralized regional pattern, with Dakar the dominant pole of attraction. Lesser poles, which are both attracting permanent settlers at rapid rates and serving as relays in the general movement toward Dakar, include the national capitals of Nouakchott, Bamako, and Banjul and the capitals of Senegal's seven predominantly rural regions. Peripheral areas of the region tend to be areas of outmigration, with a low proportion of working-age population in relation to larger dependent populations of children, women, and aged. The rural central area, by contrast, benefits from increased productivity due to the presence of working migrants with few dependents. Migrants tend to be seen as a burden in the cities, because of the larger problem of escalating urban growth without productive functions. But, in fact, new migrants are to some extent a benefit even to urban economies. They work at jobs the urban born tend to disdain, have a higher employment ratio, and express a lower demand for urban services. The crisis of the cities may be due primarily to escalating natural growth rates, in the context of postcolonial "parasitic" city roles.

Rates of out- and inmigration in zones and countries within the region depend primarily on their geographic location. The peripheral countries, Guinea, Guinea Bissau, Mali, and Mauritania, all show net emigration, while Senegal and Gambia experience net immigration. The border regions of each country tend to be areas of outmigration, while expanding cash-crop zones and cities are receiving migrants. Rural farming areas closest to the colonial capitals, which attracted dense populations during the 1920s through the 1950s, are the primary source of rural exodus toward each national capital today. In Senegal, this means the old peanut basin, along the Dakar-Saint-Louis road and railroad. In Gambia, it is the western division; for Mauritania it is the Sixth, Fifth, and Fourth regions along the lower and middle river; and in Mali it is the Bamako region.

The policy of centralization has contributed both to the rate of urbanization overall and to the pattern of primacy for Dakar and other regional capitals. See Map 13.1. A system of centralized decision making, government appointments, party structure, and education, health, and economic planning was both inherited from the colonial governments and felt as a need by the new governments in order to build coherent nations. This pattern has been illustrated in detail in Chapter 4, Table 4.7. France had a similar system at home and applied it directly to the colonies. Britain, although much less centralized at home, instituted centralized colonial administration for the sake of efficiency. And most leaders of new nations argued convincingly in the 1960s that centralization was the only means to both create a modern nation out of a disparate variety of traditional cultures and to bring about the economic development that was sought. An unwanted and largely unanticipated consequence of this policy of centralization was the attraction of unmanageable population concentrations at the center.

The creation of political frontiers during the colonial era and particularly since independence has made the border provinces of each country into neglected hinterland, last to be served by paved roads and modern marketing systems. (The only exception is the Senegal/Gambia border, where the natural barrier of the Gambia River has had more impact on rural settlement patterns than the international borders.) Outmigration from peripheral areas such as the Senegal river basin, the upper Faleme/Bafing area, Futa Jallon, and, more recently, the Casamance began in the colonial period and has become so solidly established a tradition as to pose serious obstacles to rural development efforts.

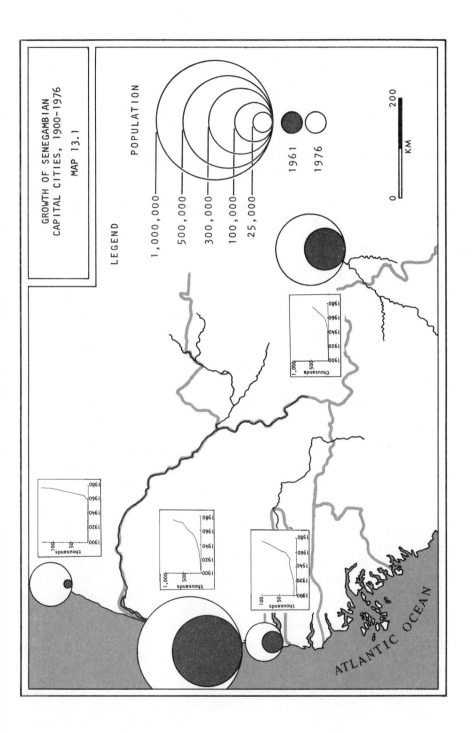

GROWTH OF SENEGAMBIAN
CAPITAL CITIES, 1900-1976

MAP 13.1

LEGEND

POPULATION

1,000,000
500,000
300,000
100,000
25,000

1961   1976

0   200

KM

ATLANTIC OCEAN

The regional geographic perspective has generally been neglected by planners and decision makers in the area; preoccupation with nation building since independence has had priority over regional coordination. Policy and projects are made and implemented in a national framework, with customs, price policy, and, to a lesser extent, such areas as road building, educational systems, and rural development taking on a competitive rather than cooperative regional dynamic. The statistics that guide planners are collected according to national boundaries and planning cycles, so that even compiling a regional picture is an arduous time-consuming task.

Near the center, the oldest areas of intense cash-crop farming in the region are experiencing soil exhaustion and overpopulation, so that they also have high rates of outmigration. Most of those who leave go to the city; a small stream heads for the frontier. Rural receiving areas include the historic expanding frontier of the Senegalese peanut basin, which continues to attract settlers and client farmers (nawetani). It seems to be expanding today as rapidly as ever, and a second cotton frontier in the Casamance-Upper Gambia area is also developing. But the end is in sight. The hitherto sparsely populated "virgin" lands of Senegal Oriental are being settled, before the peanut/cotton frontiers reach them, by migrants from the still poorer, further out Futa Jallon area of Guinea and the Kayes province of Mali.

The "virgin" lands were not virgin either. Until the last decade they were pastoral grazing lands and drought refuge. Their increasing occupation by farmers has squeezed out pastoralists, who, since they occupy the land only seasonally and sparsely, can rarely persuade encroaching farmer settlers to respect their land and water rights. This trend, which also affects the Sahel zone of Mauritania, the Kayes province of Mali, and all of the river basins, is obliging pastoralists to abandon transhumance. The recent major drought escalated this tendency to a sudden mass movement, for most families a permanent one.

Mauritania is the only one of these countries to have published recent census statistics on nomadic pastoralists. There the pastoral proportion of the entire population has dropped from 75 percent to 35 percent in just 12 years. In Senegal and Gambia, which have long been primarily sedentary, nomadic pastoralism is virtually disappearing. In the Kayes region, it appears to be surviving better, mainly because government efforts to develop cash-crop agriculture have had so little success. Pastoralists from Mauritania and a few from Senegal are converging there.

The medium-sized family herds, which were ideally suited to transhumant pastoralism in the Sahel, are becoming untenable, even where pasture land is recovering from the drought. As the nomads sedentarize along the roads and around water holes, they can maintain only very small or much larger herds. The majority are being pauperized, and many are leaving, either for farming or for the cities. Government and donor intervention would have to come much more rapidly and massively than it has so far if this tendency were to be slowed. A more likely scenario is that intervention, when it does come, will aim at making livestock profitable and will assure an urban meat supply, but it will involve many fewer herding families than in the past. The majority of those forced out of pastoralism, like the other uprooted of the western Sahel, will drift to the cities, and a small minority will enroll in rural projects offering cash incomes.

One of the major questions this study originally posed for research was whether and how the virgin lands pioneer settlement might provide relief from overpopulation in the old peanut basin of Senegal. We conclude that it is currently an alternative for a very small portion of peanut-basin outmigrants and that it will continue to be so over the short term—for no more than two decades. Over the long term, perhaps as soon as a decade from now, it will cease to be an option, since all of the arable land will have been occupied. It is this perspective that obliges us to focus on the transformation of the cities to productive functions.

Nevertheless, over the next decade, Senegal may want to encourage a larger stream of migrants to choose pioneer settlement instead of the cities. It has, together with the World Bank, already invested substantial funds in the "New Lands" settlement scheme designed to do so. The project, while succeeding in planting the seed colony upon which an expanding migratory current is building, has been expensive and entirely inadequate in scale compared with the magnitude of the peanut-basin population. Perhaps its major contribution has been to involve the Serer in the colonization process and give them a foothold on the eastern frontier. Neighboring Wolof have historically migrated spontaneously, encircling the Serer homeland.

Now that both of these ethnic groups whose homelands face soil exhaustion problems have become involved in pioneer colonization, migration policy can look away from settlement projects toward large-scale intervention that will allow eastward colonization to expand. What might be appropriate is a "sites and services" approach to rural resettlement. The interventions that we conclude would facilitate this include

Paving of trunk roads and grading of market feeder roads. The current lack of roads is a major obstacle to settlement and the growth of production in all peripheral areas.

The provision of a rural water supply. Lack of roads and the necessity of beginning settlement by hand digging deep wells are the two main ardors faced by pioneers. They are correspondingly top among the advantages rural residents in all areas cite for city life. The balance has to be equalized.

The implementation of a marketing system providing cash income.

The development of at least one outlying city in each area, with retail marketing, dry-season cash-income opportunities, schools, health care, and government services.

This sites and services approach should be the most cost-effective short-term means of accelerating the development of under-utilized provinces. It must be stressed, however, that it can at best hope to attract a slightly larger proportion of the swelling stream of outmigrants from the old peanut basin than it presently does. This would be valuable over the short term, since the cities cannot presently absorb the flow of migrants or find them productive activities. Every migrant who chooses frontier settlement over urban drift contributes to national production and costs the country far less for services. But rural-rural diversion is only a partial solution, since a majority of outmigrants, even over the short term, will continue to choose the higher potential of city residence. And it is only a short-term alternative since the frontier areas will within the next two decades be filled.

Another important aspect of the regional geography is the system of paved roads. There is currently a spoke-type road network in the center, focusing on Dakar, and single-axis isolated segments in the other national and provincial capitals. The first semicircular connectors in Senegal have just been built, and two additional semi-circles are currently being paved. The road from Kaffrine to Tambacounda is being paved, and links south around the Gambia to Velingara, Kolda, and Ziguinchor are in the pipeline. The route chosen for this project is a good example of a competitive rather than cooperative approach to infrastructure within the region. Annoyed by Gambian delays in building a bridge on the trans-Gambia, the Senegalese are going around the Gambia. And since Mali, Mauritania, and Senegal have all been more interested in linking their provinces to their capitals than in linking to one another, no paved junction is planned to Mali or Mauritania. While the paving of a major road through this hinterland area is valuable in that it will permit expansion of the rural economy, that was not its main purpose. It was built to link the two cities of Dakar and Ziguinchor. And the opportunity to open up a much larger hinterland to rural development by building connections to neighboring provincial road systems of Mali and Mauritania has so far been ignored.

Road strategy in Mali and Mauritania has been similarly dominated by exclusively national concerns, adopted by donor-advisors
as well as the governments. As an example, Mali wanted to open
up its first (Kayes) region by paving the road from Kayes to Bamako.
AID commissioned a consulting firm to evaluate the project in terms
of current traffic levels, which, not surprisingly, resulted in a negative recommendation. No one argued that the road could and should
connect to the rapidly developing Senegalese road network, as part
of a regional strategy to improve Mali's economic viability. Bamako
is in a position to be a hub of West African interior communications
if road and rail links were completed on its three most viable routes
to the sea—Ivory Coast, Guinea, and Senegal. The route through
Bamako would then be a viable option for trade and travel among
those three countries, as well as bilaterally. This could enable
Mali to overcome the awkward situation in which it finds itself today, with four zones of its rural economy oriented toward three different dynamic coastal areas—the center toward Ivory Coast, the
west toward Senegal, the east toward Nigeria, and the north toward
Algeria.

Mauritania similarly, in a narrow national perspective, decided to build the trans-Mauritania highway through the sparsely
populated pastoral zone of the Sahel rather than through the Tukulor/
Soninke zone just to the south of it, with rich agricultural potential
and strong historic ties to Senegal. The decision is understandable
in terms of the defensive political situation in which the peripheral
countries have found themselves vis-à-vis Senegal's centrality, but
it is economically less useful to the zone served, to Mauritania's
national production goals, and to the Senegambia region as a whole.

A priority for newly vital regional organizations such as the
OMVS, OMVG, CILSS, and the Club des Amis du Sahel could be coordination of regional customs/tax/price policy. In this framework,
a regional transport network could be developed, beginning with
paved spurs to the two great semicircles that Senegal is now paving.
Mali and Mauritania would both open access to potentially wealthy
but currently isolated areas of their own countries by paving routes
connecting to the Dakar-Tambacounda-Bakel-Podor-Saint-Louis
circle, through Kenieba for Mali and through Selibaby or Kaedi for
Mauritania. The mineral-rich upper Faleme area is likewise very
attractive to Senegalese planners, but they are currently stymied by
the inaccessibility of the area—again because they look at the utility
of a road or rail link in a national framework.

The upriver provinces of the Gambia could benefit substantially by the very short paved road links necessary to join Georgetown
and/or Basse to Senegal's circling road. But again, so long as
competitive national marketing systems and customs collection

persist, the government may prefer to keep the transportation system of the upriver provinces focused on Banjul. With the coordination of a regional transportation network, the governments will have to work toward coordinated economic policies.

Dakar serves as a port for Mauritania, Mali, parts of Guinea and Guinea Bissau, and, for some products, even for the Gambia, despite the large natural harbor and port there. Tensions over port usage have contributed to both Mali's and Mauritania's determination to have alternative outlets to the sea. Food relief supplies during the recent drought were a focus of this issue. Senegal was unable to expand Mali's or Mauritania's portions of port capacity, despite the urgent needs there, without threatening its own drought-relief supplies. The already belated relief effort suffered more delays while Mauritania's wharf was adapted and an airlift to the landlocked countries was mounted. Mauritania is now building a deep-water port at Nouakchott despite strong ocean currents, which make it very difficult technically.

Mali had already reoriented much of its transportation toward Ivory Coast during an earlier crisis in 1960, but the arrangements are still far from satisfactory. When the Mali Federation, comprising Senegal and Sudan, broke up at independence in August of 1960, Mali and Senegal closed the border and the railroad between their two countries, thus cutting off Bamako from its only regular access to a port. At this time, much of Mali's foreign trade shifted to the Bamako-Abidjan route, and it has remained there. But the port of Abidjan is strained beyond capacity, and the long road link to Bamako is difficult to maintain.

In the context of a customs/marketing agreement, the river routes to the sea could also regain some of their historic importance in the area. The most viable potential river route for large areas of Senegal and Mali is the Gambia, but in the absence of customs coordination, colonial and postcolonial traffic has been deliberately routed to bypass it. Mali currently hopes to use the Senegal River as an outlet and has insisted on navigability as a priority in the OMVS scheme. If it proves technically feasible, unlike repeated colonial navigability projects that gradually silted up, it will require the negotiation of customs agreements that could serve as a model for the Gambia River route. If the Senegal route proves too difficult technically, transshipment arrangements to the longer and larger Gambia channel should remain an option.

In a still larger geographic perspective, Mali's fragmented polarization points to the need for coordination of Senegambian plans with the other two dynamic regional economies of West Africa, centered on Nigeria and Ivory Coast respectively. The Economic Community of West African States (ECOWAS) treaty offers a utopian cover for all West Africa, but it is too abstract to have practical applicability immediately. And West Africa as a whole shows much less existing regional integrity than the smaller natural economic regions illustrated in this book (one centered on Nigeria, one on Ivory Coast, and the two smaller ones, Senegambia and Sierra Leone/Liberia). The economic and demographic statistics show real and current possibilities for regional development on the smaller scale presented in this book, which may in turn serve as components in a larger regional grouping.

THE ECONOMY

The primary cause of rural/urban drift on one level and of migration from less developed to developed countries on the other is the great disparities in income to be found between rural and urban areas and between developing and developed countries. Economic policy alternatives are therefore important to explore. It would be a mistake, however, to rely exclusively on economic explanations and solutions. No known combination of alternative economic policies can be expected to equalize rural/urban or third world and industrialized country incomes. The most that can be envisaged over the short term is an amelioration of the extremes of rural poverty and urban/industrialized privilege. As in the case of the other major causal factor in migration, rapid population growth, short-term economic policy options can have only a limited impact.

The modern sector of the Senegambian economies is inherited directly from the colonial era. In all of the countries concerned, it depends heavily on import-export trade. Commerce and services dominate the modern sector of the economy, while production and exchange of foodstuffs and other locally or regionally consumed items are relegated to largely unregulated informal sectors of the economy.

Migration and its economic causes are linked primarily to the modern sector of the economy, to the quest for cash on the part of both migrants and government policy makers. Both are operating in a cash-scarce environment. Since the introduction of European currencies into circulation in the interior during the colonial period, production and exchange in the import-export sector of the economy have been the only means by which both government and peasant could get access to cash.

The leaders of government in all four of the Senegambian countries at independence recognized the essential exploitation involved in the colonial import-export economy, with low prices to producers and commercial exploitation of crop marketing and mining. They

therefore organized government monopoly marketing systems.
While, in conception, the state marketing monopoly for each crop
has the protection of the peasant as its purpose, in practice the governments have found themselves in the same position as the colonial
economy; that is, their revenues depend too heavily on the exploitation of this sector of the economy. Therefore, they continue to pay
low prices to the producers and take a substantial proportion of government revenues out of the margin between producer prices and
world market prices.

One way to break this cycle of debt and dependence would be
to reorient the economy away from the import-export exchange sector and toward production for local exchange. Such a rethinking and
policy reorientation may be done at the national level, if that is the
only forum at which it is feasible. It would be much more efficient,
however, if it could be done at the regional level. Among its advantages, coordinated regional customs, price, and marketing policy
could reduce the currently substantial expenditures on policing,
smuggling, and debt collection.

One likely first step in such a reform would be a program of
regular increases in producer prices offered by government marketing organizations for both export crops and foodstuffs. The second would be a diversification of government revenues, moving away
from dependence on the import-export sector. Tentative steps have
already been taken in both directions. The goals of any such reforms should be to encourage both the bureaucracy and farmers to
profit from production rather than exchange and to raise rural incomes vis-à-vis urban ones.

Raising producer prices has the dual advantage of stimulating
agricultural production and raising rural incomes. The increase in
rural incomes creates a wider potential market for industrial produce and encourages, or at least allows, rural residents to stay in
rural areas. That producer prices directly affect the amount of a
particular crop produced has been shown repeatedly in Senegambian
and nearby Ivorian economies. In many cases, harvest prices are
too low to justify farmer investment in fertilizer, traction, and
other improvements. Even when the price is not raised, where the
drought decreased the reliability of the groundnut crop, Senegalese
farmers switched en masse to millet in 1969 and 1970 in order to
ensure their survival.

The mode and timing of payments to farmers for their crops
also alienates them from rural life. When their harvest is in they
want to market it immediately, pay off their debts, and be able to
use the rest during the dry season, often to make more money by
trading. But the government agencies, to whom they are required
by law to sell, are still bringing in much of the crop as the next

rainy season approaches. Farmers and government marketing
agents, in an atmosphere of mutual suspicion, are locked, much of
the dry season, in haggling over who owes whom what. This means
that some of the harvest rots in the field and that all of the farmers'
dry-season projects are held in abeyance until they are again busy
with the agricultural preparations for the new planting.

Efficient marketing of cash crops has been recognized as a
priority by the governments of the Senegambia since independence.
The granting of marketing monopolies to government agencies was
supposed to assure efficiency and, at the same time, provide a system of price stabilization that would allow agriculture to grow.
Stabilization, however, has come at artificially low levels rather
than in the form of price supports. And monopoly has reduced pressure for efficiency among the civil servants who operate the marketing system. If the stabilization funds were operated to truly support producer prices, rather than to depress them, the monopoly
provisions would not be necessary for their functioning. The existing inefficiency and continuation of exploitative patterns within these
marketing organizations suggest that smaller, nonmonopoly marketing systems should be encouraged. These may be government-
sponsored, mixed corporations, or private enterprises. The important factor is not their source of funding, but the fact that they
are allowed to compete for a share of the market based on their efficiency. Private credit and trade in foodstuffs, which currently
operate clandestinely, could also be legalized and regulated. Suppression has only accentuated the cost to the peasant and contributed
to the nonviable economic situation from which so many escape to
the city.

A final recommendation in the area of economic policy concerns decentralization of employment opportunities. At present,
government services, donor agencies and projects, and private
firms all tend to recruit and hire their personnel in the capital,
whether service is to be in the capital or in rural areas. Every
agency could contribute to overcoming the problem of overconcen-
tration of population in capitals if it recruited in local areas for
local positions and nationwide for all positions. Centralized recruiting has historically been linked to a centralized educational system.
Decentralization of the educational system is now considered.

EDUCATION

The step into the classroom is a sure first step out of the village and into urban life. Even the child who does not complete his
first year in primary school is more likely to end up an urban resi-

dent than is his counterpart who never went to school. And, the higher a student goes in the educational system, the more likely he is to end up living in a city, particularly a capital city. Thus, while only 19 percent of the total population of Senegal lives in Dakar, more than 70 percent of the employed adult males who ever attended secondary school lived there. [1] In the Gambia, 82 percent of the junior secondary school graduates lived in the Banjul-Kambo Saint Mary area, while that area represented only 18.5 percent of the total sample. [2] Educational data by residence for 1976 are not yet published for Mali and Mauritania, but similar patterns are believed to prevail. Total French literacy was only 2.9 percent in Mali in 1960/61 and 1.9 percent in Mauritania in 1965 (in Arabic it was 10 percent). [3] Nearly all of those literate in French live in cities.

The only reason the educational system is not the major national contributor to migratory patterns is that it still affects only a small proportion of the population. Between 6 and 28 percent of a school age cohort in these countries enters primary school, and less than 1 percent enters high school. With independence, the countries of the Senegambia inherited colonial educational systems. Their first concern was to increase enrollment. Only later and more gradually have they considered alterations in the basic structure and orientation of the systems. The systems are highly centralized geographically and administratively. Planning, personnel, enrollment, and curriculum decisions are made in the capital cities for the entire country.

In the Francophone countries, French is the language of instruction at all levels, and the basic goal is to produce an elite of graduates comparable to those in France. Since independence, this assimilationist heritage has received increasing rather than decreasing emphasis. The ideal has been modified to allow Africanization of the curriculum content in primary schools and, to a lesser extent, in secondary and postsecondary institutions. And the products have changed slightly. In the colonial period, the system graduated clerks, interpreters, teachers, lower-level civil servants, and chiefs. Since independence, the products have become bureaucrats and teachers, with only a sprinkling of other professionals. Forty-five percent of the licences (bachelors' degrees) granted by the University of Dakar from its inception in 1958 through 1968 (109 of 245) were in law and economics, the direct line to the civil service. Many of the 80 graduates in humanities and 56 in sciences also found administrative jobs in the government, little related to their fields of specialty. Efforts to develop a technical education to provide the skills necessary for Senegal's economic development have been frustrated by resistance among students, parents, educators, politicians, and French advisors. As of 1968, only 1,069 students were enrolled in technical lycees, about 3 percent of the total secondary school enrollment of 33,847.

Yet the formal educational system involves considerable unnecessary and unhealthy cultural uprooting. Students need not learn, for example, to despise manual labor and agriculture, simply because they attend school. That is a specific value that has to be taught. An alternative approach would be to begin decentralizing curriculum and personnel decisions through the creation of local school boards or consultation with existing rural councils. Educational administrators could consult such a local representative body as to the skills and even specific training programs most in need in their area. They could also seek specific information about local agricultural conditions to permit school calendars to be adjusted and allow students to participate in peak-season farm work.

The politically, socially, and economically most problematic school-aged population is not the vast majority who never attend but the ones who either drop out or flunk out. More than 95 percent of those who enter school never make it to high school. Thrust on the job market with only part of an elitist education, they enter the world of work with a contempt for manual labor but few skills. They swell the ranks of the urban unemployed, partially alienated from, but still dependent upon, the traditional kinship network. The modern sector has few places for them. This has created pressure to reduce the failure ratio in the secondary school entrance examination and high school graduation exams (baccalaureate and A levels).

Senegal has gone the furthest toward focusing on the problem of drop-outs, creating the enseignement moyen pratique program specifically to deal with it. In that program, drop-outs aged 12 to 14 are offered training in the skilled trades. But this program is also expensive and available to only a few. Relaxation of standards and retraining are "band-aid" reforms and do not deal with the basic problem that it is not feasible to educate the masses with an elite system.

A study of the age and geographic patterns of migration suggest that more radical directions must be taken to deal with this problem. One is that second-chance training for those who have failed in the formal school system target the age group 20-35 rather than 12-14. Even given an additional six months to four years of training, they still emerge from the system too young to be employed. Because of the young age structure of the population, there also are many more of them than of the older age group. They therefore swell the group of people seeking training and employment. It would be better to target training programs at the ages when men and women leave home to enter the cash job market in any case, that is, ages 20-40 for men and 15-30 for women.

A further criterion for the least uprooting educational programs would be that they be geographically decentralized, that is, available in a small city, in a relatively densely populated farming area, or in a rural area itself. This is because students tend to locate where they have been trained.

Senegambian countries also need to rectify the current sex imbalance in the educational system, not primarily because of their concern for human rights but because it offers the best hope of balanced population growth. It appears that the education and employment of women is essential to the success of family planning. It has already been shown that the educational level of the mother is the single greatest factor bearing on family size, in Africa as elsewhere.[4] Our study suggests also that the independent migration of young girls to the city to seek paid employment also raises the age of marriage and reduces overall family size. Studies in high fertility populations elsewhere have indicated that while employment of women per se is a factor in reduced fertility, it is a much greater factor at the higher socioeconomic levels than at the lower. The implication of this for the Senegambia is that the education of women would have much more impact than a program to increase their employment, unaccompanied by education.

The final educational recommendation comes out of the question of scale that the study of migration raises. It is clear that the formal educational system cannot expand its scale rapidly enough to provide a literate population with whom economic development can take place. One has only to set side by side the pyramidal age structure of the population and the still more sharply sloping pyramid of primary school, secondary school, and university available in the Senegambia to realize that the formal educational sector cannot introduce mass literacy in the twentieth century. It serves an essential function in producing a few highly trained people. But, if mass literacy is to be achieved, it must be done through some type of mass rural education, perhaps on the model of Iran's teacher corps. The educational qualifications of the teachers would have to be substantially below those in the formal sector, perhaps at the junior secondary level and even including bright primary school graduates. The cost would also have to be substantially below that in the formal sector and could be if the idealism of both teacher and communities were called upon. A small cash wage could be provided by the government or by local communities when possible. Even if well below the urban minimum wage, it would be an improvement over urban unemployment for many such young graduates. And local communities may be willing, as they have been in Kenya and Tanzania, to house the teacher and build classrooms.

HEALTH CARE

Health care in Senegambian countries, like education, has involved the introduction of modern Western medical education and health care delivery institutions (hospitals, pharmacies, clinics) based on Western technology rather than a traditional health care system. Since independence, considerable cost and effort has gone into expanding those institutions to reach a larger population, but there has been little restructuring. Only in Mali has there been a national effort to bring together knowledge and practitioners from the Western and traditional health care sectors. The results of expanded health care over the last two decades have been primarily to accentuate the difference between urban and rural populations. Urban areas now offer health care even to the poor among them, while rural areas are seriously lacking.

The gap between the scale of population growth and the cost of elite curative medicine again leads to the conclusion that mass programs that reach rural areas and focus on prevention are needed. The Sine-Saloum health project in Senegal is among the first to adopt this orientation. Whereas preventative medicine in rural areas has, since the colonial era, been limited to epidemic control, the Sine-Saloum project offers more balanced medical care and on a continuing basis. Another branch of programs in which preventative medicine has been implemented is maternal and child health care. These have been inspired by a humane concern for the problems of infant mortality in Senegambian countries. From an econo-demographic point of view, however, they take too limited a perspective. Men should also be offered medical care. And the women who benefit and succeed in bringing their children healthily through the dangerous years need to be able to regulate subsequent births. The woman whose several young children survive may still suffer deeply if her husband is sick or dies and is unable to support them. She herself may be unable to care for them if they are too close together in age. The extended family is indeed a refuge, but it is not an infinitely stretchable one. In fact, it is currently shrinking, in both rural and urban areas.

RURAL DEVELOPMENT

Nearly all analysts of the Senegambian economies conclude that the rural exodus stems primarily from lack of rural development. It has become common to assume that the converse is also true: rural development will stem the tide of rural exodus. There can be no quarrel with the general statement that the rural exodus comes in response to the faster development of urban areas, but the conclusion that rural development is a sufficient answer to the problem does not follow. No economic scenario can be imagined that would realistically permit rural incomes to catch up to the urban average. Also, young people are currently reaching the age of independence in rural areas faster than new land can be distributed to them or in places where no new land is available for them. Thirdly, some of the advantages of urban life cannot be duplicated in rural areas. The liberating aspect of urban life derives specifically from the coming together of diverse populations into dense concentrations. And, finally, cities are necessary for the very process of rural development to take place. Many of the things farmers need can be provided more efficiently in outlying urban centers than in rural areas themselves, including retail market outlets, schools, dry-season employment opportunities, and many government services.

Rural development will nevertheless have a substantial impact on the rate of urbanization in the Senegambia and perhaps on the final proportion of the population that eventually stabilizes in rural as opposed to urban areas. In short, the way that rural development takes place and the amount that takes place will affect migrants and migration significantly.

The contribution to rural development that would have the greatest immediate impact on migration is the development of a universal rural water supply for people, livestock, and vegetable gardening. Most of the investment in rural development is currently being put into irrigation. Yet most of the people are living in areas where only rainfall agriculture is possible. Currently, wells in many areas run dry for at least four to five months of the year. The government well-digging programs provide such villages, one at a time, with two-meter diameter concrete walled wells. Most of them are not fitted with pumps, in which case they are adequate only for people, not for animals or vegetable gardening. An estimate should be made of the cost and feasibility of alternative technology using narrow gauge bore wells and pumping through polyvinyl tubing, as has been done quite inexpensively in sparsely populated areas of the American west and southwest. The tubing is manufactured by a simple process from byproducts of petroleum refining and could therefore potentially be manufactured locally in Senegal.

An alternative to wood and charcoal cooking fuel must also be found if the denuding of the countryside of trees and resultant ecological deterioration is to come under control. Young women fleeing rural villages for a sojourn in the city cite the eternal quest for water and wood as being among the hateful burdens of rural life.

In the area of agricultural development, two different directions are currently being taken. The governments are investing primarily in cash-crop expansion, while AID and other investors are looking more exclusively at the development of food production. Both types of development sometimes ignore a basic facet of the migration process. That is, farmers have a legitimate need and a strong desire for cash incomes. Even when they are able to produce a cash crop, they are not assured cash income. And even when they are able to produce a food surplus, they still need cash income.

Dry-season work or trading may provide a substantial proportion of a farmer's income in the rainfall agricultural area. Development projects and planning could focus more on the provision of productive dry-season employment opportunities. One possible source is labor-intensive, low-capital cottage industries in outlying cities. Both donor- and host-country governments must recognize that, even currently, industrialization is the only alternative to the labor-surplus migration patterns reveal. In rural areas, existing industries in food processing, footwear, clothing, and building products need government and donor-agency encouragement.

A final aspect of rural development projects that relates to migration tendencies is the problem of social organization within the projects. Many of the migrants who flock to the cities are specifically seeking freedom, that is, escaping from autocratic rural social structures in which they are in a disadvantaged position. Yet some of the new rural development projects introduce new autocratic structures in which the opportunity for some groups is as limited or more limited than it was in the old structures. This is particularly visible for women; it may also be true for other groups whose existence is not generally recognized by outsiders: people from caste and slave-origin families, low-status ethnic groups, and even young people of the dominant strata.

URBAN POLICY

Cities in the Senegambia experienced bursts of growth in the immediate aftermath of World War II, with the coming of independence in the 1960s, and with the severe drought of 1968-73 (which still continues in some areas). After and even during each burst, planners had hoped that the end of the immediate stimulus would mean a leveling off of growth. This has not happened. There has been a steady urban growth in the Senegambia, and current population and economic structures guarantee that a high rate of growth will continue for at least several decades. Such rates of growth would cause social strains in any city. But in postcolonial societies in which cities are "parasitic" and not productive, it augurs national, family, and individual trauma.

It is urgent that each country work out a plan for giving its cities productive roles in the economy. The components would include industrialization, geographic balance, and cheap mass minimal urban services. A new overarching urban policy could aim at balancing urban and rural economies. The most effective policy tools lie in the area of customs, tax, and marketing, which have already been discussed in the section on economic policy. But some goals and plans of action must be set specifically for cities.

A key question that is already being explored in many countries is how productive jobs can be generated quickly and inexpensively. The informal sector of the urban economy (comprised of small enterprises organized spontaneously and largely outside government regulation) already generates employment at a fraction of the initial capital cost in private or government enterprises. It is the informal section which currently absorbs most new migrants to the city, as well as employing the great majority of urban born. Incomes in that sector are comparable to those in the formal sector for similar work. Yet governments have tended to look with disfavor on the informal economy as unattractive, disorderly, profiteering, or competing with officially sponsored firms. One new focus could be how to encourage the informal sector to grow alongside the formal, rather than grant monopolies or regulate to drive small firms out of interesting lines.

Donor countries, particularly the United States, tend to look at the economic demographic problem of the Senegambia as being primarily an inability to produce enough food. This is not the central problem. The Senegambian countries currently produce an agricultural surplus. That it is not in foodstuffs is due to deliberate and historic economic policy, on the part of both government and peasants, aimed at meeting the other basic needs: for clothing, fuel, housing, medicine, and other necessities. A balanced aid policy would encourage local production to meet these needs as well as food production.

The balance between centralization and decentralization is another area requiring close study in each country. In Senegal, there is a clear problem of overcentralization, which has been recognized for a number of years. Mauritania and Mali have the opposite problem: major economic sectors located far from the central bureaucracy in the capital city, and, therefore, difficulties of coordination. The balance between centralization and decentralization has to be determined for each country in relation to its particular economic history and migratory patterns. This book can merely point out that for both migrants and the cities that host them, seasonal migration is considerably less strain than permanent migration, and migration to nearby outlying cities poses fewer problems of adaptation than the concentration of a large regional population of migrants in a single central place.

The irreversibility of urbanization also suggests that urban and national administrations need to explore the least expensive approaches to urban services. Critics of government investment, which is presently far too concentrated in capital cities, have sometimes gone so far as to argue that donors and host governments should stop investing in urban services, that each new investment merely encourages more migration. The urban services are not, however, major causes of migration, nor will ignoring them stop the migratory flow. The vast majority of the urban poor are urban-born. And new migrants are among the poorest of the poor in Senegambian societies. They have left the countryside because they have no possibilities there. If they cannot be wished away, yet monies must be freed for urgently needed rural development to correct the imbalance, the middle course is to seek mass urban services in the least expensive modes possible.

MIGRATION POLICY

Senegambia's current policies concerning migration are among the most open in the world. In keeping with strong local traditions of hospitality and with ECOWAS treaty provisions for free movement of people across borders within West Africa, the land borders are generally loosely patrolled and an identity card is sufficient for access. Periodically, the borders have been closed with either Mali or Guinea, but even then people pass around, sometimes even through border points, quite freely. Immigration from overseas has been more closely controlled since independence in order to promote Africanization of skilled jobs. Since 1973, expatriate workers in Senegal have been required to have an employment permit if they are recruited locally, and a tax is imposed on firms using them. The number of French co-operants, mainly teachers in Senegal, has been reduced from about 20,000 per year in the 1960s to the current level of 800. It has never been very large in any of the other countries. Yet the drought brought a new influx of technical assistants to every capital. These policies seem to have had some success in reducing numbers, although many would dispute any claim to reduced European influence. A 1976 census shows a total of 16,830 overseas residents of Cap Vert, down from an estimated 60,000-70,000 at independence in 1960. Of these, 10,890 are French and 4,150 are Lebanese (not including those claiming Senegalese nationality).

Local policies on emigration of citizens are fairly open across land borders and subject to exit-visa control for overseas emigration.

The exit-visa system is part of the series of bureaucratic obstacles that have to be confronted by potential immigrant workers to France, Germany, or the United Kingdom. It eliminates adventurers who lack contacts in Europe but not those with either friends or jobs awaiting them.

Despite the openness of current emigration policy, there is beginning to be serious concern about current trends. The governments of all four countries want urgently to stem the rural exodus. In Dakar, as the economic situation deteriorates, there is also beginning to be noticeable complaint among the urban population that foreign emigrants take jobs that locals should have. A similar anti-foreign sentiment is emerging in the Gambia. The peripheral countries of Mali, Mauritania, Guinea, and Guinea Bissau are also concerned about preventing emigration. Guinea has launched a major campaign to persuade emigrants to return.

RECEIVING AREAS: POLICY ALTERNATIVES

Open borders are a source of pride to the governments of Senegal and Gambia, which have, through these last 50 years, received a steady stream of immigration with an adaptability and social harmony rarely matched elsewhere. In general, immigration seems to have been a plus in the development of the cash economy of the Senegambian peanut basin, allowing rapid expansion of the areas the government wanted to expand and filling labor needs in rural areas of labor shortage and urban occupations in low demand. Historical experience elsewhere, including Australia, parts of Latin America, and the United States, has shown that open immigration policies often accompany expanding agricultural frontiers. A corollary to this is that when the agricultural frontier closes or is filled up, the open immigration policy tends to end within a short time. There is nothing inherently right or wrong about this, it is merely observed that it happens. At the time, the decision to close the borders may be accompanied by xenophobic tendencies in the population as a whole and in the government. This situation may arise in Senegambia. It is worth noting, however, that closed land borders in the Senegambia will be more difficult to enforce and perhaps accompanied by some of the same abuses as attempts to limit immigration across the Mexican frontier to the United States. If a regional common market should by then become a reality, it would be possible to base population/migration policy on regional rather than national citizenship.

There is currently another flow of international immigration into the Senegambia, which is rarely discussed in studies of migration. It comprises an international elite of diplomats, expatriates, and "development assistants." Their numbers are small. However, their impact on the economy is substantial, both direct and indirect. The direct contribution comes largely through high quality housing, which either their governments or the Senegalese government has generally agreed to provide them. The general knowledge that some government will foot the bill has created a highly inflationary upper echelon of the urban housing market. This, in turn, draws up the value of all urban real estate, bringing middle-level housing out of the reach of middle-income Senegalese and lower-income housing out of reach of lower-income Senegalese. At all levels, it creates pressure for further government-subsidized housing. On what could be the positive side, it has created some small fortunes among Senegalese real estate holders, which could be the beginning of the capital accumulation needed for development. However, very little of it is currently reinvested in directly productive enterprises.

The indirect impact of the international elite is on consumption patterns and aspirations. The daily sight of a privileged class living in luxurious housing (some of it substantially above the quality the same individuals could afford at home), driving shiny cars excluded from the more than 100 percent duties Senegambians must pay, and otherwise engaging in conspicuous consumption is socially and economically unhealthy. It inspires both resentment and emulation, often from the same people and even from many members of the privileged group. It is fundamental to economic development theory that, in order for economic growth to reach a take-off point, there must be a margin of surplus, local savings, capital accumulation, and reinvestment in productive enterprises. At any stage along the way, conspicuous consumption detracts from the process, eating into the marginal surplus, the savings, or the amount reinvested.

At present, all of the approaches to the problems of migration in the Senegambia have been benign and relatively noncoercive. Most of the countries have hopes for stemming the rural exodus by accelerated rural development. Mali, for example, has tried to build its own peanut basin to keep the nawetan from going to Senegal, so that they produce within the Malian economy instead.

The concept of accelerated rural development is the most benevolent of the variety of policies that have been attempted or advocated in various areas of the world as antidotes to the rural exodus. Benign neglect of the cities has also been advocated by the more fervent students of rural/urban inequities. The inequity and inadequacy of this approach has been discussed.

The last group of migration policy options that has been used in some places includes various forms of legal and sometimes physical coercion. Governments that fail to deal with urbanization as

it happens or that try to attack the symptoms rather than the under-
lying causes of migratory trends, may in desperation adopt increasingly coercive policies. Legal coercion in some places takes the
form of required work permits issued only in accordance with government preferences and/or residence permits similarly issued.
Kenya has recently adopted such a system, but reports on its actual
functioning are lacking. South Africa, of course, has long had such
a system and is now using it as it grants "independence" to the
Bantustans, to deprive most of the African population of their South
African nationality. The governments of mainland China and the
Soviet Union have long assumed the right to assign both work and
residence to their citizens, but, again, not enough is known about
the actual functioning of the systems or their success in controlling
urbanization. The more drastic step of mass expulsions usually
only comes in times of national crisis such as war or economic collapse. Ghana trucked masses of non-Ghanian African residents to
the borders and dumped them in 1969 and 1970, when it was caught
in such an economic and political crisis. But the Pol Pot regime in
Cambodia was the first to turn such a policy on its own rural exodus,
forcibly expelling most of the populations of its cities. The human
costs of such massive and forcible techniques are invariably large.
In the Cambodian experience, the death toll has been estimated at one
million. So far, Senegal has used such expulsion techniques only on
urban beggars and prostitutes. The Senegambian countries, including Senegal, are fortunate in not facing the kind of immediate overpopulation problems that afflict southeast Asia and have provided
the demographic context in which war stimulated Cambodians' and,
more recently, Vietnamese boat people's massive exodus. But
sparse population is already a passing historical moment in the
Senegambia; high population density is immediately foreseeable.
Senegambian countries have a chance to develop balanced economic/
demographic growth policies now, before the moment passes.

COPING WITH ECOLOGICAL- AND DISASTER-RELATED MIGRATION

Migration is the major safety valve that Senegambian societies
have for coping with disaster, whether it comes in the form of ecological disaster or war. Together with organized fasting within
households, it is probably the major reason that so few people died
in the recent Sahelian drought. In countries such as Mauritania and
Mali with large nomadic populations, the migrations were sudden,
visible, and dramatic. In Senegal and Gambia and the sedentary
areas of Mali, the total numbers of migrants were almost certainly
greater, but the migration took place household by household and

into the less visible outer rims of the cities, so that officials and planners were not immediately aware of it. It shows up, nevertheless, both in contemporary census figures and in a net increase in urbanization and sedentarization of nomads in those predominantly agricultural areas. Because of the universal use of extended family hospitality, suffering was minimized for the immediate victims and the organization of relief did not pose insoluble problems for the governments or the relief agencies.

Yet most of the urbanization and sedentarization associated with the drought has been permanent. The slight reduction in swelling in some outlying cities near the end of the drought and the years at the beginning of ecological recovery in fact reappears toward the center. There seems to have been a funneling of population from the less favored cities toward the center. Each migrant forced out of a productive role in a traditional economy by disaster has been attracted to the cities, initially because of the greater possibilities of consumption there. In the first place, it was essential for survival. But no plan has yet emerged to restore productive roles to those migrants. Instead they have joined the masses of the rural exodus whose search for cash and consumption has yet to be matched by productive opportunities.

Preliminary data on the war-related migration from Guinea Bissau into Senegal, primarily the Casamance, indicate that a substantial proportion of that migration will also remain permanent. The data suggest that most migration, particularly urban migration and sedentarization of nomads initially provoked by disaster, becomes permanent. This implies that the starting point for rehabilitation programs has to be in their new circumstances, not their old. The spiral of economic and demographic circumstances that set off and feed continuing high rates of migration in "normal" times suggests that, unless the economies are reoriented through balanced development, the next major disaster is going to be much more difficult for all concerned.

NOTES

1. Senegal, Bureau National de Recensement, "Recensement général de la population d'avril 1976," mimeographed, Dakar, 1979, tables 2-4-a and 3-01-a for each region.

2. 1978 Gambian National Migration Survey, provisional results, set bi-educational attainment by enumeration area.

3. Mauritania, Enquete démographique en Mauritanie, 1965 (Paris: INSEE and SEDES, n.d.), p. 189; Mali, Enquete démographique au Mali, 1960-61 (Paris: INSEE, 1961), p. 45.

4. See, for example, S. K. Gaisie, Dynamics of Population Growth in Ghana (Accra-Tema: Ghana Pub. Corp., 1969), p. 33.

BIBLIOGRAPHY

"A New African Institute of Economic Development and Planning (Dakar)." Bull. Afr. Stud. Assoc. 1 (1964): 23; 5 (1965): 28.

Abéla de la Rivière, Marie-Thérèse. "The Soninke of Mali and Their Emigration to France." Etudes Maliennes 7 (1973): 1-12.

Adamolekun, Ladipo. "Bureaucrats and the Senegalese Political Process." Journal of Modern African Studies 9 (1971): 543-59.

Adams, Adrian. Le long voyage des gens du fleuve. Paris: Maspero, 1977.

Africa Contemporary Record. Country studies published annually.

Aghassian, Michel, et al. Les migrations africaines—réseaux et processus migratoires. Paris: Maspero, 1976.

Ames, D. W. "The Economic Base of Wolof Polygymy." Southwestern Journal of Anthropology 4 (1955).

_____. "The Use of a Transitional Cloth-money Token among the Wolof." Amer. Anthr. 57 (1955): 1016-24.

Amin, Samir. L'Afrique de l'Ouest bloquée. Paris: Editions de Minuit, 1971.

_____. Le monde des affaires sénégalais. Paris: Editions de Minuit, 1969.

_____. Neocolonialism in West Africa. Baltimore: Penguin, 1972.

_____. "La politique coloniale française à l'égard de la bourgeosie commerçante sénégalaise (1820-1960)." In The Development of Indigenous Trade and Markets in West Africa, edited by Claude Meillassaux, pp. 361-76. London: Oxford University Press, 1971.

Amin, Samir, and Daryll Forde, eds. Modern Migrations in Western Africa. London: Oxford University Press, 1974.

344

Amselle, Jean-Loup, ed. Les migrations africaines. Paris: Maspero, 1976.

Angrand, Armand-Pierre. Les lébous de la presqu'île du Cap-Vert. Dakar: La Maison du Livre, n.d.

Annales sénégalaises de 1854 à 1885. Suivies de traités passés avec les princes du pays. Paris: Maisonneuve, 1885.

"Arachides et vivres au Sénégal." Zaire 6 (1952): 1089-90.

Audiger, Jeanne. "Etude humaine du Bas-Ferlo." Bull. de la MAS 112 (November 1957): 1-139.

_____. "Les ouolof du Bas-Ferlo." Cahiers d'Outre-Mer (Bordeaux) 14, 157-81.

Ba, Alioune. "Aménagement hydroagricole et études socio-économiques de la cuvette de Dagana." Unpublished memoir, Faculté des Lettres et Sciences Sociales, Geographie, Dakar, 1976.

Ba, Boubacar. Commerce extérieur du Sénégal 1962-1970. Dakar: Direction de la Statistique, 1971.

_____. Un essai d'analyse des échanges extérieurs du Sénégal pour une politique du commerce extérieur: étude. Dakar: Ministère des Finances et des Affaires Economiques, Direction de la Statistique, 1973.

Ba, Oumar. La pénétration française au Cayor, 1854-1861. Dakar: Oumar Ba, 1976.

Ba, Sekou. L'emploi des jeunes au Sénégal. Dakar: Institut Africain de Développement Economique et de Planification, 1970.

"Baisse des prix à Dakar." Zaire 9 (1955): 308.

Balandier, G., and P. Mercier. Les pecheurs lebou: particularisme et évolution. Etudes sénégalaises no. 3. St.-Louis, Senegal: IFAN, 1952.

Balans, Jean-Louis. Autonomie locale et intégration nationale au Sénégal. Paris: Maspero, 1975.

Balans, J. L., C. Coulon, and A. Ricard, eds. Problèmes et perspectives de l'éducation dans un état du tiers-monde: le cas du
Sénégal. Bordeaux: Centre d'Etudes d'Afrique Noire, 1972.

Balde, Mamadou Saliou. "Un cas typique de migration interafricaine: l'immigration des Guinéens au Sénégal." In Les migrations africaines, edited by Jean-Loup Amselle. Paris: Maspero,
1976.

_____. "Changements sociaux et migration au Fuuta-Jalon." Un-
published thèse de 3e cycle, Sociologie, Paris V, 1975.

Banque Centrale des Etats de l'Afrique de l'Ouest. "Le commerce
extérieur du Sénégal en 1973." Notes d'information et statistiques. Paris, February 1975, pp. 1-32.

Barbour, K. M., and R. M. Prothero. Essays in African Population. New York: Praeger, 1962.

Barker, Jonathan Shedd. "Local Politics and National Development:
The Case of a Rural District in the Saloum Region of Senegal."
Ph.D. dissertation, University of California at Berkeley, 1967.

_____. "The Paradox of Development: Reflections on a Study of
Local-Central Political Relations in Senegal." In The State of
the Nations, edited by M. F. Lofchie, pp. 47-63. Berkeley:
University of California Press, 1971.

Barrows, Leland C. "Faidherbe and Senegal: A Critical Discussion." African Studies Review 19 (April 1976): 95-117.

_____. "General Faidherbe, the Maurel and Prom Company and
French Expansion in Senegal." Ph.D. dissertation, University
of California at Los Angeles, 1974.

Barry, Boubacar. Le royaume du Waalo. Preface by Samir Amin.
Paris: Maspero, 1972.

Batude, Fernand. L'arachide au Sénégal. Paris: Larose, 1941.

Beaujeu-Garnier, J. Geography of Population. New York: St.
Martin's Press, 1964.

Becker, Charles, and Victor Martin. "Le Sénégal centre-ouest et
son évolution démographique: Sine-Saloum-Bawol pays de
l'ouest." Part 1, mimeographed, July 1978.

_____. "La Sénégambie à l'époque de la traite des esclaves."
Société francaise d'histoire d'outre-mer (1977): 270-300.

_____. "Memoire Donnet." (Mimeographed, 1974).

Behrman, Lucy C. "French Muslim Policy and the Senegalese
Muslim Brotherhoods." In Boston University Papers on Africa,
vol. 5, edited by Daniel McCall. New York: Praeger, 1969-70.

_____. Muslim Brotherhoods and Politics in Senegal. Cambridge,
Mass.: Harvard University Press, 1970.

Berg, Elliot J. "Backward-Sloping Labor Supply Functions in Dual
Economies—the Africa Case." Quarterly Journal of Economics
75 (1961): 468-92.

_____. "The Economic Basis of Political Choice in French West
Africa." American Political Science Review 44 (June 1960):
391-405.

_____. "The Economics of Migrant Labor System." In Urbaniza-
tion and Migration in West Africa, edited by Hilda Kuper.
Berkeley: University of California Press, 1965.

_____. "French West Africa." In Labor and Economic Develop-
ment, edited by Walter Galenson, pp. 186-259. New York:
Wiley, 1959.

Berniard, S. Le Sénégal en chiffres: Annuaire statistique du
Sénégal, eds. for 1976 and 1978. Dakar: Société africaine
d'édition, 1977, 1979.

Betts, Raymond F. Assimilation and Association in French Colonial
Theory (1890-1914). New York: Columbia University Press,
1961.

_____. "The Establishment of the Medina in Dakar, Senegal, 1914."
Africa 49 (1971): 144-53.

Bijl, Joop. L'habitat du grande nombre. Etude socio-technique
d'un programme d'exigences pour l'habitat de la population éco-
nomiquement faible de la région du Cap-Vert au Sénégal. Dakar:
IFAN, 1974.

_____. L'habitat du grand nombre II. Description et évaluation de deux
quartiers des parcelles assainies à Pikine. Dakar: IFAN, 1974.

Binet, J. Rapport sociologique de la mission des Nations Unies pour l'étude du bassin du fleuve Sénégal. Nouakchott: Min. Planification, 1973.

Birmingham, Walter B., I. Neustadt, and E. N. Omaboe. "Regional Aspects of the Structure of the Economy." In Contemporary Ghana, edited by Walter Birmingham, I. Neustadt, and E. N. Omaboe. London: George Allen and Unwin, 1966.

Blaise Diagne: Sa vie, son oeuvre. Dakar: Nouvelles Éditions Africaines, 1976.

Bléneau, Daniel, and Gérard la Cognata. "Population Trends in Bamako." Etudes Maliennes 3 (1972): 26-46.

Boateng, E. A. "Agriculture and Population Growth in Ghana." In Population Growth and Economic Development in Africa, edited by S. H. Ominde and C. N. Ejiogu. New York: Heinemann with Population Council, 1972.

Bolibaugh, Jerry B. Educational Development in Guinea, Mali, Senegal, and Ivory Coast. Washington, D.C.: U.S. Department of Health, Education and Welfare, 1972.

Boserup, Esther. Woman's Role in Economic Development. New York: St. Martin's Press, 1970.

Bouche, Denise. "Autrefois, notre pays s'appelait la Gaulle . . . remarques sur l'adaptation de l'enseignement au Sénégal de 1817 à 1960." Cahiers d'Etudes Africaines 29 (1968): 110-22.

Boulègue, Jean. "Relation du port du fleuve Sénégal de João Barbosa par Jãol Baptista Lavanha, c. 1600." Bulletin de l'IFAN, ser. B, 24 (1967).

_____. "La Sénégambie du milieu du XVème au début du XVIIème siècle." Ph.D. dissertation, III cycle, Paris, 1968.

Boulègue, Marguérite. "La Presse au Sénégal avant 1939." Bulletin de l'IFAN, ser. B, 22 (1965): 715-54.

Boutillier, J. L. "La croissance démographique et économique en Côte d'Ivoire." Cahiers ORSTOM 8 (1971): 73-79.

_____. "The Productivity of Toucouleur Farmers—Its Contemporary Evolution from the Traditional Social and Economic System." In African Agrarian Systems, edited by D. Biebuyck, pp. 116-36. London: Oxford University Press, 1963.

Boutillier, Jean Louis, et al. La moyenne vallée du Sénégal: étude socio-économique. Paris: Presses Universitaires de France, 1962.

Brass, William, et al. The Demography of Tropical Africa. Princeton, N.J.: Princeton University Press, 1968.

Brasseurd, Gérard. "Le Mali." In Notes et études documentaires, nos. 4081-83. Paris: La Documentation Française, 1974.

Brigaud, F. "Le Sénégal économique." Et. Sénég. 9 (1967): 3-146.

British Ministry of Overseas Development. Land Resource Study. Banjul: Gambian Ministry of Agriculture and Rural Development, 1977.

Brooks, George E. "Peanuts and Colonialism: Consequences of the Commercialization of Peanuts in West Africa 1830-70." Journal of African History 16 (1975): 29-54.

Brunschwig, Henri. La colonisation française. Paris: Calmann-Lévy, 1949.

_____. Mythes et réalités de l'impérialisme colonial français, 1871-1914. Paris: Colin, 1960.

Bugincourt, J. "Migration, Growth of Shanty Towns and Educational Alternatives." "Population-Education-Development in Africa South of the Sahara." Mimeographed, BREDA, Dakar, 1971, pp. 241-325.

C., J. "Perspectives minières en Mauritanie." Zaire 9 (1955): 172.

Cahiers de l'ORSTOM 12 (1975) and 18 (1971), entire issues on migration in Senegal and the Colloque sur la démographie Africaine, respectively.

Caldwell, John C. African Rural-Urban Migration: The Movement to Ghana's Towns. New York: Columbia University Press, 1969.

_____. "Population Change." In A Study of Contemporary Ghana, vol. 2, edited by Walter Birmingham, I. Neustadt, and E. N. Omaboe. London: George Allen and Unwin, 1967.

_____. The Sahelian Famine and Its Demographic Consequences, paper no. 8. Washington, D.C.: Overseas Liaison Committee of the American Council on Education, December 1975.

Caldwell, John C., ed. Population Growth and Socioeconomic Change in West Africa. New York: Columbia University Press for the Population Council, 1975.

Caldwell, John C., and Chukuka Okonjo, eds. The Population of Tropical Africa. New York: Columbia University Press, 1968.

Cantori, Louis, and Steven Spiegel. The International Politics of Regions: A Comparative Approach. Englewood Cliffs, N.J.: Prentice-Hall, 1970.

Cantrelle, P. "Etude démographique dans la région du Sine-Saloum (Sénégal) état-civil et observation démographique 1963-1965." Paris: Travaux et Documents, no. 1, 1969.

_____. "Orientations de la recherche démographique au Sénégal." Cah. ORSTOM 4 (1969): 3-10.

_____. "Procédé pour obtenir des taux de mortalité de l'enfance dans les pays ne disposant pas d'un système complet d'état-civil." L'enfant en milieu tropical (Dakar) 37 (1967): 19-29.

_____. "Variations annuelles de la mortalité de l'enfance en milieu rural au Sénégal (1963-1978)." Unpublished paper, Bondy: ORSTOM, December 1979.

Cantrelle, P., M. Diagne, et coll. "Mortalité de l'enfant dans la région de Khombole-Thiénaba." Cah. ORSTOM 6 (1969): 43-74.

Cantrelle, P., B. Ferry, and C. Guitton. "Etude relative à l'évolution démographique urbaine: Application à Dakar (Sénégal)—projet 1972—fécondité-mortalité." Paris: ORSTOM, 1972.

Cantrelle, P., and H. Leridon. "Breast-feeding, Child Mortality and Fertility in a Rural Zone of Senegal." Population Studies 25 (1971): 505-33.

Cantrelle, Pierre, et al. Population and African Development, 2 vols. Dolhein, Belgium: Ordina Editions, 1974.

Cattin, J. Benoit, and Jacques Faye. "Projet Terres Neuves II: rapport sur le suivi agro-socio-économique de la campagne 1976-77." Mimeographed, ISPA-CNPA, Bambey, May 1978.

Center for Research on Economic Development, University of Michigan. "Marketing, Price Policy, and Storage of Food Grains in the Sahel: A Survey. Ann Arbor: Center for Research on Economic Development, University of Michigan, August 1977.

Chailley, Marcel. Histoire de l'Afrique occidentale française, 1639-1959. Paris: Hachette, 1968.

Chamard, Philippe Claude. Le Sénégal: Géographie. Dakar: Nouvelles Editions Africaines, 1973.

Charles, Eunice A. "Shaikh Amadu Ba and Jihad in Jolof." The International Journal of African Historical Studies 8 (1975): 367-82.

Chauleur, Pierre, ed. "The Senegalese Market." Marches tropicaux et méditerranéens (Paris) 989 (October 24, 1964): full issue.

Childe, V. Gordon. What Happened in History. Baltimore: Penguin, 1964.

CILSS-Club du Sahel Working Group on Marketing, Price Policy and Storage. Marketing, Price Policy and Storage of Food Grains in the Sahel: A Survey, 2 vols. Ann Arbor: University of Michigan, Center for Research on Economic Development, 1977.

Clément, Léonce. "French Residents Abroad." In Notes et Etudes Documentaires, no. 3975. Paris: La Documentation Francaise, 1973.

Clement, W. The Economic Structure of Education. Dakar: University of Dakar, 1967.

Club Nation et Développement du Sénégal, 1972. Paris: Présence Africaine, 1973.

Cohen, Michael, S.A. Agunbidae, Danielle Antelin, and Anne De Mautort. "Urban Growth and Economic Development in the Sahel." Washington, D.C.: World Bank staff working paper no. 315, January 1979.

Cohen, William B. "A Century of Modern Administration: From Faidherbe to Senghor." Civilisations (Brussels) 20 (1970): 40-49.

_____. Rulers of Empire: The French Colonial Service in Africa. Stanford, Calif.: Hoover Institution, 1971.

Colloque de Démographie Africaine, organized by ORSTOM, INSEE, and INED. Paris, October 6-9, 1970. Proceedings in Cahiers de l'ORSTOM 8 (1971): full issue.

Colvin, Lucie Gallistel. "Kajor and Its Diplomatic Relations with Saint-Louis of Senegal, 1763-1861." Ph.D. dissertation, Columbia University, 1972.

_____. Kajor and the French, a Study of Diplomacy from the Slave Trade through the Conquest. New York: Nok, forthcoming.

_____. "Theoretical Issues in Historical International Politics: The Case of the Senegambia." Journal of Interdisciplinary History 8 (1977): 23-44.

Comité d'Information Sahel. Les migrations africaines. Paris: Maspero, 1976.

_____. Qui de se nourrit de la famine en Afrique? Paris: Maspero, 1975.

Compagnie d'Etudes Industrielles et d'Aménagement du Territoire. Rapport général sur les perspectives de développement du Sénégal, 3rd ed. Dakar: Remis au gouvernement par les sociétés CINAM et SERESA, 1963.

Copans, J., Ph. Couty, J. Roch, and G. Rocheteau. "Maintenance sociale et changement économique au Sénégal. I. Doctrine économique et pratique du travail chez les mourides." Paris, ORSTOM, Travaux et Documents, 1972.

Coppet, Marcel de. "Aspects sociaux de l'attraction exercé par les centres urbains en voie d'industrialisation de Dakar et de Thiès, au Sénégal et au Soudan." International Institute of Political and

Social Science Concerning Countries of Differing Civilisations 27 (1952): 297-303.

Coquéry-Vidrovitch, Catherine. L'Afrique noire de 1800 à nos jours. Paris: PUF, 1974.

Costa, E. "Problèmes et politiques de l'emploi au Sénégal." Revue internationale du travail 5 (1967): 461-97.

Cottingham, Clement. "Clan Politics and Rural Modernization: A Study of Local Political Change in Senegal." Ph.D. dissertation, University of California at Berkeley, 1969.

Coulon, Christian. "Political Elites in Senegal, I." Mazawo (Kampala) 3 (1970): 9-22.

_____. "Political Elites in Senegal, II." Mazawo (Kampala) 3 (1970): 29-37.

Coutumiers Juridiques de l'Afrique Occidentale Française, I: Sénégal. Publications du Comité d'Etudes Historiques et Scientifiques de l'Afrique Occidentale Française, ser. A, no. 8-10. Paris: Larose, 1939.

Cros, C. Enquêtes sur les migrations relative au peuplement du delta—Opération 30,000 ha. Campagne de recrutement 1965-1966. Dakar: Ministry of Planning and Development, July 1965.

Crowder, M. "French Senegal." Contemp. Rev. 190 (1956): 287-91.

_____. "West Africa and the 1914-18 War." Bulletin de l'IFAN ser. B, 30 (1968): 227-47.

_____. West Africa under Colonial Rule. Evanston, Ill.: Northwestern, 1968.

_____. West African Resistance: The Military Response to Colonial Occupation. New York: Africana, 1971.

Culmann, Henri. L'Union française. Paris: Presses Universitaires de France, 1950.

"La culture du riz au Sénégal." Zaire 6 (1952): 1090-91.

Curtin, Philip D. Economic Change in Precolonial Africa: Sene-gambia in the Era of the Slave Trade. Madison: University of Wisconsin Press, 1975.

Danfakha, Marakary. "Kédougou, ville originale d'une région enclavée." Mémoire de Maîtrise de Géographie, Université de Dakar, 1972.

Davis, Shelby C. Reservoirs of Men: A History of the Black Troops of French West Africa. Chambéry: 1934.

de Jonge, Klaas, Jos van der Klei, Henk Meilink, and Jan Rockland Storm. "Sénégal: Projet d'une recherche multidisciplinaire sur les facteurs socio-économiques favorisant la migration en Basse Casamance et sur ses conséquences pour le lieu de départ. Rapport provisoire." Mimeographed, Leiden, Afrika-Studicen-trum, October 1976.

Delafosse, Maurice. Afrique Occidentale Francaise. Histoire des Colonies Françaises, vol. 4. Paris: Larose, 1931.

Delavignette, Robert. Afrique Occidentale Française. Paris: Larose, 1931.

_____. Freedom and Authority in French West Africa. London: Oxford University Press, 1950.

Delbard, B. Les dynamisme sociaux au Sénégal; les processus de formation de classes sociales dans un état d'Afrique de l'ouest. Dakar: ISEA, 1966.

Deloisy, E. "1969—la crise universitaire à Dakar." Projet 37 (1969): 864-68.

Demaison, André. Faidherbe. Les grandes figures coloniales, no. 9. Paris: Plon, 1932.

Denis, P. A. "Les anciennes contributions directes au Sénégal." Annales Africaines (1961): 129-249.

de Sapir, Olga Linares. "Agriculture and Diola Society. In African Food Production Systems, edited by Peter F. M. McLoughlin. Baltimore: Johns Hopkins Press, 1970.

Deschamps, Hubert. The French Union. Paris: Berger-Levrault, 1957.

_____. Méthodes et doctrines coloniales de la France. Paris: Colin, 1953.

La désertification au sud du Sahara. Colloque de Nouakchott, December 17-19, 1973. Dakar: Nouvelles éditions africaines, 1976.

Deutsch, Karl. The Analysis of International Relations. Englewood Cliffs, N.J.: Prentice-Hall, 1968.

Deutsch, Karl, and Haywood Laker. Mathematical Approaches to Politics. San Francisco: Jossey-Bass, 1973.

Dia, Mamadou. The African Nations and World Solidarity. New York: Praeger, 1961.

_____. Contribution à l'étude du mouvement coopératif en Afrique noire, 3rd ed. Paris: Présence Africaine, 1962.

_____. L'économie africaine; études et problèmes nouveaux. Paris: PUF, 1957.

_____. Islam, société africaine et culture industrielle. Dakar: Nouvelles Editions Africaines, 1975.

_____. "Le Président Dia trace un programme pour la politique d'indépendence." L'unité africaine, June 11, 1960.

_____. Réflexions sur l'économie de l'Afrique noire—Nouvelle édition revue et augmentée. Paris: Présence Africaine, 1961.

Diagne, Papa Syr. "Le delta du fleuve Sénégal: Problèmes de développement." Ph.D. dissertation, Paris, June 1974.

Diagne, Pathé. African Languages, Economic and Cultural Development. Notes Africaines no. 129. Dakar: IFAN, 1971.

_____. Pouvoir politique traditionnel en Afrique occidentale. Paris: Présence Africaine, 1967.

Diakite, Guimbala. "Le colonat à l'office du Niger." Mouvements du populations et systèmes d'education dans les pays Sahelo-Soudainiens. UNESCO seminar, Dakar, May 26-June 7, 1975.

Diallo, Ibrahima Papa. "Border Migrations: A Survey in Rural Senegal/Gambia Border Areas, 1970-1971." Unpublished paper,

Dakar: Institut Africain de Développement Economique et de Planification, 1972.

_____. "L'immigration des Guinéens à Dakar: Problèmes d'intégration d'une minorité étrangère." Doctorat de 3e cycle, Ph.D. dissertation, sociology, University of Lille, 1975.

_____. Les migrations frontalières entre le Sénégal et la Gambie." Mimeographed paper, IDEP, Dakar, November 1971.

Diallo, Mamadou. Galandou Diouf, homme politique sénégalais 1875-1941. Dakar: Nouvelles Éditions Africaines, 1972.

_____. Projet de développement de l'élévage au Sénégal Oriental—Rapport sociologique. Dakar: SATEC-SODEVA, 1974.

Diarassouba, Valy C. L'évolution des structures agricoles du Sénégal, déstructuration et restructuration de l'économie rurale. Paris: Editions Cujas, 1968.

Diarra, Fatoumata Agnes. Relations inter-raciales et inter-ethniques au Sénégal. Dakar: Nouvelles Editions Africaines, 1969.

Diarra, Mamadou. Justice et développement au Sénégal. Dakar: Nouvelles Éditions Africaines, 1973.

_____. Le Sénégal, concession royale: Histoire de la colonie. Dakar: Nouvelles Editions Africaines, 1973.

Diawara, Bibi, and Sekou Traore. "Population and Economic Activity in the Transformation of the Rural Sector of Mali: Forces of Inertia and Factors of Change." Les Annales de l'IFORD (Yaounde) 1 (1975).

Dieng, Amady Aly. "L'accumulation du capital et la répartition des revenus au Sénégal." Présence africaine 93 (1st quarter, 1975): 25-57.

Diop, Abdoulaye Bara. "Enquête sur la migration toucouleur à Dakar. Bull. IFAN ser. B, 23 (1960): 393-418.

_____. "La famille rurale wolof: Mode de résidence et organisation socio-économique." Bulletin de l'IFAN ser. B, 36 (1974): 147-63.

_____. Société toucouleur et migration. Dakar: IFAN, 1965.

_____. "La société wolof: Tradition et changement." Doctorat d'Etat dissertation, Université de Paris V, 1978.

_____. "La tenure foncière en milieu rural wolof: Historique et actualité." Notes africains 118 (April 1968): 50.

Diop, Cheikh Anta. Black Africa: The Economic and Cultural Basis for a Federated State. Westport, Conn.: L. Hill, 1976.

Diop, Majhemout. Contribution à l'étude des problèmes politiques en Afrique noire. Paris: Présence Africaine, 1959.

_____. Histoire des classes sociales dans l'Afrique de l'ouest. Le Sénégal, vol. 2. Paris: Maspero, 1972.

Diop, Papa A. "Senegal: The Battle to Create Employment." ILO Panorama (Geneva) (March-April 1970): 18-27.

Diouf, Abdou. " 'African Socialist' Path to Development Outlined." U.S. Joint Publications Research Service JPRS 49218, Washington, D.C., 1969. Translation of a speech published in Dakar-Matin, September 22, 1969, p. 8.

Doob, Leonard W. Becoming More Civilized: A Psychological Exploration. New Haven, Conn.: Yale University Press, 1960.

_____. Communication in Africa. New Haven, Conn.: Yale University Press, 1961.

d'Oxby, Jean Daramy. Le Sénégal en 1925. Paris: Larose, 1925.

_____. Les sociétés indigènes de prévoyance, de secours de prêts mutuels agricoles en Afrique Occidentale Française. Paris: Larose, ca. 1936.

Dubois, Jean Paul. "L'émigration des sérères vers la zone arachidière orientale: Contribution à l'étude de la colonisation agricole des Terres Neuves." Mimeographed. Dakar: ORSTOM, 1971.

_____. "Les Sérères et la question des Terres Neuves au Sénégal." Cahiers de l'ORSTOM 12 (1975): 81-120.

Dubois, J. P., and P. Milleville. "Le projet-pilote Koumpentoum-Maka; situation et résultats après la seconde campagne agricole." In "Deuxième projet de colonisation de la région des Terres Neuves," edited by J. Maymard. Mimeographed, Dakar: ORSTOM, 1974.

Dubois, J. P., P. Milleville, and P. Trincaz. "Opération Terres Neuves, étude d'accompagnement. Rapport d'activités scientifiques de l'équipe ORSTOM, et premières réflexions sur le déroulement de l'opération au cours de l'année 1972." Unpublished paper, ORSTOM, Dakar, 1973.

_____. "Opération Terres Neuves, étude d'accompagnement. Rapport de fin de campagne 1972-1973." Unpublished report, ORSTOM, Dakar, 1973.

_____. "Opération Terres Neuves, étude d'accompagnement. Rapport de fin de campagne 1973-1974." Unpublished report, ORSTOM, Dakar, 1974.

Duchêne, Albert. Histoire des finances coloniales de la France. Paris: Hachette, 1938.

_____. La politique coloniale de la France. Paris: Hachette, 1928.

Dujarric, M. L'habitat traditionnel au Sénégal. Dakar: Nouvelles Editions Africaines, 1976.

Dumont, Pierre. Politique linguistique et enseignement au Sénégal. Dakar: CLAD, 1975.

Dunsmore, J. R., et al. Land Resource Study: The Agricultural Development of the Gambia: An Agricultural, Environmental and Socioeconomic Analysis. London: Land Resources Division, Ministry of Overseas Development, 1976.

Dupont, J. F. "Tambacounda: Capitale du Sénégal oriental." Cahiers d'Outre-Mer 6 (1964): 175-204.

Echenberg, Myron J. "Military Recruitment and Labor Mobility in French West Africa, 1923-1946." Paper presented to the African Studies Association annual meeting, Philadelphia, November 3-6, 1976.

Elkan, W. "Rural Migration, Agricultural Practice and Resettlement in Senegal." Working paper no. 4, Department of Economics, University of Durham, 1976.

ENDA-IAI. "L'environnement africain." Cahiers d'étude du milieu
et d'aménagement du territoire 2 (April 1975).

Faidherbe, Louis Léon César. Considérations sur les populations
de l'Afrique septontrionale. St.-Louis: Imprimèrie du Jour,
1856.

_____. Le Sénégal: la France dans l'Afrique occidentale. Paris:
Hachette, 1889.

Falade, Solange. "Women of Dakar and the Surrounding Urban
Area." In Women of Tropical Africa, edited by Denise Paulme,
pp. 217-29. London: Routledge and Kegan Paul, 1963.

Féral, Gabriel. Annex to "Migration and Employment in Senegal:
An Introductory Report." World Bank confidential report no.
1302-SE. Washington, D.C., September 24, 1976.

_____. "L'emploi dans les pays du Sahel: Esquisse sur la situation
de l'emploi en Mauritanie." Mimeographed, ILO, Geneva, February 1977.

Ferry, B. "Charactéristiques et comportements de la famille à
Dakar (Sénégal)." Paper presented to the séminaire international de recherche sur la famille, Lomé, January 3-10, 1967.

Flis-Zonabend, Françoise. Lycéens de Dakar, essai de sociologie
de l'éducation. Paris: Maspero, 1968.

Foltz, William J. From French West Africa to the Mali Federation.
New Haven, Conn.: Yale University Press, 1965.

_____. "Senegal." In Political Parties and National Integration in
Tropical Africa, edited by James S. Coleman and Carl G.
Rosberg, Jr., pp. 16-64. Berkeley: University of California
Press, 1964, 1970.

_____. "Social Structure and Political Behavior of Senegalese
Elites." Behavior Science Notes 4 (1969): 145-63.

Forde, Daryl, and Samir Amin. Drought and Migration in the Sahel. New York: Oxford University Press, 1978.

Fougeyrollas, Pierre. L'éducation des adultes au Sénégal. Dakar: IFAN, 1966.

_____. Modernisation des hommes: l'exemple du Sénégal. Paris: Flammarion, 1967.

Fougeyrollas, Pierre, and F. Valladon. "Sénégal." Monographies Africaines, no. 11. Paris: UNESCO Institut International de Planification de l'Education, 1966.

Fouquet, J. La traite des arachides dans le pays de Kaolack et des conséquences économiques, sociales et juridiques. Saint-Louis: IFAN, 1958.

France. Coutumiers juridiques de l'Afrique Occidentale Française— Sénégal, vol. 1. Paris: Librarie Larose, 1939.

Gaisie, S. K. Dynamics of Population Growth in Ghana. Accra-Tema: Ghana Pub. Corp., 1969.

The Gambia. Census Commissioner. Population Census, 1963. Bathurst: Government Printing Office, n.d.

_____. Census Commissioner. Report of the Census Commissioner for the Colony, 1951. Bathurst: Government Printing Office, 1952.

_____. Central Bank of the Gambia. Annual Report 1973-74. Banjul: Government Printer, 1974.

_____. Central Statistics Division, Ministry of Economic Planning and Industrial Development. Population Census of 1973, Statistics for local government areas and districts, vols. 1 and 3. Banjul: Government Printer, 1976.

_____. Ministry of Economic Planning and Industrial Development. Five-Year Plan for Economic and Social Development, 1975/76-1979/80. Banjul: Government Printer, 1975.

Gamble, David P. The Wolof of Senegambia. London: International African Institute, Oxford University Press, 1967.

Gaucher, Joseph. The Beginnings of Education in French-Speaking Africa—Jean Dard and the Mutual School at Saint-Louis in Senegal. Paris: International University Booksellers, 1968.

Gautron, Jean-Claude, and Michel Rougevin-Baville. Droit public du Sénégal. Paris: Editions Pedone, 1970.

Gayet, Georges. "Les Libanais et les Syriens dans l'Ouest africain." In Ethnic and Cultural Pluralism in Intertropical Communities, pp. 161-72. Brussels: International Institute of Differing Civilizations, 1957. Report of the thirtieth meeting of the International Institute of Differing Civilizations, Lisbon, April 15-18, 1957.

Gerry, Chris. Petty Producers and the Urban Economy: A Case Study of Dakar. Geneva: International Labour Office, ca. 1974.

Gerteiny, Alfred G. Mauritania. London: Pall Mall Press, 1967.

Girard, Jean. "De Communauté traditionnel à la collectivité moderne en Casamance: Essai sur de dynamis du droit traditionnel." Annales africaines 11 (1964): 135-65.

_____. Génèse du pouvoir charismatique en Basse Casamance. Dakar: IFAN, 1969.

Girault, Arthur. Principes de colonisation et de législation colonial. Paris: Hachette, 1943.

Godinho, Vitorina Magalhaes. "Economics of the Portuguese Empire in the XVth and XVIth Centuries." SEVPEN (Paris) (1969).

Grenier, Philippe. "Les Peul du Ferlo." Cahiers d'Outre-Mer 49 (1960): 28-58.

_____. "Rapport de mission dans la région du Ferlo." St. -Louis, Service Hydr. AOF, Arrond-Hydr. Sénégal Etude Géographie Humaine, 1956-1957.

Grosmaire. Eléments de politique sylvopastorale au Sahel Sénégalaise. Unpublished report, St. Louis, Service des Eaux et Forêts, 1957.

Guèye, Lamine. Etapes et perspectives de l'Union française. Paris: Présence Africaine, 1955.

_____. Itinéraire africain. Paris: Présence Africaine, 1966.

_____. De la situation politique des sénégalais originaires des communes de plein exercice. Paris: Larose, 1922.

Guide du commerce au Sénégal. Dakar: Société Africaine d'Edition, n.d.

Guiraud, Xavier. L'arachide sénégalaise. Paris: Larose, 1937.

Guitton, C. "Etude de la fécondité à Dakar, premiers résultats." Unpublished paper, Dakar, ORSTOM, May 1973.

Hadj, Amadou. "Les inoculations agricole et les problèmes démographiques dans le Sud Saloum: Etude de cas dans la communauté rurale de Keur Saloum Diane." Dakar: IDEP, February 1977.

Hafkin, Nancy J., and Edna G. Bay. Women in Africa: Studies in Social and Economic Change. Stanford, Calif.: Stanford University Press, 1970.

Hamadtto, A. F. Interregional Migration and Urbanization in Ghana, 1960-70. Legon: Regional Institute for Population Studies, University of Ghana, 1975.

Hance, William. Population, Migration, and Urbanization in Africa. New York: Columbia University Press, 1970.

Hardy, Georges. Une conquête morale: l'enseignement en A.O.F. Paris: Larose, 1917.

_____. Histoire de la colonisation française, 4th ed. Paris: Larose, 1943.

_____. La mise en valeur du Sénégal de 1817 à 1854. Paris: Larose, 1921.

_____. Nos grands problèmes coloniaux. Paris: Larose, 1942.

Harris, J., and R. Sabot. "Urban Employment in LDCs: Toward a More General Search Model." Paper presented to the research workshop on Rural-Urban Labor Market Interactions, Employment and Rural Development Division, Development Economics Department, IBRD, Washington, D.C., February 5-7, 1976.

Harris, J., and M. Todaro. "Migration, Unemployment, and Development: A Two-Sector Analysis." American Economic Review (March 1971).

Hasselmann, K. H. "Preliminary Reflections on the Development of the Urban System in Liberia." Unpublished memoir, Monrovia, University of Liberia, Department of Geography, 1975.

Hauser, A. "Absenteeism and Labour Turnover in the Manufacturing Industries of the Dakar Area." Interafrican Labour Institute, Human Factors of Productivity in Africa (Brazzaville) (1962): 113-29.

_____. "Les industries de transformation de la région de Dakar." Et. Sénég. 5 (1954): 69-83.

_____. Les ouvriers de Dakar: Etude psychosociologique. Dakar: ORSTOM, 1968.

Hervouet, Jean Pierre. "Les éleveurs-riziculteurs du moyen delta du Sénégal (les peul et l'aménagement)." Mémoire de maîtrise de géographie, Dakar, Faculté des Lettres et Sciences Humaines, 1971.

Hopkins, A. G. An Economic History of West Africa. New York: Longman, 1973.

Hossenlop, J. "Trends in Urban Development in 14 Black African States and Madagascar, with Projections up to 1985." Cahiers de l'ORSTOM 8 (1971): 25-36.

Howard, Allen. "The Relevance of Spatial Analysis for African Economic History: The Sierra Leone Guinea System." Journal of African History 17 (1976): 365-88.

Idowu, H. Oludare. "The Conseil Général in Senegal, 1879-1920." Ph.D. dissertation, Ibadan, University of Ibadan, 1966.

_____. "The Establishment of Elective Institutions in Senegal, 1869-1880." Journal of African History 9 (May 1968).

IFAN and the Institut National de Géographie (France). Atlas régional de l'Afrique de l'Ouest. Dakar and Paris: IFAN and ING, n.d.

_____. Ethno-demographic Maps of West Africa. Dakar: IFAN, 1952.

"The Institut d'Etudes Administratives Africaines, University of Dakar." Int. Soc. Sc. J. 12 (1960): 448-49.

"The Institut des Science Economiques et Commerciales Appliquées à l'Afrique Noire, University of Dakar." Int. Soc. Sc. J. 12 (1960): 445-48.

Institut National de la Statistique et des Etudes Economiques, Service de la Coopération. Unpublished data from the Mali Demographic Survey, 1960-61, Paris, n.d.

International Bank for Reconstruction and Development. Some Economic Interpretations of Case Studies of Urban Migration in Developing Countries. Working paper no. 151, Washington, D.C.

Ivory Coast. La Côte d'Ivoire en chiffres. Annuaire statistique de la Côte d'Ivoire, 1975 edition. Dakar: Société Africaine d'Edition, 1976.

_____. Unpublished data from the 1975 population census of Ivory Coast, n.d.

Jacolin, P. "Acteurs et force sociales: La dynamique du changement dans un quartier de Dakar." Environnement africain 2 (1976): 21-37.

Jalloh, Abdul A. Political Integration in French-Speaking Africa. Berkeley: Institute of International Studies, University of California, 1973.

Johnson, G. Wesley. "The Development of Local Political Institutions in Urban Senegal." In Nations by Design: Institution-Building in Africa, edited by Arnold Rivkin, pp. 208-27. Garden City, N.Y.: Anchor, 1968.

_____. The Emergence of Black Politics in Senegal: The Struggle for Power in the Four Communes, 1900-1920. Stanford, Calif.: Stanford University Press for the Hoover Institution, 1971.

_____. "The Senegalese Urban Elite 1900-1945." In Africa and the West: Intellectual Responses to European Culture, edited by Philip D. Curtin, pp. 139-88. Madison: University of Wisconsin Press, 1972.

Johnson, G. Wesley, and William Foltz, eds. The Political Tradition of Senegal. Forthcoming.

Joshi, Heather, Harold Lubell, and Jean Mouly. "Abidjan: Urban Development and Employment in the Ivory Coast." Unpublished paper, Geneva, ILO, 1976.

Kane, F., and A. Lericollais. "L'émigration en pays Soninke." Cah. ORSTOM 12 (1975): 177-89.

Kanya-Forstner, Alexander Sydney. The Conquest of the Western Sudan: A Study in French Military Imperialism. London: Cambridge University Press, 1969.

Keita, Rokiatou Ndiaye. Kayes et sa région. Etude de géographique urbaine au Mali, 3 vols. Bamako: Editions Populaires, 1972.

Kirk, Dudley. "World Population Numbers and Rates: The Range of Difference." Presentation to the Population Association of America annual meeting, Philadelphia, April 26, 1979.

Klein, Martin. Islam and Imperialism in Senegal: Sine-Saloum, 1847-1914. Stanford, Calif.: Stanford University Press, 1968.

_____. "The Moslem Revolution in 19th Century Senegambia." In Western African History, edited by Daniel McCall, Norman Bennett, and Jeffrey Butler. New York: Praeger, 1969.

_____. "Servitude among the Wolof and Serer of Senegambia." In Slavery in Africa, edited by Suzanne Miers and Igor Kopytoff, pp. 335-63. Madison: University of Wisconsin Press, 1977.

_____. "Social and Economic Factors in the Muslim Revolution in Senegambia." Journal of African History 13 (1972): 419-41.

Kohler, J. M. The Mossi of Kolongotomo and Collectivization under the Office of Niger. Paris: ORSTOM, Travaux et Documents, 1974.

Kuczynski, R. R. Demographic Survey of the British Colonial Empire, vol. 1 (West Africa). London: Oxford University Press, 1948.

Labouret, H. Les paysans d'Afrique Occidentale. Paris: Gallimard, 1941.

Lacombe, B. "Etude démographique des migrations 1963-65 relevées dans l'enquête du Sine Saloum." Cahiers ORSTOM 9 (1972): 393-412.

_____. "Fakao: Dépouillement de registres paraoissiaux et enquête démographique retrospective. Méthodologie et résultats." Paris: ORSTOM, Travaux et Documents 7, 1970.

_____. "Le groupe des migrants comme mode de description des caractéristiques de la migration, application aux migrations relevées en 1969 dans une commune suburbaine de Dakar, Pikine (Sénégal)." Paper presented to the Congrès Régional Africain de Population, December 9-18, 1971, Accra, ORSTOM, Tananarive.

_____. "Mortalité et migration. Quelques résultats de l'enquête du Sine-Saloum." Cah. ORSTOM 6 (1969): 11-42.

_____. "Utilisation des registres paraoissiaux et des registres d'état civil en démographie africaine." Paper presented to the Congrès Régional Africain de Population, December 9-18, 1971, Accra, ORSTOM, Tananarive.

Lacombe, B., B. Lamy, and B. Vignac. "Aperçus sur la démographie de la zone de Thysse Kayemor/Sonkorong (Sine-Saloum)." Unpublished paper, Bambey, CRA, 1959.

Lacombe, B., and J. Vaugelade. "Mortalité au sevrage, mortalité saisonnière. Un exemple: Fakao (Sénégal)." Population 2 (1969): 339-43.

Ladd, William C., and James F. McClelland. Francophone Africa: A Report on Business Opportunities in Senegal. Washington, Overseas Private Investment Corporation, 1975.

Lamy, B., and J. C. Roux. "Espace et société traditionelle en zone rurale de colonisation." Dakar, ORSTOM, 1969.

Laurent, O. "Une banlieue ouvrière: l'agglomération suburbaine de Grand-Yoff." Bull. de l'IFAN, ser. B, 32 (1970): 518-57.

_____. "Dakar et ses banlieues." Paper presented to the Colloque in Talence, "La croissance urbaine en Afrique noire et à Madagascar," CNRS, 1972, pp. 763-84.

Laville, Pierre. Associations rurales et socialisme contractuel en Afrique Occidentale: Etude de cas: le Sénégal. Paris: Editions Cujas, 1972.

Leary, Francis. "Islam, Politics and Colonialism. A Political History of Islam in the Casamance Region of Senegal (1850-1914)." Ph.D. dissertation, Northwestern University, 1969.

LeBlanc, Colette. "Un village de la vallée du Sénégal: Amadi Ounaré. Bordeaux." Les Cahiers d'Outre-Mer (Avril-Juin 1965): 117-48; Bull. Chambre de Commerce (St.-Louis) 426, 438 (Fev.-Mai 1965).

Leede, J. de, W. Elkan, etc. La situation de la migration et de l'emploi au Sénégal. World Bank working paper, June 1976.

Le Maire, n.f.n. Voyages du sieur Lemaire aux Iles Canaries, au Cap Vert, au Sénégal, et en Gambia. Paris: 1695.

Léricollais, A. "Essai d'expression cartographique dans la vallée du Sénégal." Cah. ORSTOM 10 (1972): 211-20.

_____. "Les migrations." Unpublished paper, Paris, MISOES, Document de travail, 1959.

_____. "Peuplement et migrations dans la vallée du Sénégal." Cah. ORSTOM 12 (1975): 123-97.

_____. "SOB, étude géographique d'un terroir Sérèr (Sénégal)." Atlas des Structures agricoles au Sud du Sahara 7 (1972).

Léricollais, A., and C. J. Santoir. "Répertoire code des principaux terroirs de cultures de décrue de la vallée du Sénégal." Unpublished document, Dakar, ORSTOM, July 1975.

Léricollais, A., and M. Vernière. "L'émigration Toucouleur du Fleuve Sénégal à Dakar." Cah. ORSTOM 12 (1975): 161-77.

Leroux, M. La saison des pluies 1973 au Sénégal. Dakar: ASECNA, public. no. 32, 1974.

Lorimer, Frank. Demographic Information on Tropical Africa. Boston: Boston University Press, 1961.

Ly, Abdoulaye. La Compagnie du Sénégal de 1673 à 1696. Paris: Présence Africaine, 1958.

Ly, Boubacar. L'état et la production paysanne ou l'état et la révolution au Sénégal 1957-58. Paris: Présence Africaine, 1958.

_____. "L'honneur et les valeurs morales dans les sociétés ouolof et toucouleur." Thèsis, IIIe cycle, Sorbonne, Paris.

Mabogunje, Akin. "Migration and Urbanization." In Population Growth, edited by John C. Caldwell, chap. 7. New York: Columbia University Press, 1975.

_____. Regional Mobility and Resource Development in West Africa. Montreal: McGill University Press, 1972.

_____. "Systems Approach to a Theory of Rural-Urban Migration." Geographic Analysis 2 (1970): 1-18.

_____. Urbanization in Nigeria. London: University of London Press, 1968.

MacGregor, Ian, K. Williams, W. Billewica, and R. Holiday. "Mortality in a Rural West African Village (Keneba), with Special Reference to Death Occurring in the First Five Years of Life." Medical Research Council Laboratories, Fajara, the Gambia.

Makannah, T. J. "Guinean and Liberian Immigrants and Return Migrants of Sierra Leone: A Comparative Analysis of Their Demographic and Economic Profiles, 1975: A Note." In International Migration and Tourism Statistics, 1975, Central Statistics Office, pp. 1-30. Freetown: Central Statistics Office, 1975.

Mali. Enquête démographique au Mali, 1960-61. Paris: INSEE, 1961.

_____. Bureau national du recensement. "Résultats provisoires du recensement national de la population, 1976." Bamako, n.d.

_____. Ministry of Transportation and Public Works. Etude de transports, Bamako-Kayes. Bamako, n.d., about 1977.

_____. Service de la Statistique. Enquête démographique du Mali, 1960-61. In cooperation with France, Institut de la Statistique et des Etudes Economiques, Service de Coopération. Prepared by Monique Bonjou and others, under the direction of Andreé Serre. Paris: Republique Française, Secretariat d'Etat aux Affaires Etrangères, 1967.

Mansell, R. Geography of Africa. Boston: Routledge and Kegan Paul, 1973.

Mark, Peter. "Economic and Religious Change among Diola of Boulouf 1890-1940: Trade and Cash Cropping and Islam in South-west Senegal." Ph.D. dissertation, Yale University, 1979.

Markowitz, Irving L. Leopold Sedar Senghor and the Politics of Negritude. New York: Atheneum, 1969.

_____. "Leopold Sedar Senghor: The Technician's Politician." Pan-African Journal 3 (1970): 179-98.

_____. "Traditional Social Structure: The Islamic Brotherhoods and Political Development in Senegal." Journal of Modern African Studies (April 1970): 73-96.

MAS. "Hommes du Fouta Toro." Bull. MAS 121 (1960): 1-21.

Mauny, Raymond. Tableau géographique de l'ouest africain au moyen age. Dakar: IFAN, 1961.

Maurel, Jean. Bordeaux et la pacification du Sénégal. Bordeaux: 1953.

Mauritania. Enquête démographique en Mauritanie, 1965. Paris: INSEE and SEDES, n.d.

_____. Direction de la Statistique. Bureau Central du Recensement. "Recensement général de la population de la Mauritanie au 1 janvier 1977; Seconds résultats provisoires." Novakchott, n.d.

Mbodj, Mohamed. "Aspects économiques de la phase de transition (1870-1895) au sud-est du basin arachidier sénégalais." Unpublished memoir, History Department, University of Dakar, 1979.

_____. "Le Sénégal et la dépendance: le cas du Sine-Saloum et de l'arachide, 1887-1940." Unpublished paper, History Department seminar, University of Dakar, April 14, 1978.

Meillassoux, Claude. Femmes, greniers et capitaux. Paris: Maspero, 1975.

Mercier, Paul. L'agglomération dakaroise. St.-Louis du Sénégal: IFAN, 1954.

_____. "Evolution of Senegalese Elites." International Social Science Bulletin 8 (1956): 441-51.

Mersadier, Yves. Budgets familiaux africaine. Etude chez 136 familles de salariés dans trois centres urbains du Sénégal. St.-Louis: IFAN, 1957.

_____. "La Crise de l'arachide sénégalaise du début des années trente." Bulletin de l'IFAN 27 (1966): 826-77.

_____. "Structure de budgets familiaux à Thiès. Bulletin IFAN, ser. B, 17 (1955): 388-432.

Metge, Pierre. "Le peuplement du Sénégal: Essai d'intégration du facteur population dans la politique d'aménagement du terri- toire." Unpublished lère partie, Dakar, 1966.

_____. Le peuplement du territoire. Dakar: Ministry of Planning and Development, 1966.

Meunier, P. Organisation et fonctionnement de la justice indigène en Afrique Occidentale Française. Paris: Hachette, 1914.

Michel, Pierre. "Les bassins des fleuves Sénégal et Gambia: Etude géomorphologique." Unpublished thèse d'etat, University of Strasbourg, 1969.

"Migrations sénégalaises." Cahiers de l'ORSTOM 12 (1975): full issue.

Milcent, Ernest. "Senegal." In African One-Party States, edited by Gwendolyn M. Carter. Ithaca, N.Y.: Cornell University Press, 1962.

Milcent, Ernest, and Monique Sorde. Léopold Sédar Senghor et la naissance de l'Afrique moderne. Paris: International University Booksellers, 1969.

Milleville, P. "Enquéte sur les facteurs de la production arachidière dans trois terroirs de moyenne Casamance." Cah. ORSTOM, ser. B, 24 (November 1974): 65-99.

MISOES. Les migrations: Documents de travail. Dakar: IFAN, 1959.

Mitchell, Peter K. "Numbers, Location and Demographic Characteristics of Immigrants in Sierra Leone, An Exploitation of the 1963 Census Data." In Population in African Development, edited by Pierre Cantrelle et al., pp. 129–40. Dolhain: Ordina Editions for the IUSSP (1971).

Le Monde, January 1, 1973.

Monnier, J. "Le travail dans l'exploitation agricole sénégalaise." Unpublished paper, Bambey, CNRA, 1974.

Monnier, J., C. Ramond, and R. Cadot. "Etude de systèmes techniques de production pour le Sine-Saloum et Est (Systeme 8-12 ha)." Unpublished paper, Bambey, IEMVT and CNRA, June 1974.

Moral, Paul. "Le climat du Sénégal." Revue de Géographie de l'Afrique Occidentale 1 (1965): 49–70, and 3 (1966): 26–35.

Morgenthau, Ruth Schachter. "African Socialism: Declaration of Ideological Independence." Africa Report 8 (May 1963): 3–6.

_____. Political Parties in French-Speaking West Africa. Oxford: Clarendon Press, 1964.

Mortimer, Edward. France and the Africans, 1944-1960: A Political History. New York: Walker, 1969.

Mourer, Henry. "Administrative Problems of Urbanization in Africa—Additional Note on Senegal (Dakar)." Workshop on Urbanization in Africa, Addis Ababa, 1962.

Mouton, and Cie, eds. "Villes africaines." Cahiers d'études africaines 51 (1973).

"Mouvements de population et systèmes d'éducation dans les pays sahelo-soudaniens (Haute-Volta, Mali, Mauritanie, Niger, Sénégal, Tchad)." Unpublished, mimeographed proceedings of the UNESCO colloquium, Dakar, May 26-June 7, 1975.

Ndao, Serigne, Amadou Sall, and Mbalo Kasse. "Monographie de Mbacke." Memoire de stage du College d'Aménag. du Territoire, Dakar, October 1969.

NEDECO. "Study on the Dakar Water Supply." Dakar, 1970.

Newbury, Colin. "The Formation of the Government General of French West Africa." Journal of African History 1 (1960): 111-28.

Niane, Bokar. Le régime juridique et fiscale du code des investissements au Sénégal. Dakar: Nouvelles Editions Africaines, 1976.

O'Brien, Donal B. C. "Co-operators and Bureaucrats: Class Formation in a Senegalese Peasant Society." Africa 49 (October 1971): 263-78.

_____. Saints and Politicians: Essays in the Organization of a Senegalese Peasant Society. Cambridge: Cambridge University Press, 1975.

O'Brien, Rita Cruise. "Lebanese Entrepreneurs in Senegal: Economic Integration and the Politics of Protection." Cahiers d'études africaines 57 (1972): 95-115.

_____. White Society in Black Africa: The French of Senegal. London: Faber and Faber, 1972.

O'Brien, Rita Cruise, ed. The Political Economy of Underdevelopment: Dependence in Senegal. New York: Sage, 1979.

Obichere, Boniface I. "Colonial Education Policy in Senegal: A Structural Analysis." Black Academy Review 11 (1970): 17-24.

Office de la Recherche Scientifique et Technique Outre-Mer (ORSTOM). "Enquête sur les mouvements de population à partir du Pays Mossi (Haute Volta)." Fasicule I. Mimeographed report, Ouagadougou, 1975.

Oloruntimekin, R. Olatunji. "Senegambia—Mahmadou Lamine." In West African Resistance: The Military Response to Colonial Occupation, edited by Michael Crowder, pp. 80-110. New York: Africana, 1971.

Ominde, S. H., and C. N. Ejiogu, eds. Population Growth and Economic Development in Africa. New York: Population Council, 1974.

OMVS. Bassin du fleuve Sénégal. Examen préliminaire des données de base et programme d'études envisagé. Par le Bureau de Mise en Valeur des Terres du Min. des Ress. Naturelles et des parcs nat., Dakar, April 1976.

Pélissier, Paul. "L'arachide au Sénégal." In Problèmes agricoles au Sénégal. St.-Louis: IFAN, 1953.

_____. Les paysans du Sénégal, les civilisations agraires du Cayor à la Casamance. St. Yrieux: Fabrèque, 1966.

_____. La région arachidière: Etude régionale, 2 vols. Dakar: Grande Imprimerie Africaine, n.d.

Persell, S. Michael. "The French Colonial Lobby, 1899-1914." Ph.D. dissertation, Stanford University, 1969.

Person, Yves. "Senegambia." Proceedings of a colloquium at the University of Aberdeen, April 1974.

Peterec, Richard J. Dakar and West African Economic Development. New York: Columbia University Press, 1967.

_____. The Port of Ziguinchor: The Direct Ocean Outlet for Casamance (Senegal). New York: Columbia University, Division of Economic Geography, 1962.

_____. The Position of Kaolack (Senegal) and Other Ports of the Saloum Estuary in West African Trade. New York: Columbia University, Division of Economic Geography, 1962.

_____. Saint-Louis de Senegal: The Natural Ocean Outlet for the Senegal River Valley. New York: Columbia University Press, 1966.

Pfeffermann, Guy. Industrial Labor in the Republic of Senegal. New York: Praeger, 1968.

Pheffer, Paul Edward. "Railroads and Aspects of Social Change in Senegal 1878-1933." Ph.D. dissertation, University of Pennsylvania, 1975.

"La plaque tournante du Sénégal." Zaire 5 (1971): 750-51.

Pollet, E., and G. Winter. La Société Soninke (Kyahunu Mali). Brussels: Université Libre de Bruxelles, Editions de l'institut de sociologie, 1969.

Popovic, U. Le tourisme au Sénégal. Addis Ababa: Commission Economique des Nations Unies pour l'Afrique, 1974.

Poquin, Jean-Jaques. Les relations économiques des pays d'Afrique noire de l'Union Française, 1925-1955. Paris: Colin, 1957.

Priestley, Herbert F. France Overseas: A Study in Modern Imperialism. New York: Appleton-Century, 1938.

Pye, Lucian W. "The Non-Western Political Process." Journal of Politics 20 (August 1958): 468-86.

Quellien, Alain. La politique musulmane dans l'Afrique Occidentale Française. Paris: Larose, 1910.

Rajaoson, François. Enseignement supérieur et besoins en main d'oeuvre: le cas du Sénégal. Dakar: U.N. African Institute for Economic Development and Planning, 1972.

Ramond, C., M. Fall, and T. M. Diop. "Moyen terme Sahel; Main d'oeuvre et moyens de production et terre, material et cheptel de traction des terroirs de Got-Ndiamsil Sessene-Layabe." Mimeographed, Bambey, CNRA, March 1976.

Remy, Gérard, et autres. "Mobilité géographique et immobilisme social: Un exemple voltaique." Revue Tiers Monde 18 (July-September, 1977): 617-53.

Renault, François. L'abolition de l'esclavage au Sénégal, l'attitude de l'administration française 1848-1905. Paris: Maspero, 1972.

_____. "KANEL. L'exode rural dans un village de la vallée du Sénégal." Les Cahiers d'Outre-Mer, 1964.

_____. Libération d'esclaves et nouvelle servitude. Dakar: Nouvelles Editions Africaines, 1975.

Reports Showing the Present State of Her Majesty's Colonial Possessions, 1870. Annual report of the Gambia, 1869. London: Her Majesty's Stationery Office, 1870.

"La repression et l'usure et du 'Bouki' au Sénégal." Notes d'information et statistiques (February 1971): 1-4.

Riley, J. Paul, Jay C. Andersen, A. Bruce Bishop, David S. Bowles, and John E. Keith. "Cost Allocation Alternatives for the Senegal River Development Program." Unpublished report, International Programs Office of Utah State University and AID, Logan, Utah, August 1978.

Ritchie, Carson I. A. "Deux textes sur le Sénégal, 1673-1677." Bulletin IFAN, ser. B, 30 (January 1968).

Roberts, Stephen H. History of French Colonial Policy, 1870-1925, 2 vols. London: P. S. King, 1929.

Robin, J. "Le Marbat: Marché au betail de Louga." Africa 15 (1945): 47-60.

Robinson, David W. Clerics and Chiefs: The History of Abdul Bokar Kan and Futa Toro, 1853-1891. New York: Oxford University Press, 1976.

Robson, Peter. "Problems of Integration between Senegal and Gambia." In African Integration and Disintegration, edited by Arthur Hazlewood, pp. 115-28. London: Oxford University Press, 1967.

_____. "The Problems of Senegambia." Journal of Modern African Studies 3 (1965).

Roch, J. "Les migrations économiques de saison sèche en bassin arachidier sénégalais." Cah. ORSTOM 12 (1975): 55-81.

_____. "Les mourides du vieux bassin arachidier sénégalais: Entretiens recueillis dans la région du Baol." Unpublished paper, Dakar, ORSTOM, March 1971.

Roch, J., and G. Rocheteau. "Economie et population: le cas du Sénégal." Cahiers Sc. Hum. 8 (1971).

Roche, Christian. Conquête et résistance des peuples de la Casamance. Dakar: Nouvelles Editions Africaines, 1976.

Rocheteau, G. "The Modernisation of Agriculture: Land Utilization and the Preference for Consumption Crops in the Groundnut Basin of Senegal." In Population in African Development, edited by P. Cantrelle, pp. 461-69. Ordina: Editions Dolhain, 1974.

_____. "Mouridisme et économie de traite: dégagement d'un surplus et accumulation dans une confrérie islamique au Sénégal." Thèmes d'anthropologie économique. Paris: Maspero, 1974.

_____. "Pionniers mourides au Sénégal: Colonisation des Terres Neuves et transformations d'une économie paysanne." Cah. ORSTOM 12 (1975): 19-53.

_____. "Société wolof et mobilité." Cah. ORSTOM 12 (1975): 3-18.

_____. "Terroirs africains." Environnement africain 1 (1974): 95-103.

Rocheteau, G., and J. Roch. "Le role de l'état dans le controle du crédit au Sénégal." Cah. ORSTOM 12 (1975): 221-34.

Rodney, Walter. A History of the Upper Guinea Coast, 1545-1800. New York: Oxford University Press, 1970.

Rougevin-Baville, Michel. "La coordination interministérielle au Sénégal." Institut International d'Administration Publique, Bulletin 2 (1968): 69-80.

Roussel, Louis. "Comparative Demography; Temporary Displacements and Migrations." Institut National de la Statistique et des Etudes Economiques, Service de la Coopération, and Institut National d'Etudes Economiques, Paris, 1967.

_____. "Ivory Coast." In Population Growth and Socioeconomic Change in West Africa, edited by J. C. Caldwell, pp. 657-78. New York: Population Council, 1975.

Roux, Emile. Manuel à l'usage des administrateurs et du personnel des affaires indigènes de la colonie du Sénégal. Paris: Larose, 1911.

Rumnwe, Jean. Les droits politiques des indigènes des colonies. Paris: Larose, 1927.

Sabot, R. Economic Development, Structural Change and Urban Migration. Oxford: Clarendon Press, 1976.

Sagna, Basse Augustine. "Le Bilan des pluies au Sénégal de 1944 à 1973." Mémoire de maitrise de géographie, Faculté des Lettres et Sc. Humaines, Dakar, 1976.

Sankale, M., L. V. Thomas, and P. Fougeyrollas, eds. Dakar en devenir. Paris: Présence Africaine, 1968.

Sanneh, Lamin O. The Jakhanke. London: International African Institute, 1979.

Santoir, C. J. "L'émigration maure: une vocation commerciale affirmée." Cah. ORSTOM 12 (1975): 137-61.

_____. "Les sociétés pastorales du Sénégal face à la sècheresse (1972-73). Réaction à la crise et degré au rétablissement deux ans après. Le cas des Peul du Galodjina." Unpublished report, ORSTOM, Bondy, August 1976.

Sarr, Moustapha. Louga: La ville et sa région. Dakar: IFAN, initiations et études africaines, 30, 1973.

Savage, I. R., and Karl W. Deutsch. "A Statistical Model of the Gross Analysis of Transaction Flows." Econometrica 28 (July 1960): 551-72.

Saxe, Jo W. "The Changing Economic Structure of French West Africa." Annals of the American Academy of Political and Social Science (March 1955): 52-61.

Schefer, (Louis Armand) Christian. La France moderne et le problème colonial. Paris: F. Alcau, 1907.

_____. Instructions générales données de 1763 à 1870 aux gouverneurs et ordonnateurs des établissements françaises en Afrique occidentale, 2 vols. Paris: Champion, 1921.

Schumacher, Edward K. Politics, Bureaucracy, and Rural Development in Senegal. Berkeley: University of California Press, 1975.

Sebire, R. P. A. Plantes utiles du Sénégal. Paris: Baillère, 1895.

Seck, Assane. Dakar: Métropole ouest-africaine. Dakar: IFAN, 1970.

_____. "La formation d'une classe moyenne en Afrique Occidentale Française." In Development of a Middle Class in Tropical and Sub-Tropical Countries, pp. 159-63. Brussels: International Institute of Differing Civilizations, 1956.

Seck, Mansour. "Etude des principaux facteurs agrométéorologiques au Sénégal." L'agronomie tropicale (Paris) 25 (March 1970): 241-76.

Senegal. Atlas National. Paris: Institut de Géographie National, 1978.

_____. Bureau National du Recensement. "Recensement général de la population d'avril 1976." Résultats définitifs (données brutes), for Casamance, Diourbel, Louga, Senegal Oriental, Sine-Saloum, and Thiès. Mimeographed, Dakar, 1979.

_____. Bureau National du Recensement. "Résultats provisoires du recensement général de la population d'avril 1976." Mimeographed, Dakar, 1976.

_____. Bureau National du Recensement. Unpublished data from the 1970-71 National Demographic Survey, Dakar, n.d.

_____. Bureau National du Recensement. Unpublished data from the 1976 Census, Dakar, n.d.

_____. Direction de l'Aménagement du Territoire. Sample Survey.

_____. Direction de la Statistique. Les activites du secteur économique modern au Sénégal en 1974 et 1975 d'après les résultats du recensement général des entreprises, 3 vols. Dakar: SONED, 1977.

_____. Direction de la Statistique. Enquête démographique nationale, 1970-1971: Analyse des résultats du 2ème passage, portant sur la population active. Dakar: Ministère des Finances et des Affaires Economiques, Direction de la Statistique; Ministère du Plan et de la Coopération, Div. des Ressources Humaines, 1973.

_____. Direction de la Statistique. Enquête démographique nationale, 1970-1971: Résultats définitifs.

_____. Direction de la Statistique. Répertoire des villages du Sénégal. Dakar: Min. Plan. et Dévelopt, Direction de la Statistique, 1958, 1964, 1972.

_____. Direction de la Statistique. Situation économique du Sénégal. Dakar: since 1962.

_____. Direction des Transports. Bureau d'Etudes. Les flux et les moyens de transport de marchandises au Sénégal. Dakar: 1971.

_____. Ministry of Planning and Cooperation. Atlas pour l'aménagement du territoire. Dakar: Nouvelles Editions Africaines, 1977.

_____. Ministry of Planning and Cooperation. Etude d'un plan de développement régional intégré du Sénégal Oriental. Etude complémentaire rapport de fin de 1ère phase. Annexe I: le milieu humain, July 1977.

_____. Projet Rul-12 Sénégal. L'habitat du grande nombre VI, Sam et Diamagueune-Yeumbel. Habitation et autres équipements. Dakar: IFAN, 1975.

"Le Sénégal." Marchés nouveaux, February 10, 1978. Paris: Groupe Jeune Afrique, 1978.

Senegal: Tradition, Diversification and Economic Development. A World Bank Country Economic Report. Washington, D.C.: World Bank, 1974.

Senghor, Léopold Sédar. On African Socialism. Translated by and with an introduction by Mercer Cook. New York: Praeger, 1964.

_____. Les Fondements de l'africanité ou négritude et arabicité. Paris: Présence Africaine, 1967.

_____. Liberté—Négritude et humanisme. Paris: Seuil, 1964.

_____. Nation et voie africaine du socialisme. Paris: Présence Africaine, 1961.

Sene, Malick. "Exode rural et insertion de la jeunesse dans les structures socio-économiques du monde rural—Zone Operation Riz—Segou." Mouvements de population et systemes d'education dans les pays Sahelo-Soudaniens. UNESCO Seminar, Dakar, May 26-June 7, 1975.

Shapiro, Kenneth H., ed. "Livestock Production and Marketing in the Entente States of West Africa: Summary Report." Center for Research on Economic Development, University of Michigan and AID, Ann Arbor, March 1979.

Shyrock, Henry S., and Jacob S. Seigel. The Methods and Materials of Demography, vol. I. Washington, D.C.: U.S. Government Printing Office for the U.S. Department of Commerce, 1973.

Silla, Ousmane. "Les castes dans la société ouolof: Aspects traditionnels, persistances actuelles." Mémoire pour l'obtention du diplome de l'Ecole Pratique des Hautes Etudes, Paris, Sorbonne, May 1965.

_____. "Les Partis Politiques au Sénégal." Revue française d'études politiques africaines (April 1968): 78-94.

Skinner, Snider William. Senegal's Agricultural Economy in Brief. Washington, D.C.: Economic Research Service, USDA, 1966.

Skurnik, W. A. E. The Foreign Policy of Senegal. Evanston, Ill.: Northwestern University Press, 1972.

Songre, Ambroise. "Mass Emigration from Upper Volta: The Facts and Implications." International Labour Review 108 (1973): 209-25.

Sonolet, Louis. L'Afrique Occidentale Française. Paris: Hachette, 1913.

Soumah, Moussa. "Culture cotonnière et développement régional au Sénégal." Annales de la Faculté des Lettres et Sciences humaines de Dakar 7 (1977): 243-68.

Sow, Fatou. Les fonctionnaires de l'administration centrale du Sénégal. Dakar: IFAN, 1967.

_____. Le logement au Sénégal. Dakar: IFAN, 1974.

Sow, Samba. "Intégration de l'élevage et des éleveurs dans la zone pionnière du delta." Mémoire de stage, Dakar, ENEA, 1965.

Speckmann, J. D. Rapport final. Projet inter-universitaire pour une recherche inter-disciplinaire sur la planification des extentions urbaines au Cap-Vert Sénégal. Université de Dakar, Université d'Etat de Leiden: IFAN, 1975.

Stengers, Jean. "L'impérialism colonial de la fin du XIXe siècle: mythe ou réalité." Journal of African History 3 (1962): 469-91.

Suret-Canale, Jean. Afrique noire occidentale et centrale. l'ère coloniale (1900-1945), vol. 2. Paris: Editions Sociales, 1968.

_____. La République de Guinée. Paris: Editions Sociales, 1970.

_____. La Sénégambie à l'ère de la traite." Revue canadienne des études africaines 11 (1977): 125-34.

Swindel, Kenneth. "A Report on Migrant Farmers in the Gambia." In "Demographic Aspects of Migration in West Africa," edited by K. C. Zachariah and Julien Condé, The Gambia, Annex I. Mimeographed, World Bank and OECD, Washington, D. C., June 1978.

Talence, M. "Urban Growth in Black Africa and Madagascar," vol. 2. Paris: Editions du CNRS, 1972.

Tautain, L. Etudes critiques sur l'éthnologie et l'éthnographie des peuples du bassin du Sénégal. Paris: Ernest Leroux, 1885.

Terrisse, André. "Aspects du malaise paysan au Sénégal." Revue française d'études politiques africaines 55 (July 1970): 79-91.

Texeira da Mota, A. "Un document nouveau pour l'histoire des Peuls au Sénégal pendant les XVème et XVIème siècles." Boletim cultural da Guiné Portuguesa 96 (1969): 814 ff.

_____. "Fulas e Beafadas no Rio Grande no seculo XV." Academia das ciencias de Lisboa (1970): 921.

Thiam, Doudou. The Foreign Policy of African States. New York: Praeger, 1965.

Thomas, Benjamin E. "Railways and Ports in French West Africa." Economic Geography 33 (January 1957): 1-15.

Thomas, Louis V. "Analyse dynamique de la parenté sénégalaise." Bulletin de l'IFAN, ser. B, 30 (1968): 1005-56.

_____. Les Diola: Essai d'analyse fonctionelle sur une population de Basse Casamance, 2 vols. Dakar: IFAN, 1958-59.

_____. "Essai sur quelques problèmes relatifs au régime foncier des Diola de Basse-Casamance (Senegal)." International African Seminar, Leopoldville, 1960. African Agrarian Systems. London: International African Institute, 1963.

Thoré, Luc. Dagoudane-Pikine. Etude sur l'évolution et les problèmes du groupe familial en ville. Dakar: ORSTOM, 1974.

Toupet, C. "Agrarian and Social Transformations in the Tamourt
Basin, Mauritania." Malayan J. Tr. Geog. 8 (1956): 82-86.

_____. "Le problème des transports en Mauritanie." Bull. IFAN
25 (1963): 80-106.

_____. La sédentarisation des nomades en Mauritanie centrale
sahelienne. Lille: Universite III, repr. de theses, 1977.

Toure, Kiba. Environment. Les problèmes de la détérioration et
de la protection de la nature dans le départment de Vélingara.
Dakar: Nouvelles Editions Africaines, 1976.

Traoré, Bakary, Mamadou Lo, and Jean-Louis Alibert. Forces
politiques en Afrique noire. Paris: Presses Universitaires de
France, 1966.

UNESCO. "Mouvements de population et systèmes d'éducation dans
les pays sahelo-soudaniens (Haute-Volta, Mali-Mauritanie,
Niger, Sénégal, Tchad)." Unpublished, mimeographed proceedings of the UNESCO colloquium, Dakar, May 26-June 7, 1975.

_____. Two Studies on Ethnic Group Relations in Africa: Senegal,
The United Republic of Tanzania. Paris: UNESCO, 1974.

UNESCO-MAB. Notes techniques. Le Sahel: Bases écologiques
de l'aménagement. Dakar 1974. Développement des régions
arides et seminarides: Obstacles et perspectives. Dakar,
1977.

United Nations. Methods of Measuring Internal Migration, United
Nations Manual VI. New York: United Nations, 1970.

_____. UN Demographic Yearbooks 1970-1977. New York: United
Nations.

_____. World Trade Annual Supplements. New York: United
Nations, 1974.

_____. Population Division, Department of Economic and Social
Affairs of the UN Secretariat, 1975. "Selected World Demo-
graphic Indicators by Countries, 1950-2000," ESA/P/WP.55.
New York: United Nations, May 28, 1975.

U.S. Bureau of Census. World Population, 1977. Washington, D.C.: Bureau of Census, 1979.

U.S. Department of State, Bureau of Public Affairs. "International Population Policy." Current policy no. 171, April 29, 1980.

U.S. Walter Reed Army Hospital. "Health Data Publications: Republic of Senegal. Unpublished report no. 26. Washington, D.C., June 1965.

Van der Vaeren, Aguessy D. "Les Femmes commerçantes au détail sur les marchés dakarois." In The New Elites of Tropical Africa, edited by P. C. Lloyd, pp. 244-55. London: Oxford University Press, 1966.

Vanhaeverbeke, A. Renumération de travail et commerce extérieur: Essor d'une économique paysanne exportatrice et termes de l'échange de producteurs d'arachides au Sénégal. Louvain: Centre de Recherches de Pays en Développement, Université Catholique de Louvain, Faculté des Sciences Economiques, Sociales et Politiques, 1970.

van Loo, Henk L., and Nella J. Star. La Basse Casamance, Sud-Ouest Sénégal: données de bases démographiques et socio-economiques. Leyde: University of Leyde, July 1973.

Verdier, J. "Enquête sur le fichier enfants de Khombel-Thiènaba." Unpublished paper, Dakar, ORSTOM, 1972.

Vernière, Marc. "Anyama: Study of Population and the Cola Nut Trade." Cahiers ORSTOM 6 (1969): 83-112.

_____. "Etapes et modalités de la croissance de Dagoudane Pikine Banlieue de Dakar." Unpublished paper, Juillet, ORSTOM, 1971.

_____. "L'expulsion des Bidonvilles dakarois: Bouleversement d'une société urbaine de transition. Leçon d'enquêtes réalisées à Fann Paillote et Guedj Awaye." Psychopathologie africaine 10 (1974): 321-51.

_____. "A Propos de la marginalité: Réflexions illustrées par quelques enquêtes en milieu urbain et suburbain africain." Cahiers d'études africaines 51 (1973).

_____. "Résultats de l'enquête par sondage au 1/20° des parcelles de Pikine (Grand-Dakar) 1966-1967." Unpublished report, Dakar, ORSTOM, 1970.

_____. "Volontarisme d'état et spontanéisme populaire dans l'urbanisation du Tiers-Monde." Paris, Ecole Pratique des Hautes Etudes et CNRS, 1973.

Verrière, Louis. "La population du Sénégal." Dissertation, Doctorat de IIIe cycle, University of Dakar, 1963.

Vígnac-Buttin, B. "Résultats de recensement de Nioro du Rip (Sine-Saloum) Sénégal." Unpublished, Dakar, ORSTOM, 1970.

Vignon, Louis. Un programme de politique coloniale. Paris: Hachette, 1919.

Villard, André. Histoire du Sénégal. Dakar: Maurice Viale, 1943.

Wane, Amadou Taminou. Etude sur la race toucouleur. Unpublished, Dakar, n.d.

Wane, Yaya. Les toucouleurs du Fouta Tooro (Senegal). Dakar: IFAN, 1969.

_____. Les toucouleurs du Fouta Tooro, stratification sociale et structure familiale. Paris: CNRS; Dakar: IFAN, 1966.

Westebbe, Richard M. The Economy of Mauritania. New York: Praeger, 1971.

Witherell, Julian. "The Response of the Peoples of Cayor to French Penetration, 1850-1900." Ph.D. dissertation, University of Wisconsin, 1964. Published on demand by University Microfilms, Ann Arbor, Michigan.

Wolfson, Margaret. Changing Approaches to Population Problems. Paris: Organization for Economic Cooperation and Development, 1977.

World Bank, Sierra Leone. Current Economic Position and Prospects (in 5 volumes), vol. 5, Statistical Appendix, Western Africa Region. Washington, D.C.: World Bank, November 27, 1974.

_____. Migration and Employment in Senegal: An Introductory Report. Working paper, Washington, D.C., September 24, 1976.

_____. "Rapport sur la situation de la migration et de l'emploi au Senegal." Mimeographed, Washington, D.C., June 1976.

_____. Urban Growth and Economic Development on the Sahel. Working paper no. 315, Washington, D.C., 1979.

_____. World Bank Atlas. Washington, D.C.: World Bank, 1975.

_____. World Bank Atlas. Washington, D.C.: World Bank, 1976.

_____. World Tables 1976. Baltimore: Johns Hopkins University Press for the World Bank, 1976.

Zachariah, K. C., and Julien Condé. "Demographic Aspects of Migration in West Africa." Mimeographed, World Bank and OECD, June 1978.

Zachariah, K. C., and N. K. Nair. "Senegal: Patterns of Internal and International Migration in Recent Years." In Demographic Aspects of Migration in West Africa. Washington, D.C.: OECD/World Bank, 1978.

Zuccarelli, François. Un parti politique africain: l'Union Progressiste Sénégalaise. Paris: Pichon et Durand-Auzias, 1971.

Zuccarelli, R. "Le régime des engagés à temps au Sénégal de 1817 à 1848." Cahiers d'études africaines 7 (1962).

ABOUT THE AUTHORS

LUCIE GALLISTEL COLVIN is associate professor in the African American Studies Department of the University of Maryland Baltimore County. She is author of the Historical Dictionary of Senegal, as well as of Kajor and the Frènch: Diplomacy in Precolonial Senegambia, English and French versions of which are forthcoming, and of several articles.

CHEIKH BA is maître assistant in the Department of Geography at the University of Dakar. His research focus has been on the pastoralists of the Ferló in northern Senegal.

BOUBACAR BARRY is maître assistant in the Department of History of the University of Dakar. He is author of Le Royaume du Waalo: le Sénégal avant la conquete, of Bakar Biro, le dernier grand almany du Fouta Djalon, and of numerous monographs and articles. He is a contributing author to UNESCO, General History of Africa; J. F. Ade Ajayi and Michael Crowder, History of West Africa, vol. I; and Rita Cruise O'Brien, The Political Economy of Underdevelopment: Dependence in Senegal. His current research includes a manuscript on Islam and social change in the history of the Senegambia and a monograph on Futa Jallon from 1850 to 1920.

JACQUES FAYE is a sociologist currently serving as director of the Kaolack branch of the Institut Senegalais de Recherches Agronomiques. He has conducted survey research and applied studies on multiple facets of the socioeconomy of rural Senegal.

ALICE HAMER, a Ph.D. candidate at the University of Michigan, is interested in economic history and women and development. Her dissertation on Jola women is currently in progress.

MOUSSA SOUMAH is assistant in the Department of Geography at the University of Dakar. His research has focused on the human geography and development potential of the upper Casamance area.

FATOU SOW is chargé de recherches at the Centre National de la Recherche Scientifique (Paris), affiliated with the Social Science Department at the Institut Fondamental d'Afrique Noire in Dakar. She is author of Les fonctionnaires de l'administration centrale du Sénégal and numerous scholarly articles and consultant reports. Her current research interests include the women of the Senegal river valley and an ongoing project on the phenomenon of opinion in Africa.